Variorum Revised Editions and Reprints:

JOSEPH R. STRAYER
The Royal Domain in the Baillage of Rouen

JOHN WILLIS CLARK
The Care of Books. An Essay on the Development of Libraries and their
Fittings, from the Earliest Times to the End of the 18th Century
Cambridge 1902 definitive edition

In the Collected Studies Series:

WALTER ULLMANN
The Church and the Law in the Earlier Middle Ages

WALTER ULLMANN
The Papacy and Political Ideas in the Middle Ages

WALTER ULLMANN
Scholarship and Politics in the Middle Ages

BERNHARD BLUMENKRANZ
Juifs et Chrétiens — Patristique et Moyen-Age

PAUL MEYVAERT
Benedict, Gregory, Bede and Others

EDMOND-RENE LABANDE
Spiritualité et vie littéraire de l'Occident. Xe-XIVe s.

GILES CONSTABLE
Religious Life and Thought (11th-12th Centuries)

MICHEL MOLLAT
Etudes sur l'économie et la société de l'Occident médiéval (XIIe-XIVe s.)

DAVID HERLIHY
The Social History of Italy and Western Europe, 700-1500

PAUL J. ALEXANDER
Religious and Political History and Thought in the Byzantine Empire

HENRY MONNIER
Etudes de droit byzantin

MILTON V. ANASTOS
Studies in Byzantine Intellectual History

Church Law and Constitutional Thought
in the Middle Ages

Professor Brian Tierney

Brian Tierney

Church Law and Constitutional Thought in the Middle Ages

VARIORUM REPRINTS
London 1979

FL79/9197   10/79

262.9 TIE   X1

British Library CIP data

Tierney, Brian
Church law and constitutional thought in the
Middle Ages.
– (Collected studies series; CS90)
1. Canon law – History
2. Constitutional history, Medieval
I. Title   II. Series
262.9'90'022   BV760.2

ISBN 0-86078-036-8

Published in Great Britain by   Variorum Reprints
21a Pembridge Mews London W11 3EQ

Printed in Great Britain by   Kingprint Ltd
Richmond Surrey TW9 4PD

VARIORUM REPRINT CS90

CONTENTS

This volume contains a total of 340 pages

PREFACE

In 1960 David Knowles wrote that the study of medieval canon law had recently become a "fashionable" subject among historians. Some of the reasons for this renewed interest in the Decretists and Decretalists are discussed in the first of the following essays, "Some Recent Works on the Political Theories of the Medieval Canonists," originally published in 1955. Medievalists had never wholly neglected the canonists. The study of their works always attracted the interest of a number of distinguished scholars. But, particularly in English-speaking countries, such study was often seen as constituting a rather specialised field, outside the main stream of historical writing. Between 1935 and 1955 the situation changed. Stephan Kuttner's *Repertorium der Kanonistik* (1937) provided the first adequate guide to the manuscript sources. Then, especially in the years just after World War II, historians in many different countries came to realise that the great mass of still-unexplored canonistic writings provided invaluable source material for the study of medieval thought and medieval institutions. Important contributions came from England and America (notably in the works of Walter Ullmann and Gaines Post) as well as from the more traditional centers of canonistic studies. Since then a great body of new work in the field has enhanced our understanding of the religious, political, and economic life of the Middle Ages.

My own work has been concerned mainly with a continuing endeavor to understand the constitutional law of the medieval church. All the essays that follow relate to this theme in one way or another. But the theme is a very broad one. The influence of the church touched every aspect of medieval life and thought, and the law that regulated the church's activity reflected this universality. A historian who studies canon law nowadays can hardly be a narrow specialist. In pursuing my central theme, I was led sometimes to studies on comparative law as in the essays on Accursius and Bracton, sometimes to classical problems of political theory as in the essays on Grosseteste and on "Divided Sovereignty," sometimes to the borderland of theology as in the essays on "Sola Scriptura" and on "A Scriptural Text in the Decretales . . . . "

Hence these papers may perhaps have enough variety to interest scholars in more than one field of medieval studies. I hope they will have enough unity to express a coherent point of view on the problems discussed.

BRIAN TIERNEY

Cornell University,
Ithaca, N.Y.
June, 1978

SOME RECENT WORKS ON THE POLITICAL THEORIES
OF THE MEDIEVAL CANONISTS

During the past decade there has been a significant shift of emphasis in work on the medieval canonists. The traditional studies on the literary history of canonistic sources and on problems of specifically ecclesiastical jurisprudence continue to flourish, and, indeed, have been stimulated by the plans for a new edition of Gratian's *Decretum*; but alongside this work, and complementary to it, there has appeared a new trend, a lively interest in the content and influence of canonistic doctrine concerning public law and political theory. This trend, moreover, shows all the international diffusion — and even, perhaps, something of the interplay of national susceptibilities — that its exponents have discerned in the work of the medieval canonists themselves. It is especially interesting that notable contributions have come from England and the United States as well as from the more established centers of canonistic studies.

The political aspects of the canonists' teaching have never been entirely neglected of course. Pioneer workers like Maassen and Schulte often found occasion to print relevant material in their textual studies and, more recently, writers on medieval political theory like the Carlyles, Rivière, Lecler, have all made some limited use of canonistic sources. The work of the past few years has been marked by a more systematic treatment of broad tracts of canonistic thought, and by a more painstaking investigation of manuscript sources, accompanied by the publication of many new texts. It has also been marked — and this is its very *raison d'être* — by a new awareness of the vitality and importance of canonistic thought on major questions of ecclesiastical and secular government. The problems which have recently engaged the attention of scholars in this field are not peripheral ones, and in drawing together the threads of recent research one is not concerned merely with a sort of abstruse 'legal archaeology '; it is a question rather of assessing the results of a fresh approach to the great central issues of medieval politics. Among those issues the problem of *Regnum* and *Sacerdotium* remains a principal focal point of research, but recent workers have gone beyond this familiar field — or battlefield — to investigate the canonistic contribution to the medieval idea of sovereignty in all its aspects. There are three main themes that are being explored, each with its own unresolved problems. We might define them as the problems of *Regnum* and *Sacerdotium*, of *Regnum* and *Imperium*, of *Regnum* and *Rex*, and it will be convenient to review the recent work under those headings.

All these topics, the relations of Church and State, the external organization of states, the internal sovereignty of states, involve problems that are very much alive in the modern world, and that fact may help to explain both the growing interest in canonistic teaching concerning them and the sharp divergencies in current interpretations of that teaching. Such divergencies, however, would also arise almost inevitably from the nature of the source material itself, and one can hardly explain the current controversies without some account of the difficulties inherent in handling medieval canonistic texts. It happens that one of the most able scholars in the field, Fr. Alfons M. Stickler, has devoted his last article to precisely this point,[1] and so a summary of his conclusions will provide a most suitable introduction to a survey of the main problems that are being discussed.

Fr. Stickler sets out to provide rules of guidance for a student embarking on research into the canonists' theories of Church and State, and in laying down sound precepts he indicates very plainly (by the argument *a contrario sensu* as the canonists would say) the pitfalls that gape for the unwary novice. He puts forward six 'methodological considerations' which seem important enough to be summarized *seriatim*. (1) In considering a canonistic text the student must pay careful attention to the content of the law that was being glossed. The canonists did show great freedom in interpretation, in marshalling opposing arguments, in suggesting particular exceptions to general rules, but they did not feel free to maintain a personal position in defiance of established law. (2) It is essential to take into account the literary form of any particular text. For instance, *Notabilia*, observations introduced by some expression like *arg(umentum)*, *no(ta)*, *ita habes*, did not necessarily reflect a personal opinion of the author. He was merely pointing out that the text could be used in support of a certain position without committing himself. Others forms of canonistic argument presented the case for and against a given proposition, but, again, without always reaching a definite conclusion. Only when there is such a conclusion can one be sure of the author's own opinion. (3) Neither in the *Corpus Iuris Canonici* nor in the glosses on it does one find any single section devoted to a systematic exposition of public law. The various problems arose in different contexts, and sometimes the most important canonistic glosses were evoked by a chance word or phrase in some text dealing with a quite different issue. Therefore it is necessary to study the whole of a canonist's work to arrive at a just appreciation of his view on any disputed point. Moreover, 'theory without practice is like a vessel without content'; one cannot arrive at a balanced view of the canonists' teaching on Church and State merely

---

[1] A. M. Stickler, 'Sacerdotium et Regnum nei decretisti e primi decretalisti: Considerazioni metodologiche di ricerca e testi,' *Salesianum* 15 (1953) 572-612.

by quoting statements of abstract principle from their work. It is necessary also to consider what concrete applications of legislative, judicial, and executive power they envisaged. (4) To evaluate the contribution of an author to the growth of canonistic thought one must have a clear understanding, not only of his own doctrines, but also of those of his predecessors and contemporaries and successors. (5) It is also useful to consider the affiliation of the author to a particular school of canonistic thought, of which three main ones have been distinguished in the twelfth century, that of Bologna, that of Paris, and the Anglo-Norman school. Where there was a strong international element, as at Bologna, the nationality of a canonist may also be a significant factor. (6) For a complete and perfect understanding of canonistic teachings on Church and State one must consider the contributions of contemporary theology, philosophy, and especially of Roman legal science; but, so far as theology and philosophy are concerned, one must also be on guard against over-estimating the influence of their abstract conceptions on the concrete and practical thought of the canonists.

Of all these various considerations No. 2 is perhaps the most important. It may serve to remind us that, by an adroit selection of texts, one can 'prove' well-nigh anything out of any of the major canonistic works. For an objective enquiry it is essential to bear in mind that the innumerable arguments advanced in the course of a canonistic gloss do not necessarily represent the opinions of the author or, sometimes, of anyone else. There is no field of study where patience and docility to the texts are more essential; and even when those qualities are not lacking there is still room for sharp differences of opinion concerning the teachings of individual canonists, and the general trends of canonistic thought.

I. *Regnum and Sacerdotium*

Such differences of opinion are very much in evidence in recent work on the canonists' theories of Church and State. The problems involved can be introduced by a description of one of the most lively contributions to the debate, Dr. Walter Ullmann's *Medieval Papalism*.[2] This book presents a vigorous and trenchant statement of the view that the medieval canonists were primarily responsible for the growth of 'the theory of political omnipotence of the pope as Boniface VIII propounded it in *Unam Sanctam*' (p. 11). After an introduction emphasizing the vitality and prestige of canonistic scholarship in the high Middle Ages — all the participants in the discussion are at any rate agreed on that point — Dr. Ullmann begins his argument with an analysis of canonistic ideas on natural law. He distinguishes several different conceptions: natural law as the mere instinct of all 'animalic creatures'; as the moral judgments of the natural reason; as the precepts of the Old and New Testaments, in which sense natural law was equated with divine law.[3] This con-

---

[2] W. Ullmann, *Medieval Papalism: The Political Theories of the Medieval Canonists* (London 1949).

[3] The concept of natural law in Gratian and the early Decretists has attracted much attention recently. See J. Gaudemet, 'La doctrine et les sources du droit dans le Décret de Gratien,' *Revue de droit canonique* 1 (1951) 5-31; M. Villey, 'Sources et portée du droit naturel chez Gratien,' *ibid.* 4 (1954) 50-65; P. Delhaye, 'Morale et droit canonique dans la *Summa* d'Étienne de Tournai, '*Studia Gratiana* 1 (Bologna 1953) 435-49 at 440f.; F.

ception of natural law as a set of Christian principles 'was in fact the chief tenet of the canonists' (p. 47) and, accordingly, 'the natural (divine) law was throughout conceived of as unalterable and immutable' (p. 46). All this, however, turns out to be only a sort of elaborate range-finding for the artillery blast that follows in the next chapter. B efore the omnipotence of the pope the immutability of the natural law was 'but a hollow name.' The pope could do whatever God could do; the canonists, Dr. Ullmann holds, set him above natural law just as the civilians set the emperor above human law.[4] This assertion is supported by examples of canonistic teaching on the pope's power to deprive a person of his 'natural' liberty, dissolve marriages, absolve from oaths.

Moreover, the canonists claimed 'not only a supremacy of the pope in spiritual matters ... but also, and to an equal degree, his supremacy in all temporal matters' (p. 77). Dr. Ullmann therefore undertakes an analysis of the 'transcendental ideas' upon which this claim was based, suggesting that, for the canonists, the struggle between Church and State was simply 'the political aspect of the ancient antagonism between mind and matter' (p. 81). The ecclesiastical power was identified with mind, the civil power with matter and 'the inequality of mind and matter was faithfully reflected in the corresponding inequality of pope and emperor' (p. 82). But it was not merely a question of inequality. The temporal power existed for the sake of the spiritual, and so 'the spiritual authority had complete and unrestricted power over the temporal' (p. 84).[5] The emperor was a mere instrument of the pope, delegated to perform those tasks that were 'of too mean a character,' too 'vile,' too 'sordid,' too 'menial' to be dealt with by the spiritual power. This conception of the relations of mind and body was derived from Aristotle's *De anima*, supported by Holy Writ, with the Donation of Constantine providing a useful auxiliary argument on the level of human law for the canonists' position. The practical corollaries of that position were the exemption of clerics and ecclesiastical affairs from all secular authority, and the extension of the Church's jurisdiction over 'every conceivable aspect of human life' (p. 107). (Various examples are given of the extension of spiritual jurisdiction beyond the purely ecclesiastical sphere, e.g. to cases involving dowries, wills, legitimation of children, all criminal cases — since they involved sin —, breaches of peace treaties, temporal disputes between kings.)

Dr. Ullmann goes on to argue that the jurisdiction of the pope was not limited to Christendom but extended over the whole world, and to examine the im-

---

Arnold, 'Die Rechtslehre des Magisters Gratianus,' *ibid.* 450-482 at 460f.; A. Wegner, 'Über positives göttliches Recht und natürliches göttliches Recht,' *ibid.* 503-18; D. Com posta, 'Il diritto naturale in Graziano,' *ibid.* 2 (to be published); S. Kuttner, 'New Studies on the Roman Law in Gratian's Decretum,' *Seminar* 11 (1953) 12-50 at 42f.

[4] Dr. Ullmann strongly emphasizes an ideological conflict between civilians and canonists, the one school exalting the emperor, the other the pope. The theme is developed further in his article, 'Honorius III and the Prohibition of Legal Studies,' *The Juridical Review* 60 (1948) 177-86. For another interpretation of Honorius' attitude see S. Kuttner, 'Papst Honorius III und das Studium des Zivilrechts,' *Festschrift für Martin Wolff* (Tübingen 1952) 79-101.

[5] To the present writer the weakest point in the whole argument is the lack of canonistic documentation for these assertions.

plications of this view for the juristic theory of the crusade. He returns in his last chapter to the core of his argument, describing in greater detail the development of the theory that the emperor received his authority from the pope as a mere subordinate agent. According to Dr. Ullmann this theory took root during the pontificate of Innocent III. Before that time the views of Innocent's old teacher, Huguccio, had prevailed, and Huguccio held that, since the time of Christ, spiritual and temporal power had been divided 'in order to promote humility and prevent pride.' The emperor, therefore, did not receive the power of the sword from the pope but from the princes who elected him; papal consecration conferred only the title of emperor, not the reality of power. These views were repeated by the Spaniard Laurentius and by the Englishman Ricardus; their decisive defeat was due to the vigorous pontificate of Innocent himself and to the influence of another Englishman, Alanus, 'who may well be considered the scientific framer of the extreme papalist point of view' (p. 147). Sharply rejecting the dualist position of Huguccio, Alanus maintained that the pope conferred the *gladius materialis* on the emperor, for the Church formed one body and it ought to have only one head. Christ possessed both swords and he conferred them both on Peter; if He had not done so it would have been impossible for Pope Zacharias to have deposed King Childeric. In fact, the pope as *iudex ordinarius ... quoad spiritualia et quoad temporalia* could depose the emperor or any other temporal ruler, or even exercise temporal power himself. Alanus did not create this theory *ex nihilo* but it was through his influence that it gained general currency; his views were repeated by Tancred and afterwards became universally accepted among the canonists. It only remained for later glossators like Bernardus Parmensis, Goffredus Tranensis, Innocent IV, Hostiensis to strengthen the scriptural and historical basis of the argument — and for the popes to put it into practice in their relations with emperors and kings.

There have been a number of recent studies which, without going over precisely the same canonistic ground as Dr. Ullmann, suggest different interpretations of some of the papal documents that he cites,[6] and there has been

---

[6] M. Maccarrone, *Chiesa e stato nella dottrina di papa Innocenzo III* (Lateranum N.S. 6 iii-iv; Rome 1940). Maccarrone argues that all Innocent III's claims on behalf of the papacy and all his interventions in secular affairs were consistent with the dualist doctrine taught by Huguccio. His views were accepted by A. Fliche, in *La Chrétienté romaine (1198-1274)* (Fliche and Martin, Histoire de l'Église 10; Paris 1950) 30-43. Maccarrone has also discussed the expression *Vicarius Christi*, much emphasized by Ullmann, and concludes that, for Innocent III, it did not imply a claim to temporal power, though it acquired a hierocratic connotation later in the thirteenth century, 'Il papa « Vicarius Christi »,' *Miscellanea Pio Paschini* (Rome 1949) 427-500; *Vicarius Christi: Storia del titolo papale* (Lateranum N.S. 18 i-iv; Rome 1952). On papal *plenitudo potestatis* see G. Ladner, 'The Concepts of « Ecclesia » and « Christianitas » and Their Relation to the Idea of Papal « Plenitudo Potestatis » from Gregory VII to Boniface VIII,' *Miscellanea historiae pontificiae* 18 (Rome 1954) 49-77. Ladner maintains that in the papal letters of the thirteenth century *plenitudo potestatis* referred to the universal spiritual authority of the pope, together with his indirect power in temporal affairs and his direct lordship over the Papal States, but that it did not refer to direct universal temporal authority, as Ullmann claims. G. Le Bras has argued that even Boniface VIII took up a moderate and balanced position on the temporal power of the pope: 'Boniface VIII, symphoniste et modérateur,' in

one substantial review article challenging his interpretation of the canonistic doctrines themselves.[7] Fr. Stickler offers a considerable number of detailed criticisms on particular points,[8] and, besides this, he castigates Dr. Ullmann's whole method of enquiry.

> The reader is bidden to accept a good many statements without any, or without adequate textual support. And where the texts are provided, this is usually done without any systematic criteria: without regard to the chronological order, without distinguishing the schools, or the respective importance, or the common acceptance of a view... This method is certainly not apt to give a correct impression of the *communis opinio* of the period... (p. 454).

Dr. Ullmann is especially blamed for having failed to investigate adequately the sources of Alanus' theories and for having consequently exaggerated his importance as a founder of the hierocratic doctrine.[9] Altogether, a good deal of Fr. Stickler's criticism amounts to a complaint that Dr. Ullmann's work does not conform to the 'methodological criteria' that we have outlined. There is some truth in this, but it must be remembered that *Medieval Papalism* was composed as a course of lectures. They were very stimulating to those who heard them, and that was partly because, like another eminent legal historian, Dr. Ullmann availed himself of 'the lecturer's right to pick and choose, to be aphoristic.' He did not attempt or pretend to provide a detailed chronological history of the development of canonistic ideas. He presented instead a bold and vivid picture of the basic aspects of canonistic political thought, concentrating especially on the period of greatest vitality, the first half of the thirteenth century. Fr. Stickler's most damaging criticism, therefore, is that, precisely for that period, the whole picture is out of focus. To him 'it appears more than doubtful that from Alanus on both the canonists and the Curia abandoned the dualist theory which prevailed up till then.' He quotes a number of texts from Alanus, Tancred, and Hostiensis in support of this statement, but obviously, in the course of a review, could not embark on a synthesis that would reconcile them with the texts on which Dr. Ullmann relies, which certainly do seem to present the pope as a kind of universal overlord.

Mélanges d'histoire du moyen âge... Louis Halphen (Paris 1951). On the other hand, G. De Vergottini, like Ullmann, emphasizes the growing insistence on a direct power of the pope in temporal affairs in the decretals of the thirteenth century, *Il diritto pubblico italiano nei secoli XII-XIV* 1 (2nd ed. Milan 1954) 79-104. The development of the claim to lordship over all islands in the letters of the medieval popes has been traced by Luis Weckmann, *Las Bulas Alejandrinas de 1493 y la Teoria Politica del Papado Medieval* (Mexico 1949).

[7] A. M. Stickler, 'Concerning the Political Theories of the Medieval Canonists,' *Traditio* 7 (1949-51) 450-463.

[8] e.g. that Dr. Ullmann has misunderstood the canonistic doctrine on papal dispensation in his chapter on 'The Pope and Natural Law'; that he has strained the meaning of his texts in presenting the canonists as merely contemptuous of temporal power and of the laity in general; that he has misrepresented the papal and canonistic teaching on appeals from a secular court to an ecclesiastical one.

[9] In this connection Fr. Stickler points out that 'the characteristic utterances of *Unam Sanctam* can be found *verbatim* in two of Gratian's contemporaries, Hugh of St. Victor and Bernard of Clairvaux...' (p. 457).

Fr. Stickler is content to observe that 'in this conflict of utterances there lies a real problem which may eventually be solved.' For an attempt at a full-scale alternative synthesis, presenting conclusions radically different from those of Dr. Ullmann, we must turn to a recent work of Professor Sergio Mochi Onory, *Fonti canonistiche dell' idea moderna dello stato.*[10] Dr. Ullmann holds firmly at the center of his thought two ideas which should indeed always be present to students of medieval political theory — the idea of Christian society as a united organism; the idea of the primacy of the spiritual within that society. It is certainly true that, for the canonists, the temporal was inferior to the spiritual, but Dr. Ullmann takes it for granted that inferiority meant hierarchical subordination, and that that in turn meant utter subjection. It may be that, in emphasizing the unity of Christian society, he has oversimplified the subtleties of its articulation. This articulation of Christian society in all its aspects is precisely the theme that Mochi Onory has chosen to develop. His work spreads over all three departments into which our survey is divided, and we shall perhaps do an injustice to his closely interwoven arguments by separating them for purposes of analysis; but this seems the best way of comparing his conclusions in each field with those of other workers.

In the matter of Church and State his main contention — diametrically opposed to Dr. Ullmann's — is that canonistic doctrine respected the essential integrity of the secular power. Temporal rulers and their peoples were subject in spiritualities to the pope as head of the Church, but in the conduct of secular affairs the canonists conceded to them a sphere of *autonomia e sufficienza di vita,* to use the author's favorite phrase. Mochi Onory's work differs from Ullmann's in method as well as in conclusions. He has relied almost entirely on printed material whereas Ullmann based his work largely on manuscripts; and, unlike Ullmann again, he has attempted a chronological development, tracing the threads of canonistic thought decade by decade from the appearance of Gratian's *Decretum.* We can, therefore, illustrate from the texts cited in his work the main stages in the development of canonistic doctrine, and thus provide a historical background for the evaluation of Dr. Ullmann's conclusions as well as his own.

The best starting point is provided by a comment in the *Summa* of Rufinus (1157-1159) on a text of St. Peter Damian, incorporated in the *Decretum* and there attributed to Pope Nicholas II.[11] In this text the saint, apparently paraphrasing Matthew 16.19, used the words, 'qui beato Petro aeternae vitae clavigero terreni simul et coelestis imperii iura commisit.' There seems no reason to suppose that Peter Damian intended anything but a reference to the familiar doctrine that sins forgiven by the apostle on earth would be forgiven in Heaven. Rufinus, however, suggested that *coeleste imperium* referred to the clergy and spiritual affairs, *terrenum imperium* to the laity and secular affairs[12]

---

[10] S. Mochi Onory, *Fonti canonistiche dell' idea moderna dello stato* (Milan 1951). Mochi Onory died soon after his book was published, and it is an invidious task to criticize the work of a scholar who can no longer reply. But works of synthesis often advance our knowledge as much by the discussions they stimulate as by their own immediate contribution. Mochi Onory, with his enthusiasm for the canonists and their works, would surely have wished the discussion to continue.

[11] *Dist.* 22 c.1.

[12] *Fonti* 87; 'Celeste imperium celestium militum i.e. clericorum universitatem cum

— and thereby shaped the course of the whole subsequent controversy. He explained that the papal *ius terreni imperii* was expressed in two-fold fashion; the Pope confirmed the earthly power of the emperor by consecrating him, and subsequently imposed penances for his sins and granted absolution to him as to any other layman.

> Summus itaque patriarcha quoad auctoritatem ius habet terreni imperii, eo scil. modo quia primum sua auctoritate imperatorem in terreno regno consecrando confirmat, et post tam ipsum quam reliquos seculares istis secularibus abutentes, sola sua auctoritate pene addicit et ipsos eosdem post penitentes absolvit.[13]

This gloss contains the seeds of much future doctrine. The function of consecrating the emperor, in fact the heritage of a particular historical situation, was treated as an inherent part of the authority divinely conferred on Peter from the very beginning of the Church. Again, the power to judge the emperor *ratione peccati*, presented by Rufinus traditionally enough as simply a power to remit sin, would be shown to have far-reaching political implications once it became associated with the idea of a wordly *imperium* of the pope. Rufinus himself, however, went on to draw an important distinction between *auctoritas* and *amministratio* explaining that the pope could not actually exercise the temporal power that he confirmed in the emperor.[14] Mochi Onory emphasizes this element in his teaching and feels able to conclude that Rufinus envisaged an effective division of powers in the Gelasian tradition.

In 1186, the *Summa Lipsiensis*, reflecting the movements of thought of the preceding generation, presented both a significant development of Rufinus' argument and a clear statement of a sharply opposed point of view. The relevant gloss was again on the words, *terreni simul et coelestis imperii*. After repeating Rufinus' suggestion that these words referred to a papal *imperium* over clergy and laity, the author of the *Summa* introduced into this interpretation of the power of the keys that other scriptural metaphor of the two swords which henceforth would become almost inextricably associated with it.

> ... *terreni simul et celestis*. Celeste vocat imperium celestium militum, id est clericorum universitatem cum hiis, que ad eos pertinent. Terrenum regnum vocat homines seculares cum rebus secularibus. Per hoc ergo videtur, quod summus pont(ifex) utrumque habet gladium... et quod ab eo suum habet imperator et quod posset deponi ab eo, si abutatur sua potestate ut XV. q. VI. Alius.[15]

Rufinus had written of consecration and confirmation, but here the pope was presented as the direct source of the emperor's power, endowed also with the

---

his, que ad eos pertinent, dicit; terrenum vero regnum vel imperium seculares homines secularesque res appellat: per hoc ergo videtur, quod summus pontifex, qui beati Petri est vicarius, habet iura terreni regni' (*Summa ad Dist.* 22 c.1). On Peter Damian's meaning see Maccarrone, *Chiesa e Stato* 64-5, referring to the views of Rivière, Voosen, and Arquillière.

[13] *Ibid.*

[14] *Ibid.* 'Ipse vero princeps post ipsum auctoritatem habet seculares regendi et preter ipsum officium amministrandi; etenim nec apostolicum secularia nec principem ecclesiastica procurare oportet...'

[15] *Fonti* 110 (*Summa ad Dist.* 22 c.1). 15 q.6 c.3 *Alius* referred to the 'deposition' of Childebert, king of the Franks, by Pope Zacharias.

I

602

authority to take away that power. At the end of the gloss it was added that those who held this opinion distinguished between *auctoritas* and *administratio* and denied to the pope the right of actually administering secular affairs.[16]

The author of the *Summa Lipsiensis* did not commit himself to the support of this opinion however, and presented along with it a very different point of view. According to this second interpretation the emperor's power could not be derived from the pope since there had been emperors before there were popes; the real source of imperial power, under God, was the *populus*. The pope possessed both swords only in the sense that he exercised spiritual authority over the laity as well as over the clergy; his anointing of the emperor served only to confirm a power already conferred by election. The exercise of the spiritual authority could, however, have repercussions in the temporal sphere. When, for instance, the pope was said to have deposed a king, it meant that he had excommunicated the king and so caused his subjects to withdraw their allegiance from him.[17]

We have here in embryo the two classical positions that later canonists would develop in more detail. Neither is quite uncompromising. Even the 'hierocratic' argument denied to the pope the normal exercise of temporal power; even the 'dualist' argument acknowledged that the pope, by the exercise of his spiritual authority, might on occasion intervene decisively in matters of secular government. Mochi Onory extracts from the glosses of this period many cases in which such interventions were justified on the ground of the pope's spiritual jurisdiction in the moral sphere — e.g. it was maintained that the pope could revise unjust sentences of a secular ruler, annul feudal arrangements repugnant to equity or Christian moral principles, decide issues involving internal peace or peace between states, determine the licitness of a war, summon a prince to the defense of Christendom. Mochi Onory maintains that all this did not destroy the autonomy of a ruler in the conduct of secular affairs, since these were all exceptional cases involving issues properly pertaining to the spiritual power.

He devotes several chapters to Huguccio as the greatest exponent of the dualist tradition.[18] After the argument concerning the two swords discussed

---

[16] *Fonti* 111: 'Nota, qui primam tenent sententiam, dicunt quod summus pon(tifex) utrumque habet gladium: alterum non admin(i)stratione, set tantum auctoritate, ut materialem: celestem vero et ecclesiasticum plena auctoritate.'

[17] *Fonti* 110-1: 'Alii dicunt in contrarium et hiis rationibus: ante enim erant imperatores quam summi pon(tifices) et tunc habebant potestatem, quia omnis potestas a deo est. Item nonne potest uti gladio quem consequitur in electione populi, quia populus ei et in eum omne ius et potestatem transfert? Item quomodo posset ei papa dare potestatem vel executionem gladii, cum non habeat, nec habere vel exercere possit... Quod ergo hic dicitur quod habet utrum(que) gladium, id est tam super clericos, quam super laicos imperium habet spirituale, ut quem ligat in terra, ligatus sit in celis. Regem autem deposuisse dicitur papa, cum ipsum pro sua contumacia excommunicaret et ita subditos ab eius obedientia subtraxit, cum nulli debeant domino excommunicato obedire... Item quid ergo accepit a papa cum inungitur imperator? Confirmationem potestatis vel ut ei tanquam imperatori hec liceant.'

[18] For a judicious discussion of Huguccio's views see also Maccarrone, *Chiesa e Stato* 68-78. On his alleged Ghibellinism see G. Catalano, 'Contributo alla biografia di Uguccio da Pisa,' *Il diritto ecclesiastico* 65 (1954) 3-67 at 49-60.

by Dr. Ullmann, Huguccio went on to raise the delicate question, who was greater, pope or emperor. He first replied that the pope was greater than the emperor *in spiritualibus*, the emperor greater than the pope *in temporalibus*. But he hastened to modify this deceptively simple formula. The superiority of the pope lay in the fact that he possessed spiritual power over the emperor, could judge him and condemn him; but the emperor could not judge the pope in any circumstances. He had more temporal power than the pope but not temporal power over the pope.[19] In another context Huguccio wrote that secular power was as inferior to spiritual as lead to gold, and indeed, although he so firmly defended the dualist theory of the origin of the two powers, he also clearly maintained a certain subordination of the temporal power to the spiritual. This recognition of the intrinsic superiority of the spiritual power was, moreover, developed into a doctrine that the pope could assume the functions of a secular judge to prevent a failure of justice in circumstances where no established temporal authority was competent to act. Thus, in discussing the deposition of a secular ruler, he not only referred to a subtraction of obedience brought about by sentence of excommunication, but also suggested that the pope, as a superior judge, could confirm and thereby validate a sentence of deposition promulgated by princes or barons. Likewise the pope could remedy injustices arising from the neglect of the emperor and compel the emperor to make restitution to an injured party, this again because there was no other competent judge — 'et in secularibus etiam papa imperatorem iudicare potest, si alterius iudicium subire nolit.'[20] On the other hand, the pope could not depose a king or baron subject to emperor or king because in that case there did exist a legitimate secular judge:

---

[19] *Fonti* 149: 'Set queret aliquis uter utro sit maior? Et quidem in spiritualibus papa maior est imperatore, imperator maior papa in temporalibus... Set aliter, et aliter; papa sic est maior in spiritualibus, quod habet iurisdictionem in spiritualibus super imperatorem, ut in eis possit eum ligare, condempnare ... sed imperator non sic est maior papa in temporalibus ... nullam enim iurisdictionem vel prelationem habet imperator super papam: set dicitur esse maior in temporalibus quam ille quia maiorem potestatem et iurisdictionem habet in eis quam ille, non tamen super eum...' (*Summa ad Dist.* 96 c.6).

[20] *Fonti* 155: 'Set numquid papa potest deponere imperatorem vel regem qui non subest imperatori? Sic, si de voluntate principum coram eo accusetur et convincatur, et convinctus et admonitus nolit satisfacere, tunc debet excommunicare, ut si sic non respicit recte sententiam depositionis percellitur a papa vel a principibus de voluntate pape, est enim papa maior ei et preest ei... Sed nonne principes et barones si coram eis convincatur possunt eum deponere? credo quod sic, set habeant assensum pape, aliter non, cum iudex superior, id est papa, invenitur' (*Summa ad* 15 q.6 c.3); *Fonti* 153: 'Principaliter, ergo neutrum pendet ex aliquo, verum est quo ad institutionem, sed in multis imperialibus (sic!) potestas pendet ex pontificali, rationem, de negligentia habita circa eos corrigendos, nam si negligentes fuerunt in corrigendo eos luent penas pro suo delicto ut XVII q.II cognovimus, et quia gravius, nosti itaque et infra pendere, quo ad spiritualia, et in secularibus etiam papa imperatorem iudicare potest, si alterius iudicium subire nolit...' (*Summa ad Dist.* 96 c.10). (In some of the passages transcribed from Huguccio it seems that either Mochi Onory's manuscripts or his readings are at fault.) Huguccio's idea of the pope as *iudex superior* is by no means identical with the idea of an indirect influence of the spiritual power in temporal affairs, *ratione peccati*.

Set queret aliquis, an papa posset similiter deponere comites et alios barones qui subsunt regibus vel imperatoribus sine consensu illorum quibus subsunt. Credo quod non, quia non debent sub eo conveniri vel accusari, set sub suo rege vel imperatore. Simile est de metropolitano, qui licet possit iudicare episcopos suos ... non tamen eorum clericos.[21]

Mochi Onory presents these arguments at length, and in commenting on them, draws a series of interesting comparisons between Huguccio's theory of the relations between pope and emperor and his views on the structure of the ecclesiastical hierarchy itself. The implied analogy between a bishop and a king in the passage just cited gains added interest when we turn to Huguccio's explanation of the relationship between pope, metropolitan, and bishop, which Mochi Onory also explored. The metropolitan, Huguccio maintained, was the ordinary judge of the bishops of his province, but he was not the ordinary judge of the clergy subject to those bishops (just as the pope could depose a king but not the subject of a king). But, within the ecclesiastical hierarchy, the pope, in virtue of his *plenitudo potestatis*, was the *iudex ordinarius* of every one, of prelates and their subjects alike.[22] Evidently, even though Huguccio was prepared to countenance a considerable influence of the spiritual power over the temporal, he attributed to the pope a quite different type of authority in the ecclesiastical sphere from that conceded to him in temporal affairs. Mochi Onory naturally emphasizes this dualism and finds no difficulty in arguing that Huguccio's doctrines left to the secular state an essential core of autonomous life.

After dealing with Huguccio, however, he was faced with the more difficult problem of Alanus. For Dr. Ullmann the work of Alanus was the spring from which flowed the main stream of hierocratic tradition through Tancred and Bernardus Parmensis to the full flood of Innocent IV and Hostiensis. Mochi Onory does not carry his study down to include the glossators of the Gregorian Decretals, but he does deal with Alanus and Tancred, and he, in a quite different spirit, endeavors to accomodate their doctrines to his own view that the canonists generally favored a dualist theory of divided powers. We have seen how Alanus claimed that the pope possessed the *gladius materialis* and conferred it on the emperor. His gloss continued:

Si ergo papa iudex ordinarius est et quoad spiritualia et quoad temporalia, potest ab eo deponi imperator et eodem modo quilibet laicus habens potestatem vel dignitatem aliquam sub imperatore, si plenitudinem [?] potestatis suae uti vellet.[23]

---

[21] *Fonti* 156 (*Summa ad* 15 q.6 c.3).

[22] *Fonti* 166: '... metropolitanus non est iudex ordinarius nisi in parrochia sua, et licet sit iudex ordinarius suorum episcoporum non tamen illorum qui subsunt episcopis ... in papa tamen speciale est, qui est iudex ordinarius omnium, scilicet maiorum et minorum prelatorum et subditorum ... ipse enim solus habet plenitudinem potestatis...' (*Summa ad* 6 q.3 c.2).

[23] *Fonti* 191-2: 'Verius est quod gladium habeat a papa. Est enim corpus unum ecclesiae, ergo unum solum caput habere debet. Item, dominus utroque gladio usus est... Sed Petrum vicarium suum in terris in solidum constituit ergo utrumque gladium ei reliquit... Item si quoad temporalia imperator sub papa non fuisset, ergo de eis sub papa respondere non teneretur, at in neutra princeps a papa depositus, ut XV q.VI alius. Propter hoc dicatur, quod gladium materialem habet a papa. Canonica tamen canonicorum electio sibi tribuit. Si ergo papa iudex ordinarius est...' (Gloss *ad Comp.* I 2.20.7).

Alanus was using *plenitudo potestatis* in the same sense as Huguccio to describe a power of ordinary jurisdiction extending beyond the second rank of a hierarchy to embrace inferiors at all levels. But whereas Huguccio had attributed to the pope this universal jurisdiction only in the ecclesiastical sphere, Alanus extended it to the temporal sphere as well. This might seem to demolish any possible claim to autonomy of the secular ruler, but Mochi Onory makes considerable play with the next words of the gloss:

> Sed numquid pro omni crimine potest deponi imperator? Respondeo: immo pro nullo, nisi persistere in illo contenderit. Sed nec tunc forte pro omni, sed solum pro tali, quod scandalum inducit, ut est haeresis, symonia, discordia continua et si qua sunt similia... Sed numquid papa materialem gladium sibi posset retinere? Resp. non, dominus enim gladios divisit, ut XCVI. di. cum ad verum, et praeterea ecclesia ex hoc plurimum turbaretur.

According to Mochi Onory's interpretation of this passage the emperor could be deposed only for persistent 'crimen (= peccatum)' and so, 'In this fashion canonistic thought reached a secure conclusion: the *ratio criminis* (= *peccatum*) constituted the title in virtue of which the pope intervened in the deposition of a prince...'[24] Mochi Onory's argument does seem to become rather strained at this point. Alanus stated clearly enough that the pope's power of deposition stemmed from his possession of supreme temporal authority, not from any indirect effect of his spiritual authority, and contemporaries of Alanus sometimes held that a ruler who was merely *inutilis* could be deposed without any question of *peccatum*. Mochi Onory seems on firmer ground in pointing out that the denial to the pope of the actual exercise of temporal authority still provided some possibility of *autonomia e sufficienza di vita* for the secular power.[25]

It is true that the 'monistic' theory could leave to the prince a real freedom of action in his own sphere (even though his authority was derived from the pope) provided that the exclusion of the pope from the actual exercise of temporal power was rigorously maintained. But it is also true that the 'dualist' theory could be developed in a fashion that would make temporal rulers no more than servants of the pope (although he was not the source of their power). The practical content of the canonists' theories would depend on the policies actually pursued by the popes, and on the material that their decretal letters provided for the canonistic collections. The last part of Mochi Onory's book is therefore devoted to an exposition of the interplay of canonistic thought around certain crucial decretals of Innocent III, especially

---

[24] *Fonti* 194.

[25] It will be seen that there is a direct conflict on this point between Mochi Onory and Ullmann. Ullmann, relying on MS Aug. XL, Badische Landesbibliothek, Karlsruhe, wrote: 'The pope if he wished could use both swords: « Utroque gladio uti potest »' (*Medieval Papalism* 149). These words do not occur in Mochi Onory's version (Schulte's transcription from MS Ye.52, Universitätsbibliothek, Halle). The nearest parallel is 'dominus utroque gladio usus est,' but there *dominus* referred to Christ. That Mochi Onory's text reflects Alanus' true viewpoint is proved by a recently printed text from Alanus' apparatus on the *Decretum* (*Ius Naturale*), 'Sed nunquid papa posset materialem sibi retinere si vellet. R(espondeo) non, quia dominus gladios divisit, ut hic, et ecclesia ex hoc plurimum turbaretur': Gaines Post, 'Two Notes on Nationalism in the Middle Ages,' *Traditio* 9 (1953) 281-320 at 304.

Per Venerabilem, Licet, Novit, and *Venerabilem.*[26] The first three decretals provided concrete examples of the pope claiming temporal jurisdiction where there was no competent lay judge, or where justice had been denied, or where a moral issue was involved. (In the decretal *Novit* Innocent defended his intervention *ratione peccati* in a feudal dispute between the king of France and the king of England.) *Venerabilem* set out the papal theory of the *translatio imperii,* and Innocent's claim that he could examine and reject the candidate for the imperial title elected by the princes. We are here working over the same ground that Ullmann covered in his last chapter, but Mochi Onory harvests a very different crop of inferences from the same material. He insists — following Maccarrone — that all Innocent's claims were consistent with a dualist theory on the origins of spiritual and temporal power, and he does show that canonists committed to a dualist position were able to assimilate them into the framework of their thought without undue strain.

But there still remains a real difficulty in reconciling Innocent's legislative and political activity with Mochi Onory's pattern of thought. It is not so much that Innocent committed the papacy, and in its wake the canonists, to an uncompromising hierocratic monism, but rather that he showed how even the dualist doctrine of Huguccio could justify such vast encroachments into the sphere of secular jurisdiction as to undermine any effective independence of the temporal power. If the pope could take cognizance of any secular case where a plaintiff pleaded that he had been denied justice, if he claimed the final say in any matter of criminal jurisdiction involving sin, if this jurisdiction *ratione peccati* was to be extended even to the intricacies of feudal disputes, what then became of the state's *autonomia e sufficienza di vita*? Even canonists more moderate than Alanus and Tancred were led to defend a great expansion of papal claims over the lay power, and, if one takes into account the developments of Innocent III's arguments by Innocent IV and Hostiensis, it becomes well-nigh impossible to imagine any kind of significant political action over which the pope did not claim ultimate jurisdiction on one ground or another. In the works of the thirteenth-century canonists the autonomy of the secular power does indeed come to appear as 'a vessel without content.'

Mochi Onory does not ignore this tendency of canonistic thought, but, we think, does not assimilate it adequately into the framework of his theory. He shows no inclination to minimize the popes' interventions in the secular sphere, nor the canonists' claims arising out of them; he even seems to document such claims with a certain enthusiasm. To the argument that they destroy that independence of the secular power which, he claims, the canonists were anxious to defend, he has a simple answer, repeated several times in the course of his work. The papal *imperium spirituale* did not violate the essential autonomy of the secular power since, whenever the pope intervened in the secular sphere, he acted from spiritual motives — *di motivi d'ordine spirituale e religioso.* And so we reach the conclusion that the nations of Christendom were to be ruled by 'Catholic monarchs, sovereign in the bounds of their own kingaoms, subject only to the authority of one who, from motives pertaining to the spiritual world, approves and guides, judges and controls, confirms and deposes' (p. 226). It might seem that the question whether a ruler who is subject to 'judgment,' 'control,' 'deposition' can be called sovereign in any

---

[26] In the Gregorian Decretals respectively 4.17.13, 2.2.10, 2.1.13, 1.6.34.

normal sense of the word is more a problem of semantics than of political theory. But, in any case, the idea that the motive of a superior provides a proper citerion for determining the degree of independence of an inferior seems open to criticism. St. Louis was presumably actuated by spiritual motives in his government of France; every medieval king was supposed to rule 'from spiritual motives.' One cannot help feeling that some recent writers who have sought to defend the thirteenth-century pontiffs against charges of excessive wordly ambition are at times not certain whether they wish to prove that the popes did not pursue temporal power or that they pursued it with the very best of intentions.

The most paradoxical feature of Mochi Onory's conclusion is that he seems to be saying the same thing that Ullmann does in the last pages of *Medieval Papalism* — 'It was the spiritual power who directed and guided the temporalities of life to the end recognized as true and fitting for man.'[27] It might remove much confusion if we could come to understand how two gifted writers could cover so much common ground, and even reach a verbal similarity in their conclusions, yet really hold such radically different views concerning the whole temper and tendency of canonistic thought. The solution may lie in the fact that the papal decretals and canonistic glosses of the Middle Ages readily lend themselves to two different types of interpretation. One can seek in them abstract principles of general validity, perennially relevant to the problems of Church and State, or one can turn to them simply for help in understanding the particular policies that medieval pontiffs were led to adopt, and the canonists to defend, by the exigencies of contemporary politics. Each type of enquiry will have its own methods and emphases. We may agree, for instance, that Boniface VIII was a very ambitious prelate but still find *Unam Sanctam* a very ambiguous document. Again, Fr. Stickler takes Dr. Ullmann to task for failing to state clearly that, in principle, there could be no appeal from a secular court to an ecclesiastical one, that such an appeal was only allowed in certain exceptional cases. It is well to have the principle stated; but it is also useful to be reminded that, in canonistic doctrine, the 'exceptions' became almost all-embracing. The relevance of either consideration depends on what one is trying to prove.

On this basis we might argue that Ullmann and Mochi Onory have each used a method of analysis that would have been more appropriate in pursuing the objective of the other. Ullmann has proved convincingly enough that if one takes together all the divers claims and arguments that the popes, and the canonists on their behalf, put forward in the Middle Ages, often in the heat of bitter disputes with the secular power, they do add up, for all practical purposes, to an assertion of papal overlordship. But what he asserts is that the canonistic doctrine of papal world monarchy was a necessary corollary of a papally-inspired monistic philosophy of politics. Mochi Onory, on the other hand, has devoted great ingenuity and diligence to proving that, even in the most extreme hierocratic utterances down to the time of Tancred, there is always some loop-hole in the formulation of the abstract principle involved that makes it just possible to reconcile these texts with a dualist theory of Church and State. But he will have it that these canonists were all aglow with enthusiasm for the effective independence of secular rulers in the real world

---

[27] *Medieval Papalism* 194.

of affairs. Each writer has constructed a strong and in its way convincing argument, but in neither case does the argument prove exactly what the author intended.

There is one great merit in Mochi Onory's work which requires some further discussion. More than any other writer in the field he has shown himself aware that the medieval problems of *Sacerdotium* and *Regnum* cannot be considered adequately in a vacuum. He has sought instead to treat the structure of Church-State relations as an integral element in the pattern of medieval society as a whole. Above all he has emphasized how often the canonists borrowed analogies from within the ecclesiastical hierarchy itself to define relations between the spiritual and temporal powers, and how receptive they were too to conceptions derived from secular systems of government. A continuation of this line of thought might even suggest a solution to the central problem of current dispute — whether canonistic thought was essentially 'monist' or 'dualist' in its orientation. The real problem is not so much that some canonists seem to be monists and some dualists, but that no canonist whose works have been explored so far is consistent in defending a position of absolute monism or of absolute dualism. The real solution may be that in seeking to identify the canonists' doctrines with one doctrinaire position or the other we are imposing on them categories of thought that have little relation to the real sources and content of their work. The problems that most interested the canonists were practical rather than speculative ones — what authority had the pope to confirm, appoint, depose secular rulers? to intervene in the internal affairs of kingdoms? hear appeals? exercise authority during vacancies? The mass of accumulated jurisprudence on the relations of superiors and subordinates within the Church and within the State provided the obvious raw material from which the answers could be quarried. Such material could of course provide a variety of answers, but it remains true that the substantial content of the canonists' teaching was probably influenced more by their working experience of the structure of medieval societies than by any disposition to press abstract principles to logical conclusions.[28] It is odd that so much has been written on the canonists' theories of Church-and-State, but so little about their theory of the Church, or, for that matter, of the State. This situation may account for some of the current difficulties of interpretation.[29]

It might seem that the power relations involved in the subordination of temporal authority to spiritual were much more subtle and elusive than any that would occur in the straight-forward hierarchical subordination of inferior to superior within either society. But we should not allow ourselves to become even more hypnotized than were medieval thinkers themselves by the impressive simplicity of the Dyonisian celestial hierarchy, with its omnipotent head, and power flowing from the head downwards from rank to rank in a pyramid of perfect symmetry. Whatever lip-service was paid to the idea,

---

[28] Hence, the conclusions of the medieval canonists are not likely to prove very relevant in the discussion of the same problems against the backgrounds of quite different societies.

[29] Modern partisans of the dualist theory too readily interpret the texts asserting that the temporal power was not derived from the spiritual as excluding any sort of direct hierarchical subordination; their adversaries too readily see in the claims that the pope did confer authority on the emperor an assertion of the unqualified subjection of the temporal power.

medieval hierarchies of government were not so simple as that in practice; in fact their complexities provided the canonists with analogies for most of the problems involved in defining the pope's powers over a secular ruler.[30] It is true that analogies of this sort could provide no adequate answer to the enduring philosophical and theological problems involved in the relations of spiritual and temporal power; but it may also be true that the solution of such problems was not a major preoccupation of the medieval canonists. They did have the idea of an indirect power of the spiritual authority in temporal affairs, *ratione peccati*, but they showed little inclination to probe into the perennial problems concerning the relations between secular law and moral law that such a concept implies. They did take sides on the central philosophical issue: whether, in virtue of its inherent superiority, spiritual authority was necessarily the source of temporal power. But when one looks for a rational defense of one side or the other, one usually encounters only a string of pre-cedents and metaphors — all too often dubious precedents and muddled metaphors.

We are not suggesting that the epic clashes of *Regnum* and *Sacerdotium* in the Middle Ages stimulated no profound reflections on the deepest problems involved; but, if one is looking for universally valid principles rationally de-fended, there is much richer material to be found in the medieval philosophers and theologians than in the lawyers. Still less are we suggesting that the canonists' contribution in this field was negligible and unworthy of the attention it has been receiving. For the historian who seeks simply to understand the workings of thirteenth-century ecclesiastical polity — and politics — a know-ledge of the canonists is becoming indispensable. We are only on the thresh-old of the work that needs to be done.

A number of articles by Fr. Stickler provide good examples of the sort of work that can be most useful now that the broad lines of the subject have been opened up. Although we have mentioned some of Fr. Stickler's views already, we have reserved for a separate discussion his own original contributions to the discussion since they are rather different in purpose and temper from the

---

[30] Thus, some canonists held that temporal power was subordinate to spiritual, yet not derived from it. This was not a unique relationship; writers like Huguccio and Joannes Teutonicus were by no means certain that, within the ecclesiastical hierarchy, a bishop's authority was derived from the pope, but they had no doubt that the bishop was hier-archically subordinate to the pope. (The point is discussed in my forthcoming book, *Foun-dations of the Conciliar Theory*.) Again, we have seen how Huguccio borrowed an analogy from within the ecclesiastical hierarchy to explain the position of the pope in relation to the subjects of a temporal king; if he had turned to the temporal sphere he would have found similar examples in the relations of lords to sub-vassals. C. C. Bayley has recently shown how Innocent III, in developing his doctrine on the powers implied by his right to confirm the election of the emperor, closely followed the law relating to confirmation of episcopal elections (*The Formation of the German College of Electors in the Mid-Thirteenth Century* [Toronto 1949] 124-8). So too, the whole papal argument concerning vacancy of the empire or negligence of the emperor is paralleled in the canon law relating to de-volution of authority to superiors in the ecclesiastical hierarchy. And here, again, the claim that a ruler who did not normally exercise jurisdiction over the subjects of his sub-ordinates could do so on a complaint of denial of justice, was a commonplace in the sphere of secular government.

works already considered. Ullmann and Mochi Onory have each built up an imposing synthesis and defended it with a certain warmth. Fr. Stickler's articles have been severely analytical, concerned with the clarification of certain technical terminology used by the canonists in their discussions on *Regnum* and *Sacerdotium*. His great theme is the interpretation of the allegory of the two swords, and he has patiently pursued this theme from Gregory VII through Anselm of Lucca and St. Bernard to the canonists of the twelfth century.[31] As regards the canonists, the article which best conveys the essence of his thought is one on Gratian himself,[32] in which Fr. Stickler reaches the striking conclusion that the terms *gladius spiritualis* and *gladius materialis*, commonly assumed by thirteenth-century canonists and modern scholars alike to refer to ecclesiastical and secular power, had no such connotations for Gratian. To him they meant rather the powers of spiritual coercion and of physical coercion which both belonged to the Church as a juridically perfect society. The highest form of spiritual coercion was excommunication while there were two extreme forms of physical coercion, sentence of mutilation or death (*effusio sanguinis*) and the making of war (*vis armata*). However, since it was considered improper for clerics to have any part in the shedding of blood, the Church could not itself use the *gladius materialis*[33] which it possessed but had to call on the lay power to do so. This delegation to lay rulers of the *gladius materialis* of the Church made possible all the subsequent confusions of thought and terminology. The chances of such confusion were heightened by the fact that a lay ruler did have an obligation to use his own secular power in the service of the Church at the request of pope or bishop. Hence, when we read of a prince using force on behalf of the Church, it is often not clear whether he was exercising the delegated authority of the Church or his own authority at the request of the Church. But it is clear that when Gratian used a phrase like *papa dat gladium imperatori*, he did not mean that the pope bestowed temporal power on the emperor — only that he delegated to the emperor the exercise of the material sword of the Church.

Fr. Stickler has applied these conclusions in another paper where he undertakes a systematic analysis of Gratian's views on the relations of *Sacerdotium* and *Regnum*.[34] It is the most detailed study of Gratian that has been undertaken from this point of view, and provides a model of scholarly method even if the conclusions have not been universally accepted.[35] The result of the ana-

---

[31] 'Il potere coattivo materiale della Chiesa nella Reforma Gregoriana secondo Anselmo di Lucca,' *Studi Gregoriani* 2 (1947) 235-85; 'Il gladius nel Registro di Gregorio VII,' *ibid.* 3 (1948) 89-103; 'Il « gladius » negli atti dei concilii e dei RR. Pontefici sino a Graziano e Bernardo di Clairvaux,' *Salesianum* 13 (1951) 414-45.

[32] 'De ecclesiae potestate coactiva materiali apud magistrum Gratianum,' *Salesianum* 4 (1942) 2-23, 97-119.

[33] There was a distinction here between *effusio sanguinis* and *vis armata*. A cleric could not exercise the first power even indirectly; he could not, that is, delegate the jurisdiction of the Church to a lay judge with the demand that death or mutilation be inflicted. He could, however, exercise the *vis armata* indirectly by summoning lay rulers to make war on behalf of the Church.

[34] 'Magistri Gratiani sententia de potestate ecclesiae in statum,' *Apollinaris* 21 (1948) 36-111.

[35] Dr. Ullmann has expressed sharp disagreement. See 'The Medieval Interpretation

lysis is to rank Gratian very definitely among the adherents of the Gelasian dualist tradition. According to Fr. Stickler, 'the father of the science of canon law' taught that both powers were instituted by God, separate in offices and functions, neither dependent on the other. Lay princes were subject to the jurisdiction of the Church in spiritual matters and the sentences of the Church in such matters might have an influence (*influxus*) on secular affairs. Nevertheless, in principle, 'the temporal power is in no way juridically dependent on the spiritual; neither by divine law nor by human law.'

This work on Gratian provides a firmer foundation than has hitherto been available for investigating the development of thought among the glossators of the *Decretum*. In a discussion of the *Quaestiones Bambergenses* Fr. Stickler notices some hints of a confusion of terminology, but his major contribution to the unravelling of Decretist thought is an article on Huguccio.[36] In the work of this great canonist the idea of the *gladius materialis* as temporal power, the 'political' sword-idea existed side by side with the older 'coercive-jurisdiction' idea, both being fully developed in different contexts. It is not clear whether Huguccio was himself conscious of the double meaning he attached to the allegory of the sword. He showed no awareness of the problem and he never discussed it; if he had done so he might have provided an invaluable clarification at a critical moment in the development of canonistic thought. On the other hand, he never fell into confusion; he did not, that is, cite passages referring to the old idea of the sword when he was using the term as a symbol of temporal power. However, it is easy to see how such confusion could arise in the works of his successors and, perhaps, distort their whole outlook on the relations of Church and State.

These articles are full of penetrating and valuable insights. It is evident that a development of the line of argument they suggest might undermine the theory that the canonists regarded the emperor as a mere *minister*, a servant of the pope, and Fr. Stickler promises to come to grips with this problem in an article on 'Imperator vicarius Papae.'[37] It is also true, however, that his technical articles as yet provide no irresistible evidence for his general views on the development of canonistic thought, for he has not yet dealt in detail with the major canonists of the mid-thirteenth century. Fr. Stickler has shown himself a formidable critic but he has not yet followed Dr. Ullmann onto his own ground.

For a final evaluation of thirteenth-century canonistic teachings on Church and State we shall need a new survey of those teachings themselves, based on all the available texts.[38] We shall also need a broader study setting the

---

of Frederick I's Authentic « Habita »,' *Studi in memoria di Paolo Koschaker* 1 (Milan 1953) 101-36 at 106.

[36] 'De potestate gladii materialis ecclesiae secundum « Quaestiones Bambergenses » in-editas,' *Salesianum* 6 (1944) 113-140; 'Der Schwerterbegriff bei Huguccio,' *Ephemerides iuris canonici* 3 (1937) 201-42.

[37] 'Sacerdotium et Regnum,' *Salesianum* 15 (1953) 577 n. 2. The article is to appear in the centenary *Festschrift* of the *Institut für österreichische Geschichtsforschung* (1954). See *infra*, Additional Note.

[38] Before a new synthesis is undertaken it seems desirable that other expressions prominent in the controversy should be subjected to the same sort of stringent analysis that Fr. Stickler has applied to the allegory of the swords. We would suggest especially *potes-*

doctrines of the high Middle Ages against the background of earlier ecclesiastical tradition. Dr. Ullmann has lately been devoting all his attention to this second task.[39] It is to be hoped that Fr. Stickler will bear in mind the saying of Fustel de Coulanges that an hour of synthesis is worth a life-time of analysis, and will eventually undertake the first.

II. *Regnum and Imperium*

Contemporary interest in the origins of the European system of nation states has no doubt been stimulated both by the recent perversions of nationalism and by the current attempts to re-create some form of supra-national authority. The problem has many aspects and the juristic approach has not been neglected in recent work.[40]

When the Roman Empire collapsed, independent kingdoms established themselves in its ruins. From the time of Charlemagne there existed a rather vague theory that all kings should again be subject to one emperor who was thought of as the temporal head of Christendom; with the revival of the study of Roman law in the twelfth century the theory acquired sharper outlines, the contemporary German emperor of course being cast for the role of *dominus mundi*, though, needless to say, no emperor actually exercised universal authority in the Middle Ages. The juristic problem is to determine when the *de facto* independence of the national kings became supported, not only by effective military power, nor even by conscious patriotic sentiment, but by a coherent legal theory opposed to the universalism of the classical Roman law. One of the main themes of Mochi Onory's *Fonti canonistiche* is that the canonists of the twelfth and early thirteenth centuries were responsible for creating such

---

tas clavium, still very obscure when applied to the public power of the pope in spite of the work of Van de Kerckhove, *La notion de juridiction dans la doctrine des décrétistes et des premiers décrétalistes* (Assisi 1937); and, above all, that much-misunderstood term *plenitudo potestatis*, for which a beginning has just been made in Dr. Ladner's article cited n. 6 above.

[39] See his articles, 'The Origins of the Ottonianum,' *Cambridge Historical Journal* 11 (1953) 114-28; 'Cardinal Roland and Besançon,' *Miscellanea Historiae Pontificiae* 18 (Rome 1954) 107-125; 'Frederick's Opponent, Innocent IV, as Melchisedek,' in *Atti del Convegno internazionale di Studi Federiciani* (Palermo 1952); 'Cardinal Humbert and the Ecclesia Romana,' *Studi Gregoriani* 4 (1952) 111-27; 'Nos si aliquid incompetenter...', *Ephemerides Iuris Canonici* 9 (1953) 279-287.

[40] The best recent survey of the whole subject is that of F. A. F. von der Heydte, *Die Geburtstunde des souveränen Staates* (Regensburg 1952). The author has based his study mainly on the theologians, publicists, and civilians of the thirteenth and fourteenth centuries. He mentions the canonists incidentally but was not able to use the recent work emphasizing the importance of their contribution. — Dr. Rolf Most, who was killed in the recent war, was working up to the time of his death on ideas cocerning the empire and national statehood in the glosses of the canonists. His only published work in this field was a study on Lupold of Bebenburg, in which he compared the historical and juristic approach of Lupold with the theological basis of Ockham's thought, 'Der Reichsgedanke des Lupold von Bebenburg,' *Deutsches Archiv für Geschichte des Mittelalters* 4 (1940) 444-85. He left unfinished a projected thesis, *Studien zur abendländischen Geltung des deutschen Kaisertums im ausgehenden Mittelalter, insbesondere in Spanien*. On his work see H. Heimpel, *Deutsches Archiv* 5 (1941-42) 511-13.

a theory. Alert to the actual trends of political development and, as partisans of the papacy, hostile to the empire, they built a new doctrine around the idea *rex, imperator in regno suo, superiorem in temporalibus non recognoscit.* The kingdoms were to be loosed from the bond of legal subjection to the empire, the unity of Christendom maintained by the universal *imperium spirituale* of the pope, which respected the autonomy of the king in secular affairs.

In presenting these views Mochi Onory was saying the last word — or almost the last word — in an argument that has been going on for the past forty years about the origins of the phrase, *rex est imperator in regno suo.* In 1913 Sidney Woolf traced the expression from Bartolus to Oldradus da Ponte (d. 1335). Ercole next showed that it was employed in France in the controversies between Philip the Fair and Boniface VIII and attributed the earliest use of it to the French canonist Gulielmus Durandus. In 1921 Paul Fournier noticed a similar usage in the work of a contemporary Sicilian jurist, Andrea d'Isernia. Nine years later Calasso entered the fray and from then on it became mainly a duel between him and Ercole, the one claiming an Italian, the other a French origin for the crucial formula. Calasso first supported the claim to priority of the Neapolitan jurist Marinus da Caramanico; Ercole riposted with the French writer Jean de Blanot, whose work appeared before that of Marinus in 1256.[41] In his latest book Calasso has argued that the idea of the king as emperor in his own kingdom was current among the canonists and legists of Bologna in the earliest years of the thirteenth century, and that it was developed scientifically into a theory of the independence of national kings by the civilian glossators of South Italy, most especially by his favorite author, Marinus.[42]

As evidence for the early currency of the idea in Bologna Calasso cites two canonistic texts and one civilian one. Stephanus Tornacensis, glossing the words, *Constitutio, vel edictum est quod rex vel imperator constituit vel edicit,* wrote: '(Rex) in regno suo, vel eundem vocat regem et imperatorem.'[43] Calasso does not lay much emphasis on this, and rightly so, for, properly understood, it has nothing whatsoever to do with the question at issue. The second canonistic text is much more important. It is from Alanus, and it occurs at the end of the famous passage where he claimed that the pope conferred power on the emperor and could depose him. After presenting his arguments Alanus concluded: 'Et quod dictum est de imperatore, dictum habeatur de quolibet rege vel principe, qui nulli subest. Unusquisque enim tantum juris habet in regno suo quantum imperator in imperio.'[44]

The importance of this passage for the controversy about the idea of the king as emperor was pointed out by Rivière as long ago as 1926.[45] Calasso wel-

---

[41] For the bibliography of this controversy see Mochi Onory, *Fonti* 9 n. 1.

[42] F. Calasso, *I glossatori e la teoria della sovranità* (Milan 1945). In subsequent notes references are given to the second edition, Milan 1951.

[43] *I glossatori* 35 (*Summa ad Dist.* 2 c.4). Stephanus was explaining that either the word *rex* in his text meant a local king who could issue only local edicts or else the word *rex* was used to designate the emperor. He did not mean that every local king had imperial power.

[44] *I glossatori* 35 (Gloss *ad Comp. I* 2.20.7). The gloss continued: 'Divisio enim regnorum de jure gentium introductum a papa approbatur, licet antiquo jure gentium imperator unus in orbe esse deberet' (*cit. Fonti*, 192).

[45] *Le problème de l'église et de l'état au temps de Philippe le Bel* (Louvain-Paris 1926) 424-30.

comed it as evidence for the currency of the idea in Italy long before its appearance in France. But it could not have been completely satisfactory from his point of view to find the first germs of a theory of national sovereignty in the works of a Frenchman and an Englishman even if they were both professors at Bologna. He therefore argues that the context of Alanus' passage makes it impossible to read into his words any such implication. It was precisely in propounding the theory of papal overlordship that Alanus referred to the independence of kings and princes; he wished to maintain the doctrine of a universal empire, and merely to substitute the pope for the emperor as its head. Calasso lays far more emphasis on his civilian text, from the great Azo himself. It was a question of defining the powers of the king of France in a feudal dispute. In arguing the case for the king, Azo wrote: 'Item quilibet (rex) hodie videtur eandem potestatem habere in terra sua, quam imperator, ergo potuit facere quod placet.'[46]

As for the canonists, apart from explaining away the text of Alanus, observing that Joannes Teutonicus upheld the authority of the emperor, and discerning the seeds of the hierocratic theory in Huguccio, Calasso has little to say about them, and he certainly does not attribute to them a major part in the evolution of the idea of national independence. All through the thirteenth century, according to him, 'il principio d'ordine universale manteneva sempre, nella dialettica della Chiesa, la sua integrità originaria.'

At this point Mochi Onory stepped in to state the case for the canonists. In his opinion, the text of Azo is without significance,[47] that of Alanus a most important contribution to a broad movement of canonistic thought that established a firm juristic basis for a theory of national sovereign states. The validity of this claim depends partly of course on the correctness of Mochi Onory's view that the canonists did not claim for the pope a universal temporal *imperium*. A great deal of his argument rests also on another presupposition which is again controversial, namely that the attribution to a king of the powers of an emperor within his own territory necessarily implied that the king was independent of any external authority. Calasso has expressed doubt on this point. As Gaines Post observes,

> Francesco Calasso refuses to believe that *rex imperator in regno suo* meant independence of the Empire, for in a sense every local administrator was king or emperor in his sphere of jurisdiction... But I find this argument weak: some canonists and legists, and theologians, held that the king, who had the powers of the emperor in his own realm, recognized *no* superior.[48]

Calasso's argument is weak if it is exaggerated to exclude as irrelevant all early expressions of the *rex-imperator* idea — which is what Gaines Post had in mind — but, taken in a more moderate sense, it is not without substance. The claim that a subordinate exercised in a limited territory the same powers that a superior exercised universally did not in fact necessarily imply that the subordinate recognized no superior. Canonists of the early thirteenth

---

[46] *I glossatori* 38.

[47] *Fonti* 65-7. Mochi Onory points out that Azo, in his final decision on the case, did not accept the principle of the text cited.

[48] Gaines Post, '« Blessed Lady Spain » - Vincentius Hispanus and Spanish National Imperialism in the Thirteenth Century,' *Speculum* 29 (1954) 198-209 at 199, referring to *I glossatori* 172f.

century could write that the difference between the *plena auctoritas* which only the pope possessed and the authority of any other bishop lay simply in the universal extension of the papal power; apart from this universality the bishop possessed in his own diocese the elements of power that made up *plena auctoritas*.[49] Again, some of the canonistic glosses which most clearly developed the claims of kings to exercise the public authority attributed to the emperor in Roman law were written on the canons *In apibus* and *Scitote*, of which the first specifically laid down that there was one single emperor, and the second dealt with the organization of an ecclesiastical province, with the obvious implication that the province was part of wider unity.[50]

If the phrase, *rex, imperator in regno suo, superiorem in temporalibus non recognoscit*, had been a commonplace in canonistic glosses, then indeed it would be reasonable to suppose that any reference to the king as emperor carried some hint of independent authority, but in fact the phrase never occurs at all in the works with which we are concerned. It is formed by a conflation of two ideas which were at first quite separable. Certainly, there were some canonists who held that there were kings who recognized no superior, and when we find a clear-cut statement of that view in their works together with the assertion that the king exercised the powers of an emperor *in regno suo*, it is reasonable to assume that the second claim was intended to buttress the first. When for instance, we find Vincentius Hispanus defending the fiscal and legislative powers of the king of Castile, we may with some reason suppose that he was eager to demonstrate the self-sufficiency of the Spanish kingdom, perhaps in order to refute the claim of Joannes Teutonicus that a kingdom separated from the empire was 'headless' and 'monstrous.' But such an inference is only justified by the fact that other glosses of Vincentius decisively repudiate imperial claims over Spain. The mere attribution to a king of public authority in his own kingdom no more proved that the king was independent of the emperor than the parallel descriptions of a bishop's jurisdiction in his diocese proved that the bishop was independent of the pope.

If this criticism is well founded it upsets all Mochi Onory's claims for the twelfth-century canonists up to and including Huguccio. In the first part of his work he has taken great pains to gather together glosses referring to the powers of kings and magistrates of cities over their own peoples, and he attaches great importance to the gloss of Stephanus Tornacensis already quoted. But none of this is really relevant to the problem of *rex* and *imperator*. He also discusses the claim of local communities to enact laws or maintain customs contrary to the universal written law. Here he does seem to be coming to grips with the problem of local autonomy, but it has been pointed out that in the texts he cites the canonists were merely echoing earlier controversies among the civilians, not making an original contribution of their own.[51]

---

[49] MS 676, Caius College, Cambridge *ad Dist.* 11 c.2: 'Plena potestas consistit in precepto, necessitate observantie, generalitate. Quilibet episcopus duo istorum habet in sua diocesi scil. preceptum et necessitatem observantie. Summus vero pontifex habet tres, scil. preceptum, necessitatem et generalitatem.' (On this MS see S. Kuttner and E. Rathbone, 'Anglo-Norman Canonists of the Twelfth Century,' *Traditio* 7 [1949-51] 279-339 at 317f.). There are similar passages in Huguccio and the *Glossa Palatina ad Dist.* 11 c.2.

[50] 7 q.1 c.41 and 6 q.3 c.2.

[51] E. M. Meijers, Book Review, *Tijdschrift voor Rechtsgeschiedenis* 20 (1952) 113-25.

I

616

The weaknesses in the earlier part of Mochi Onory's work can be illustrated best from his chapter on Huguccio, who receives more attention than any other canonist, and who is presented as a great figure of transition, half-committed to the old ideas, yet reaching forward towards a new synthesis. Mochi Onory begins by asserting (but without adequate textual support) that Huguccio attributed to each king *plenitudo potestatis* in his own kingdom,[52] then proceeds to cite two texts in which, he claims, Huguccio referred to a king as emperor *in regno suo*.[53] But in fact both texts really stated that the *imperator* could be called *rex*, not that every *rex* was an *imperator*. Then, relying on Huguccio's glosses on *In apibus* and *Scitote*, Mochi Onory points out that he insisted on the need for one single sovereign power — supreme judge and supreme legislator — in each realm. Moreover he explicitly referred to the existence of kings independent of the emperor. This is the one valid point in the argument. Huguccio actually did write, in discussing the deposition of an emperor by the pope, 'potest deponere imperatorem vel regem qui non subest imperatori'; but when one considers this passing phrase in the whole context of his work, it seems extremely improbable that he had in mind anything but *de facto* independence. Whenever he discussed the question explicitly he maintained that all kings were *de iure* subject to the emperor — 'solus enim romanus dicitur iure imperator, sub quo omnes reges debent esse.'[54] Mochi Onory, having extracted from Huguccio's glosses a picture of the king as equal to the emperor, sovereign in his own territory, finds this very paradoxical, and even sees Huguccio as 'tormented with doubt.' He lays great emphasis on a text in which Huguccio first observed that the French and English were, or ought to be, subject to the Roman empire, and then added:

> Item, saltem ratione pontificis subsunt romano imperio; omnes enim christiani subsunt apostolico et ideo omnes tenentur vivere secundum leges romanas, saltem quas approbat ecclesia.[55]

Mochi Onory sees in this text a crucial stage in the development of the doctrine of papal *imperium spirituale*; Calasso sees in it the beginning of the hierocratic theory. We are inclined to think that Huguccio was not intending any subtle novelty, but merely observing that, while the French and English ought to be subject to the emperor, they certainly were subject to the pope *de facto* as well as *de iure*. For the immediate controversy the main relevance of the text would seem to be that Huguccio again firmly asserted the universal authority of the emperor as a matter of right. His position on this question was quite consistent and thoroughly conservative. Naturally he knew that some kings did not recognize the emperor's authority *de facto*, but he never suggested that this state of affairs could be justified *de iure*.

Mochi Onory's arguments have recently been criticized in rather astringent

---

[52] *Fonti* 164. Mochi Onory discusses at some length Huguccio's use of *plena potestas* and *plenitudo potestatis* (158-61), but none of the texts cited apply *plenitudo potestatis* to royal authority.

[53] *Fonti* 165, 167 (*Summa ad* 7 q.1 c.41, Dist.2 c.4). Mochi Onory's misinterpretations of these texts were noticed independently by Meijers, *art. cit.* 123 n. 2 and by Kuttner, 'Papst Honorius und das Studium des Zivilrechts' (*supra* n. 4) 97 n. 2.

[54] *Fonti* 165 (*Summa ad* 7 q.1 c.41).

[55] *Fonti* 175 (*Summa ad* Dist.1 c.12).

fashion by E. M. Meijers.[56] All his criticisms are valid and documented — he concentrates on Mochi Onory's neglect of Roman law doctrines and his misunderstanding of the *rex-imperator* equation in Huguccio. Yet the review as a whole seems a little harsh in tone, for Mochi Onory did make a substantial contribution in the latter part of his book. Once Huguccio is left behind we have a much more firmly based argument with sufficient material on the direct point at issue to show, at least, that Calasso dismissed the canonists far too casually.

The first canonistic gloss which clearly defended the independence of the national kings, and associated the claim to independence with the assertion that the king possessed the powers of an emperor in his kingdom, came from the Englishman Ricardus. After stating the traditional point of view that all kings were subject to the emperor, he continued:

> Set contra: Patet reges multos imperatori non subici. Videtur enim quod sicut per violentiam essent subditi, quod violenter possint ad propriam redire libertatem. Nam universitas civitatis, multo magis regni, iurisdictionem et imperium conferre potest ... et exercitus eligit imperatorem, pari ratione et regem... Item cum uterque tam imperator quam rex eadem auctoritate, eadem consecratione, eadem crismate inungitur, unde ergo potestatis diversitas?[57]

This was written in the last years of the twelfth century. A decade later, Alanus, another Englishman, produced the gloss already quoted, and, however one interprets Alanus' doctrine of papal power, this gloss certainly upheld the independence of kings from the emperor. In the meantime there had appeared Innocent III's decretal *Per Venerabilem* (1201), which stated that the king of France acknowledged no temporal overlord (*cum ... superiorem in temporalibus minime recognoscat*). Comment on this was at first cautious. Laurentius merely wrote dryly, de facto,[58] Joannes Galensis also wrote, de facto, with the added explanation that *de iure* the king was subject to the pope in spiritualities and temporalities; Joannes Teutonicus, a strong defender of the German *imperium*, observed, 'de iure tamen (rex) subest romano imperatori,' referring to his gloss on *Venerabilem* where he had written that the pope transferred the *regimen mundi* to the Germans.[59] But, finally, the Spanish canonist Vincentius carried the argument to a new conclusion with the terse comment, 'De facto, Jo. Inmo de iure'; and thereby, according to Mochi Onory, 'inserì

---

[56] *Supra* n. 51.

[57] *Fonti* 253. The text was also cited by Ullmann, 'The Development of the Medieval Idea of Sovereignty,' *English Historical Review* 64 (1949) 1-33. In this article Dr. Ullmann analyzed the contributions of the French school of jurists emphasized by Ercole and of the Italian school emphasized by Calasso, and showed how their ideas flowed together in the work of Oldradus da Ponte.

[58] Mochi Onory followed Tancred in attributing this gloss to Laurentius. It is in fact almost certainly by Joannes Galensis. See F. Gillmann, 'Des Johannes Galensis Apparat zur Compilatio III in der Universitätsbibliothek Erlangen,' *Archiv für katholisches Kirchenrecht* 118 (1938) 179-80, 180 n. 2, 199.

[59] He upheld the same point of view in his *glossa ordinaria* on the *Decretum ad Dist.* 63 c.22. Mochi Onory notes that he made a special exemption in the case of Spain, but G. Post has pointed out that the words referring to Spain may be a late interpolation, as was definitely a similar phrase in Joannes' *apparatus* to the *Comp.* III: 'Two Notes on Nationalism' (cited *supra* n. 25) 299 n. 10, 300.

nel dibattito delle idee contrastanti il vero e proprio elemento decisivo per la soluzione di tutto il problema.'[60]

Meijers has pointed out that the arguments in favor of national independence occur in canonistic glosses more frequently than in civilian ones, not because of a doctrinal evolution which the canonists as such contributed to without distinction of nationality, but because there happened to be representatives of various nations among the canonists, while all the leading civilians were Italians. 'Le sentiment national était ici le facteur décisif.' Mochi Onory would perhaps not regard this as inconsistent with his own position. It is part of his general argument that canonistic scholarship — precisely because of its international character — was especially alert and sensitive to the political realities of the age. Certainly it was important for the future that the Church did not become rigorously committed to the doctrine of universal empire — an attractive position after all in view of the especially strong claims of the pope over the emperor — and Mochi Onory's work serves a very useful purpose in showing how the canonists kept the question at least open to discussion.[61]

In two recent articles, Professor Gaines Post has published a considerable number of new glosses from the early thirteenth-century canonists which tend to confirm Mochi Onory's claim that these writers were much preoccupied with the problem of national sovereignty.[62] In a study of the idea *pugna pro patria*, he provides some canonistic documentation for a theme recently treated from non-legal sources by E. Kantorowicz, and emphasizes especially a tendency of the canonists to use *patria* in the sense of kingdom. In the other study, on the *rex-imperator* idea, he prints for the first time the full text of Joannes Teutonicus' gloss on the decretal *Venerabilem* and a new text from Alanus' apparatus on the *Decretum*. Both confirm the views attributed to the authors on the basis of texts previously known; Joannes appears again as the champion of empire, Alanus as the defender of national independence. Most interesting of all is a newly published gloss from the *Apparatus* of Vincentius Hispanus on the Gregorian Decretals, in which the laconic comment cited by Mochi Onory was expanded into a full-blooded, patriotic protest against the claims of the German emperors. Joannes Teutonicus said that the Germans merited the empire by their virtues. Vincentius replied that they had lost it by their stupidity and that the Spaniards had acquired empire by their valor and probity. He concluded with an eloquent panegyric on Spain, and, in another context, modestly claimed that Spain was the greatest of the provinces of

---

[60] *Fonti* 282.

[61] The attitudes of subsequent popes varied according to the political situation. De Vergottini has pointed out that in 1220 at a moment of rapprochement, Honorius III regarded Frederick II's legislation on the defense of the Church as valid for the whole of Christendom, *Studi sulla legislazione di Federico II in Italia: Le leggi del 1220* (Milan 1952) 159-66. In another work De Vergottini has restated at length the arguments of Mochi Onory, with modifications suggested by recent criticisms of them: *Il diritto pubblico* (cited *supra* n. 6) 210-36.

[62] Cited *supra* n. 25, n. 48. Post's own conclusion is that, for the twelfth and most of the thirteenth century, 'Mochi Onory goes too far, Calasso not far enough, in finding expressions of independence of the greater kingdoms from the Empire' ('Two Notes on Nationalism' 319).

Christendom. Professor Post has devoted a separate article to a more detailed study of these glosses of Vincentius, setting them against the whole background of the Spanish *Reconquista*, and arguing that Vincentius was not claiming universal empire for the Spaniards, but rather a 'national empire' of their own.[63]

The legal technicality of exemption from imperial jurisdiction gains new meaning and life when it is thus related to the great contemporary currents of thought and action; and, as more and more texts become available, the main need will be for studies that aim to integrate the canonistic material into broader surveys of the growth of nationalist ideas. It is especially to be hoped that the focus of future discussion will shift from the question where the phrase *rex in regno suo est imperator* originated, and who is to have the credit for inventing it. That argument is becoming a little threadbare. So far as the equation *rex-imperator* is concerned, the indications are that some such terminology will be found as far back as scholars care to press the research. If we concentrate on the more significant problem, the adaptation of the phrase to support national claims to independence from the empire, it now seems clear that the critical time was around 1200, that the canonists played a very considerable part in the development, and that, among the canonists, Englishmen and Spaniards were mainly responsible for the new theory.

---

[63] '« Blessed Lady Spain ».' The texts printed in this article are valuable, but Professor Post's interpretations seem to require some emendations. In the following notes the Latin text is given first, then his comment, then our own comment. (1) 'Et si vinco vincentem te, vinco te, ff. de diver. et temp. prescrip. de accessionibus (*Dig.* 44,3) *Vinc.*' ('The last sentence is not clear... The reference to the Digest 44,3 seems to have no bearing on the words': 203 n. 28). The meaning seems clear enough though the argument is a little naive. The pope had praised the French above the other provinces, but the Spaniards had defeated the French; therefore Spain was greater than the other provinces — because 'if I beat someone who beats you, I beat you.' The Roman law text is *Dig.* 44.3.14.3 and does refer to this principle. (2) 'Nec aliquid regnum eximi potuit ab imperio, quia illud esset acephalum.' ('... the empire would be a headless monster if any kingdom were independent of it...': 206). Evidently it is not the empire that would be made headless by the defection of a single kingdom, but the kingdom that would lose its proper head in being cut off from the empire. (3) 'Sed ego Vinc. dico quod theutonici per busnardiam perdiderunt imperium. Quodlibet enim thigurium sibi usurpat dominium, et quelibet civitas de dominio cum eis contendit.' ('For every hut usurps lordship (*dominium*) for itself and every city contends with others for the same': 206). The true meaning is that every city contends with the Germans, not with other cities. (4) 'Iuvantur ergo Yspani meritis et probitate; nec indigent corpore prescriptionum vel consuetudinum sicut theutonici.' ('Unlike the Germans they have no need of a body of prescripts and customs': 206; 'Presumably because the Spanish have the Roman law. But is Vincentius obivious to the customary law in Spain?' 206 n. 43). Vincentius would not have argued that the Spanish were independent of the empire because they had Roman law; that argument was always used by the canonists in just the contrary sense. The text means, 'Nor do they lack a body of prescripts and customs...'

III. *Regnum and Rex*

We have said that little has been written on the canonists' theory of the State. That is not quite true, since nearly all the discussions on *Regnum* and *Imperium* involve some consideration of a king's authority in relation to his subjects; but there has been no *ex professo* treatment of the canonists' ideas concerning the internal government of secular states. The richness of the material available for such a study can be gathered from the texts assembled by Mochi Onory even though he neither explored in detail the manuscripts of the twelfth century nor used the printed editions of the great canonists from mid-thirteenth century onwards. Among the topics he discusses, and illustrates with canonistic texts, are the *populus* as the source of political authority; elective versus hereditary monarchy; the right of the *populus* to exercise jurisdiction, enact legislation, consent to legislation; the right of resistance to tyranny. He also discusses sovereignty, in the sense of the need in each community for one single authority charged with the supreme direction of public affairs, and, in considering the nature of this authority, he shows how the canonists emphasized especially the legislative and fiscal aspects — an interesting point, since we still sometimes read that 'in the Middle Ages all law was custom,' the function of a king merely to declare the law and judge according to it. It seems that when the medieval canonists considered the content of political authority they thought at once of the power to make law and the power to raise taxes.

The very listing of topics discussed by the canonists reveals the influence of Roman law doctrines on their political thought, and indeed, in this field, the works of the canonists and of the civilians can hardly be considered separately with any profit. But, even if it proved that the main contribution of the canonists was the assimilation and diffusion of Roman law concepts, their work would hardly be the less important for that; and, in fact, if the research were extended to include writers like Hostiensis, whose vast *Lectura* contains much relevant material, one would probably find distinctively canonistic ideas applied to the analysis of political authority. Another factor which certainly influenced canonistic thought was the actual practice of political life in the Italian city-states, for, when the great Italian canonists of the mid-thirteenth century thought of a political community, it was the city-state that came most naturally to mind, though they did on occasion discuss the position of a king in a feudal monarchy. In the history of medieval government the greatest change of all was from feudal hierarchy to corporate state, and the canonists, with their way of considering all political groupings against a background of Roman law, ecclesiastical corporation structure, and Italian communal organization, probably contributed much to the movement of ideas that accompanied the change.

A whole chapter of medieval political theory remains to be written. A sort of preview of the probable contents of that chapter has been provided by Professor Gaines Post in a paper on the medieval theory of public law and the State.[64] He first criticizes the view, which he associates especially with Gierke,

---

[64] 'The Theory of Public Law and the State in the Thirteenth Century,' *Seminar* 6 (1948) 42-59. On the argument from necessity in Roman and canon law see also C. C. Bayley, 'Pivotal Concepts in the Political Philosophy of William of Ockham,' *Journal of the History of Ideas* 10 (1949) 199-218.

Kern, and de Lagarde, that in the thirteenth century there was no public law, only an interlocking mass of private rights, and consequently no State, that is to say, no public authority charged with the protection of the common welfare even, if necessary, at the expense of private rights. On the contrary, Post maintains, the civilian glossators of the thirteenth century, starting out from Ulpian's dictum 'Public law pertains to the *status rei Romanae,*' built up a theory that the prince could levy extraordinary taxation for the protection of the *status regni,* the common welfare of the community, and could make new laws when 'evident utility' required them. The canonists too conceded to civil rulers the right to tax the clergy if this was necessary for the common welfare and the pope's consent was obtained; and the popes themselves appealed to the principle of necessity in demanding subsidies from the clergy. Hence, while 'normally the ruler was preserving the *status* of all in the realm when he was ruling according to the law which protected all private rights and interests,' in exceptional emergencies, 'the common welfare of the community was above all private rights, privileges, and immunities.' Already in the thirteenth century the adage, *necessitas legem non habet,* was becoming a principle of public law.

Professor Ernst H. Kantorowicz has recently turned aside from his valuable studies in political theology to illustrate the importance of canonistic influence on the developing idea of public authority from another angle. His contribution deals with a question much disputed among constitutional historians, the oath sworn by medieval English kings at their coronation to preserve inviolate the rights of the crown — with an implied distinction between the crown and the person of the king. Kantorowicz argues very convincingly that the oath against alienation — which in canonical practice and juristic theory was already required from bishops directly dependent on the pope — was added to the oath sworn in 1216 by King Henry III, the pope's feudal vassal, through the influence of the papal legate, Guala. Subsequent papal letters and canonistic commentaries on them treated it as a normal part of any king's coronation oath.[65] The argument from thirteenth-century canonistic doctrines on alienation (which Kantorowicz did not have occasion to explore thoroughly in this article) could certainly be developed much further in this context.

The growth of a theory of public authority could enhance the authority of a ruler; but it had other implications as well. To revert to Professor Post's argument, he points out that, although the king could demand extra-ordinary taxes in case of necessity, the subjects could claim a right of consent precisely because, in a common emergency, all their interests were involved. Post himself has not been content to pursue the hackneyed argument that Roman and canon law principles paved the way for Renaissance despotism. On the contrary, the whole theme of his specialist articles in this field has been the contribution of Roman and canon law to the growth of medieval constitutionalism,[66] especially in connection with the rise of representative assemblies.

---

[65] E. H. Kantorowicz, 'Inalienability: A Note on Canonical Practice and the English Coronation Oath in the Thirteenth Century,' *Speculum* 29 (1954) 488-502. M. David also has studied the influence of the canonistic doctrine on oaths and promises on the coronation oaths of medieval kings, 'Le serment du sacre,' *Revue du moyen âge latin* 6 (1950) 5-272, especially at 158-80.

[66] C. C. Bayley has used a somewhat similar approach in showing how canon law doctrines

Many factors contributed to the growth of such institutions, he points out, but their emergence would hardly have been possible at all without a procedure of 'corporate representation' — the representation of a corporate group by a proctor equipped with full powers to act on its behalf.[67] The formula commonly used to define the powers of representatives in medieval assemblies was *plena potestas*, and Professor Post shows that this formula was first given general currency in the Middle Ages, and applied to the representation of corporations as well as individuals, by the legists and canonists — especially the canonists — of the second half of the twelfth century. He denies that the *procuradores* attending the twelfth-century *Cortes* of the Spanish kingdoms (where the two laws were little studied at that time) were true 'corporate representatives, empowered by mandates to carry the will of their communities to the king in his council,' and he finds the first certain example of such representation in a letter of Innocent III (1200) commanding six cities in the March of Ancona to send to the papal curia *procuratores* equipped with *plenaria potestas*. The first secular ruler definitely known to have summoned representatives with mandates from their communities was Frederick II (1231), again in Italy.

By the middle of the thirteenth century the procedure of proctorial representation was spreading to assemblies in Spain, England, and France, and in the meantime the canonists and legists had much elaborated the terminology used in the definition of proctorial mandates.[68] There was a distinction between a special mandate which empowered a proctor to act in one case only, and a general mandate which gave him authority for a whole series of cases. Even the proctor equipped with a general mandate had to refer back to his principal for instructions in certain circumstances, but when the mandate was strengthened with a clause conceding *plena potestas* (or with a similar formula), the proctor was held to be *sufficienter instructus*, able to do all that his principal could have done had he been present in court. It still happened sometimes that a proctor was granted a delay to consult his principal, but this was at the discretion of the court. All this has an obvious relevance to the claims of representatives in national assemblies to refer back to their constituencies for instructions. Post discusses the attempts of constituents to protect their interests by limiting the mandates of their representatives, but concludes that usually the kings were able to thwart such attempts by insisting on mandates conferring *plena potestas*. There is, however, a far more important issue involved in the relation between everyday procedural *plena potestas* and parliamentary *plena potestas*. In private law, *plena potestas* 'expressed the consent of the interested parties both to the representation and to the authority of the court to decide the issue, after judicial process, and pass sentence.' The question arises whether the *plena potestas* of a parliamentary representative implied a right of 'political' consent, limiting the royal authority (in other words a right to refuse consent), or whether, as in private law, it signified rather a consent in advance to whatever decisions the king should promulgate in his

---

influenced the organization and procedure of the thirteenth-century German college of electors, *op. cit. supra* n. 30.

[67] 'Roman Law and Early Representation in Spain and Italy,' *Speculum* 18 (1943) 211-32.

[68] 'Plena Potestas and Consent in Medieval Assemblies,' *Traditio* 1 (1943) 355-408.

parliament. Gaines Post holds that, when a king sought extraordinary taxes or extraordinary powers for the defense of the realm, he had a duty to obtain consent but a right to exact that consent. The representative might argue that the proposed subsidy was unnecessary, or that his community was unable to bear the burden — like a proctor defending his principal's interests in court — but he had no right to refuse consent when the royal decision was finally promulgated.

This problem could not be analyzed in all its aspects, however, in an article on *plena potestas*, since it involves not only the nature of the representatives' mandates, but the nature of the assembly itself. The argument was therefore carried further in an article which took as its theme the Roman law dictum, *quod omnes tangit ab omnibus approbetur*, found in certain election writs of Edward I of England.[69] Professor Post maintains that the phrase was not merely 'a rhetorical flourish of some scribe in the royal chancery' but an introduction into the sphere of public law of an equitable principle already well established in English private law. He first shows how the legists and canonists of the thirteenth century developed from the classical texts two legal principles — no right held by several persons in common could be alienated without the consent of them all, and no one could be deprived of a right in which he shared without being summoned before a court to accept its judgment. These principles Post defines as 'voluntary consent' and 'procedural consent.' There were certain refinements of each. As regards 'voluntary consent,' the vote of the greater part of a corporation was held to bind the whole body; and as regards 'procedural consent,' it was not essential that a defendant should actually appear in court. If he was duly summoned and failed to appear or present a valid excuse, the case against him could proceed as if he were present (his 'consent' to the jurisdiction of the court being presumed.)

The precise situations of Roman law did not arise in England but there were numerous cases of co-ownership and common rights to which the same principles could be applied. Professor Post's main purpose in this article is to establish that Bracton did know the Romano-canonical doctrines on the *quod omnes tangit* principle and did adapt them in their varied applications and meanings to the procedure of the common law. Once established in English private law they were in a position to influence the development of parliament considered both as a high court of justice and as a tax-granting assembly; as a high court of justice because tenants-in-chief could claim that suits involving their estates touched the king as an interested party and could only be settled in his presence; as a tax-granting assembly because the magnates could protest that the business of a tax touched the knights and burgesses and could not be decided unless they were summoned.[70] (In summoning them, however, the king would intend to exact only 'procedural consent.') Again, the principles of private law could explain why boroughs that failed to send

---

[69] 'A Romano-Canonical Maxim, "quod omnes tangit," in Bracton,' *Traditio* 4 (1946) 197-251.

[70] Or, as Post points out, the initiative might well have come from the knights themselves. In his most recent article (a revised version of a paper read at the meeting of the American Historical Association in 1949) Professor Post has applied these conclusions to an analysis of the terminology of the Statute of York, 'The Two Laws and the Statute of York,' *Speculum* 29 (1954) 417-32.

624

representat:ves were held liable for taxes granted in parliament; if they were properly summoned and failed to respond they were guilty of default, 'their silence being interpreted as consent.' And, finally, the private law doctrine of corporate consent seems reflected in the acceptance of majority decisions in parliament.

Gaines Post does not press his arguments further than the evidence warrants, and promises further studies on a number of debatable points, but his articles already provide a substantial contribution to a central problem of medieval constitutional history. The nature of the topics he has discussed has led him to emphasize mainly the curial aspects of parliament; it is likely that further investigation of canonistic material would provide evidence favorable to the less orthodox views of Miss Clarke and of Professor Wilkinson.

John Higham has recently offered a neat definition of two complementary approaches to intellectual history.[71] There is an internal approach which 'seeks the connection between thought and thought' and an external approach which seeks rather 'the connection between thought and deed.' Most of the work that we have been considering belongs to the first category (though obviously enough the canonists' theories on Church and State had far-reaching practical repercussions in an age when nearly every great pope was also a great lawyer). Post's studies on representation and consent exemplify rather the second approach or, more accurately, a fusion of both types of argument. There is need for more work of the same kind, and, indeed, the study of canonistic influence on the growth of medieval institutions is perhaps the most fertile field for research in medieval canon law outside the sphere of pure literary history. Such research could have a special value at a time when, in America, the 'history of ideas' has been raised to the status of an independent discipline and, in England, an influential school of historians seems anxious to 'take the mind out of history' altogether. These may seem odd developments of historiography for an age bedeviled by clashing ideologies whose impact on the world of practical affairs is all too painfully apparent; but it is certainly true that both methods of enquiry have achieved some brilliant results. It would be regrettable, all the same, if they came altogether to dominate the study of medieval history, and especially if the second approach should come to dominate the study of medieval institutions, where the source material is far less suited to this kind of enquiry than that of later epochs. It is all very well to take the mind out of a collection of eighteenth-century English gentlemen; one does not lose much perhaps, and there is still plenty of fascinating material left for the historian. But if we take the mind out of the Middle Ages, then indeed all is chaos and night.

Canonistic studies provide a useful bridge between the realm of pure theory and the world of hard facts, both because canonistic thought was concrete and realistic, moving close to the real world of events, and because the canonists themselves were often practical men of affairs engaged in the actual conduct of government in Church and State. Obviously no one imagines that medieval parliaments came into existence because canon law provided a convenient procedure of corporate representation and Roman law a principle that all interested parties in a case should be consulted. But when, in the great national

---

[71] 'Intellectual History and its Neighbours,' *Journal of the History of Ideas* 15 (1954) 339-368.

monarchies of the Middle Ages, there arose urgent political and economic reasons why the substantial classes of the realm should be associated with the king in the conduct of major fiscal, judicial, and political business, there arose also the need for legal formulas and procedures which could define the form that that association should take. If Roman and canonist procedures had not been available, no doubt something else would have been improvised. But since the doctrines of the two laws were at hand and were used, they did come to play a part in shaping the development of medieval representative assemblies. The essential nature of institutions, as well as the essential substance of law, is sometimes secreted in the interstices of procedure.

.*.

It is strange that, in the past, so great and potent an influence on European civilization as the law of the Church Universal has been widely regarded — even among medievalists — as something recondite, if not repugnant, outside the main stream of medieval life and thought. The recent work should help to dispel that illusion. In all three fields that we have considered striking advances have been made in the past few years; and in each much remains to be done. Indeed the most stimulating aspect of canonistic studies in their present stage is the challenge of the vast mass of unedited and unused manuscript material. The preliminary voyages of exploration have brought back treasure from this half-forgotten land; we must now look forward to a systematic conquest.

The Catholic University of America.

Additional Note. — Since this article went to press, two new papers by Father Stickler have become accessible, in which he further develops his arguments, ' Imperator vicarius Papae,' *Mitteilungen des Instituts für österreichische Geschichtsforschung* 62 (1954) 165-212; 'Sacerdozio e regno nelle nuove ricerche attorno ai secoli XII e XIII...,' *Miscellanea historiae pontificiae* 18 (1954) 1-26. There has also appeared an important book by Father F. Kempf, S. J., *Papsttum und Kaisertum bei Innozens III.* (Miscell. hist. pont. 19 ; Rome 1954). This work will require detailed assessment in some future Bibliographical Survey. Like Maccarrone, Fr. Kempf denies that Innocent III claimed direct temporal power for the papacy, and he has used the numerous texts published by Fr. Stickler to present Innocent's position against a detailed background of contemporary canonistic theory.

II

Pope and Council: Some New Decretist Texts

IN recent studies on the idea of sovereignty in the Middle Ages there has been no lack of emphasis on the contribution of the mediaeval canonists. A substantial literature has grown up concerning canonistic theories on the relations between church and state and between the national kingdoms and the empire. Moreover, several recent works have called attention to the influence of canonistic doctrine and ecclesiastical practice on the development of secular institutions of government. It even seems that canonistic studies may contribute to our understanding of some of the classic problems of the constitutional historians—the significance of coronation oaths, the origins of parliament and, *mirabile dictu*, the terminology of the Statute of York.[1]

Even before the recent growth of interest in the canonists and their works it was often pointed out as a standard platitude of the text-books that mediaeval theories of papal authority greatly influenced subsequent doctrines of secular kingship.[2] It is surprising therefore that the greatest gap in modern work on the political theories of the canonists occurs precisely at this point. The subject that has been least studied is the one that was after all the canonists' own proper business, that is to say the juridical structure of the church and the nature and limits of papal sovereignty within the church. In a work on the early background of conciliar thought I discussed a few of the texts of the twelfth century Decretists touching on these questions.[3] The purpose of this article is to present a more adequate and representative selection of texts from the various canon law schools of the twelfth century, and to reconsider some problems of papal sovereignty in the light of them.[4]

---

[1] For a discussion of recent contributions in these fields see 'Some Recent Works on the Political Theories of the Medieval Canonists,' *Traditio* X (1954) 594-625. Since the article was written a number of important books dealing with various aspects of mediaeval sovereignty has appeared: L. Buisson, *König Ludwig IX der Heilige und das Recht* (Freiburg, 1954), R. Castillo Lara, *Coacción eclesiástica y sacro romano imperio* (Turin, 1956), M. David, *La souveraineté et les limites juridiques du pouvoir monarchique du IXe au XVe siècle* (Paris, 1954), J. W. Gough, *Fundamental Law in English Constitutional History* (Oxford, 1955), M. Pacaut, *'Alexandre III. Etude sur la conception du pouvoir pontifical dans sa pensée et dans son oeuvre* (Paris, 1956), P. N. Riesenberg, *Inalienability of Sovereignty in Medieval Political Thought* (New York, 1956). Of these Buisson, David, Pacaut and Riesenberg make use of canonistic material.
[2] E. H. Kantorowicz has some fresh and penetrating observations on this theme in his article, "Mysteries of State: an Absolutist Concept and its Late Medieval Origins," *Harvard Theological Review*, XLVIII (1951), 65-91.
[3] *Foundations of the Conciliar Theory* (Cambridge, 1955).
[4] Besides discussing the new material presented in this article I have also considered texts published by A. M. Landgraf, "Scattered Remarks on the Development of Dogma and on Papal Infallibility", *Theological Studies*, VII (1946), 577-82; A. Stickler,

"Sacerdotium et Regnum nei decretisti e primi decretalisti", *Salesianum*, XV (1953), 575-612; and J. Watt, "The Early Medieval Canonists and the Formation of Conciliar Theory", *Irish Theological Quarterly*, XXIV (1957), 13-31. My own transcriptions are taken from microfilms in the library of the Institute of Research and Study in Medieval Canon Law. The following manuscripts have been cited: Admont, Stiftsbibliothek, MS 7; Arras, Bibliothèque municipale, MS 271; Augsburg, Kreis- und Stadtbibliothek, MS I; Barcelona, Archivo de la Corona de Aragón, MS S. Cugat 55; Cambridge, Trinity College, MSS O.5.17 and 0.10.2; Douai, Bibliothèque municipale, MS 649; Dublin, Trinity College, MS 275; Erfurt, Stadtbücherei, MS Amplon quart. 117; Göttingen, Universitätsbibliothek, MS iur. 159; Halle, Universitätsbibliothek, MS Ye 52; Liége, Bibliothèque de l'Université, MS 127E; London, British Museum, MS Royal 11.D.II; Montecassino, Biblioteca Abbaziale, MS 396; Munich, Staatsbibliothek, MS 16084; Paris, Bibliothèque Nationale, MSS 3009, 14997, 15994; Rouen, Bibliothèque municipale, MS 743 (E.74). For information concerning the canonists and anonymous works mentioned in the text see S. Kuttner, *Repertorium der Kanonistik* (Vatican City, 1937), idem "Bernardus Compostellanus Antiquus", *Traditio*, I (1943), 277-340, S. Kuttner and E. Rathbone, "Anglo-Norman Canonists of the Twelfth Century", *Traditio*, VII (1949-51), 279-358.

These problems were posed for the commentators on Gratian by the dialectical structure of the Decretum itself. On the one hand Gratian vigorously asserted that the pope was the supreme judge in the church and himself to be judged by no one, that the pope alone could define articles of faith, that his legislation was to be obeyed by all, that he could even over-rule the decisions of previous general councils.[5] But, on the other hand, many of the texts that Gratian cited seemed to support the opposite conclusions. The ones that became the principal focal points of discussion were these: *Dist.* 15 c. 2, where Pope Gregory I, referring to the first four general councils, declared, *dum universali sunt consensu constituta se et non illa destruit quisquis praesumit aut soluere quos religant aut ligare quos soluunt*; C. 25 q. 1, in which Gratian explicitly discussed the question whether the pope was bound by statutes of general councils; *Dist.* 40 c. 6, which laid down the rule that a pope was immune from human judgement but added as a qualification, *nisi deprehendatur a fide deuius*; and finally *Dist.* 19 c. 9, which declared that Pope Anastasius II had been deserted by his clergy and smitten by God because he entered into communion with a condemned heretic *sine concilio episcoporum uel presbyterorum et clerici cunctae ecclesiae catholicae*. These texts could give rise to all kinds of subtle problems, but the central difficulties are obvious enough. If the pope was the final arbiter in matters of faith how could any teaching of his be held heretical? And if the pope was the supreme judge how could any-one condemn him?

It is evident that in discussing issues of this kind we are dealing with extreme and exceptional cases. In the days of Alexander III or Innocent III the pope did indeed preside over the day to day conduct of ecclesiastical affairs as supreme judge and legislator, and all the canonists thought it right and proper that this should be so. When one deals with limiting cases, in the nature of things one is far from the mean, from normal everyday situations; but in problems of constitutional theory an emphasis on limiting cases seems inescapable if we are to understand the underlying principles of any given system of thought.[6] It may also seem that, since the canonists' central problem was so much concerned with the definition of articles of faith it was in essence a theological issue which cannot properly be discussed in constitutional terms. In a sense this is very true. The point is that the theologians of the day made little attempt to cope with the problem and, in the absence of adequate theological guidance, the canonists debated it in strictly juristic terms.[7] The pope's power to define articles of faith was conceived of simply as one aspect of his authority as supreme judge.

Gratian himself made this clear when he posed the question whether greater authority was to be attributed to the opinions of revered theologians like Augustine or Jerome or to the pronouncements of a pope. He held that in theological studies the opinion of a writer like Augustine was to be preferred on a point of scriptural exegesis since the great theologians were especially gifted with wisdom (*scientia*), but in deciding cases the courts had to judge according to the definitions of the pope since the pope possessed the *clavis potestatis*, the power of jurisdiction that Christ had conferred on Peter.[8] The canonists, while commonly accepting Gratian's view that the fathers were

[5] These affirmations of papal authority are scattered all through the Decretum. See especially D.12, D.19, D.22, C.2 q.6, C.9 q.3, C.24 q.1, C.25 q.1.

[6] However, the problems discussed were not altogether remote from real life. When we find the canonists discussing whether schism was equivalent to heresy or affirming that, when there was doubt as to who was true pope, the issue could be settled by human judgment we may remember that in the days of Barbarossa and the anti-pope Victor these were not merely theoretical questions.

[7] Landgraf remarked on the paucity of theological writing on this theme, *art. cit.* p. 577.

[8] D.20 *ante* c. 1. On the canonists' interpretation of the famous text *Tu es Petrus* . . . see now M. J. Wilks "Papa est nomen iurisdictionis", *Journal of Theological Studies*, VIII (New Series) (1957), 71-91.

greater in *scientia*, sometimes took occasion to explain in this context that the pope's power of pronouncing authoritative decisions included the definition of articles of faith.[9] Some of them also sugested that, if a dispute arose as to whether the pope's teaching was orthodox or not, the pope ought voluntarily to appoint another as judge *et sub eo de hoc litigare*.[10] The only way they could conceive of settling a disputed point of doctrine was to conduct litigation under a judge. When the issue was being discussed in these terms, the question whether there was any authority in the church competent to over-rule the pope's decision in matters of faith or to pass judgement on the pope himself did present itself precisely as a constitutional problem, a problem of sovereignty. Huguccio even used the doctrine that a pope could be condemned for heresy as an argument to prove that a tyrannical king might be deposed by his barons.[11]

A theologian might well maintain that the ecclesiology of the late twelfth century was radically flawed by this tendency to force essentially theological propositions into a juristic mould, and it may be that the study of these problems of constitutional law cannot take us to the most profound levels of mediaeval thought on the nature and functions of the papacy. But it can teach us a very great deal about the origins and developments of 'mediaeval constitutionalism', for the constitutional problems that the canonists were already debating in the second half of the twelfth century were substantially similar to those that would arise in the sphere of secular government in the thirteenth century and afterwards.

In the fully developed constitutional theories of the later Middle Ages there existed divers elements of thought inextricably interwoven with one another. In the works of the earlier canonists we can see some of the doctrines that would be used in later systems of thought evolving separately and then, by the end of the twelfth century, being brought tentatively into relationship with one another to form comprehensive theories of authority within the church. The problems to be considered can be arranged in logical sequence, each leading on to the next. There is first the question of fundamental law, whether there existed any 'natural' or customary law, not created by the will of the ruler and unchangeable by him. The tendency in much recent work has been to de-emphasize the importance of this conception in the secular sphere, to point out that mediaeval kings did in fact make new laws changing old customs and knew perfectly well that they were doing so. There has never been much doubt that this was also true of the popes. Indeed, a scholar as perceptive as J. N. Figgis once referred to 'the Canonist theory of sovereignty (substantially the same as Austin's)'.

If, however, a theory of fundamental law did exist, there next arose the question of who was competent to define and declare that law. If men believed in the existence of a fundamental law but assumed that the individual ruler—king, emperor, or pope—had the sole power of declaring the tenets of that law, the practical result was much the same as if they had indeed attributed

[9] Sicardus, "In expositionibus uero scripturarum preponuntur (patres) quia ibi scientia sine potestate requiritur excentis articulis fidei in quibus maior est apostolici quam alicuius sancti patris auctoritas." (MS Augsburg I, fol. 80va); *Summa Antiquitate et tempore*, "In scripturas autem exponendo maioris sit auctoritatis quod amplioris scientie esse constiterit . . . Nota tamen quod in obscuris scripturis et maxime circa articulos fidei maioris auctoritatis esset interpretatio pape quam augustini. Set alias, in libro componendo uel exponendo, maioris auctoritatis esset augustinus quam apostolicus." (MS Göttingen, iur. 159, fol. 25vb); *Summa Prima primi*, "Cum enim in questione fidei eius interpretationi standum est ut 24 Q. 1 *Quocies*, ergo et morum, quia sine illis fides mortua est. Item generaliter difficiliores questiones ad papam sunt referende." (MS London BM Royal 11.D.II, fol. 321rb). See also the gloss *ad Dist.* 20 of the Caius glosses cited by Watt, *art. cit.* p. 28.

[10] *Summa Duacensis*, *Summa Prima primi*. *Infra*. Appendix C.10, C.11.

[11] *Ad* C.15 q.6. C.3. Cited by Mochi Onory, *Fonti canonistiche dell' idea moderna dello stato* (Milan, 1951), p. 156.

to him a kind of Austinian sovereignty, even though the theoretical basis of his power was different. The common mediaeval alternative to this view was the doctrine that the highest authority for the promulgation of law was not the ruler alone but the ruler surrounded by an assembly, a parliament, estates-general, or general council, whose decisions the individual ruler could not annul. This doctrine raises a third question. If a dispute arose between the members of such an assembly and its head, which party possessed the higher authority? This is of crucial importance since it involves also the problem of the deposition of a ruler who has become intolerable to his subjects. If, in the last resort, supreme authority lay with the members of the assembly, they could judge and depose the ruler; but if, in case of dispute, ultimate authority lay with the ruler, then it would seem that, as one of the canonists put it, *non restat nisi dolor et gemitus.*[12]

It happens that the chronological order in which the canonists took up the problems mentioned corresponds precisely with the logical sequence in which we have presented them. The first point, the existence of some fundamental law existing outside the will of the legislator, need not detain us over long. The canonists did very clearly attribute to the pope a legislative function. There was never any suggestion that every time he promulgated a new decretal he was or ought to be merely declaring pre-existing law.[13] But, equally, there was a general consensus of opinion that this legislative authority was not unlimited. The very first words of the Decretum itself were,

> Humanum genus duobus regitur, naturali videlicet iure et moribus. Ius naturale est quod in lege et evangelio continetur, quo quisque iubetur alii inferre quod sibi uult fieri.

And a little further on Gratian added,

> Quaecumque enim vel moribus recepta sunt, vel scriptis comprehensa, si naturali iuri fuerint adversa, uana et irrita habenda sunt.[14]

The canonists were to point out that the term 'natural law' could have many other connotations, and that there were some varieties of natural law that could be modified by papal authority.[15] But no one dissented from the view that natural law in Gratian's own sense of the term, that is to say the fundamental moral principles laid down in the Old and New Testaments, was immutable. It could not be changed by the pope or any-one else.[16]

It was not until about 1160 that the canonists began to concern themselves with our second question, whether there was any institution of church government that could limit the authority of a pope. Then two major works, one from the school of Bologna and one from the French school raised the question of the relations between papal decretals and the canons of general councils.

---

[12] *Summa Duacensis, Infra,* Appendix C.11.
[13] The Decretists did, however, regard custom as an important source of law. See the remarks of F. Arnold, "Die Rechtslehre des Magisters Gratians, *Studia Gratiana* I (Bologna, 1953), 451-82 and of L. Buisson, *op. cit.,* pp. 71-79. On the closely related question whether popular acceptance was necessary to validate enacted law there is a detailed study by L. de Lucca, "L' accetazione popolare della legge canonica nel pensiero di Graziano e dei suoi interpreti", *Studia Gratiana* III (Bologna, 1955), 194-276.
[14] D.8 ante c.2.
[15] This was emphasized especially by W. Ullmann, *Medieval Papalism* (London, 1949),

pp. 50-75.
[16] Quite recently an extensive literature has grown up concerning the doctrine of natural law in Gratian and his commentators. The older work of O. Lottin, *Le droit natural chez Saint Thomas d' Aquin et ses prédécesseurs* (2nd ed. Bruges, 1931) remains valuable and the article "Naturel (Droit)" by C. Lefebvre and G. Simon in *Dictionnaire de droit canonique* provides an excellent introduction to the subject. See also contributions of Delhaye and Wegner, *Studia Gratiana* I (Bologna, 1953); de Tejada, Composta and Rota, *ibid.* II (1954); Villey and Gualazzini, *ibid.* III (1955). Delhaye (p. 440 n. 8) gives references to other recent work on this subject.

Rufinus taught that, while not every conciliar canon was inviolable, those 'statutes of the ancient and venerable fathers that were promulgated with full authority to preserve the state of the universal church' could not be annulled by papal authority. The *Summa Parisiensis* held that the immutable canons were those that pertained specially to articles of faith.[17] Then, about 1169, the *Summa Elegantius in iure divino*, another work of the French school, combined both arguments. The popes could abrogate old canons and found new ones provided that *nichil contra fidem presumant uel in quo uniuersalem ecclesiam offendant*. The author added that the pope should not be regarded as acting contrary to the general statutes of councils when he granted particular dispensations against them which did not establish binding precedents.[18]

These three glosses set the tone for future canonistic discussion. In the 1170s both Johannes Faventinus in Bologna and the *Summa Antiquitate et tempore* in France taught that papal decretals were not to be obeyed if they were 'contrary to the precepts of the Gospel or the decres of the holy fathers'.[19] The author of the *Distinctiones Monacenses* held that the pope was bound by existing statutes concerning matters that were essential to salvation but not by those that dealt with points that had been morally indifferent before the law concerning them was promulgated. The French *Summa Tractaturus magister* offered a more elaborate analysis. There were some statutes that pertained to the general state of the church and that were essential to salvation. These the pope could not modify in whole or in part. Other universal statutes were not essential to salvation and these he could modify in part, but could not destroy altogether without the consent of a general council. Those that referred only to the special privileges of some particular church he could change in whole or in part.[20] The *Summa Et est sciendum* declared that the pope was bound by the statutes of councils *in his que spectant ad articulos fidei et statum ecclesie.* This formula was used repeatedly by Huguccio and had become very generally accepted by the early thirteenth century.[21] It may be added that the Decretists consistently rated the canons of councils as superior to the decretals of popes when they listed in order of precedence the different sources of ecclesiastical law.[22]

---

[17] *Die Summa Decretorum des Magister Rufinus*, ed. H. Singer (Paderborn, 1902), p. 13; *The Summa Parisiensis on the Decretum Gratiani*, ed. T. P. McLaughlin (Toronto, 1952), p. 230.
[18] *Infra*, Appendix A.1.
[19] *Infra*, Appendix A.2.
[20] For the text of the *Distinctiones Monacenses* see Landgraf, art. cit., p. 579 and for that of the *Summa Tractaturus Magister* Watt, art. cit., p. 28. On the right of resistance to unjust papal commands see "Grosseteste and the Theory of Papal Sovereignty", *Journal of Ecclesiastical History*, VI (1955), 1-17.
[21] A selection of illustratvie texts is given in Appendix A. By the early thirteenth century it was very commonly accepted that the pope could not go against the canons of general councils in matters touching articles of faith or affecting the general state of the church, but it remained a matter of controversy whether and within what limits he could over-rule other general laws of the councils. The controversy was particularly concerned with the limits of the pope's dispensatory authority. See J. Brys, *De dispensatione in iure canonico* (Bruges, 1925), pp. 122-134, 195-226.

[22] Such lists were commonly included in glosses *ad* D.20; several of them have been printed by C. Munier, *Les sources patristiques du droit de l'église* (Mulhouse, 1957), p. 200. By way of example we give another; *Summa Antiquitate et Tempore ad* D.20 *ante* c.1, "Talis hic adhibenda videtur distinctio ut in causis decidendis primum locum et principalem obtineat lex naturalis, vetus testamentum et nouum, postea statuta generalium conciliorum, deinde decretales epistole, postea statuta primatum, patriacharum, deinde statuta archiepiscoporum, postea episcoporum, et ut ad unum dicere sit (!), quanto altiorem locum habent in iudicando tanto digniorem locum obtineant eorum statuta in causis decidendis." The order of authorities varied slightly from canonist to canonist but in all the cases known to me the canons of general councils were preferred to the decretals of popes, and this in spite of a statement by Gratian himself that "Decretales itaque epistole canonibus conciliorum pari iure exequantur." (D.20 *ante* c.1). On this the *Summa Animal est substantia* commented, "i.e. sicut ista seruanda sunt sicut et illa. Utrumque debet obseruari. Maxime canones conciliorum preferuntur decretalibus quia illi equiparantur euangelio,, xv di. *Sicut*

The canonists seem to have considered that the meaning of the phrase *status ecclesiae* was self evident for they seldom gave specific examples of the limitations on papal authority that it implied. A *Quaestio* of Bazianus recently published by Fr. Stickler provides a significant exception. The problem discussed was whether the church courts provided a universal forum for all, clergy and laity alike. As a corollary Bazianus inquired whether, if this was not already the situation, the pope could enact a law establishing them as such for the future. The case was posed in an interesting fashion for the author explicitly raised the issue of papal *plenitudo potestatis* in opposition to a general statute of the church.

> In secunda questione videtur quod dominus papa non potest statuere quod ecclesia sit generale forum. Est enim preceptum apostoli ut laici sint iudices secularium rerum: in epistola ad corinthios . . . Item hoc esset generale statutum ecclesie perturbare. Set numquid posset hoc papa, numquid posset destruere omnes leges, numquid faciet omnes clericos vacare foro et causis emere Iustinianum et Ulpianum et dimittere Paulum et reliquos sanctos, quorum scriptis ecclesia regitur, numquid usurpabit officium alienum, quod fieri non debet . . . ?
> Contra: papa habet plenitudinem potestatis . . . Videtur ergo quod per voluntatem suam possit disponere tam de laicis quam de clericis.

The conclusion was that the church courts were not a general forum for all cases, that the pope could make them so only if he acted by direct revelation and inspiration of the Holy Spirit, and that such inspiration could be presumed only if every-one, clergy and princes alike, willingly consented to the change —an unlikely contingency.[23]

It has recently been argued that the limitation of papal authority suggested by the texts on *status ecclesie* 'is not a limitation in any real sense at all' because, 'The sovereign of any juridical society is "limited" to the extent that, however absolute he may be held to be, it is inadmissible that he might use his power to subvert the foundations of the society with whose government he is entrusted.'[24] But this is to take altogether too optimistic a view of the intrinsic nature of political institutions. A thirteenth century pope was so limited; a twentieth century dictator often is not. For a student of constitutional theory it is important to know whether any such limitation does or does not exist in a given society. The issue is not a merely academic one and still less is it merely mediaeval. The question whether a sovereign government can be bound by a pre-existing fundamental law defining the constitutional structure of the state has been a burning political issue in the Union of South Africa in very recent years.

What we can say with confidence is that the various texts which attributed to a general council superiority in questions of faith and in matters touching the general state of the church did not in themselves carry any anti-papal connotation, for the canonists always insisted that the pope himself or his legate had to preside in a general council. Just as, later on, the English judges were

---

sancti." (MS Liége 127E, fol. 13vb. On this manuscript see G. Fransen, "Manuscrits des décrétistes dans les bibliothèques liégoises", *Studia Gratiana*, I. (Bologna, 1953), 289-302 at p. 298).

[23] The *Quaestio* is printed in full in A. Stickler, *art. cit.* pp. 607-8. The text is given as published there though the manuscript actually has *generalē statutum* which one would normally extend as *generalem statutum*. This is grammatically impossible but *generalem statum* would be correct. There are similar ambiguities, probably arising out of scribal errors in some of the manuscripts of Huguccio (*Foundations* p 52 n. 3). In this case I think that the general sense of the passage and the wording of it make *generalem statum* the more likely reading. The problems of terminology connected with the canonists' and civilians' use of the phrases *status ecclesie*, *status regni* are being investigated by Gaines Post.

[24] J. Watt, *art. cit.*, p. 17.

to tell Henry VIII that he at no time stood so high in his estate royal as in time of parliament so the canonists were teaching, in effect, that the pope at no time stood so high in his estate pontifical as in time of general council.

We are therefore left with our third problem. Where did ultimate authority reside in case of disagreement between the pope and the members of a council? And, if the pope was supreme, how was the deposition of a heretical pope to be brought about? We must emphasize here that the common canonistic doctrine that a man who became a heretic *ipso facto* ceased to be pope did not eliminate the need for a juridical superior to pass sentence on him. No man, pope or peasant, became a heretic simply by making a mistake in a matter of doctrine. The crime of heresy consisted in pertinaciously resisting the sentence of the church after the disputed doctrine had been condemned. If the error was one that had already been condemned a prelate might indeed incur automatic excommunication and consequent loss of jurisdiction by adhering to it, but only if the original sentence had been promulgated by a superior. An inferior could not bind a superior, nor an equal an equal.[25] As the author of the *Summa Et est sciendum* observed, it could not be assumed that a pope had ceased to be pope and so had lost his immunity from judgement simply because some-one had flung a charge of heresy at him. *Non enim qui accusatur reus est set qui convincitur . . .*[26] And the one point that was common to virtually every canonistic commentary on the problem of a heretical pope was an insistence that a pope who erred could not be condemned at once, but only if he pertinaciously continued in his error after correction. Again, who was to 'correct' the teaching of a pope?

In a previous study, based largely on the *Glossa Ordinaria* of Johannes Teutonicus, I suggested that the Decretists did not deal adequately with these difficulties and that, instead of developing a systematic theory of the relations between pope and council, they took refuge in the confusions arising out of their own ambiguous use of terms like *Romana ecclesia*. The texts from Huguccio and Alanus recently published by John Watt, together with further material now available from manuscript sources, necessitate some modification of that judgement. Although there was a good deal of confusion in some quarters a few of the most clear sighted canonists did thoroughly comprehend and systematically resolve all difficulties surrounding the case of a heretical pope.

The Decretists were slow to come to grips with this problem. Forty years after the Decretum itself had appeared glosses on the case of Anastasius were still concerned only to define the precise nature of the pope's offence,[27] without making any reference to the implied problem of the relationship between the pope and the *concilium . . . cunctae ecclesiae catholicae* which, according to the critical text, he ought to have consulted. Two major works of the Bolognese and French schools written around 1180, the *Summae* of Simon de Bisignano and of Sicardus scarcely mention the constitutional ambiguities inherent in Gratian's texts.[27a] Then, quite suddenly in the 1180s, the whole issue exploded

---

[25] On excommunication *latae sententiae* at this period see P. Huizing, "The Earliest Development of Excommunication latae sententiae by Gratian and the Earliest Decretists", *Studia Gratiana* III, 278-320.

[26] *Summa ad* D.40 c.6 *Infra*, Appendix C.7.

[27] The letter of Anastasius given by Gratian (D.19 c.8) acknowledged the validity of ordinations made by the condemned heretic Acacius. This problem of 're-ordinations' was of course ancient (see L. Saltet, *Les Ré-ordinations* (Paris, 1907)). By the second half of the twelfth century most of the canonists held that the pope could accept as valid the ordinations

of a heretical bishop, and so it seemed that Anastasius had done nothing wrong. The Decretists sometimes explained that his offence consisted in recognizing the validity of the ordinations without insisting on the need for papal dispensation; more commonly they held that his real crime was that he secretly favored the heresy of Acacius. This led on to discussions on the need for the cooperation of a council in determining disputed articles of faith. A sequence of glosses illustrating the development of canonistic comment on the case is given in Appendix B.

[27a] On the affiliation of Sicardus with the

into life in a group of French *Summae*, and from then onwards it was discussed in detail in nearly all the major Decretist commentaries.

One factor that seems to have been important in precipitating the whole discussion was the decretal *Cum Christus* sent by Alexander III to the Archbishop of Rheims in 1177. In this decretal the pope actually did define an article of faith concerning the co-existence of the divine and human natures in Christ. Moreover, without consulting a general council, he defined it in a sense contrary to the opinion that prevailed among the theologians of Paris, and his definition came to be universally accepted as orthodox. The canonists seem to have been considerably impressed by the discomforture of the theologians.[28] For them, once they had grasped the full significance of the decretal, one effect of it was to sharpen the problem of a heretical pope; for how could the pope be a heretic when whatever he decreed, even though it ran counter to respectable theological opinion was held orthodox? Could, perhaps, the fathers of a council restrain him if he sought to promulgate as an article of faith some proposition that was clearly heretical?

The first work in which all the aspects of the problem were brought under discussion seems to have been the French *Summa Et est sciendum* (1181-85). On the authority of the pope in relation to previous general councils the comment was conventional as we have seen, *non potest derogari principalibus conciliis in his scilicet que spectant ad articulos fidei et statum ecclesie*. But, in discussing the case of Anastasius the author put forward a more radical doctrine. Here he suggested that if a dispute arose *within* a council, the authority of the members of the council was greater than that of the pope.

> Per hoc habes quod non debet papa ei communicare cui concilium censuit non communicandum. Eadem ratione si in questionibus que in concilio proponuntur a sententia pape discordat concilium maior est sententia concilii quam pape.[29]

When a canonist prefaced a statement with a phrase like, *Per hoc habes*, he was not definitively committing himself to the point of view expressed. He was merely pointing out that this was an arguable proposition that was supported by the text under discussion. In another context this author put forward the view, again without committing himself, that any opinion the pope pronounced was *ipso facto* orthodox and that it was for him alone to determine questions of faith. Finally, in his comment on *Dist.* 40 c. 6, the text which referred to the possibility of deposing a heretical pope, he drew together all the threads of the argument. The case of heresy, wrote the author, provided an exception to the general rule of papal immunity from judgement because heresy (and schism too, he added) violated the unity of the church and corrupted the foundations of the faith. Some held, however, that the pope could be accused

---

French school see S. Kuttner "Réflexions sur les brocards des glossateurs", *Mélanges de Ghellinck* (Gembloux, 1951), pp. 767-92.
[28] See *Summa Et est sciendum ad* D.17 post c.4, D.40 c.6 (*infra* Appendix C.7) and D.20 *ante* c.1, "Hic solet queri si gregorius qui et papa et expositor extitit inueniretur in sua expositione alicui expositori contrarius preponi deberet an subici uel equalis esset auctoritatis. Et forte equalis ubi non ut papa locutus est set ut expositor . . . Secus vero ubi loquitur sicut papa quo casu cunctis prefertur ut in extrav. *cum christus*." *Summa Omnis qui iuste ad* D.40 c.6 (*infra,* Appendix C.9) *Quaestiones Orielenses* (cf Stickler *art. cit.* p. 607); Huguccio ad C.9 q.3 c.17 (cf Watt, *art. cit.*, p. 30); *Summa Animal est substantia ad* D.20 *ante*

c.1, ". . . set in his que non sunt determinata in nouo uel ueteri testamento, si modo oriatur questio uel dubitatio prefertur summi pontificis sententia, extra, de hereticis, *cum christus, merentur*", ad C.24 q.1 c.13, "Arg. est hic contra theologos qui dicunt quod Christus in eo quod est homo nihil est, set aliqualiter quia papa reprobauit istam opinionem ex. de her., *cum christus*. Et tamen ipsi propter hoc nolunt acquiescere licet iterum acquieuerit papa. Nam qui opugnat romanam ecclesiam est hereticus, xii di. *nulli*." MS Liége 127E, fol. 13vb and fol. 213vb). On the theological doctrine involved see the article, "Adoptianisme au XIIe siècle", *Dictionnaire de théologie catholique*, 413-18.
[29] *Infra*, Appendix B.5.

of any crime that was notorious. Then the difficulties were fairly presented. It seemed that no statement of the pope could be heretical even if everyone disagreed with it for Alexander III had in fact successfully promulgated the decretal *Cum Christus* against great opposition. Again it could not be assumed that the pope had become automatically degraded from his office simply because his orthodoxy was suspect. (It was here that the author wrote, *Non enim qui accusatur reus est set qui conuincitur.*) And again, it seemed that even if the law did hold a pope liable to deposition for heresy, the pope could change that law.[30]

The final solution was that, if the pope propounded a new heresy, all these objections were valid. There was no authority in the church competent to dispute the orthodoxy of a papal pronouncement on an undetermined issue of faith. But if a pope adhered to a heresy already condemned by a previous general council then a new council could condemn him as one already excommunicate and guilty of heresy. The reason for this was that the pope alone did not have power to change the statutes of preceding general councils. Thus, although this canonist put forward the view that the members of a council in opposition to a pope might have a greater authority than the pope himself, he did not choose to base his arguments concerning the deposition of a pope on this assumption. Rather, he relied on the more common doctrine that the pope-in-council, as we might put it, was superior to a pope acting alone.

The Anglo-Norman *Summa Omnis qui iuste* was concerned with the question whether the clergy could licitly withdraw obedience from a heretical pope before he had been formally condemned. On the case of Anastasius the author observed that the text merely declared that the clergy deserted the pope; it did not say that their action was praiseworthy. In a later gloss, however, without expressing a personal ipinion, he reported that some held it licit for subjects to withdraw allegiance from a pope who propounded a novel heresy.[31] His long comment on *Dist.* 40 c. 6 was almost identical with that of the *Summa Et est sciendum*. The author of the *Summa Reverentia sacrorum canonum* started out from the proposition that a pope who fell into heresy was self-condemned, but without distinguishing old heresies and new ones. This left him with the difficult problem of deciding who could judge whether the pope was in fact a heretic or not. If a heretical pope was 'less than any catholic' did that mean that any catholic could judge an erring pope? That conclusion seemed unacceptable. Perhaps any bishop could judge, 'because heresy concerns all ecclesiastical judges and just as what touches all ought to be approved by all if it is good, so it ought to be rejected by all if it is evil' (an interesting variation on the *quod omnes tangit* phrase). But it was safer, the argument concluded, to hold that a case of this sort was among the *causae arduae* that could be decided only by the Roman church—presumably by the cardinals since it was the pope himself who was on trial. This author evidently had in mind a sharp distinction between the jurisdictional primacy of the Roman church and the personal authority of the pope.[32]

All the previous arguments were recapitulated in the *Summa* of Huguccio, the greatest of the twelfth century commentaries on the Decretum. Huguccio explicitly committed himself to the view that, in a dispute between a pope and the members of a council, the views of the pope should prevail.[33] Accordingly,

---

[30] *Infra*, Appendix C.7.

[31] *Summa ad* C.24 q.1 c.1, "Item queritur si alius prelatus inciderit in heresim nouam et hoc fuerit notorium, an subditi debeant eo ipso recedere . . . sane dici potest quod non debent ab eo recedere nisi consulto superiore. Set quid si sumus pontifex ita incideret? Dicunt quia non est ei superior licite possunt subditi ab eo recedere ut supra di. xl *si papa*, supra di. xix, Anastasius." (MS Rouen 743, fol. 108ra). See also *infra*, Appendix, B.6, C.9.

[32] *Infra*, Appendix C.8.

[33] *Foundations*, p. 55 and Watt, art. cit., pp. 29-30.

in the long and complex gloss that he devoted to the problem of a heretical pope he maintained that no action could be taken in such a case unless (a) the pope's heresy was one already condemned (so that there was no need for any new judgement on the doctrine involved) (b) the pope publicly proclaimed himself an adherent of the condemned heresy (so that there was no need for any enquiry into the facts of the case) (c) the pope pertinaciously continued in his heresy after correction. It was virtually unthinkable that these circumstances would ever arise in practice; if a pope were to fall into heresy at all it would almost certainly be by erring in some matter of doctrine that had not been clearly defined. In another way, however, Huguccio greatly extended the possibilities of deposing an unsuitable pope, for he supported the view that had been put forward by some of his predecessors that any notorious crime which scandalized the church could be regarded as a kind of constructive heresy, and so as a ground for action against a pope.[34]

Besides the texts of Huguccio already published in which he defended the ultimate authority of a pope in opposition to 'the whole church' we can cite another in which the same point of view was uncompromisingly stated.

> s.v. *Considimus*. In prima parte uidetur dici quod non liceat pape contradicere constitutioni uniuersalis ecclesie et ita ut ecclesia potior in constituendo quam papa, set finis principium corrigit. Et nota quod constitutio solius pape potior est quam totius ecclesie . . .[35]

But against this must be set a further text of Huguccio which provides an opportunity to re-assess another important department of his thought. The passage he was commenting on here referred to the unerring faith of the Roman church.

> s.v. *Nunquam errasse*. Obicitur de Anastasio. Sed forte processit. Uel forte melius quod est, loquitur uniuersali ecclesie, que numquam desinet, licet forte possit deficere. Licet enim papa romanus aliquando errauerit, non ideo romana ecclesia, que non solus papa intelligitur, sed uniuersi fideles. Nam ecclesia est congregatio fidelium, ut (De cons.) di. I *Ecclesia*, que etsi rome non sit, est tamen in partibus gallicanis potissime uel ubicumque fideles existunt. Et ecclesia qui(dem) potest desinere esse, sed nunquam contingit. Nam petro et uniuerse ecclesie in prima petri dictum est: Non deficit fides tua . . .[36]

The attitude here seems quite different from that in the previous quotation, but when the whole of Huguccio's work is considered there is no inconsistency in his thought on this matter. He simply did not regard the doctrine of indefectibility, the divine promise that the faith of the church would never become totally extinct, as having anything at all to do with the quite different problem of the location of jurisdictional primacy within the church.[37] There is no confusion

---

[34] Huguccio's gloss *ad* D.40 c.6 was printed in Foundations, pp. 248-50 and the arguments discussed at pp. 58-63. The gloss was also printed by J. F. v. Schulte, *Die Stellung der Concilien, Päpste und Bischöfe* (Prague, 1871), pp. 262-4.

[35] *Summa ad* C.25 q.1 c.1 (MS Admont 7, fol. 331rb). On the different recensions of this section of Huguccio's work see L. Prosdocimi, "La 'Summa Decretorum' di Uguccione da Pisa", *Studia Gratiana* III, pp. 349-74.

[36] Cited by Landgraf from MS Bamberg 61, *art. cit.*, p. 581. The corresponding passage in MS Admont 7 is rendered incoherent

by homoeoteleusis. The passage occurs substantially as given by Landgraf in MS Vatican lat. 2280 and MS Lons-le-Saunier Arch. 16. For the same doctrine in other parts of Huguccio's work, see *Foundations*, pp. 41-43.

[37] Other contemporary canonists also interpreted the words "Ego rogaui pro te petre ut non deficiat fides tua" as referring to the universal church. In addition to the texts quoted in *Foundations* pp. 41-45 see *Summa Omnis qui iuste ad* C.24 q.1 c.9 (*infra*, Appendix B.6): *Summa Animal est substantia ad* C.24 q.1 c.9 (*infra*, Appendix B.7) and *ad* D.21 *ante* c.1, "*Fides tua,*

in Huguccio's handling of these concepts. That is to say, in dealing with the primacy of Rome he did not buttress his argument with texts concerning the unerring 'Roman church' which elsewhere he had interpreted as referring to the universal church.[38] In much the same way, as Fr. Stickler has shown in discussing the problems of church and state, Huguccio manipulated two quite different doctrines concerning the nature of the 'two swords', without explaining the relation between them but also without confusing them.[39] This question of indefectibility and primacy provides a good example of the way in which later 'publicists' would fuse together and adapt for their own purposes elements of thought that the canonists had maintained in isolation from one another. Orthodox theologians came to treat the words, *ut non deficiat fides tua* as a promise directed through Peter to the popes, and so were able to re-shape the canonists' teaching on the pope's authority as supreme judge in articles of faith into a doctrine of an infallible papal *magisterium*. On the other hand, conciliarists would use the doctrine that only the whole church was unerring in faith as an argument to prove the superiority of a general council over the pope.

To return to our problem of deposing a heretical pope. Huguccio's arguments were comprehensive, subtle and consistent. The surprising thing is that they did not prove acceptable to the next generation of Decretists. The Anglo-Norman *Summa Prima primi*, for instance, re-stated the view that within a general council the opinion of the pope outweighed that of the fathers of the council, but explicitly rejected Huguccio's teaching (which in fact followed as a necessary corollary) that the pope could not be condemned for a new heresy.

> Set ecce papa confingit novam heresim. Aliquis vult probare quod sit heresis. Papa dicit quod est fides catholica. Estne audiendus qui vult probare? Hu(guccio) dicit quod non, arg. 24 q. 1 *Quociens*. Set magis credo contrarium.[40]

The *Summa Animal est substantia* varied between the non-commital and the negative. The author began by suggesting that a pope who fell into heresy was to be regarded as having deposed himself, though he was doubtful whether notorious crimes in general had any such effect. The trouble with this simple solution was that it did not explain who was competent to judge whether the pope was in fact a heretic or not. The author of this *summa* denied that the cardinals were competent to judge a pope, and he even denied at this point in his work that a pope who embraced a heresy previously condemned incurred an automatic sentence of excommunication.[41] But he suggested that if a pope was in fact deposed and another instituted in his place then the cardinals should summon a council to judge the issue. The whole gloss was a tangle of loose ends.[42]

---

finaliter nam defecit in passione, i di, fidelior. Uel fides petri, i.e. ecclesie que etiam in passione fuit in beata uirgine." (MS Liége 127E, fol. 14rb).

[38] The one apparent exception is in the gloss *ad* C.9 q.3 c.17, printed by Watt, *art. cit.* p. 29, where Huguccio did cite the texts which he interpreted as referring to the faith of the whole church in a context relating to the primacy of Peter. *"pro suo principatu, quem Beatus Petrus apostolus Domini uoce et tenuit semper et tenebit. Fluctuare potest Petri nauicula sed non subiungi, quia non deficiet fides eius, nec ipse potest esse nulla ut xxi di. i et xxiiii Q.i, Pudenda, A recta."* There seems some ambiguity here, but the correct reading is

"nec *ipsa* potest esse nulla". It was the *nauicula Petri*, the church, that was referred to as unfailing, not Peter himself or his successors. Huguccio was guilty of an irrelevance here, but his doctrine was consistent enough.

[39] A. Stickler, "Der Schwerterbegriff bei Huguccio," *Ephemerides iuris canonici*, III (1947), 201-42.

[40] *Infra*, Appendix C.11. For other decretist views in the generation after Huguccio see *Foundations*, pp. 63-66.

[41] On this point the author reversed himself in a later gloss. *Summa ad* C.24 q.1, c.1. (infra, Appendix C.12).

[42] *Summa ad* D.40 c.6 (infra, Appendix C.12).

The author of the *Summa Duacensis* also found it difficult to maintain a consistent position. The general tone of this work was strongly pro-papal. It defended the unusual positions that the pope was not bound by any statutes of preceding general councils and that, contrary to Gratian's view, the opinions of a pope took precedence over those of the great doctors of the church *in expositione scripturarum* as well as *in decisione causarum*.[43] It was hard for a canonist with these views to tackle the case of a heretical pope. He began his gloss on the words *a nemine est iudicandus* by citing various cases from the Decretum in which popes had been accused of different offences and explained the reasons why they did not violate the principle of papal immunity. (In one instance the individual referred to was not really a pope, in others the popes had voluntarily submitted to judgement.) But he omitted the case of Anastasius which was the really difficult one. He then characteristically dismissed the argument that any scandalous crime could be regarded as a kind of heresy—that would be to reduce the papal privilege to little or nothing. As for heresy itself, the author acknowledged that a man could not be a pope and a heretic at the same time, but his refusal to concede any superiority to the statutes of earlier general councils left him with no basis for distinguishing between a previously condemned heresy and a novel one. He therefore held that a pope who fell into heresy automatically lost his power of jurisdiction whether the heresy had been previously condemned or not. But what if the pope claimed that his new heresy was orthodox doctrine? To avoid any trial of a man who was still regarded as pope it was suggested that the church should consider the issue *deliberatiue non iuditialiter*. If the church decided that the doctrine was heretical and the pope persisted in adhering to it, then he ceased *ipso facto* to be pope. The gloss concluded with the words, *eo (papa) invito potest ecclesia questionem fidei decidere.*[44]

It seems that this canonist set out to defend a very exalted view of papal authority, but manoeuvred himself into a position from which he could escape only by propounding a thoroughly 'left-wing' view on the definition of articles of faith.

The most interesting of these glosses written in the generation after Huguccio's *summa* appeared were those of Alanus Anglicus in his *Apparatus Ius naturale*. In discussing the case of Anastasius he wrote that the liability of a pope to judgement on a charge of heresy arose from the fact that 'in a matter of faith a council is greater than a pope'.[45] In another gloss he went further and explained that, where a matter of faith was involved, but not in any other case, the judgement of the members of a council in opposition to a pope was of greater authority than that of the pope himself. Alanus also preferred the opinion of the cardinals to that of the pope on a disputed article of faith. His insistence that, 'in all other judicial controversies I prefer the sentence of the pope to the sentence of all others' perhaps implies some realisation that the teaching authority required to define articles of faith was of a different nature

---

[43] *Summa Duacensis ad* D.19 *ante* c.1, "In hac xix di. agitur de decretalibus epistolis . . . Derogant ergo uel arrogant ueteri iuri, arg. D. De legibus, *non est nouum*, nec distinguimus in ueteri iure utrum emissum sit a conciliis uel a papa tantum quia utrique indiferentur abrogatur uel derogatur. Concilia enim a solo papa habent auctoritatem ut xvii di. per totum, et ipse ea sua auctoritate confirmat et sua moderatione custodit ut xxxv Q.i c.i Ex quo palam quia maior est eius auctoritas quam illorum ut eadem di. c.i in prin." (MS Douai 649, fol. 96vb). *Ad* D.20 *ante* c.1, "Agitur hic de expositoribus sacre scripture. Hos Gratianus sumi pontifici in causarum decisione postponit, in expositione sacre scripture preponit. Hoc nego, quia in utroque postponendi sunt. Licet enim sunt uera que dicunt non tamen sunt autentica nisi a sumo pontifice confirmata. . ." (MS Douai 649, fol. 97ra). This latter gloss also occurs in the *Summa Prima primi* (MS London BM Royal 11.D.ii, fol. 321rb).

[44] *Infra*, Appendix, C.10. The same doctrine occurs in the Anglo-Norman *Summa Quaestionem* of Honorius. MS Douai 640, fol. 10ra.

[45] *Infra*, Appendix B.8.

[208]

from the authority inhering in the office of a judge. But this thought was not developed, and the definition of faith was still treated as though it were a special variety of judicial process.[46] Alanus was no wild radical, and when he commented on *Dist.* 4c, c. 6, he rejected Huguccio's doctrine, quite commonly accepted in his day, that any scandalous crime in the pope was tantamount to heresy. The whole gloss was moderate in tone, but Alanus did not hold a heretical pope immune from judgement simply because the heresy he propounded was a new one, and, in view of his doctrine on conciliar authority, this attitude was entirely logical. In the last resort, according to Alanus, a pope was liable to judgement for heresy (and not for anything else) because a council of bishops or the cardinals possessed a superior authority in the definition of articles of faith (and not in anything else).

> Est ergo uerum quod de sola heresi inuitus potest papa iudicari, ut hic dicitur, sed hoc ideo in hoc crimine, quia circa ea que ad fidem pertinent minor est collegio cardinalium, uel concilio generali episcoporum.[47]

These glosses form a pattern of thought as consistent as that of Huguccio, but quite different in content.

Indeed, the principal conclusion that emerges from a survey of this kind is that there was no such thing as 'the Canonist theory of sovereignty'. In this, as in other matters, there was a variety of canonistic theories. It seems generally true that the 'constitutionalism' of some of the canonists, if we can call it that, did not consist in an inclination to hamper the freedom of action of the pope in the day-to-day conduct of affairs, but rather in an attempt to devise some form of legal restraint that could be applied in extreme cases where the well-being of the whole church seemed to be threatened. Another point is that there was no real correlation between 'imperialist' sympathies and 'conciliar' attitudes at this stage of doctrinal development. Alanus, who supported the authority of the bishops in council against the pope, strongly upheld the supremacy of the pope over the emperor. Huguccio, who defended the sovereignty of the pope against all other elements within the ecclesiastical hierarchy, adopted a moderate standpoint in the controversy of church and state. Both of these two were brilliant systematic thinkers. It would be possible to extract from the work of Huguccio, and perhaps from that of Alanus,[48] systems of ecclesiology and political theory comparable in strength, subtlety and coherence with anything achieved by the famous 'publicists' of the later Middle Ages. Usually, however, consistency was not the strongest point of the commentators on Gratian. That is the especially true of the best known of them all, Johannes Teutonicus, whose *Glossa Ordinaria* to the Decretum brought to a close this whole epoch of Decretist activity. One could hardly extract a coherent theory of church government from the cat's cradle of texts scattered throughout the *Glossa Ordinaria*;[49] and yet one might reasonably claim that this gloss of Johannes was one of the most influential works in the whole history of

---

[46] *Apparatus ad* C.9 q.3 c.17, cited by Watt, *art. cit.* p. 31. "Sed queritur, cum ipse concilio uel cardinalibus questionem fidei uentilat et contingit papam aliam habere sententiam, aliam cardinales, cuius sententia preualebit? Respondeo, concilii uel cardinalium si omnes in concilium opinione concordent. Immo etiam si maior pars, sed si tanta pars cum papa concordat, quanta est que consensit pape adhereo, et hec in questione fidei tantum. In aliis autem controuersiis iudicialibus omnibus pape sententiam omnium aliorum sententiis prefero."

[47] These words, cited by Watt, *art. cit.* p.30, do not occur in the 'short version' of the *apparatus* of MS Paris BN 3909, cited in Appendix C.13.

[48] The principal difficulty with Alanus arises from the substantial variations that are found in the different recensions of his *apparatus*. There can be no final assessment of his mature thought until the manuscript tradition of his work has been established. This is a problem that still awaits investigation.

[49] The relevant texts are printed in *Foundations*, pp. 250-54.

mediaeval political theory. It provided a source of arguments for thinkers as different as Ockham and Alvarus Pelagius, for Franciscus Zabarella as well as for Johannes de Torquemada. The reason it could provide intellectual ammunition for so many thinkers greater than Johannes Teutonicus himself becomes apparent only as we come to know in detail the richness and diversity of the tradition that Johannes inherited from his canonistic predecessors and rather indiscriminately transmitted to succeeding generations of lawyers and theologians.

APPENDIX

A. *Some ways of describing the limits to papal authority.*

1. *Summa Elegantius in iure diuino* (c. 1169)

> Inter uniuersalia uero concilia viii preminentem et horum iiii super-latiuam habent auctoritatem . . . Que nullo dispensationis colore uel mutare uel mutilare nec ad unum iota sancta romana ecclesia preualet. (MS Paris BN 14997, fol. 3v)
> Ergo et canones abrogare eisque derogare et nouos condere et priuilegia dare dataque tollere plenam habent potestatem dum tamen in his omnibus nihil contra fidem presumant uel in quo uniuersalem ecclesiam offendant. Possunt itaque contra generalia statuta pietatis uel necessitatis uel meritorum intuitu beneficia conferre que non personam transgrediantur nec ad exemplum trahantur, quamquam si subtiliter considerentur non est contra generalia statuta quod sic partialiter conceditur. (*Ibid.*, fol. 8r)
> Secundum hoc ergo ecclesiasticarum regularum alie mobiles alie immo-biles sunt. Immobiles dicimus quas lex eterna ita sanxit ut obseruate conferant, non obseruate adimant salutem. Talia sunt precepta noui et moralia ueteris testamenti. Preter hoc et iiii or primorum uniuersalium conciliorum instituta que neque consuetudine in contrarium faciente nec constitutione iudicari possunt. (*Ibid.*, fol. 6r)

2. Johannes Fauentinus, *Summa* (after 1171)

> *Ad D.* 19 *ante c.* 1. Sunt enim decretales epistole quas ad prouincias uel personas pro diuersis negociis sedes apostolica direxit que cum deuotione sunt custodiende nisi preceptis euangelii uel decretis sanctorum patrum inueniantur diuerse, sicut epistola illa anastasii pape. (MS Arras 271, fol. 7va)
> The same gloss occurs in the *Summa Antiquitate et tempore* (MS Göttingen iur. 159, fol. 24vb)

3. Simon de Bisignano, *Summa* (1177-79)

> *Ad C.* 25 q. 1 c. 6. Hinc collige illud que frequenter solet proponi scilicet quod apostolicus contra hominum statuta possit facere, contra ea uero que a domino uel apostolis sunt instituta nequaquam. (MS Augsburg I, fol. 50ra)

4. Sicardus, *Summa* (1179-81)

> *Ad C.* 25 q. 1

Sunt		De articulis fidei	
leges		De moribus decalogi	hiis derogari non potest
communes		De negotiis seculi	hiis derogari potest per

priuilegia conditoris earum uel maioris iudicis causa iustissima interue-
niente . . . (MS Augsburg I, fol. 124v)

5. Summa Permissio quedam (1179-87)

Ad C. 25 q. 1 *ante* c. 1. Set queritur, si autem emanauerint statuta date
sententie scilicet ut qui contra uenerit anathema sit, an in eam incidat
dominus papa si contra uenerit. Ad quod potest responderi quod si
huiusmodi statuta emanauerint a ueteri testamento uel scriptura euan-
geliorum uel ab apostolis uel a supradictis iiiior conciliis dominus papa
ueniens contra eo ipso est excommunicatus. Si aliunde poterit papa contra
uenire et ea immutare. Potest autem dici quod si papa ex certa scientia
concessit secundum contra primum priori derogatur omnino. Si ignoranter
leditur primum, alii dicunt quod si primum enormiter non leditur ualet
secundum. Sin autem non ualet, ut supra xii Q. iii *Bone rei* (c. 74) et
infra Q. e. § ult (C. 25 q. 1 *post* c. 16). Uel potest dici quod specialia
priuilegia potest apostolicus per alia contraria tollere. Set contra generalia
statuta ecclesie a domino uel apostolis eius uel iiii conciliis promulgata
nichil potest dispensare. (MS Halle Ye 52, fol. 9rb)

6. Summa Et est sciendum (1181-85)

Ad D. 15 c. 1. Hic habes que sunt illa in quibus non potest derogari
principalibus conciliis, in his scilicet que spectant ad articulos fidei et
statum ecclesie. (MS Barcelona S. Cugat 55, fol. 69r)

7. Huguccio, Summa (1188-90)

Ad C. 25 q. 1 *ante* c. 1. Et potentiam domini pape ita uolumus artare
quod ecclesiasticam constitutionem inmutare potest dummodo contra
fidem non faciat uel non obuiet his que pertinent ad salutem, etiam si
ab episcopis apostolis et prophetis statuta fuerunt dummodo non sint de
preceptis uel prohibicionibus. Nam apostoli constituerunt quod sacerdos
pro fornicatione deponatur ut in multis capitulis habere in tractatu ordi-
nandorum potes. Tamen dispensare in ordinibus remansit nam et episcopus
potest cum talibus dispensare . . . Set si precipiat quod missa non
cantetur unquam non ualet quia domini est preceptum 'hec facite in
meam commemorationem etc.' Similiter quod non legatur euangelium.
(MS Admont 7, fol. 331ra)
Ad. C. 25 q. 1 c. 7 s.v. *sententialiter diffinierunt,* dando precepta uel pro-
hibiciones, non ubi penam constituerunt, uel quod melius est in hiis que
pertinent ad salutem, et quod in euangelio et lege et prophetis inmutare
non possit. Item in hiis que statum ecclesie prospiciunt et in sacramenta!
et in articulis fidei dispensare non potest. (*Ibid.,* fol. 331rb)

8. Ricardus Anglicus, Summa Breuis (1196-98)

Ad C. 9 q. 1. Incidenter autem apponitur de potentia pape quem dico
potestatem habere ut ius commune statuat omni ecclesie dum modo non
ledat nouum uel uetus testamentum uel statum uniuersalis ecclesie.
Dispensare autem potest sine ullo termino quatenus se extendit mater
discretio ut arg. i Q. v.c. ult (c. 3). (MS Dublin, Trinity 275, p. 174)

9. Apparatus Ecce uicit leo (1202-10)

Ad D. 15 c. 2. Nec enim potest ire contra hec concilia in hiis scilicet que
ad fidem pertinent uel bonos mores set de hiis que sunt dicta de ani-
maduersionibus potest. (MS Cambridge, Trinity O.5.17, fol. 5vb)

10. *Summa Animal est substantia* (1206-10)

> *Ad* 25 q.1 c.6. Dicunt quod contra canones apostolorum qui loquuntur de moribus siue de euangelio non potest papa uenire, set contra eum (!) que pertinent tantum ad ius positiuum potest bene dispensare, et hanc solutionem bene admittimus. Nam apostoli parum statuerunt nisi de hiis que pertinent ad ius naturale siue ad bonos mores quia exponebant et interpretabantur diuinam scripturam et contra talia non potest papa dispensare quia ueniret contra ius naturale. Set si aliqua statuerunt que non sunt de iure naturali papa bene potest abrogare et uenire contra quia eamdem habet potestatem quam et apostoli, xix *Sic omnes* (D.19 c.2) (MS Liége 127E, fol. 223ra)

11. *Alanus, Apparatus Ius naturale.* (c. 1210)

> *Ad* D.15 c.2 s.v. *sic.* Quantum ad articulos fidei et ecclesie statum generalem ut ex uerbis capituli potest colligi ubi dicitur 'quia in his surgit structura fidei et norma uiuendi' . . . *uniuersali*: arg. non licere canonico suo dissentire capitulo, arg. supra di. viii *Que contra* (c.2), infra xix *In canonicis* (c.6), arg. contra infra xciii *Miratus* (c.2). (MS Paris BN 3909, fol. 3ra)

12. *Glossa Palatina* (1210-15)

> *Ad* C.25 q.1 c.3. Hinc colligunt quidam quod dominus papa non potest contra generalem statum ecclesie dispensare et hic indubitabile quidem circa articulos fidei. Etiam si tota ecclesia consentiret non posset, immo omnes essent heretici, arg. xv di. *Sicut sancti* (c.2) et sic intelliguntur infra e. *Sunt quidam* (c.6) et c. *Contra statuta* (c.7). Uerum contra generalem statum ecclesie, puta de continentia non seruanda uel de alio consimili, posset non tamen solus statuere aliud, arg. supra prox, q.1 *Memor sum* (c.10), xi di. *Ecclesiasticarum* (c.5). In aliis autem dic papam solum posse etiam contra apostolum, xxxiiii di. *Lector* (c.18), et contra euangelium et in decimis et in uoto et in sacramento, extra *De uoto,* per totum. H(uguccio)tamen dicit papam in sacramentis non posse dispensare. Tu dic contra. Peccat tamen qui facit sine causa. (MS Cambridge Trinity O.10.2, fol. 35vb)

B. *Some comments on the case of Anastasius II*

1. *Johannes Fauentinus*
   Supra, Appendix A.2.
2. *Summa Inperatorie maiestati* (1175-78)

> In hoc capitulo dicitur quod Anastasius excommunicatus est quia communicauit fotino communicanti achatio excòmmunicato, et ita uidetur excommunicatio transire in tertiam personam, cui contra in xi Q. ult. *Quoniam multos* (11 q.3 c.103). Soluo. Communicatio alia extrinseca ut in cibo et potu et oratione et salutatione etc. alia intrinseca sicut in heresi et in scismate et huiusmodi. Qui in interiori communione communicat excommunicato, scilicet ut si est hereticus cadat cum eo in heresim communicans illi excommunicatus est. (MS Munich 16084, fol. 4rb).

3. *Summa Permissio quedam* (1179-87)

> *Ad* D.19 c.9. Dicamus quod non ideo ab eo abstinendum est quia communicauit cum excommunicante(!) excommunicato. Set quia cum uoluit eum reuocare tacite eius heresi et errori consensit, quo ipse in canonem

II

date sententie incidit et ideo ab illo sicut ab aliis excommunicatis est abstinendum. (MS Halle Ye 52, fol. 1va)

4. *Summa Tractaturus magister* (1175-91)

Ad D.19 c.8. Hec decretalis anastasii non reprobatur ideo quod dixit ordinatos ab excommunicato posse in suis ordinibus recipi quod fit aliquando ex dispensatione . . . set quia dixit eos nulla lesionis portione contingi et generaliter recipiendos contra statutum generalis concilii in quo erant depositi, ut infra i Q.vii *Exigunt* (c.18). Uel propter alia que non sunt hic posita que tamen ipse dixit in illa sua decretali, unde hec portio est suspecta scilicet quia fouebat dampnatum errorem illius et uolebat eum reuocare ut habetur in sequenti capitulo. (MS Paris BN 15994, fol. 6ra)

5. *Summa Et est sciendum* (1181-85)

Ad D.19 c.8. Hic queritur quare decretalem hanc ecclesia reprobat. Licet enim dixisset papa achatium potuisse ordinare uel ab eo ordinatos de iure debuisse ministrare, non tamen erat ob hoc notandus cum ipse potuisset mutare canones in quibus dicebatur hereticos tolerari non posse nec cum hoc non sit contra articulos fidei. Soluo. Hic papa errorem defendebat achatii quare ipse conuincebatur magis errare defendendo culpam errantis ut C.xxiiii Q.iii *Qui aliorum* (c.32). Credo tamen tempore anastasii hanc decretalem fuisse autenticam, eius uero successor presumpsit illum hereticum quia est fulmine percussus ut infra c.i(x) dicitur, quare et eius scripta iniqua iudicauit ista maxime, uel quia sine uoluntate concilii hereticum uoluit reconciliare.
Ad D.19 c.9. Per hoc habes quod non debet papa ei communicare cui concilium censuit non communicandum. Eadem ratione si in questionibus que in concilio proponuntur a sententia pape discordat concilium maior est sententia concilii quam pape. (MS Barcelona S. Cugat 55, fol. 70r)

6. *Summa Omnis qui iuste* (c.1186)

Ad D.19 c.9 s.v. *Abegerunt*, infra viii Q.iiii *Nonne* (c.1) contra. Speciale est in heresi quod possunt recedere statim ab eo et hoc in odium heresis dicitur hic. Secus de aliis criminibus in quibus non potest recedi a prelato ante sententiam ut ibi dicitur. Uel dici potest quod clerici ita fecerunt, non tamen super hoc laudari debent, nec hic laudantur. (MS Rouen 743, fol. 7ra)
Ad D.19 ante c.9. Solet queri quare reprobatum est capitulum illud, quia nihil est in eo quod possit reprehendi. Dicit G. quod reprobatum est hoc capitulum non propter id quod dixit hic, set propter id quod alibi dixit, uel quia dixit ordinatos ab eo licite posse officium suum consequi quod non est uerum. Ex dispensatione enim posset non ex rigore et quia uoluit totum rigorem enuntiare reprobatur hoc capitulum. Set queri potest, nonne potuit statuere ut de iure reciperentur ordinati ab eo contra alios canones? In omnibus enim potest derogare predecessoribus suis preterquam in articulis fidei. Dici potest quod non erat receptum capitulum istud a concilio et ideo reprobatur, uel potest dici quod successor eius uidens illum nutu dei percussum reprobauit eum cum scriptis suis. (Ibid., fol. 7ra).
Ad C.24 q.1 c.9.s.v. *Nunquam errasse*, scilicet in toto corpore suo. Nunquam enim tota (ecclesia) errauit et si aliter continget in aliqua persona, specialiter ut in anastasio, ut supra di. xix *Anastasius*. Nota hic arg. non intelligi fieri quod a tota uniuersalitate(!) non fit. (*Ibid.*, fol. 108va)

[213]

7. *Summa Animal est substantia* (1206-10)

> *Ad* C.24 q.1 c.9. Ergo ecclesia romana nunquam errauit. Contra xix di. *Anastasius* (c.9) . . . Soluo. Intelligitur de uniuersali ecclesia que nunquam succubuit quia etiam in passione domini quando minima erat fides in beata uirgine nec errauit. (MS Liége 127E, fol. 213rb)

8. Alanus, *Apparatus Ius naturale* (c. 1210)

> *Ad* D.19 c.9. Argumentum quod in questione fidei maior est sinodus quam papa, ar. supra di. xv *Sicut*, et di. xvi *Sancta*, quod firmiter est tenendum. Unde accidit ex tali causa quod sinodus potest ipsum iudicare et dampnare, unde accidit quod incidit in excommunicationem latam super heresi in sinodo ut hic, quod non accideret si papa in hoc casu maior esset synodo uel equalis, ar. infra di. xxi *Inferior* Si autem ipse tamen uel ipsius predecessor alius sine concilio uel collegio cardinalium aliquam heresim dampnasset nec ipsum nec ipsius successorem in dampnatione incidere putarem, licet eumdam errorem foueret, sicut nec hodie papa uerberans clericum incideret in canonum. (Transcription of J. Watt, *art. cit.* p. 30 from MS Paris BN 15393, fol. 15a)

C. The case of a heretical pope

1. *Summa Antiquitate et tempore* (after 1171)

> *Ad* D.40 c.6. Nota quod non continuo pro heresi papa dampnandus est set si secundo uel tercio comonitus pertinax fuerit in errore. (MS Göttingen iur. 159, fol. 46va)

2. *Commentum Atrebatense* (1171-79)

> *Ad* D.40 c.6. Queritur si papa manifeste fornicaretur et comonitus noluerit desistere utrum possit a subditis accusari et dampnari. Respondeo sic. Uidetur nam ydolatrie crimen incidere ut di. lxxxi *Si quis* (c.4.). Cum enim manifeste peccat mortaliter licet expressim a fide non exorbitet alios tamen exemplo praue actionis exorbitare facit. Que ergo est differentia inter heresim et alia mortalia peccata quo ad hunc articulum? Respondeo quia super aliis non potest accusari nisi notoria fuerint et desistere amonitus noluerit. Set de heresi nonnunquam (non notoria?) accusari potest. (MS Arras 271, fol. 150rb)

3. *Summa Inperatorie Maiestati* (1175-78)

> *Ad* D.21 c.7. In causa autem fidei sedes apostolica iudicari potest. Ad hoc notandum quod prima sedes iudicari non potest nisi in articulis fidei pertinaciter errauerit ut infra di. xl *Si papa* (c.6), uel cum perseuerauerit ecclesiam corrumperit schismate ut infra xxiiii causa *Sane profertur* (24 q.2 c.6). Set . . . ibi enim papa pro patriarcha ponitur, nec uidetur quod apostolicus pro schismate sit iudicandus. (MS Munich 16084, fol. 4va)

4. Simon de Bisignano, *Summa* (1177-79)

> *Ad* D.40 c.6. Et nota quod probatur si(!) tunc demum potest condempnari papa a subditis cum errorem pertinaciter uult defendere ut infra xxiiii Q.iii *Dixit apostolus* (c.29). (MS Augsburg I, fol. 5va)
>
> *Ad* C.25 q.1 c.10. Queritur autem hic an fidem suam apostolicus huic exponere teneretur, quod ea ratione uidetur dicendum quia pro heresi potest sumus pontifex a subditis iudicari ut supra di. xl *Si papa* (c.6). Ergo et suspitionem susceptam pro heresi diluere et abolere tenetur cum sit impius et crudelis qui consciencie fidens famam negligit ut supra c.xi

q.iii *Non sunt audiendi* (c.56). Uel dici potest quod ex dispensatione et humilitate hoc fecit apostolicus non ex iuris rigore ut supra c.ii q.vii *Nos si* (c.41), unde hoc faciens non dedit successoribus formam qua id facere tenerentur ut supra c.ii q.iiii(!) *Auditum est* (2 q.5 c.18) (Ibid., fol. 50ra)

5. Sicardus, *Summa* (1179-81)

Ad D.22. Nam si ordinarius est iudex in nullo negotio iudicabit maiorem nisi in casu cum cardinales deponunt apostolicum hereticum ut di. xl *Si papa* (c.6). (MS Augsburg I, fol. 81ra)

6. *Summa Tractaturus magister* (1175-91)

Ad D.40 c.6 s.v. *A fide deuius*, contumaciter, xxiiii Q.iii *Dixit* (c.29), xxiiii Q.1 *Quoties* (c.12) . . . Set hoc de dampnata heresi. (MS Paris BN 15994, fol. 12vb)

7. *Summa Et est sciendum* (1181-85)

Ad D.17 post c.4. Apostolicus autem de quo hic dicitur accusari non poterat a subditis nec dampnari ut di. xxi *Nunc autem* (c.7) et c.ix Q.iii *Aliorum* (c.14), nisi pro fide ut di. xl *Si papa* (c.6) et tunc demum cum errorem uellet defendere ut c.xxiii Q.iii *Dixit apostolus* (c.29). Alii dicunt quod de noua heresi non potest papa accusari cum eo ipso aliquid autenticum sit quod ipse sic sentit cuius est questionem fidei terminare ut c.xxiiii Q.1 *Quocies* (c.12). Secus uero si incideret in errorem dampnatam ut c.xxiiii Q.1 c. ii et iii. Alii dicunt quod pro quolibet notorio crimine eum posse a concilio deponi. Si uero de hoc ipso esset questio utrum esset uerus papa hoc posset per homines terminari. (MS Barcelona S. Cugat 55, fol. 69r)

Ad D.21 c.9. Uidetur quod ante depositionem huius (Dioscurus of Alexandria) inquiri debuit utrum iuste excommunicauerat papam uel non, puta pro heresi. Quod tamen non prouenit. Constabat etiam eum non potuisse uel etiam pro heresi hoc fecisse cum adhuc pro papa eum haberet ecclesia. (*Ibid.*, fol. 71v)

Ad D.40 c.6. Ecce casus qui a generalitate excipitur in quo scilicet potest apostolicus accusari cum errat in fide, quod tamen tunc demum debet intelligi posse fieri cum errorem defendit ut c.xxiiii Q.iii *Dixit apostolus* (c.29). Set quare est in heresi speciale? Quia cetera peccata unitatem ecclesie non rumpunt. Cum ceteris enim uiciis potest esse homo membrum ecclesie licet putridum. Heresis uero uel scisma ipsam uiolant unitatem et fundamentum fidei maculant et corrumpunt, unde cum sit hereticus est quolibet catholico minor. Alii uero dicunt non esse speciale in hoc casu. Idem enim potest fieri pro quolibet peccato notorio. Set contra hoc totaliter obicitur. Non uidetur quod papa possit pro heresi accusari quia eo ipso uidetur aliquid esse catholice dictum quod papa sic sentit licet ab eius sententia discrepent uniuersi, quia questio fidei non nisi per petri successorem est terminanda ut C.xxiiii Q.i *Quocies* (c.12) cum uideamus quod licet omnes dicerent Christum non esse aliquid secundum quod homo preualuit tamen alexandri tercii sententia in contrarium sentientis ut in decretali *Cum Christus.* Item cum papa adhuc pro apostolico teneatur quia uel hoc factum negat uel hoc esse heresim non est certum omnis ei debetur honor a subditis et reuerentia ut ante accusationem donec obiecta sub luce constiterint ut c.viii Q.iiii *Nonne* (c.1). Non enim qui accusatur reus est set qui conuincitur criminosus ut c.xv Q. ult. c. ult. (15 q.8 c.5). Sic igitur ante a nemine accusari poterat ut c.viiii Q.iii *Aliorum* (c.14) ita nec modo. Item cum liceat ei omnia constituta predecessorum mutare, nonne potest et istud ut nec etiam pro heresi possit accusari? Item par pari legem dare non potest nec sua sententia ligare. Soluo. Si nouam heresim fingeret tunc dicerem eum non accusandum, immo eius opinio ceteris anteponeretur. De errore uero iam dampnato in conciliis hoc potest intelligi. Si enim uellet defendere errorem iam dampnatum statim eum posset dampnare concilium tanquam hereticum et excommunicatum ut c.xxiiii Q.i c.ii et tercio. Nec concedendum est eum solum absque communi consilio fratrum posse derogare statuta conciliorum. (*Ibid.*, fol. 79v)

8. *Summa Reuerentia sacrorum canonum* (1183-92)

Ad D.21 c.3. Unde et summus pontifex cum omnibus sit superior omnes iudicat et a nemine iudicatur ut infra ix Q.iii *Nemo* (c.13). Casualiter tamen ratione hereseos qui superior est ab inferioribus condempnari (potest). (MS Erfurt Amplon Quart. 17, fol. 119va)

Ad D.40 c.6. s.v. *A fide deuius*, in quo casu etiam ab aliis posset iudicari ut infra ii Q.vii § (*post* c.22). In hoc capitulo non tamen queritur, si sumus pontifex quod absit a fide deuiaret et ideo minor quolibet catholico inueniretur, an quilibet catholicus in eum animaduertere posset. Quod non uidetur quia iudex esse non potest qui nulli preest iurisditioni, et quod is statueret non haberet rei iudicate auctoritatem ut C. *De iurisditione omnium iudicum* l.iii (Codex 3.13.3). Set nunquid metropolitanus uel episcopus alius in eum animaduertere posset? Quod forte uidetur quia heresis omnes ecclesie iudices tangit et quod omnes similiter tangit ab omnibus, sicut si bonum est debet comprobari, ita si malum est improbari ut colligi potest ex eo quod dicitur in C. *De auctoritate* l. ult. (Codex 5. 59.5). Tutius tamen uidetur in hoc casu ut quia cognitio hereseos questio ardua est non nisi ad romanam ecclesiam referatur ut infra xxiiii Q.i *Quoties* (c.12), ut cuius sit promouere eius sit et causa cognita promotum deicere (*Ibid.*, fol. 125ra)

9. *Summa Omnis qui iuste* (c.1186)

Ad D.40 c.6. Set quero si esset hereticus et uellet retractare errorem suum an esset dicendum hereticus uel deberetne deponi, et dicunt quod non ut infra xxiiii Q.iii. Set quero si posset similiter accusari in crimine simonie uel si homicida esset. Et dicunt quod heresis et scisma ipsam uiolant ecclesiam et fundamentum maculant fidei. Cetera autem peccata non corrumpunt unitatem licet peccantes putrida membra sint ecclesie. Alii dicunt non esse speciale quod hic dicitur. Idem enim potest fieri pro quolibet peccato notorio et ita dicit G. Item uidetur quod nec etiam pro heresi posset accusari quia eo ipso uidetur aliquid canonice dictum quia papa sic sentit licet ab eius sententia uniuersi dissentiant, quia non nisi ad petrum referenda est questio fidei ut xxiiii Q.i *Quoties* (c.12), cum uideatur quod licet omnes dicerent Christum non esse aliquid in eo quod homo preualuit tamen Alex. iii sententia in contrarium dicentis in decreto illo *Cum Christus*. Item cum adhuc habeatur pro apostolico uel quia negat factum uel quia heresim esse non sit certum omnis debetur ei reuerencia a subditis ut viii Q.iv *Nonne* (c.1). Non enim qui accusatus reus est set qui conuincitur criminosus ut xv Q.ult c.ult. (15 q.8 c.5). Sicut igitur ante a nemine accusari poterat ut iii Q.ix *Aliorum* (c.14) ita nec modo. Item cum liceat ei omnia constituta predecessorum mutare, nonne potest et istud ut nec etiam pro heresi potest accusari? Item (par pari) legem dicere non potest nec sua sententia ligare dici potest. Si nouam heresim fingeret non posset accusari, immo opinio sua ceteris deberet preferri. Si uero errorem dampnatum uellet defendere statim posset eum consilium dampnare ut xxiiii Q.i c.i et ii. Nec est concedendum eum solum absque communi consensu concilii posse derogare statuta conciliorum. (MS Rouen 743, fol. 18vb)

10. *Summa Duacensis* (towards 1200)

Ad D.40 c.6. Quod autem dicitur papam posse accusari si fuerit in fide deuius, large accipit Y (Huguccio) nomen fidei ut etiam possit acusari de omni crimine notorio, et dicitur tunc deuiare a fide, i.e. facere contra doctrinam fidei. Largius etiam extenditur nomen fidei ut dicantur preces contra fidem i.e. contra consuetam loquendi regulam ut *de cons.* di. iv *Si non sancti fictaur* (c.72). Sic etiam omnis mortaliter peccans dicitur Christum negare ut xi Q.iii *Existimant* (c.84). Set secundum hoc nullum uel modicum esset pape priuilegium. Propterea dicendum simpliciter quod in nullo casu accusari potest propter defectum iudicis superioris arg. iii Q.i § *Patet* (post c.6). Imo uerius quia constitutum est ne accusetur ut xi Q.iii *Nemo* (c.41). Quod autem hic uidetur casus hereseos excipi, superficialiter dicitur hec exceptio. Simul enim et papa et hereticus esse non potest, arg. *de pen.* di. i *Uerbum* (c.51), di. xxiiii Q.i c.i.ii.iii, *Didicimus* (c.31), que locum habent si sequitur heresim iam dampnatam. Si nouam et eam iam predicare cepit similiter cadit a iuris-dictione sua ipso iure ut e. c. *Ait, Aperte* (24 q.1 c.35, c.36). Si uero contendat papa id heresim esse uel negauerit se heresim illam non dampnatam que ei inponitur fouere uel correctus uoluerit emendari, non potest inuitus iudicari a quoquam. Et quid si contendat heresim non esse quod predicat? Debet iudicem eligere et sub eo de hoc litigare. Licet enim legibus solutus sit debet tamen legibus uiuere . . . Et quid si nolit? Credo quia sine eo debeat ecclesia deliberatiue non iuditialiter disceptare et eo inuento quod heresis sit, papa correctus, nisi resipiscat papa desinit esse ipso iure. Secus si alias malefaciat et corrigi nolit. Tunc enim non restat nisi dolor et gemitus. Ratio diuersitatis est quoniam causa fidei omnibus indicitur esse communis ut xxvi(!) di. *Ubinam* (d.96 c.4) et eo inuito potest ecclesia questionem fidei decidere. (MS Douai 649, fol. 99ra)

11. *Summa Prima Primi* (towards 1200)

Ad D.19 *ante* c.1. Concilia enim a solo papa habent auctoritatem ut 22 di. per totum. Ex quo apparet quod maior est eius quam patrum in concilio existentium auctoritas ut infra eadem c.1 in prin. (MS London BM Royal 11.D.II, fol. 321rb)

Ad D.40 c.6. Nota quod si papa admonitus uelit resipiscere a nullo potest accusari uel dampnari ut 24 Q. 3 *Dixit* (c.29), 21 di. *Nunc autem* (c.7), et hoc siue sit heresis siue aliud crimen notorium. Secus si publice predicet et ammonitus nolit corigi ut hic. Esto ergo quod papa sequatur heresim dampnatam latenter, et cum aliqui uelint hoc probare papa negat se eam sequi. Suntne ipsi uolentes probare audiendi? Credo quod non, quia non potest accusari nisi quando scitur esse heresis quod papa sequitur et papa non negat se id sequi et ammonitus non uult resipiscere. Set ecce papa confingit nouam heresim. Aliquis uult probare quod sit heresis. Papa dicit quod est fides catholica. Estne audiendus qui uult probare? Hu(guccio) dicit quod non, arg. 24 Q.1 *Quoties* (c.12). Set magis credo contrarium. Hoc enim casu debet iudicem eligere et sub eo litigare. Licet enim legibus sit solutus debet tamen legibus uiuere . . . Quod si nolit credo quod sine eo ecclesia possit disceptare et iudicare, et eo inuento quod papa sit hereticus, nisi coreptus resipiscat, ecclesia potest ipsum condempnare et deponere. Secus si alias male faceret et corrigi nolit. Ratio diversitatis est quia causa fidei omnibus communis est ut 96 di *Ubinam* (c. 4), et eo invito potest ecclesia decidere questionem fidei. Hu(guccio) tamen dicit quod papa de quolibet crimine notorio potest accusari et dampnari . . . Hoc non credo.

12. *Summa Animal est substantia* (1206-1210)

> *Ad* D.40 c.6 s.v. *Deuius.* Quia uenit contra substantiam religionis sue unde se ipsum uidetur impugnare et deponere. Tamen si paratus sit se corrigere non uidetur quod possit accusari, xxiiii Q.iiii *Dixit* (c.29). Dicunt etiam quod de occulta heresi potest ad purgationem compelli. Set nonne accusari (potest) de alio peccato mortali notorio ut de fornicatione uel adulterio? Dicunt quod sic si nolet corrigi et ecclesia scandalizetur, ii Q.vii § *Cum Balaam* (post c.41), et hic dicendum est maxime si quis erit iudex in huiusmodi causa. Papa uero habet plenitudinem potestatis, ii Q.vi *Decreto* (c.11), ergo uidetur quod nullus alius posset habere maiorem, et ita nullus erit iudex in causa sua. Preterea uidetur quod huic decreto possit papa derogare cum habet plenitudinem potestatis. Preterea si dicatur quod cardinales sunt iudices, ergo papa potest de eis corrigi si aliquando male iudicauit et ita a papa appellabitur ad cardinales, quod non solet dici. Queritur etiam si per numerosos testes papa est depositus et alius institutus quis retractabit sententiam illam. Potest dici quod cardinales debent conuocare concilium et illud erit iudex. Et nota quod si papa incidit in heresim dampnatam non ideo est excommunicatus, set omnes alii sunt excommunicati, xxiiii Q.1 *Achacius* et c. *Audiuimus* (c.3 and c.4), quia sententia paris eum non ligat, xi(!) *Inferior* (D.21 c.4). MS Liége 127E, fol. 31vb)
>
> *Ad* C.24 q.1 c.1. Ergo uidetur quod si papa incideret in heresim iam dampnatam quod sit excommunicatus, di. xix *Anastasius* (c.9). Tamen uidetur quod non quia nullus est superior et nullus potest excommunicari nisi a superiore, xxi di. *Inferior* (c.4). Bene concedo quod est excommunicatus nam est factus inferior qui apostatando confitetur ecclesiam nullam nullam(!) esse et ita non est caput ecclesie unde inferior nullo(!) catholico, ii Q.vii § *Set queritur* (post c.26), quare potest accusari super isto crimine non super alio, xl di. *Si papa* (c.6). (*Ibid.*, fol. 212rb)

13. Alanus, *Apparatus Ius naturale* (c.1210)

> *Ad* D.40 c.6. Set nonne damasus de adulterio est accusatus ut infra ii Q.vii § *Cum balaam* in fine (post c.41)? Item si publicus fenerator esset nunquid accusari posset? Posset secundum quosdam de omni notorio, qui large accipiunt peccare in fide, i.e. contra doctrinam fidei nostre sicut omnis mortaliter peccans dicitur Christum negare ut infra xi Q.iii *Existimant* (c.84). Set secundum hoc nullum esset hic pape priuilegium. Ideo dicendum quod cum iudicem non habeat superiorem inuitus iudicari non potest nisi de crimine hereseos in quo propter criminis enormitatem et commune periculum ecclesie est statutum. Set nunquid alius pape posset legem inponere cum papa canonibus sit solutus et possit eos mutare. Forte ita est in hoc crimine quia ibi quasi per consequentiam reuocatur in dubium utrum papa sit. Uidetur enim quod si hereticus est caput ecclesie non est. Si uero de alio crimine infamatur et alius uelit eum accusare ne in eo ecclesia scandalizetur, licet cogi non possit, tamen amonitus iudicem eligere debebit et sub eo litigare. Quamuis enim legibus solutus sit secundum leges tamen uiuere debet. (MS Paris BN 3909, fol. 8va)

III

"THE PRINCE IS NOT BOUND BY THE LAWS." ACCURSIUS AND THE ORIGINS OF THE MODERN STATE *

It is just fifty years since the distinguished legal historian, Adhémar Esmein, addressing an international conference in London, discussed the interpretation of the Roman law maxim *Princeps legibus solutus est* by the medieval glossators, and the influence of their teachings on the growth of French government.[1] Esmein thought that the glossators had perverted a doctrine of classical constitutional law, which had merely exempted the emperor from the observance of certain legal rules, into a general principle of irresponsible absolutism. Certain French constitutional lawyers of the sixteenth century, he maintained, struggled stoutly against this doctrine but, none the less, its acceptance opened the way to various abuses in French public life ranging from the arbitrary decision of legal cases to the issuance of *lettres de cachet*. Esmein accordingly took advantage of the occasion to congratulate his English hosts on having escaped the glossators' baneful influence.

It also happens that this year is being celebrated as the seven hundredth anniversary of the death of Accursius, author of the *Glosa Magna* on the whole *Corpus Iuris Civilis,* the greatest glossator of them all.[2] There is, however, more than a mere coincidence of dates to render timely a reconsideration of Accursius's own interpretation of the famous maxim. Recent work on the political theories of the medieval glossators has been concerned as much with the constitutionalist as with the absolutist implications of their thought, and it has raised broad new problems for historians of Western institutions. To some scholars indeed it seems that the peculiar fusion of classical, Christian and feudal concepts which we encounter in the works of the thirteenth century Roman and canon lawyers stimulated such far-reaching developments in the theory and practice of government as to make possible then for the first time the emergence of true constitutional states, and so the

* The author was assisted during the writing of this article by a grant from the American Council of Learned Societies and wishes to express his gratitude.
[1] A. Esmein, "La maxime Princeps legibus solutus est dans l'ancien droit public français", *Essays in Legal History,* ed. P. Vinogradoff (Oxford, 1913), pp. 201-214.
[2] Accursius died between 1259 and 1263. On the chronology of his life and work see E. Genzmer, "Zur Lebensgeschichte des Accursius", *Festschrift für Leopold Wenger, Münchener Beiträge zur Papyrusforschung und antiken Rechtsgeschichte,* XXXV (1945), pp. 223-241.

beginnings of a type of polity that, after centuries of vicissitudes and adaptations, has come to be charaeteristic of modern Western society. On this view the pattern of government that was emerging by the end of the thirteenth century in Europe was different in kind from that of any previous civilization; different from the political organizations of primitive cultures because it did have written records, organized departments of state, the idea of legislation as a deliberate product of reason and will; different from ancient empires (Wittfogel's "oriental despotisms") because of its constitutional limitations on monarchy; different too from classical city-states because, for the first time, the techniques of representation and consent were so adapted as to make possible the practice of constitutional government throughout whole nations, over areas embracing many cities.

Not everyone would agree with this way of looking at things. No one indeed doubts that there were limitations on government in the Middle Ages; the important question is whether there was really any state power to be limited. It has often been argued that in medieval times the ruler was assumed to be "under the law", bound by a pre-existing fundamental law which had its roots in ancient custom, and that this presupposition stands in the sharpest contrast to the modern view that all law depends ultimately on the will of a sovereign legislator. This argument, in effect, treats medieval government as simply one additional specimen in a whole class of primitive legal systems. It has especial force when it cites by way of contrast the example of modern constitutional countries like England in which supreme power is vested in a sovereign legislature, untrammelled by any written constitution or enforceable precepts of natural law. (In our own subsequent argumentation we shall be concerned especially with this type of modern constitutionalism precisely because its underlying principles seem, at first sight, so remote from those of medieval constitutional law.) Many historians then, especially students of the Renaissance, would maintain that there is a radical discontinuity between medieval and modern concepts of government, that medieval kingdoms cannot properly be called "states" at all both because of their subordinate position in an international ordering of society and, what more particularly concerns us, because they lacked a concept of legislative sovereignty.[3]

The arguments against this point of view rest largely on recent studies of medieval Roman and canon law. It is this situation that gives point to our

---

[3] For modern literature concerning the autonomy of medieval kingdoms with respect to papacy and empire see "Some Recent Works on the Political Theories of the Medieval Canonists", *Traditio*, X (1954), pp. 594-625. On the question of internal sovereignty see M. David, *La souveraineté et les limites juridiques du pouvoir monarchique* (Paris, 1954) and, especially, Ernst H. Kantorowicz, *The King's Two Bodies* (Princeton, 1957). The present state of the whole question is reviewed by Gaines Post, "Ratio publicae utilitatis, ratio status und 'Staatsräson' (1100–1300)", *Die Welt als Geschichte*, XXI (No. 2, 1961), pp. 8-28, 71-99. Post discusses and argues against the views of various historians, including Meinecke, Kern, Gilbert, Friedrich, who, although starting from different premises, all treat the emergence of the state as a post-medieval phenomenon.

enquiry. In the whole general debate concerning the influence of Roman law on medieval constitutional theory and the relationship of that theory to the modern concept of the state there is no particular topic more significant than the ideas on sovereignty associated with the principle *Princeps legibus solutus est* in the Middle Ages, and, among the medieval jurists, there is no one more important nor, from its point of view, more neglected than Accursius. His vast gloss (completed in its first recension c. 1228) synthesised and by so doing virtually superseded a century's work by the great line of glossators that stretches from Irnerius to Azo. It was used for centuries as a standard text in all the law schools of Christendom and its words were accorded an authority second only to those of the *Corpus Iuris Civilis* itself. The gloss of Accursius was rot a work of profound originality, though throughout one has the impression of a formidable controlling intelligence at work in the selection of the comments and solutions of his predecessors that were chosen for emphasis. Its importance lies in the fact that, in an age when concepts of government were becoming permeated with the doctrines of Roman law, the Accursian gloss more than any other one work determined which interpretations of those doctrines would find general acceptance.

As we have indicated, the nature of this Roman law influence has become a matter of controversy among modern historians. An older school of thought, typified in the comments of Esmein, maintains that all Roman jurisprudence, civilian and canonist alike, was starkly absolutist in temper, and that constitutional government arose in spite of it from an original heritage of Teutonic liberty that was providentially preserved in England since there the sturdy growth of the common law excluded Roman influences. Although this view is still fairly widespread it has come under mounting criticism. Even before Esmein's paper A. J. Carlyle had suggested that "the conception of the revived study of the Roman law as unfavourable to the progress of political liberty... requires at least very considerable qualification",[4] though he did not consider the implications of our "absolutist" text. C. H. McIlwain, when he wrote his admirable *Growth of Political Thought in the West,* could still refer to "the truly absolutist Roman doctrine of monarchy", but, a few years later, reconsidering the whole question at a time when events in contemporary Germany had produced a general scepticism about theories of innate Teutonic virtue, he strongly emphasised the contribution of Roman law to the growth

---

[4] R. W. and A. J. Carlyle, *A History of Mediaeval Political Theory in the West* (Edinburgh, 1903–36), II, p. 75.

[5] C. H. McIlwain, *The Growth of Political Thought in the West* (New York, 1932), p. 383, "Esmein has shown how the truly absolutist Roman doctrine of monarchy affected the monarchy of France..."; *idem, Constitutionalism, Ancient and Modern* (Ithaca, 1940), pp. 43-68. See also McIlwain's remarks on Roman law in "Mediaeval Institutions in the Modern World", *Speculum,* XVI (July, 1941), pp. 275-283 and in "The English Common Law, Barrier Against Absolutism", *American Historical Review,* XLIX (Oct., 1943) pp. 23-31. On the same theme see also R. Neuner, "The Democratic Spirit of the Roman Law and the Common Law", *Seminar,* III (1945), pp. 57-68.

of Western constitutionalism.[5] These later pages of McIlwain remain the best brief introduction to the subject and the views expressed in them have been very influential, but they have not stimulated any general study of the political theories of the glossators—the medieval canonists have received much more attention in recent years—and no real agreement has emerged concerning the nature and influence of their teachings. Several modern works have discussed the significance of Roman law doctrines for particular aspects of constitutionalism, especially in connection with the technicalities of representation.[6] On the other hand two very recent books have vigorously re-stated the argument that France entered the modern era with a more absolute form of government than England precisely because the French assimilated more Roman law into their legal system in the thirteenth century than the English did.[7]

Thus two problems arise. The first, relatively straight-forward, is to assess the significance of the constitutionalist elements in the medieval *Glossa Ordinaria* to the *Corpus* of Roman law. The second, extremely complicated, is to determine whether there really is any continuity between the underlying principles of medieval constitutionalism and those of the modern Western state. There are certain ambiguities both in the condition of modern scholarship and in the nature of the source material itself which have impeded the development of any generally acceptable synthesis in this whole area of thought. (Not least important is the absence, among modern political scientists, of any universally accepted synthetic theory of law, sovereignty and the state.) At present a scholar who is disposed to find in the writings of the medieval civilians and canonists a significant contribution to the developing theory of the constitutional state finds himself obliged to argue on several different fronts at the same time. Against one established school of thought, which denies the very existence of the state in the Middle Ages (because then "all law was custom"), he must emphasize the broad legislative competence of the ruler which was already asserted in theory in the twelfth century and was being widely exercised in practice by the end of the thirteenth.[8] But, in

---

[6] On this see especially Gaines Post, "Plena Potestas and Consent in Medieval Assemblies", *Traditio*, I (1943), pp 355-408; *idem*, "A Romano-Canonical Maxim 'Quod Omnes Tangit' in Bracton", *Traditio*, IV (1946), pp. 197-251; Yves Congar, "Quod Omnes Tangit ab Omnibus Tractari et Approbari Debet", *Revue historique de droit français et étranger*, XXXV (No. 2, 1958), pp. 210-259. P. N. Riesenberg has dealt with the relationship between public utility and inalienability of public rights in Accursius and other medieval Roman lawyers, *Inalienability of Sovereignty in Medieval Thought* (New York, 1956), pp. 68-79. M. P. Gilmore's *Argument from Roman Law in Political Thought 1200-1600* (Cambridge, Mass., 1941), was concerned with the imperium of inferior magistrates as a factor limiting the absolute authority of the Prince. For constitutional ideas among the canonists contemporary with Accursius I may refer to my own *Foundations of the Conciliar Theory* (Cambridge, 1955) and "Pope and Council: Some New Decretist Texts", *Mediaeval Studies*, XIX (1957), pp. 197-218.

[7] John P. Dawson, *A History of Lay Judges* (Cambridge, Mass., 1960); Walter Ullmann, *Principles of Government and Politics in the Middle Ages* (London, 1961).

[8] For a general survey of the growth of legislative activity in the thirteenth century

arguing against another traditional school of thought which sees medieval Roman jurisprudence as a mere apologia for absolutism, the same scholar must emphasize the limitations on the will of the sovereign that were implicit in medieval conceptions of the "rule of law". Finally, he has to show that, if there is a paradox involved in pursuing these two lines of argument simultaneously, it is a perennial one, that the tension between a concept of legislative sovereignty and a conviction that the sovereign should be in some meaningful sense "bound by the law" is not peculiar to the Middle Ages.

In fact, this tension arises in all modern constitutional countries that attribute sovereign power to a particular organ of government.[9] We would maintain, therefore, that in discussing such matters the medieval jurists were not dealing with problems essentially alien to the nature of the modern state. On the contrary they were pre-occupied with issues quite similar to those raised by contemporary constitutional lawyers who have tried to reconcile the theory of legislative sovereignty with the practice of constitutional government. The real persistence of this problem has sometimes been obscured in the past by the widespread acceptance (especially in England) of philosophies of sovereignty that really were incompatible with the principles of medieval constitutionalism. The point that has been becoming more and more apparent in recent years is that such philosophies are also incompatible with the practice of modern constitutional democracy. In the nineteenth century the two most influential doctrines were those derived from Austin, who treated law as positive command, and from Rousseau and Hegel who treated it as a manifestation of general will. If the pre-suppositions of either system are accepted it is possible (in theory) to eliminate the "tension" to which we have referred. But both systems of thought are widely regarded as untenable or at least as quite inapplicable to Western constitutional states in the writings of contemporary jurists, philosophers, anthropologists and political theorists who have concerned themselves with the problems of law and sovereignty.[10]

---

with references to the modern literature, see Sten Gagnér, *Studien zur Ideengeschichte der Gesetzgebung* (Uppsala, 1960). On England in particular see T.F.T. Plucknett, *Legislation of Edward I* (Oxford, 1949) and J. W. Gough, *Fundamental Law in English Constitutional History* (Oxford, 1953); for France G. I. Langmuir, "'Judei Nostri' and the Beginning of Capetian Legislation", *Traditio*, XVI (1960), pp. 203-239 and M. J. Odenheimer, *Der christliche-kirchliche Anteil an der Verdrangung der Vorherschaft des staatlich gesetzen Rechts* (Basle, 1957).

[9] The problems to be considered do not arise in the same way in countries with written constitutions that provide for judicial review of legislation. In these cases it is much easier to see analogies with medieval concepts of fundamental law.

[10] G. Marshall, *Parliamentary Sovereignty and the Commonwealth* (Oxford, 1957), pp. 267-272 provides a good bibliography of modern writing on the problems of sovereignty in England and the Commonwealth, much of it critical of Austinian concepts. He includes some of the work by analytical philosophers as well as that of the constitutional lawyers. See too R.F.V. Heuston, *Essays in Constitutional Law* (London, 1961). Bertrand de Jouvenel, drawing on French rather than English constitutional experience and on anthropological data, has also criticised positivist conceptions of sovereignty as in-

This rather obvious fact has not always been noticed sufficiently by historians who are interested in investigating the origins of the modern state. Too often, indeed, the argument that there was no really "modern" theory of sovereignty in the Middle Ages seems designed merely to prove that medieval ways of thinking about politics were different from those of Rousseau or Austin. Recently it has become more fashionable to maintain the opposite point of view, that those thinkers did have "precursors" in the thirteenth and fourteenth centuries and that, accordingly, a genuinely modern idea of the state did exist then.[11] For a historian of constitutionalism the whole debate

---

consistent with the real structure of modern states in his *Sovereignty*, transl. J. F. Huntingdon (Cambridge, 1957). In America Jacques Maritain even suggested that, since the word "sovereignty" is inextricably associated in our minds with the ideas of Hobbes, Rousseau and Austin, and since these ideas are essentially alien to the nature of the modern Western state, we ought to abandon the use of the word altogether, *Man and the State* (Chicago, 1951), pp. 28-53. For the latest round in the continuing argument concerning the nature of governmental authority between American upholders of "classical natural right" and exponents of "empirical social science" see S. Rothman, "The Revival of Classical Political Philosophy: A Critique", and J. Cropsey, "A Reply to Rothman", *American Political Science Review*, LVI (June, 1962), pp. 341-352 and pp. 353-359. It is unnecessary for us to take sides in this dispute. Neither a commitment to the doctrine of natural rights nor, I trust, an enthusiasm for empirical observation could lead to the conclusion that Austin's system or Rousseau's provides an adequate model for understanding the structure and functioning of modern constitutional states.

[11] J. N. Figgis, in his Birkbeck lectures of 1900, was perhaps the first to challenge the view that "there is no Austinian sovereign in the medieval state", finding a doctrine "substantially the same as Austin's" in medieval canonistic theories of papal authority. See his *Political Thought from Gerson to Grotius* (Reprinted, New York, 1960), pp. 20, 65-66. He was no doubt influenced by Gierke's view that Innocent IV's legal theory of corporations opened the way for the growth of "antique-modern" conceptions of the state in place of the pre-existing "properly medieval" ones. More commonly Marsilius of Padua has been favored as a candidate for the role of "the prophet of modern times . . . the most modern of mediaeval thinkers" (as Previté-Orton called him). A. P. D'Entrèves, *Natural Law* (London, 1951), p. 75, found in the *Defensor Pacis* an anticipation of the general will theory and considered Marsilius "a striking and untimely fore-runner" of Rousseau. The relationship between the two thinkers was examined in more detail by S. Stelling-Michaud, "De Marsile de Padoue à Jean-Jacques Rousseau", *Bulletin de l'Institut National Genevois*, LIV (1951), pp. 1-35. Gewirth preferred to emphasise the novelty of the Austinian element in Marsilius, "Thus in contrast to the entire medieval tradition which insisted that a law which is not just . . . is not a law at all, Marsilius makes the positivist aspect of coerciveness basic", *Marsilius of Padua. The Defender of the Peace*, II (New York, 1956), p. xxxvi. Most recently M. J. Wilks has discovered anticipations of both Austin and Rousseau in the works of Augustinus Triumphus, "The Idea of the Church as 'Unus homo perfectus' and Its Bearing on the Medieval Theory of Sovereignty", *Miscellanea Historiae Ecclesiasticae. Stockholm 1960* (Louvain, 1961), pp. 33-49 at pp. 33-34, "This theory of sovereignty . . . was a true theory of sovereignty in the Austinian sense, and went far beyond the hesitations and retractions of a Bodin or Hobbes . . . The theory of sovereignty is, in fact, not the least of the contributions which the Medieval Church had to make to the modern world." For Rousseau see p. 46. S. Z. Ehler, in his essay "On Applying the Modern Word 'State' to the Middle Ages", *Medieval Studies Presented to Aubrey Gwynn, S.J.* (Dublin, 1961), pp. 492-501, is concerned mainly with external sovereignty. He strongly emphasises the "universalist organising forces" of the Middle Ages but blankly ignores developments in contemporary Europe. In writing about the "modern" state his gaze

seems a singularly sterile one. The point is that the theories most favored in the nineteenth century simply did not define adequately the characteristics of law and sovereignty as they actually exist in modern constitutional societies, and the fact is now widely recognized. In England legal complexities arising out of the enactment of the Statute of Westminster and the constitutional structure of the Commonwealth have begun to produce, among the more intelligent students of the common law, a certain disenchantment with the simplicities of Austinian theory, while the behavior of modern totalitarian despotisms has rendered merely grotesque the view that organs of state necessarily pursue exalted ethical ends or translate into law the higher will of their citizens. Hence the cruder varieties of Hegelianism are happily unfashionable and there are relatively few simple unreconstructed Austinians left even in England. Recently, indeed, there have been most interesting attempts (to which we shall return), by writers working within the English common law tradition, to develop theories of law and sovereignty based on Kelsen's jurisprudence rather than Austin's, that is to say on a jurisprudence that treats legal systems as structures of inter-related norms rather than as mere collections of commands.[12] The re-thinking concerning these questions that is going on in many quarters and from many points of view is healthy and welcome, but it is rendering obsolete a considerable body of historical writing which contentedly concludes to the existence or non-existence of a truly "modern" idea of sovereignty in the Middle Ages by demonstrating that a selected group of thinkers did or did not succeed in anticipating the ideas of Austin or Rousseau.

The difficulties of constructing a theory of sovereignty applicable to Western constitutional states are especially evident in discussions on the particular point to be investigated, the significance of our familiar phrase, the "rule of law", and the relationship of such a concept to that of legislative sovereignty. Dicey, a convinced Austinian, presented a famous definition of the rule of law which emphasised the exclusion of mere caprice from the exercise of governmental authority, "the absolute supremacy or predominance of regular law as opposed to arbitrary power". De Jouvenel has criticised this by calling attention to the wide discretionary powers of officials in modern states and has suggested instead that the rule of law can be said to exist only when the enacted laws themselves are in conformity with the deep-lying convictions shared by members of a political community.[13] It would seem that both points of view must be combined to achieve a satisfactory definition.

---

seems firmly fixed on mid-nineteenth century European realities rather than on mid-twentieth century ones.

[12] The most explicit attempt along these lines was the fine essay of R. T. E. Latham, *The Law and the Commonwealth* (Oxford, 1949). On his views see below, p. 397.

[13] A. V. Dicey, *The Law of the Constitution* (8th ed., London, 1927), p. 198. De Jouvenel, *op. cit.*, pp. 297-298.

However wide the discretionary powers of officials may be, the limits of those powers are defined by law in constitutional countries, and the courts would not uphold actions outside the defined limits. There could certainly be no rule of law if we ever abandoned the principle, "What is done officially must be done in accordance with law". At the same time we would not normally speak of the rule of law existing in a land where legislation was scrupulously enforced but the laws themselves were grossly unjust, imposed by a tyrant on unwilling subjects. In constitutional states the eliciting of a consensus is just as important as the exclusion of caprice. But this involves the further implication that, however great the power attributed to a sovereign government in a constitutional state, that power must be regarded as bound at least by the law that defines its own mode of functioning, and this in turn implies that the acts of such governments must themselves be regarded as justiciable at least in some exceptional circumstances. It is not only that orders of particular officials may contravene established laws, but also that situations can arise in which there is doubt whether a given decree emanating from a sovereign legislature has been duly promulgated in accordance with the rules specifying how laws may legitimately be enacted in a given society.

It was precisely this possibility of subjecting a sovereign government to any kind of legal limitation that Austin rejected as logically incompatible with his whole system of thought,[14] for, he argued, if any rules existed specifying limits on the exercise of sovereign authority, those rules themselves could be abrogated at the pleasure of the sovereign. The absence of any tradition of formal judicial review in England made the argument acceptable to most common lawyers there until recently, but it seems most improbable that Austin himself was led to his conclusions by any profound meditations on the spirit and history of English law. On the contrary, it was the Roman Pandects that he studied during the years in Germany when he was preparing to take up his chair of jurisprudence at London. Moreover, his doctrine might well be regarded as a simple re-phrasing of our Roman law text, "The Prince is not bound by the laws" taken together with its well known counterpart, "What has pleased the Prince has the force of law". It would be no task at all to show that the medieval civilians had at their disposal the raw materials from which an Austinian theory of sovereignty could have been constructed. But, to repeat, if one is interested in investigating the origins of the modern Western state, the problem is not to find out how far medieval lawyers succeeded in anticipating the conclusions of Austin; the more interesting question is how far they succeeded in avoiding them. We cannot hope to understand the origins of the constitutional state by seeking out

<hr />

[14] J. Austin, *The Province of Jurisprudence Determined*, ed. H. L. A. Hart (New York, 1954), Lecture VI, p. 254, "Now it follows ... that the power of a monarch properly so called, or the power of a sovereign number in its collegiate and sovereign capacity, is incapable of *legal* limitation."

386

medieval anticipations of nineteenth century aberrations from the Western constitutional tradition.

When one turns to the source material itself it is at once apparent that the texts of the *Corpus Iuris Civilis* are ambivalent.[15] Some passages suggested that the emperor's power was of divine origin. Others asserted most explicitly that it came from the people.[16] At one point we find the simple statement that what has pleased the Prince has the force of law. At another a complex process of senatorial counsel and consent was laid down as necessary for an act of general legislation.[17] The maxim that we are especially concerned with, "The Prince is not bound by the laws" seems to have a precise antithesis in the *lex Digna* which asserted that "It is a statement worthy of the majesty of a ruler for the Prince to profess himself bound by the laws".[18] A modern student of classical Roman law would naturally and properly seek an explanation for these inconsistencies by investigating the historical development of the Roman constitution. The task for a medievalist is to discover what was made of them by jurists whose minds were saturated with the preconceptions of a feudal and Christian society and who were more at home with the techniques of dialectical argumentation than with those of historical research.

The very dialectical structure of the glossators' works has tended to discourage a systematic use of them by recent historians of political theory. Accursius did use the word state (*status*) and in something very like the modern sense of the term,[19] but at no point did he offer a detailed explanation of his views on state sovereignty or on possible limitations of it. His glosses typically consists of a few words of comment surrounded by an intricate structure of cross-references to other sections of the *Corpus Iuris Civilis*. The substance of the argument can only be appreciated by checking all the contexts referred to. At those points one finds more glosses with further references. By exploring them in turn one is introduced to a whole network of texts, some of which seem to have little to do with one another at first glance, but which were all interconnected in the mind of the glossator and, indeed, were held to be fully intelligible only by virtue of their interconnections. It is much simpler to read John of Salisbury—and that presumably is why several widely used-text book histories of political thought do not so much as mention the

---

[15] Several aspects of this ambivalence have been intricately worked out by Ernst H. Kantorowicz, *op. cit.*, pp. 97-192.
[16] E.g. on divine origin *Dig.* Prologue (*Constitutio Deo auctore*) and *Nov.* 73.1; on popular origin *Inst.* 1.2.6, *Cod.* 1.17.1, *Dig.* 1.4.1. In subsequent notes quotations from Accursius are taken from the glossed edition of the *Corpus Iuris Civilis* of Lyons, 1627. But since the numeration of titles varies in the different early editions all references to texts of Roman law are given to the standard modern edition of Mommsen, Krueger, Schoell and Kroll (Reprinted, Berlin, 1954).
[17] *Inst.* 1.2.6 and *Cod.* 1.14.8.
[18] *Dig.* 1.3.31 and *Cod.* 1.14.4.
[19] Gloss *ad Dig.* 1.1.1.2. Accursius wrote that public law existed to preserve the state, lest it perish, "ad statum conservandum, ne pereat."

name of Accursius. On the other hand the labor involved in this kind of work is trivial compared with that of the glossators themselves who had to hew out, through the stubborn undergrowth of conflicting texts, the paths of argument that we can follow at leisure.

* * *

The purpose of our enquiry then is to explore the network of ideas that Accursius associated with the apparently absolutist text, *Princeps legibus solutus est,* to explain the implications of those ideas for his theory of law and sovereignty and to consider briefly their relationship to the views of some modern constitutional lawyers who have concerned themselves with analogous problems. The words of our maxim obviously might mean many things. They could at most form the foundation for a theory of arbitrary and irresponsible despotism; they must at least raise the question whether the attribution of legislative sovereignty to an organ of government is compatible with the existence of any over-riding rule of law. The central issue might be put like this. Did Accursius think that the maxim, *Princeps legibus solutus est* designated a sovereign standing outside of and above the community, bound to it by no reciprocal legal ties? (Walter Ullmann has recently described the medieval theory of theocratic kingship in such terms and there is ample evidence in the *Corpus Iuris Civilis* itself that Justinian, who initiated the whole work of codification, so conceived of his office.) Or did Accursius rather maintain that the relevant texts of Roman law, taken as a whole, required the prince to operate within a framework of fundamental rules that corresponded to the basic pre-suppositions of the society which he governed? In the simplest terms, did he favor an absolutist or a constitutionalist theory of law?

Let us turn to the text itself. Accursius's gloss on the words *Princeps legibus solutus est* ran like this:

Princeps legibus, ab alio conditis ut infra *de arbit. 1. nam et magistratus,* vel a seipso ut infra *de arbit. 1. penul.* Voluntate tamen sua seipsum subiicit ut *Cod. eod. 1. digna* et *Institu. quibus modis test. infir. in fi.* et facit *Cod. de testa. 1. hac consultissima § ex imperfecto* et *Cod. de bon. quae lib. 1. cum multa* et infra *de leg. iii 1. ex imperfecto* et in *decret. dist. 8 c. quae contra.*

Transposing the references into a modern form we can render it thus:

The Prince is loosed from the laws. That is from laws founded by another as at *Dig.* 4.8.4, or by himself as at *Dig.* 4.8.51. Nevertheless by his own will he subjects himself as at *Cod.* 1.14.4 and *Inst.* 2.17.8, and also relevant are *Cod.* 6.23.3, *Cod.* 6.61.7, *Dig.* 32.1.23 and *Dist.* 8. c.2 of the Decretum.[20]

[20]   Gloss *ad Dig.* 1.3.31. In all subsequent quotations in the text Accursius's references (which cited Book and Title by name and the first words of the relevant law) have been

We can dispose first of the concluding reference to canon law which seems appended almost as an afterthought to the list of civil citations. The canon mentioned was a text of St. Augustine incorporated in Gratian's *Decretum*, where it was adduced to support the principle. "No one is permitted to act against natural law." [21] We do not propose to attempt in this paper an analysis of Accursius's theory of natural law—our concern is with the role of a legislative sovereign within the framework of human law—but we may insert at least a word of caution against the widely held view that juristic theories of natural law constituted a significant limitation on the legislative competence of medieval governments. Accursius certainly did believe that, in case of conflict, the will of God should be followed rather than the will of any man (which was what the text of St. Augustine actually said). But there is nothing peculiarly medieval about that. He certainly did not think, in the manner of some modern enthusiasts for natural law theories, that natural law was a kind of detailed pattern of legislation laid up in Heaven or in the hearts of the judges, authorizing them to set aside as invalid any enactments of human legislation which they thought departed from its tenets. A detailed examination of the whole question would suggest that, for the glossators of Accursius's generation, natural law provided a moral basis for deciding whether a given enactment was a good and just law, not for determining whether it was a valid one. If an act of legislation proved to be unjust there was a duty for the legislator to change it, not a right for the judge to annul it.

In any case the main substance of Accursius's thought on the problem at issue was conveyed in his list of civil law references. Of these the first two defined Accursius's interpretation of the text he was commenting on. All the rest were concerned with the modifications of the *legibus solutus* principle implied by the *lex Digna* (*Cod.* 1.14.4) and related passages.

At *Dig.* 4.8.4 we read that magistrates could not be subjected to coercion by equal or inferior magistrates.[22] A praetor could not issue a coercive command to a consul for instance. The gloss at this point did not draw any further conclusions about the status of the emperor, but the implication was obvious. There was no magistrate superior to the emperor; therefore he was not subject to legal coercion. *Dig.* 4.8.51 declared that a man could not give an arbitration award in a case where he was an interested party "since no one can command himself to perform an act or prohibit himself from doing it".[23] Here too the gloss made no further reference to the problems of sover-

---

transposed into modern numerical references. In the passage quoted above the reference to *Cod.* 6.23.3 is given incorrectly, though this is certainly the law intended. The reference should read *Cod. de testa. 1. ex imperfecto.*

[21] *Dist.* 8 c.2 (Rubric), "Adversus naturale ius nulli quidquam agere licet."

[22] *Dig.* 4.8.4, "Nam magistratus superiore aut pari imperio nullo modo possunt cogi."

[23] *Dig.* 4.8.51, "Si de re sua quis arbiter factus sit, sententiam dicere non potest, quia se facere iubeat aut petere prohibeat: neque autem imperare sibi neque se prohibere quisquam potest."

eignty, but again the meaning of Accursius is plain enough. Evidently an emperor could not bind himself by his own laws in the sense that he could not, in any meaningful way, issue coercive comands to himself.

Of the four civil law texts mentioned after the *lex Digna* three referred to the fact that the emperors refused to accept inheritances from invalidly drafted wills although, as *legibus solutus,* they could have ignored the technicalities of the law. "Although we are loosed from the laws, nevertheless we live by the laws," declared the emperors Severus and Antoninus (*Inst.* 2.17.18). Similarly Paulus at *Dig.* 32.1.23, "It is shameful for an emperor to claim an inheritance from an invalid will . . . It is fitting for such majesty to observe the laws from which it seems to be loosed." The glosses on these two laws gave cross-references to one another and to still other laws where the same principle about invalid wills was asserted, and they both referred also to the *lex Digna* with its generalised statement that it was proper for the Prince to live in accordance with the law.[24] But the most interesting development of Accursius's thought in this second layer of glosses occurs in his comment on the third law of the group, *Cod.* 6.23.3. This declared, "It has often been laid down that the emperor cannot claim an inheritance from an invalid will, for although the law concerning the imperium exempted the emperor from the technicalities of the law, nevertheless nothing is so proper to the imperium as to live according to the law." On this Accursius commented:

The Law concerning the imperium, that is the *lex regia* giving supreme power to the Prince as at *Inst.* 1.2.6. And it exempts him from the technicalities of the law inasmuch as, if he should not observe those technicalities in wills and other things there is no one empowered to invalidate his acts, as at *Dig.* 4.8.4.[25]

This is the first reference that we have encountered to the *lex regia,* the law that had originally conferred imperial authority on the Prince. It is clear that Accursius regarded this *lex* as the basis of the emperor's exemption from the laws, but it is also apparent throughout these discussions that he had no conception of the real historical *leges de imperio* of classical times, which had conferred specific powers on the emperors together with specific exemp-

[24] Gloss *ad Inst.* 2.17.8, "*Vivimus,* id est vivere volumus ut hic et *Cod. de leg. et consti. prin. 1. digna vox* et facit *ff de leg. ii 1. quod principi et 1. seq.* et *ff de leg. iii 1. ex imperfecto* et *ff de inoffi. test. 1. Papinianus § si Imperator.*" Gloss *ad Dig.* 32.1.23, "*Inverecundum,* i.e. valde verecundum, sic *supra de liberis postu. 1. Gallus § illo,* et facit *C. de testament. i. iii* et *qui testamenta facere possunt l. cum heres* et *Institut. quibus modis testamenta infirmantur § fin.* et *C. de legibus et const. 1. digna* et *sup. de iud. 1. non quicquid.*" An investigation of these references produces no more glosses of major significance except those on the *lex· Digna* discussed below.

[25] Gloss *ad Cod.* 6.23.3, "*Lex imperii,* id est lex regia, dando supremam potestatem principi ut *Instit. de iur. na. § sed et quod principi.* Et eximit eum a solennibus iuris, ut licet non observet in testamentis et in aliis solennia iuris, tamen nemo sit qui ea possit infirmare ut *ff de arbit. 1. nam magistratus.*"

tions from the observation of particular laws.[26] There is of course no such *lex de imperio* incorporated in the *Corpus Iuris Civilis*. The text at *Inst.* 1.2.6 which Accursius cited, and from which he had derived his own conception of the *lex regia,* simply declared without reservation that the people had conferred on the emperor all their own authority and power.[27] This made Accursius's task more complicated but, in a way, more interesting. Since the only *lex regia* he could envisage was a general mandate of authority containing neither specific limitations on imperial power nor specific exemptions from particular laws, he could only investigate its significance by attempting to construct a pure theory of sovereignty. That is to say, his task was to work out all the implications of attributing an unlimited legislative capacity to the Prince for a legal system that was conceived of as a structure of interdependent rules (and the very glossatorial technique that we have been describing shows that the *Corpus* of Roman law was so regarded).

In the texts considered so far Accursius had succeeded in achieving a decidedly minimalist interpretation of the phrase, *Princeps legibus solutus est.* The references to *Dig.* 4.8.4. and *Dig.* 4.8.51, together with the gloss at *Cod.* 6.23.3, make it clear that for Accursius the emperor was "loosed from the laws" only in the sense that there existed no legal machinery for bringing him to justice if he broke them. He did not associate the words *legibus solutus* with any ideas of arbitrary government. There was no suggestion in any of the laws cited to elucidate them that the Prince, because he was "loosed from the laws", could change the law at his own whim or set it aside in individual cases to please his favorites. (Accursius did know of course that the emperor possessed legislative and dispensatory powers but, for reasons to be considered, he did not associate their exercise with the *legibus solutus* principle.) Again, we find in the texts cited no trace of the doctrine developed by later theoreticians of absolutism, that, since every wish of the Prince could be constitutive of new law, all his actions were necessarily in accordance with the law (since each fresh whim created law for the occasion). On that argument it would be logically impossible for a sovereign ever to offend against the existing laws. But Accursius quite obviously believed that the Prince could break the law. The point was that, if he did so, there was no superior magistrate set over him who could exercise jurisdiction in his case. His teaching so far amounts to no more than an assertion of the principle, familiar

[26] On the *leges de imperio* see F. Schulz, "Bracton on Kingship", *English Historical Review*, LX (May, 1945), pp. 136-176 and, for a surviving example, S. Riccobono, *Fontes Iuris Romani Antejustiniani* I (Florence, 1941), pp. 154-156. Schulz argued that it was Justinian's compilers, not the glossators (as Esmein asserted), who first substituted an absolutist principle for the constitutional law of classical times. He maintained, however, that the glossators faithfully adhered to the absolutist doctrine that they found ready-made in their texts.

[27] *Inst.* 1.2.6, "Sed et quod principi placuit legis habet vigorem, cum lege regia, quae de imperio eius lata est, populus ei et in eum omne suum imperium et potestatem concessit."

in many modern constitutional states, that the government cannot be sued in its own courts without its own consent. Justice Holmes thought that for a citizen to claim such a right was "like shaking one's fist at the sky when the sky furnishes the energy to enable one to raise the fist". Having made this modest point Accursius hastened to add that, in fact, the Prince did adhere to the laws, adding several legal references to establish the fact.

In pursuing Accursius's further arguments on this theme we are led to the heart of his doctrine of law and sovereignty. The original gloss on the words *Princeps legibus solutus* contained seven references to civil law texts. One of them was the *lex Digna* and three of the others were equipped with glosses that also referred back to the same law.[28] Accursius seems to be insistently shepherding towards the *lex Digna* anyone who seeks to understand his interpretation of the term *legibus solutus*. His glosses at that point do indeed provide the best explanation of his thought on the subject.

The *lex Digna* itself ran like this:

It is a statement worthy of the majesty of the ruler for the Prince to profess himself bound by the law. So much does our authority depend on the authority of the law. And indeed it is greater for the imperium to submit the principate to the laws. And by the declaration of the present law we indicate what we do not permit to ourselves.[29]

In his first gloss on this text Accursius attacked the central problem posed by it. How could it be called worthy for the Prince to profess himself bound by the law when the statement was on the face of it false, since several texts explicitly mentioned that the emperor was "loosed from the laws". The emperors, Accursius explained, did not formally decree that they were bound by the laws. (This would have violated the principle encountered earlier, "No man can issue a command to himself.") Rather they declared their will to live in accordance with the law.[30] This explanation was merely a restatement of the point already made in the gloss on the text, *Princeps legibus solutus est* — "Nevertheless by his own will he subjects himself." Accursius's

---

[28] Gloss *ad Dig.* 4.8.4, "*Imperio,* scil magistratus. Et sic nota quod par parem cogere non potest ut hic et *C. de ap. 1. praecipimus § penult.* et *i. ad Treb. 1. ille a quo § tempestivum* et *C. de leg. et const. 1. digna.*" See also the glosses *ad Dig.* 32.1.23 and *Inst.* 1.2.6 quoted above. The other law cited in this group, *Cod.* 6.61.7, referred to the special privileges attached to donations from the emperor. The gloss there has nothing relevant to our theme.

[29] Cod. 1.14.4, "Digna vox maiestate regnantis legibus alligatum se principem profiteri: adeo de auctoritate iuris nostra pendet auctoritas: et re vera maius imperio est submittere legibus principatum: et oraculo praesentis edicti quod nobis licere non patimur indicamus."

[30] Gloss *ad Cod.* 1.14.4, "*Digna vox.* Ponit casum et eius rationem et commendationem et exemplum. Sed quomodo est digna vox cum sit falsum ut *ff eo. 1. princeps* et *ff de leg. iii 1. ex imperfecto* et in *auth. de consulibus § fin. col. iiii* et *i. de testa. 1. ex imperfecto*? Resp. digna est si dicat se velle non quod sit ut *Instit. quib. mod. testa infir. § fin* et in praealleg. *l. ex imperfecto.* Alii dicunt quod hic permittitur mentiri ut *Instit. de act. § aliae,* quod non placet."

language here has been much misunderstood. It has been argued that his glosses had an absolutist connotation since they implied that the Prince was not required to obey the law except when he wanted to, or that, at most, they referred to a merely moral obligation rather than to a strictly legal one. But Accursius did not suggest that it would be an act of supererogatory virtue for the Prince to subject himself to the laws. He laid down as a legal fact, supported by legal references, that the emperor did in fact do so. In his view fidelity to the law was just as much an intrinsic attribute of the princely office as freedom from coercion, and both attributes, he thought, could be deduced equally well from the texts of Roman law itself. He never argued that it could be licit for an emperor to break the law, nor would he have countenanced such a suggestion. The point he was making in this first gloss on the *lex Digna* was that this fidelity to the law, which was required of all men, had to be maintained in the case of the Prince alone through internal rather than external discipline.

The argument was carried further in another gloss on the same text. Theodosius and Valentinian had declared vaguely that their obligation to obey the laws was related to the fact that their own authority depended on the authority of the law. Accursius chose to interpret this as a specific reference to the *lex regia*.

On the authority (of the law). This is the rational basis for the first statement, and the words "of the law" refer to the *lex regia* which concerns the transfer of imperium from the people to the Prince as at *Inst.* 1.2.6 and *Cod.* 1.17.1.[31]

We are confronted by an apparent paradox for we have seen that the *lex regia*, which here is supposed to explain why the Prince should profess himself bound by the laws, was also cited in a precisely contrary sense at *Cod.* 6.23.3 to show how the Prince came to be loosed from the laws. It has often been observed that the Roman law doctrine of a transfer of power from people to Prince contributed to the growth of democratic theories from the Middle Ages onward by keeping alive the idea of a popular origin of sovereignty. But Accursius's position is not so simple. He is apparently arguing that a democratic origin of power necessarily involves a constitutional limitation on it; and such a conclusion is by no means self-evident. The argument might indeed have seemed to have some practical if not logical validity a century ago. Nowadays we are all accustomed to the idea that "totalitarian democracy" can be the most oppressive form of despotism. Again, quite apart from modern experience, the problem was inherent in the Roman law text itself. How could an act which supposedly conferred "all power and imperium" on the emperor be held to constitute a limitation on his authority?

---

[31] Gloss *ad Cod.* 1.14.4, "*De auctoritate.* Haec est ratio primi dicti et quod dicit iuris, scilicet legis regiae quae est de imperio transferendo de populo in principem ut *Instit. de iur. nat. § set et quod princ.* et *i. de vete. iu. enu. 1. i § hoc etiam.*"

To resolve the paradox we must note that, in the gloss just cited, Accursius was not simply asserting that imperial authority came from the people but rather insisting that it rested on a duly constituted *lex*; and we must also recall in what an extremely limited sense he regarded the emperor as loosed from the law by the enactment of the *lex regia*. His argument must be given full weight. He did not assert that the *lex regia* freed the Prince from the coercive power of the law in the merely *de facto* sense that no forces were available to restrain him. It was also true that there was no superior magistrate who could *de iure* issue commands to him. By just such an argument Austin reached his conclusion that legislative sovereignty was of its nature illimitable by law, and on his own premises the argument is irrefutable. If a *lex* was merely a coercive command then indeed no *lex* could, even in principle, bind the emperor (for there was no one qualified to issue commands to him). If legal obligation rested merely on fear of coercion then there could be no such obligation in the Prince (for he was set above the coercive sanctions of the law); and, on these assumptions, Accursius's whole pattern of thought falls apart in a muddle of self-contradictions. But the crux of the whole matter is that Accursius, like all other thirteenth century thinkers (and most modern ones), did not define law as merely coercive command, though coercion was often mentioned as one element among others in the definitions that were favored. Something of the way in which he did feel about the nature of law emerges in the final gloss on the *lex Digna* that we have to consider:

(*It is greater to submit the principate to the laws*). That is than the laws to the principate, which is to say it is more honorable and fitting; for the imperium comes by fortune, whence it is said, "If Fortune wills a rhetorician becomes a consul. And if she wills a consul becomes a rhetorician;" but the laws are promulgated by the divine will, as at *Cod*. 7.33.12, and so are immutable." [32]

Law, then, was for Accursius something sacrosanct. The text to which he referred, *Cod*. 7.33.12, again mentioned the divine origin of law, and in his gloss at that point Accursius gave a reference to the definition of *lex* attributed to Demosthenes in the first Book of the Digest.[33] "Law is something that all men ought to obey for many reasons, and especially because every law is a device and gift of the gods, a decree of learned men, a restraint of those who either voluntarily or through ignorance are guilty of crime. It is also a

---

[32] Gloss *ad Cod*. 1.14.4, "*Principatum*, sub. quam leges principatui sive imperio, q.d. maior est honor, et maior est convenientia cum imperium sit de fortuna, unde dicitur "Si fortuna volet, fies de rhetore consul. Si volet haec eadem, fies de consule rhetor." At leges sunt divino nutu prolatae ut *i. de praescrip. long. tem. 1. fin.* et sic immutabiles." The last words can only mean that laws which actually existed were to be rigorously observed, not that existing laws could never be changed. The latter position would have been impossible for any interpreter of Roman law.

[33] Gloss *ad Cod*. 7.33.12, "*Divino*. Nota divinitus leges factas *ff de legib. et senatusc. 1. lex est* (*Dig*. 1.3.2)..."

common engagement of the state, by whose rules everyone in the state ought to regulate his life." [34] We have started out to trace Accursius's interpretation of a famous "absolutist" text, and at the end of the trail we find ourselves led to a sort of rhapsody on the rule of law.

Accursius's arguments on this whole question are typical of thirteenth century juristic thought, but they also have parallels in contemporary legal philosophy. Amid all the divers modern views on the nature of legal systems, perhaps the most frequently recurring insight is a recognition that the concept of obligation is essential for an adequate definition of law, and that this concept cannot be extracted by any process of logical argumentation from the quite different ideas of command and coercion. For example, in a recently published posthumous work on the definition of law, Hermann Kantorowicz has suggested a modification of Kelsen's "pure theory" along these lines. Kelsen argued that law must be conceived of as a system of inter-related norms, the validity of any norm being established by its dependence on some other accepted norm. However, to avoid a circular argument, he postulated that there had to be a basic norm, a *Grundnorm,* on which the whole system depended, whose validity could not be established in this fashion. It was a norm deriving its validity from extra-legal considerations. Kelsen himself accepted as a *Grundnorm* simply the will of the first promulgators of a constitution, but Kantorowicz has observed that "this pre-supposes a still more basic rule to the effect that this arbitrary decision ought to be obeyed". He himself suggested that a basic norm could be found in the proposition, "Thou shalt abide by the laws", which, he thought, could be validated extra-legally as a precept of morality. [35] To a medieval Christian like Accursius it was natural to regard it also as a manifestation of the divine will. Indeed, while Kantorowicz conducted his whole argument in terms of modern linguistic analysis, it leads to exactly the same conclusion that we have reached by following the thread of Accursius's medieval glosses. According to Accursius, the command of the Prince could not be the ultimate basis of law in the Roman legal system since his authority to command rested on a preceding law and the validity of that in turn on the principle to which we have been led, "Law is what all men ought to obey". The essence of the argument was that law logically preceded sovereignty since sovereignty was a product of law. It is a point that has often been made in more recent writings.

[34] *Dig.* 1.3.2, "Lex est cui omnes decet obedire, propter alia multa et maxime quia omnis lex inventum ac munus deorum est, decretum vero prudentum hominum, coercitio eorum qui sponte vel ignorantia delinquuntur, communis sponsio civitatis, ad cuius praescriptum omnes qui in ea respublica sunt, vitam instituere debent."
[35] Hermann Kantorowicz, *The Definition of Law* (Cambridge, 1958), pp. 32, 50. Kantorowicz understood of course that there could be a conflict between some particular law and some particular tenet of a moral or religious system. His point was that virtually all ethical systems ascribe a value to the maintenance of law in general, and that if any society adopted a system of belief that failed to do so, e.g. radical anarchism, "law would cease to function."

If, following the line of argument of the *Glossa Ordinaria,* we regard the whole complex of Roman law texts that has been considered as a structure dependent on the basic principle that law was "a common engagement of the state", which created a universal obligation of obedience, then all the parts of Accursius's argument fall into place without self-contradiction. The legislative acts of the Prince deserved obedience precisely because a *lex* had been enacted conferring on him the authority to legislate.[36] That is why Accursius did not associate the legislative activity of the Prince with the *legibus solutus* principle. When the Prince legislated he was not acting as one *legibus solutus*; rather he was acting in accordance with the law that defined his office. Again, he could change a law by due exercise of his legislative authority but if, in his own person, he broke a law while it actually existed his action was just as illegal as a similar act by a subject (though, because of the Prince's peculiar position, no magistrate could sit in judgment on him). On these premises there was no inconsistency in maintaining that the same *lex regia* which freed the emperor from coercive sanctions also obliged him to respect the laws. The emperor's obligation to obey the law indeed rested on exactly the same foundation as the subject's obligation to obey the emperor. They stood or fell together.[37]

The arguments considered so far do not altogether settle the question whether Accursius's outlook was compatible with a theory of the rule of law in any properly understood sense of the term, for it would seem an empty doctrine to proclaim the ruler obliged by the law if that same ruler could, from moment to moment, change the content of the laws to suit his own convenience. It is no doubt impossible to devise a legal structure that, by its own terms, excludes all possibility of its own subversion. In the last resort, if a people becomes corrupt, its laws will be corrupted. But it is possible to impede the subverting of a system of law through the arbitrary will of a sovereign by imposing requirements of counsel and consent for the promulgation of new law, and we have suggested that some such procedure is of the essence of the rule of law in constitutional states. This, however, raises another problem concerning the nature of sovereignty. It would seem that a sovereign could not bind himself or his successors by promulgating or accepting any rules limiting his own powers. As Austin put it, "The immediate author of a law of the

---

[36]   It should be noted that, although the Institutes stated that the emperor's will was a source of law, they did not by any means assert that it was the only source. The words, "Sed et quod principi placuit legis habet vigorem" came after several sections describing other modes of legislation. The significance of the particle *et* has recently been discussed by Ernst H. Kantorowicz *The King's Two Bodies,* p. 103.

[37]   Accursius did not discuss in detail the problem of tyranny, of persistent disobedience to the law by the Prince, but it must have been obvious enough to any writer in the first half of the thirteenth century that illegal actions by the ruler were likely to evoke extra-legal remedies. The point is that, unless the law was maintained, the whole system —which included the powers of the Prince—was not viable in theory or practice.

kind or any of the sovereign successors to that immediate author may abrogate the law at pleasure", or, in the language of the Roman lawyers, "Par in parem non habet imperium".

This particular issue, which is so important for understanding the temper of Accursius's medieval pattern of thought, has also arisen in acute form for modern constitutional lawyers in their discussions on the nature of parliamentary authority. There always have been persuasive common-sense reasons against accepting Austin's doctrine of illimitable sovereignty as an adequate theoretical formulation of the principles underlying English constitutional practice, and one can sympathise with A. L. Goodhart when he declares flatly that the English parliament is in fact limited by fundamental laws which are universally recognized as binding even though they are not set down in a written constitution.[38] (He might say with old Glanvill, "It does not seem absurd to call these laws of England laws although they are not written . . .") Quite apart from moral and philosophical arguments, however, specific constitutional problems have arisen during the past generation which can hardly be handled adequately within the framework of Austin's jurisprudence. As Geoffrey Marshall observed, ' . . . the traditional linguistic garb in which the theory of sovereignty has been clothed is an embarrassing apparel for a Parliament which passed the Statute of Westminster . . ."[39]

This Statute of Westminster, enacted by the British Parliament in 1931, codified previous legislation conferring self-government on the Dominions of the Commonwealth. Now, in Austin's theory, no act of a sovereign legislature can bind its successors; it would seem then, according to his principles, that a future British Parliament might repeal the Statute of Westminster and begin to legislate once more for Canada or Australia. But no one really supposes that such an act would be of any force either in law or in fact. Again, each independent country of the Comonwealth has its own sovereign Parliament, but the authority of each of them is derived from a statute of the British Parliament which may specify the rules according to which legislation can be enacted in the Dominion Parliament. The question then arises—and it has arisen in practice—whether the Dominion Parliament can change those rules. The controversies on this point have given rise to much elaborate discussion concerning the relationship of a sovereign legislature to the rules that define its mode of functioning. It is unnecessary for us to enter into the detail of these disputes. The point is that they are leading many constitutional lawyers to abandon as grievous over-simplifications those doctrines of sovereign power as inherently illimitable and of law as mere command which are often supposed to set a gulf between medieval concepts of government and modern ones.

From the recent discussions on these practical problems (which sometimes

[38] A. L. Goodhart, *English Law and the Moral Law* (London, 1953), pp. 50-62.
[39] G. Marshall, *op. cit.*, p. 39.

resemble Kantorowicz's purely abstract argument in preferring the language of Kelsen's jurisprudence to that of Austin's) a theory of parliamentary sovereignty has emerged which distinguishes between the rules defining the mode of enactment of legislation by a sovereign legislature and the actual content of its laws, with the corollary that issues arising out of the former rules may be justiciable before the courts even when there is no general provision for judicial review of legislation. The argument has especial relevance in cases involving self-limitation by a sovereign legislator. Thus, if Parliament decreed that a certain statute could never be enacted without a prior referendum and then did indeed enact it without referendum, on strictly Austinian principles the validity of the second statute could not be challenged in the courts since the sovereign could not bind itself. In the newer view the matter would be regarded as justiciable because, as one of the most brilliant contributors to the debate explained, "Where the purported sovereign is any one but a single actual person, the designation of him must include the statement of rules for the ascertainment of his will, and these rules, since their observance is a condition of the validity of his legislation, are rules of law logically prior to him." [40]

This last phrase brings us back to the line of thought that we have been pursuing in Accursius. He too thought that law was logically prior to sovereignty. It might be argued, moreover, that when the purported sovereign *is* a single actual person it is still more important that the designation of him should include a statement of rules for the ascertainment of his will if government by mere arbitrary caprice is to be avoided. Accursius developed precisely this argument. The laws of the Prince were indeed to be obeyed, but not every act of the Prince was lawful (as we have seen), and, we can now add, not every statement of the Prince was constitutive of law. Accursius pointed this out in commenting on the text, "What has pleased the Prince has the force of law."

Pleased. For the sake of making a common and general law as at *Cod.* 7.45.7, for there it is said, "Not every statement of the judge is a sentence. So too not every statement of the Prince is a law". [41]

The distinction could be applied in considering either the validity of general enactments or the enforceability of specific administrative orders of the sovereign that ran counter to established law.

As to the former, one text of Roman law (*Cod.* 1.14.8) did lay down a detailed procedure of counsel and consent to be followed in the enactment of general legislation which, if literally adhered to or adapted to medieval

---

[40] R. T. E. Latham, *op. cit.*, p. 523.

[41] Gloss *ad Inst.* 1.2.6, "*Placuit,* causa faciendi communem legem et generalem: alias non esset lex communis ut sequitur et C. *de sent. et interl. om. iud. 1. ex stipulatione.* Nam ibi dicitur, non omnis vox iudicis est sententia: et sic non omnis vox principis est lex."

conditions, could have provided an effective safeguard against outrageous or perverse legislation. But the question obviously arose whether future emperors could be bound by its terms. There was, moreover, a subsequent text of Justinian which, in a quite contrary fashion, declared that any sentence promulgated by the Prince constituted a new general law for the class of cases involved, and this because it was established that decrees of the Prince had the force of law. In commenting on this second text Accursius made clear his view that the law requiring counsel and consent could not be changed except by a procedure in accordance with its own terms. Consistently with this view he interpreted the second decree in a very limited sense as referring only to judicial decisions settling doubtful points of law not covered in existing legislation.

This law is to be understood as referring to points which are not decided in the laws such as feudal matters. For in other things we would rather follow the written law, for this decision is not a law established as a law should be established in accordance with *Cod.* 1.14.8.[42]

As to the validity of particular imperial commands contrary to established laws, there was again a provision in Roman law itself that individual rescripts contrary to general laws were to be set aside by the judge as invalid.[43] Accursius's predecessors had raised the logical question whether any such rescripts *contra ius* promulgated by the Prince, whose decrees had the force of law, would not implicitly set aside the prior law prohibiting such rescripts;[44] but Accursius himself, consistently with his whole pattern of thought, took it for granted that the general prohibitory rule was to be applied so long as it had not specifically been repealed, and he discussed at some length the kinds of rescripts that were to be rejected in accordance with its terms. They included rescripts depriving a subject of his property or his right to bring suit or ones which were contrary to public utility.[45] These rules should not be regarded as constitutive of formal limitations on the power of the sovereign

---

[42] Gloss *ad Cod.* 1.14.12, "*Si imperialis.* Hanc legem intellige in his quae non sunt decisa per leges ut in feudo et similibus: in aliis enim potius legem servaremus scriptam cum haec sententia non sit lex constituta sicuti debet constitui ut *s. eo. 1. humanum* (*Cod.* 1.14.8)."

[43] *Cod.* 1.22.6, "Omnes cuiuscumque maioris vel minoris administrationis universae nostrae rei publicae iudices monemus, ut nullum rescriptum, nullam pragmaticam sanctionem, nullam sacram adnotationem, quae generali iuri vel utilitati publicae adversa esse videatur in disceptatione cuiuslibet litigii patiantur proferri, sed generales sacras constitutiones modis omnibus non dubitent observandas."

[44] On the related principle, "The Prince has all the laws in the shrine of his breast", see F. Gillmann, "Romanus pontifex iura omnia in scrinio pectoris sui censetur habere", *Archiv für katholisches Kirchenrecht*, XCII (1912), pp. 3-17 and Ernst H. Kantorowicz, *op. cit.*, pp. 153-154. The medieval argumentation about "implicit" repeal of legislation by subsequent contrary acts of the sovereign has been repeated (unconsciously of course) in the modern constitutional disputes to which we have referred. See G. Marshall, *op. cit.*, pp. 33ff.

[45] Gloss *ad Cod.* 1.22.6. The whole subject was considered at length there and then again at *Dig.* 1.4.1.

to legislate. In the last resort, where public necessity was involved, even individual property rights could be set aside and, by the use of *non obstante* clauses, the Prince could cut through any technicalities of existing law. But neither should Accursius's arguments be dismissed as mere academic theorising, devoid of practical implications. The conclusions of the glossators concerning rescripts *contra ius* were taken over with little change by the canonists and, through the influence of their works, they became the basis of endless litigation in ecclesiastical courts which turned precisely on the validity of particular papal decretals. They did in fact provide a workable set of rules for ensuring that the practice of government was regularly carried on in accordance with the norms of law.

To sum up, we may say briefly that, although no judge could challenge an act of the sovereign legislator, there were many occasions, according to Accursius, when a judge might be called upon to decide whether a given command emanating from the imperial government was or was not such an act. R. F. V. Heuston, in a recent book discussing the modern work on parliamentary sovereignty in England, reached the conclusion that the courts might on occasion pronounce on the validity of a law emanating from Parliament since the issue to be decided could be, not whether a given statute was valid, but whether a given enactment was indeed a statute. (He had in mind the problems we have mentioned concerning parliamentary self-limitation.) Heuston summarised the implications of this doctrine with enthusiasm. "It appears that the lawyer can, without reservation or evasion, subscribe not only to the unlimited power of Parliament, but also to the possibility of legal restraints upon (at least) the mode of user of that power." He added that, "So Anglican a solution cannot fail to be agreeable to many" and hailed it as not only a new theory of sovereignty but an important development in the history of political thought, "a striking affirmation of the supremacy of law in times of stress", which had the added attraction of being couched "in the calm, hard, tightly knit style of the common lawyer." [46] It will be seen that Accursius, with only Latin to write in, and, what is worse, only Roman law to expound had succeeded in developing a strikingly similar theory seven centuries ago.

* * *

We have been rather wilfully emphasising modern parallels, not by way of presenting a spurious anachronistic argument that our thirteenth century glossator was really a twentieth century jurist "born out of due time", but rather to call attention to certain perennial elements in the Western tradition

---

[46] R. F. V. Heuston, *op. cit.*, pp. 6, 28.

III

of government and to the problems that they raise for modern investigators of the origins of the constitutional state. The concept of legislative sovereignty was not lacking in the thirteenth century; the peculiar difficulties of reconciling that concept with any meaningful definition of the "rule of law" have not disappeared in the twentieth.

To return to our starting point, the traditional opinion expounded long ago by Esmein must evidently be abandoned. Accursius did not give an absolutist interpretation to constitutionalist maxims of Roman law. Rather he displayed considerable ingenuity in extracting a constitutionalist doctrine from a structure of texts that was originally intended to buttress Justinian's theocratic absolutism. The eventual divergence between the constitutional traditions of France and England is indeed a matter of great moment but it must be explained by legal and historical factors (and geographical ones) other than those discussed by Esmein, for the French constitutional lawyers of the sixteenth century whom he quoted were not reacting against the doctrine of the glossators, but were faithfully following the tradition of interpretation established by Accursius. Moreover there was no significant difference between England and France in the reception of these doctrines in the thirteenth century. On the contrary, Bracton took over from Accursius the whole structure of thought that we have been describing and incorporated it into his own treatise on the laws of England.[47] Hence English common lawyers were fortunate in having built into the foundations of their system the same structure of constitutional public law that the French exponents of limited monarchy strove to defend. After a century of Austinian aberration the most recent work on sovereignty in the common law tradition shows a refreshing return to the spirit of the founders.

Cornell University

[47] The position of Bracton is discussed in detail in the article "Bracton on Government", *Speculum*, XXXVIII (1963).

IV

BRACTON ON GOVERNMENT*

A PROPERLY descriptive title for this paper might be something like "Notes on Schulz on McIlwain on Bracton on kingship." That would describe its purpose accurately and would also have the advantage of telling something about the present state of Bractonian studies. In approaching their problems it is all too easy to be reminded of the fifteenth-century philosopher who complained that his contemporaries were no longer writing glosses on glosses but "glosses on glosses on glosses." Yet the convolutions of modern Bractonian scholarship are not the result of a merely perverse academic game. The growth of Western constitutionalism is an intrinsically important subject for historians, Bracton's treatise on English law marked an important stage in that growth, and the understanding of Bracton's constitutional thought depends to a quite exceptional degree for a mediaeval jurist on the unravelling of purely technical problems of textual criticism.

Probably the two most influential contributions to the study of Bracton's theories on government that have appeared in the past generation are Schulz's article, "Bracton on Kingship" and McIlwain's book, *Constitutionalism Ancient and Modern*.[1] Schulz's contribution was, as Lapsley wrote, a "magisterial article" which "marks a turning point in the history of Bractonian studies."[2] McIlwain's book, on the other hand, was a very successful work of popularization, but it included an important chapter on Bracton which presented the author's final evaluation of certain crucial texts. The qualities of the two historians were different and complementary. Schulz brought to his work a truly magisterial knowledge of classical Roman law, McIlwain a lifetime's study of constitutional history and political theory. Modern scholars are fortunate to be able to take up the discussion from the point where they left it.[3]

* The author was assisted during the writing of this article by a grant from the American Council of Learned Societies and wishes to express his gratitude.

[1] F. Schulz, "Bracton on Kingship," *English Historical Review*, LX (1945), 136–176; C. H. McIlwain, *Constitutionalism Ancient and Modern* (Ithaca, N. Y., 1940). Textual studies on Bracton multiplied in the wake of Hermann Kantorowicz's controversial *Bractonian Problems* (Glasgow, 1941). For discussion of the immediate reactions to Kantorowicz's criticism of Woodbine's edition see McIlwain, "The Present Status of the Problem of the Bractonian Text," *Harvard Law Review*, LVII (1943–1944), 220–240, and Schulz, "Critical Studies on Bracton's Treatise," *Law Quarterly Review*, LIX (1943), 172–180. The whole problem of Bracton's "redactor" was reconsidered by T. F. T. Plucknett, *Early English Legal Literature* (Cambridge, 1958), pp. 61–79. It is unnecessary for us to enter into the detail of these disputes, but one aspect of them is important for our enquiry. That is the controversy about Bracton's proficiency in the handling of Roman and canon law sources. On this I agree entirely with the conclusion of Schulz, "As far as Roman and canon law is concerned students must always bear in mind that Bracton, though he was neither a legist nor a canonist, had a good knowledge of Roman and canon law, and certainly knew more of this law than some of his critics. Of course he handled the legal texts in the traditional medieval way; in particular he always read them *adiuncta glossa*." ("Bracton on Kingship," p. 176).

[2] G. Lapsley, "Bracton and the Authorship of the 'addicio de cartis'," *English Historical Review*,

QUOD PRINCIPI PLACUIT

It is convenient to begin with a text from Glanvill's prologue that formed a model for Bracton:

Glanvill	*Bracton*
Leges namque Anglicanas licet non scriptas leges appellari non videatur absurdum, (cum hoc ipsum lex sit, quod principi placet legis habet vigorem, eas scilicet quas super dubiis in concilio definiendis, procerum quidem consilio et principis accedente auctoritate constat esse promulgatas). Si enim ob scripturae solummodo defectum leges minime censerentur, maioris proculdubio auctoritatis robur ipsis legibus videretur accommodare scriptura, quam decernentium aequitas aut ratio statuentis.	Sed non erit absurdum leges Anglicanas licet non scriptas leges appellare, cum legis vigorem habeat quidquid de consilio et consensu magnatum et rei publicae communi sponsione, auctoritate regis sive principis praecedente iuste fuerit definitum et approbatum.[4]

Schulz maintained that in Glanvill's text the words in parentheses were an interpolation which interrupted and spoiled the argument. He thought that Bracton had the interpolated text before him, saw the corruption and remodelled his own text accordingly.[5] McIlwain was concerned to defend Glanvill against the charge of absolutism and described the citation of "Quod principi placet . . . " as a "left-handed reference." He assumed that the text was quoted in a contemptuous spirit and apparently took the general meaning of the passage to be — even such a statement as "Quod principi placet . . . " is a *lex*; how much

---

LXII (1947), 1–19, at p. 18. Lapsley sharply attacked H. Kantorowicz's views on the authenticity of the *addicio*. The question is discussed below pp. 310–316.

[3] The most important works on Bracton's constitutional theory up to 1945 were listed by Schulz (*art. cit.*, p. 136, n. 2). Since then several studies have appeared besides Lapsley's. H. G. Richardson, "Studies in Bracton," *Traditio*, VI (1948), 61–104, at pp. 75–78, pointed out that Bracton used the *Leges Edwardi Confessoris* as the framework for a long passage on kingship. M. David, *La souveraineté et les limites juridiques du pouvoir monarchique* (Paris, 1954), pp. 246–251, considered Bracton's thought but seems to have added nothing to the earlier studies, and S. J. T. Miller, "The Position of the King in Bracton and Beaumanoir," SPECULUM, XXXI (1956), 263–296, was generally content to follow McIlwain on the particular points that concern us. The whole problem of the relationship between king and law in Bracton was re-opened in brilliant fashion by Ernst Kantorowicz in *The King's Two Bodies* (Princeton, 1957), pp. 143–192. The special distinction of this work was that, for the first time, it discussed Bracton's views against the whole background of contemporary European law and theology. There is a good unpublished doctoral thesis (Göttingen, 1957) by Wiebke Fesefeldt, "Englische Staatstheorie des 13. Jahrhunderts: Henry de Bracton und sein Werk." This provides more detailed discussion than is available elsewhere on Bracton's relationship to John of Salisbury, on his use of the terms *ius*, *lex*, *consuetudo*, and on his conception of the judicial office.

[4] Glanvill, ed. G. E. Woodbine, *De Legibus et Consuetudinibus Regni Angliae* (New Haven, 1932), p. 24; Bracton, ed. G. E. Woodbine, *De Legibus et Consuetudinibus Angliae*, 4 vols. (New Haven, 1915–1942), II, 19 (f. 1).

[5] *Art. cit.*, p. 171. This involves the assumption that, having noticed a corruption in Glanvill, Bracton preferred to base his own argument on the corruption rather than on Glanvill's text.

more the ancient laws of England.[6] Both critics seem to have misunderstood Glanvill's text. His argument is straightforward enough as it stands. "It would not seem absurd to call the laws of England *leges* although they are unwritten, for this itself is a law, 'What the Prince approves has the force of a *lex*.'" And English laws were indeed supported by the authority of the Prince. Therefore, according to the Roman text itself, they could reasonably be called *leges*. Bracton did not curtail his own exposition because he had detected a corruption. Rather he took carful note of the argument that the doctrine, "Quod principi placet . . . " was itself an expression of *lex* for deployment in another context.

The place where he chose to present his own version of this argument has become one of the most famous cruxes in his work. Bracton was arguing at this point that the king had no equal or superior in his realm but that still, as a minister of God, he could do nothing except what he could do *de iure*.

Nihil enim aliud potest rex in terris, cum sit dei minister et vicarius, nisi id solum quod de iure potest, nec obstat quod dicitur quod principi placet legis habet vigorem, quia sequitur in fine legis cum lege regia quae de imperio eius lata est, id est non quidquid de voluntate regis temere praesumptum est sed quod magnatum suorum consilio, rege auctoritatem praestante et habita super hoc deliberatione et tractatu, recte fuerit definitum.[7]

So far as the textual problem is concerned a definitive solution was provided by Schulz. He pointed out that the words "cum lege regia quae de imperio eius lata est" were a direct quotation from the Institutes of Justinian, that the reader was expected to supply from memory the other half of the famous text, "populus ei et in eum omne suum imperium et potestatem concessit," and that this was indeed a quite normal way of citing familiar legal maxims in the Middle Ages.[8] It should be noted in passing that, as Schulz observed, the phrase "Quod principi placuit . . . " in Roman law and in Bracton referred quite unambiguously to the legislative authority of the ruler.

McIlwain erred in his interpretation of this passage (though erring in the best of company) and became enmeshed in a host of difficulties. Taking the word *cum* as a preposition he wrote,

Justinian says the prince's will is law, because (*cum*) the people have conceded all their power to him; Bracton says the prince's will is law together with, or if in accordance with the *lex regia* (*cum lege regia*); and this *lex regia* admits of nothing beyond a true definition of what the law already is, promulgated by the king's authority only after discussion with the magnates and on their advice. Justinian's is a doctrine of practical absolutism, Bracton's a clear assertion of constitutionalism.[9]

[6] *Op. cit.*, pp. 66–68.

[7] Woodbine, II, 305 (f. 107–107b).

[8] *Art. cit.*, pp. 153–156. Cf. *Inst.* 1.2.6 and the parallel passage at *Dig.* 1.4.1. This seems to me like one of those brilliant emendations that would be obvious to everyone once it had been pointed out. But, in fact, Miller remains unconvinced (*art. cit.*, p. 271), and Ehrlich tentatively suggested the same emendation long before Schulz without apparently convincing anyone (even himself). Cf. L. Ehrlich, *Proceedings Against the Crown, Oxford Studies in Social and Legal History*, XII (Oxford, 1921), p. 39 n. 3.

[9] *Op. cit.*, p. 73.

It might seem that, lacking a true reading of his text, McIlwain was merely blundering, and yet he was blundering around a problem of central significance in Bracton's constitutional theory whose importance he had intuitively grasped and whose very existence was not apparent to Schulz. There is no difficulty about the first part of Bracton's argument. The king can do nothing but what he can do *de iure*, and the fact that he can change the law by legislation is not contrary to this, for his legislative authority was itself conferred on him by law. The problem lies in the words immediately following the citation of the *lex regia*, "id est non quidquid de voluntate regis temere praesumptum est sed quod magnatum suorum consilio . . . fuerit definitum." The source of the words themselves is plain enough. They were suggested by the text of Glanvill already cited, they carried a reminiscence of *Cod.* 1.14.8, and they no doubt described the actual practice that Bracton was familiar with. But how did Bracton come to imagine that a *lex regia* which conferred "all imperium and power" on the ruler could be cited to support an argument that the king's personal authority was limited by the counsel of his magnates? The text of the Institutes said nothing of the sort; rather it emphasized the personal power of the emperor:

Sed et quod principi placuit legis habet vigorem, cum lege regia quae de imperio eius lata est, populus ei et in eum omne suum imperium et potestatem concessit. Quodcumque igitur imperator per epistulam constituit vel cognoscens decrevit vel edicto praecepit, legem esse constat.

Schulz's brief comment on this point was, for him, oddly naive. He himself knew, because he was learned in classical law and Roman constitutional history, that there had once been a *lex de imperio* which conferred on the emperor substantial but not unlimited powers. He seems to have simply attributed this twentieth-century insight to Bracton, suggesting that the thirteenth-century English lawyer inferred from the Roman law text just cited the meaning, "the *potestas* of the *princeps* depends on the *lex de imperio* which cannot possibly have given him absolute freedom of action."[10] This is highly unconvincing. McIlwain was right to see that, in the text under discussion, there was an odd conjunction of an apparently absolutist text and a constitutionalist sentiment which requires explanation.

The problem is complicated by the fact, that, in this same section of his work, Bracton went on to use the existence of a *lex regia* in the course of an explicit argument that the king should be bound by the law, though this time, according to Schulz, he quite failed to grasp the meaning of the other Roman law texts which he cited in order to reach that conclusion. The assertion that the king should

[10] *Art. cit.*, pp. 154–155. Fesefeldt (*op. cit.*, Ch. ii, n. 56), accepted Schulz's emendation but rightly called attention to the words "id est" in Bracton's text as posing a problem that required further elucidation. She went on to raise the question whether Bracton might have deliberately presented his Roman law quotation in truncated form in order to render it as innocuous as possible, but concluded that this could hardly have impressed any student of Roman law. S. B. Chrimes, *English Constitutional Ideas in the Fifteenth Century* (Cambridge, England, 1936), p. 327, merely observed that Bracton reached his conclusion "by assuming, unwarrantably, that the expression 'what is pleasing to the prince' really meant 'what is agreed upon after deliberation with his council of magnates'."

exercise his legislative function in accordance with accepted legal forms is indeed only a particular example of the general problem of the relationship between the king and the law. We must therefore consider the broader problem before returning to this particular instance.

REX AND *LEX*

After distinguishing between a king and a tyrant in the manner of John of Salisbury, Bracton continued his argument thus:

Temperet igitur potentiam suam per legem quae frenum est potentiae, quod secundum leges vivat, quod hoc sanxit lex humana quod leges suum ligent latorem, et alibi in eadem, digna vox maiestate regnantis est legibus, scilicet alligatum se principem profiteri. Item nihil tam proprium est imperii quam legibus vivere, et maius imperio est legibus submittere principatum, et merito debet retribuere legi quod lex tribuit ei, facit enim lex quod ipse sit rex.[11]

Schulz provided most valuable information on the sources of this passage, though, again, his discussion of its implications for political theory was not altogether satisfactory.

He began his exposition by describing the growth of the doctrine, *princeps legibus solutus*, in the period before Justinian's *Corpus Iuris*. Briefly, there is extant a *lex de imperio Vespasiani* which conferred on the emperor legislative authority and exempted him from the observance of various legal rules. There must have been other such laws in classical times and no doubt the number of exemptions increased, though the emperors sometimes made a virtue of not taking advantage of them. In post-classical times, when the absolute power of the emperor was more and more taken for granted as normal and necessary, it came to be assumed that some earlier *lex de imperio* must have conferred on the emperor exemption from all laws in general, not just from some specified legal rules in particular. Schulz insisted that this principle did not enter Roman law before the time of Justinian himself. However that may be, it is agreed that it grew out of a juristic rationalization of the *de facto* situation that existed under the dominate.[12]

All this is interesting in itself, though I am not sure that Schulz's expertise in these matters helped him to understand the thought of mediaeval lawyers whose knowledge of them was so much more rudimentary than his own. In any case it is most important to bear in mind that the *Corpus Iuris Civilis* did not contain any text of a purported *lex regia* conferring on the emperor both governmental authority and a license to disobey all laws. Schulz's assumption that the mediaeval glossators were all thinking of an imperial authority constituted in such terms became a source of confusion in his account of the relationship between Bracton and the latter's civilian sources. What the *Corpus Iuris* did provide

---

[11] Woodbine, II, 305 (f. 107b). Schulz *art. cit.*, p. 141) pointed to parallels with Isidore of Seville, John of Salisbury, Azo and *Dig.* 2.2.1; also to direct quotations from *Cod.* 1.14.4 and *Cod.* 6.23.3. Cf. Woodbine, II, 33 (f. 5b): "Ipse autem rex non debet esse sub homine sed sub deo et sub lege, quia lex facit regem. Attribuat igitur rex legi, quod lex attribuat ei, videlicet dominationem et potestatem. Non est enim rex ubi dominatur voluntas et non lex."

[12] *Art. cit.*, p. 154. Cf. S. Riccobono, *Fontes Iuris Romani Antejustiniani*, I (Florence, 1941), 154–156.

was the statement in two contexts (*Inst.* 1.2.6 and *Dig.* 1.4.1) that the people had conferred *imperium,* including legislative authority, on the prince and in several others the assertion that the prince was *legibus solutus.* The *locus classicus* for this latter view was *Dig.* 1.3.31, where the flat statement, "Princeps legibus solutus est," was attributed to Ulpian. To complicate matters further the Code contained an edict of the Emperors Theodosius and Valentinian which (in the form that we have it) declared that it was worthy for the emperor to profess himself bound by the laws: "Digna vox maiestate regnantis legibus alligatum se principem profiteri: adeo de auctoritate iuris nostra pendet auctoritas."[13]

Schulz maintained that the thirteenth-century civilians, with their thorough grasp of the whole network of texts in the *Corpus Iuris* perfectly understood the absolutist intentions of Justinian's compilers and consistently taught that the emperor was only morally bound by the laws, not legally bound. But Bracton, we are told, took the *lex digna* to mean literally, "The emperors declare that henceforth the emperor is legally bound by the law." According to Schulz, Bracton had derived this view of a ruler legally bound by the law in the first place from an ecclesiastical source, a text of St Isidore inserted in Gratian's *Decretum* as a *palea,* and he adhered to it quite consistently, though his attempts to defend it by citing Roman law texts that really had quite different implications were unfortunate. It must be said that Schulz was able to uphold this interpretation of Bracton's thought only by simply ignoring all the Bractonian texts which to other scholars have seemed to imply the opposite point of view, that the king was *legibus solutus.* McIlwain, on the other hand, emphasized such passages. He thought that Bracton's reference to the *lex digna* could imply only a self-imposed limitation and that a limitation that was merely self-imposed could be legitimately disregarded. He further pointed out that, according to Bracton, the king had no equal in his kingdom, much less a superior, and that no judge could void his acts. Faced by such texts, McIlwain was driven to ask, "Was Bracton, then, an absolutist or a constitutionalist, or was he just a blockhead?"[14]

Thus McIlwain's argument called attention to apparent internal contradictions in Bracton's work, while Schulz, ignoring these internal disharmonies, emphasized a crude contradiction between Bracton and his Roman law sources (though such a view seems hardly compatible with Schulz's own estimate of Bracton's juristic acumen). The difficulties center around Bracton's use of the Roman law expression "princeps legibus alligatus," a phrase that could have had several different connotations. The problem remains of determining whether any particular meaning was consistent with all Bracton's texts and, if so, whether

---

[13] *Cod.* 1.14.4. For a far-ranging discussion on the whole medieval concept of a ruler at once above and below the law, with abundant citations of secondary references, see Ernst Kantorowicz, *op. cit.,* pp. 81–192. My own purpose is more modest but, I hope, complementary. It is not to explore again all the associations and significances that could be implied by Bracton's terminology, but rather to try to define with precision which particular meaning, out of all the possible ones, he did intend to convey in the particular passages considered.

[14] *Op. cit.,* pp. 74–76, 87.

that meaning could have been extracted from his civilian sources without gross blundering or wilful perversity.

It seems to me arguable that Bracton's views really were based on passages of Roman law and on the interpretations of them that he found in the *Glossa Ordinaria*; that it is incorrect to suppose that he merely tricked out an essentially ecclesiastical theory with civilian texts which he interpreted in a sense different from that of the civilians themselves; and that most difficulties of interpretation disappear when the Roman law basis of his thought is properly understood. Schulz's distinction between a Roman theory of a prince morally bound by the law and an English theory of a king legally bound by the law was not very felicitous. It does not correspond precisely to mediaeval categories of thought. As we are often told, mediaeval lawyers did not distinguish as sharply as modern ones betwen moral law and legal law, between moral obligation and legal obligation; and of course the phrase "legally bound by the law" does not occur in the relevant text of Isidore or in Bracton or in his civilian sources. A distinction that mediaeval jurists were familiar with had arisen out of the canonists' difficulties over the *forum internum* and the *forum externum*. There were cases in which a man was obliged by ecclesiastical law and could legally be coerced by the ecclesiastical courts; there were other cases where he was no less obliged in which he could not be so coerced. The fulfilment of the law then depended on his voluntary observance of it (and on his voluntary submission to a confessor in case of delict). The difference did not lie in the kind of obligation but in the nature of the appropriate sanction. It is an analogous kind of distinction that we find in Bracton and also in the gloss of Accursius. Both writers held that the ruler had a duty to obey the law, but that the fulfilment of the duty could be ensured only by his will to adhere to its provisions, not by legal coercion. It goes without saying that mediaeval jurists, unlike some modern ones (though their number is happily decreasing), did not regard sanction as the sole ground of legal obligation.[15]

In his commentary on the *lex digna* Accursius first wrote that it seemed false to state flatly that the emperor was bound by the law and that it was better to say that he willed himself to be bound (*se velle*). But he also wrote in another gloss on the same law that it was more honorable to subject the principate to the laws than the laws to the principate.[16] When Bracton came to read the *lex digna* he could hardly have supposed (as Schulz would have it) that this statement by two fifth-century emperors professing themselves bound by the laws constituted of itself an edict legally binding all future emperors, for the *Glossa Ordinaria* pointed out that the maxim "par in parem non habet imperium" excluded such

---

[15] For a discussion of some modern views see A. L. Goodhart, *English Law and the Moral Law* (London, 1953). Schulz (*art. cit.*, p. 163, n. 1) disposed of the mediaeval civilians by quoting a series of texts in which they stated that the emperor conformed to the law of his own will. But, if Schulz assumed that a voluntary rather than a coerced observance of the laws implied a ruler who was merely "morally bound by the law" as distinct from one who was "legally bound by the law," then he should have seen that precisely the same argument applied to Bracton's king.

[16] Gloss *ad Cod.* 1.14.4 s.v. *Principatum* in *Corpus Iuris Civilis* (Lyons, 1618).

an interpretation; and Bracton knew that maxim well and cited it himself.[17] If
the law had any permanent force for future rulers, it could only be because it was
based on an argument which had enduring validity. The rational basis for the
lex digna, its *ratio* as the *Glossa Ordinaria* explained, was contained in its second
clause, "so much does our authority depend on the authority of the law." Accursius explained this as a reference to the *lex regia* and so did Azo, adding that since
the emperor's authority was derived from the law he should repay the law by
keeping it.[18] If, then, Bracton thought that the *lex regia* could be cited as an argument for binding the king to the law, so did his civilian sources. Schulz was
content to observe that he found the logic of the argument obscure. It is indeed
hard to see how the civilians could have propounded it at all, and so have provided a textual basis for Bracton, if they thought of the *lex regia* as precisely
that law which licensed the prince in advance to disobey all laws. Evidently we
need to know more precisely just what they did understand by the phrase
"princeps legibus solutus."

The structure of cross-references in the *Glossa Ordinaria* is especially helpful
here. We need not assume that Bracton was familiar with all the inter-relations
of the different texts of the *Corpus Iuris* in the fashion of a professional civilian.
It is enough to suppose that at some time he glanced at the *lex digna* and read
it *adiuncta glossa*, which seems a reasonable assumption. His attention would
then have been directed to other passages of the *Glossa Ordinaria* which are of
great interest in the interpretation of his thought. The very first reference given
by Accursius in his gloss on the *lex digna* was to Dig. 1.3.31 which proclaimed the
apparently contrary principle, "Princeps legibus solutus est." When we turn to
that passage we find a gloss in which Accursius explained his understanding of
these words by referring to two other sections of the Digest, *Dig.* 4.8.4 and *Dig.*
4.8.51. Of these, the first stated that a superior magistrate could not be coerced
by an inferior or an equal, the second that a man could not act as arbiter in his
own case since he could not issue coercive commands to himself.[19] Accursius's

---

[17] Gloss s.v. *Indicamus:* "Scilicet successori nostro, et non dicit praecipimus quia par in parem non
habet imperium." On Bracton see n. 21 below.

[18] Gloss s.v. *De auctoritate:* "Haec est ratio primi dicti, et quod dicit iuris, scilicet legis regiae, quae
est de imperio transferendo de populo in principem." Azo, *Summa Codicis* (Lyons, 1530) ad rubr.
1.14, f. viib: "Quis debeat observare leges: et quidem observande sunt ab omnibus hominibus . . .
Imperator tamen unus successori suo imperare non potest sed suadere ut leges servet et suasionis
causam proponere: ut quia de lege scilicet regia pendet auctoritas principalis: quia per eam populus
transtulit omne imperium in principem, merito et ipse hoc retribuat legi ut servet eam." Cf. Azo,
Ad Singulas Leges . . . Codicis Iustinianei Commentaria (Paris, 1577) ad 1.14.4, p. 40: "Quia haec est
causa quare debet legibus alligari quia imperium habuit a populo lege Hortensia lata, nam ei et in
eum omne ius suum transtulit." The error of citing the *lex Hortensia* in this context may have arisen
from the fact that the *lex Hortensia* was mentioned in the *Institutes* just before the passage on the *lex
regia*. Azo's *Summa* may very well have been (as Schulz suggested) the immediate source of Bracton's
famous little rhyme, "Debet retribuere legi quod lex tribuit ei. Facit enim lex quod ipse sit rex." But
so many manuscript sources of Roman and canon law in the early thirteenth century remain inade-
quately explored that it is impossible to be certain about such things.

[19] *Dig.* 4.8.4: "Nam magistratus superiore aut pari imperio nullo modo possunt cogi." *Dig.* 4.8.51:
"Si de re sua quis arbiter factus sit, sententiam dicere non potest, quia se facere iubeat aut petere
prohibeat; neque autem imperare sibi neque se prohibere quisquam potest."

argument, then, was not that some supposed *lex regia* had contained clauses licensing the emperor to disobey the laws, but that the very act of setting up a supreme magistrate necessarily removed the chosen person from the sphere of coercive jurisdiction since, by definition, there was no equal or superior who could lay down the law to him with coercive sanctions. After making this point Accursius added that the emperor submitted himself to the law of his own will, and added a list of citations to prove this, starting with a reference back to the *lex digna*.[20]

Bracton's position was exactly the same. No person in the realm was the equal or superior of the king, and so no judge could dispute his acts.[21] No writ ran against the king. He was indeed *sub lege* in that he had a duty to live according to the laws; nothing in his position licensed him to disobey them; but his observance of the law could be ensured only by his own good will, not by judicial coercion.[22] This view was expressed quite clearly in a passage where Bracton compared the role of the king to that of Christ and of Mary in that they had conformed to the law because of their regard for justice and humility, not because they were subject to coercive sanctions.[23]

There is, then, no reason to suppose that Bracton was merely eccentric in his handling of Roman law material. The implications that he saw in his civilian texts could very well have been suggested by Accursius himself. Nor does it seem necessary to maintain that his argument lacked internal consistency. In connection with this point it is interesting to note that Bracton's great contemporary, Thomas Aquinas, reflected on the same texts of Roman law as Bracton and came to precisely the same conclusions, though he preferred to found his own interpretation on the *Glossa Ordinaria* of the Psalms rather than on the *Glossa Ordinaria* of the Code. It would be possible of course to find many other parallels

---

[20] Gloss *ad Dig.* 1.3.31 s.v. *Princeps legibus:* "Ab alio conditis ut infra *de arbit. l. nam magistratus* (4.8.4), vel a seipso ut infra *de arbit. l. penultim.* (4.8.51). Voluntate tamen sua seipsum subiicit ut *Codic. eodem l. digna* . . . " This gloss and other relevant passages of the *Glossa Ordinaria* are analysed in detail in a forthcoming article, " 'The Prince Is Not Bound by the Laws.' Sovereignty and the Rule of Law in Accursius," *Comparative Studies in Society and History,* v (1963).

[21] Woodbine, II, 33 (f. 5b): "Parem autem non habet rex in regno suo quia sic amitteret praeceptum cum par in parem non habet imperium. Item nec multo fortius superiorem . . . Si autem ab eo petatur, cum breve non currat contra ipsum, locus erit supplicationi . . . "; II, 157 (f. 107): "Et haec locum habent inter privatas personas: inter regem et privatas personas non tenet istud quia rex parem non habet, nec vicinum, nec superiorem."; III, 43 (f. 171b): "Si autem princeps vel rex vel alius qui superiorem non habuerit nisi deum, contra ipsum non habebitur remedium per assisam, immo tantum locus erit supplicationi ut factum suum corrigat et emendet, quod si non fecerit, sufficiat ei pro poena quod deum expectet ultorem . . . nisi sit qui dicat quod universitas regni et baronagium suum hoc facere possit et debeat in curia ipsius regis" (cf. n. 52 below): IV, 281: " . . . et pares non habent neque superiores."

[22] Woodbine, IV, 159 (f. 368): " . . . nec poterit (regi) aliquis necessitatem imponere quod illam corrigat vel emendet nisi velit, cum superiorem non habeat nisi deum . . . "

[23] Woodbine, II, 33 (f. 5b). Schulz thought the passage might well be an interpolation but his reading is impossible. The last sentence as he gives it, "Sic ergo rex ne potestas sua maneat infrenata, igitur non debet esse maior eo in regno suo in exhibitione iuris," is neither good grammar nor good sense. The words "Sic ergo rex . . . " refer back to the immediately preceding sentences that Schulz would omit. A new sentence begins with "Igitur . . . " The passage is correctly punctuated in Woodbine.

between Bracton and the jurists and theologians of the mid-thirteenth century and, as we have indicated, the investigation of such parallels has been undertaken with considerable *élan* by Ernst Kantorowicz. It seems worth quoting this particular text of St Thomas because a comparison with it serves to bring out with special clarity certain aspects of Bracton's thought that are important for our argument. Thomas was discussing the problem whether the prince was to be regarded as *legibus solutus* in accordance with *Dig.* 1.3.31 which he had previously quoted.

> It may be said that the prince is called freed from the law as regards the coercive force of the law; for no one properly speaking is coerced by himself; but the law does not have coercive force except from the power of the prince: thus therefore the prince is said to be freed from the law because no one can pass a judgment condemning him if he acts against the law: whence on Psalm 50 "To you alone have I sinned" the gloss says that no man may judge the acts of the king: but as regards the directive force of the law the prince is subject to the law by his own will as it is said in *extra, de constitutionibus*, cap. cum omnes (Decretals, 1.2.6), "Whatever anyone has established as law for another he should adhere to himself . . . " and in the Code . . . " It is a declaration worthy of the ruler for the prince to profess himself bound by the laws. . . . " . . . The prince is also above the law in that, if it is expedient, he can change the law, or dispense from it according to time and place.[24]

It should first be noted that neither Bracton, nor Thomas in this particular passage, was operating with the very familiar distinction between divine and natural law on the one hand and positive law on the other. They were not making the point that the ruler was above positive law because such law was merely an expression of his own will; he was held "loosed" from the law only in the sense that there was no judge to impose coercive sanctions on him. To understand Bracton at all one must bear in mind that when he wrote of the king being under the law it was the real complicated earthy law of England he had in mind, not some hypothetical reflection of an ideal pattern laid up in heaven. His teaching on this point was very simple and quite consistent. It is perhaps precisely because he did not choose to avail himself of the more subtle distinctions that mediaevalists expect to find in thirteenth-century authors that it has sometimes seemed puzzling. Bracton had no need of them. The propositions that a man is "under the law" and at the same time answerable to no judge who can enforce the law with coercive sanctions will seem contradictory only if one starts out from a modern positivist theory of legal obligation.

Finally, the passage of St Thomas illustrates very plainly that, for men of his age, the obligation of a king to live according to the laws as they actually existed did not in the least exclude the possibility that he might licitly undertake to change those laws by new legislation. Even nowadays an English sovereign, at his coronation, swears to govern his peoples "according to their respective laws and customs." The next day he might be signing new laws into existence. No

---

[24] *Summa Theologica*, 1.2.96.5. Cf. Ernst Kantorowicz, *op. cit.*, p. 136, n. 153, Miller, *art. cit.*, p. 271, n. 36. Also R. W. and A. J. Carlyle, *A History of Mediaeval Political Theory in the West*, v, 2nd. ed. (London, 1938), 475–476, and J.-M. Aubert, *Le droit romain dans l'oeuvre de Saint Thomas* (Paris, 1955), p. 83.

one thinks of the two things as contradictory; nor did mediaeval jurists. In thirteenth-century legal texts the phrases *rex sub lege* or *rex legibus alligatus* are never, or scarcely ever, used in such a fashion as to imply a denial of the king's legislative function. The assumption that such phrases normally did carry that connotation has been a fruitful source of misunderstandings in modern scholarship. In particular McIlwain raised up a host of unnecessary difficulties for himself by his reluctance to attribute a consciously exercised legislative capacity to thirteenth-century monarchs.[25]

Bracton, as we have seen, plainly attributed a legislative function to the king, but held that that function itself was to be exercised in accordance with the law of the land (which, in England, required counsel and consent).[26] We can finally return to his argument that the king's obligation to adhere to the law arose from the fact that the royal authority itself was derived from a *lex regia*. Schulz, as we have noted, found Bracton's formulation of this view logically unconvincing. But if we bear in mind that Bracton and his civilian source were thinking in terms of a *lex regia* that freed the king from the sanctions of law, not from obligations to the law, the argument is plain and sensible enough. Bracton started from the assumption of a land ruled by laws, among which was a law establishing the authority of the ruler. He urged that in these conditions a king who undermined the authority of law in general by contemptuously disregarding it undermined the source of his own authority — for "law makes the king." A king who did follow his own naked will without respect for the law could not expect to remain an effective ruler. That path led only to anarchy — "where there is no law there is no king." It seems good sound practical advice for any constitutional ruler.

Historians have a habit of reproving their colleagues in the other "social sciences" for constructing imposing chains of argument that result in merely trite conclusions. In this case our own analysis has led only to a common-sense interpretation, of the kind that an intelligent reader might perhaps extract from the *De Legibus* without benefit of source criticism or textual analysis. But, in dealing with the thought of Bracton, one would hope for no other result. The task of clarifying the sources and structure of his argument is indeed especially rewarding when its fulfilment serves to assure us that the necessary pre-occupation with technical problems need not exclude the satisfaction of reaching common-sense conclusions.

---

[25] Every lawyer and administrator with a smattering of civilian learning was familiar with the idea that new law could be created by deliberate legislation, and every cleric engaged in the conduct of ecclesiastical affairs took for granted the enactment and application of such new law. Of course in the Middle Ages, as nowadays, changes in the law were brought about in several different ways — by the framing of a new law, by judicial interpretations or by administrative decisions. Mediaeval Roman and canon lawyers were much concerned with the analysis of these procedures. For a general survey of the growth of legislative activity at the end of the thirteenth century, see Sten Gagnér, *Studien zur Ideengeschichte der Gesetzgebung* (Uppsala, 1960) and the remarks of Walter Ullmann, "Law and the Medieval Historian," XIe Congrès des Sciences Historiques, Rapports III (Uppsala, 1960), 34–74. On England see J. W. Gough, *Fundamental Law in English Constitutional History* (Oxford, 1955), pp. 12–29, and T. F. T. Plucknett, *Legislation of Edward I* (Oxford, 1949).

[26] Woodbine, II, 21 (f. 1b), and IV, 285 (f. 413b).

GUBERNACULUM

We still have to consider McIlwain's own solution for the problems that he raised. His confrontation of "absolutist" and "constitutionalist" texts in Bracton led him to formulate the problem of their conflict in this way:

It seems impossible that the same man, if a sane man, could declare that the king has no peer on earth, much less a superior, and that no subject, not even a judge, can question or ought to question the legality of any of his acts; and could then go on to add that the king's will is not law except in the form of a definition to which the assent of the magnates is absolutely essential.[27]

There is really no contradiction in these propositions. The first refers to the king's immunity from civil suit or criminal prosecution, the second to the mode of exercise of his legislative capacity.[28] There is no logical or practical difficulty in conferring immunity from suit on a head of state without conferring on him arbitrary and unlimited powers of legislation. Such a situation has indeed often existed. Altogether, it seems to me, far too much has been made of the king's judicial immunity as an "absolutist" element in Bracton's thought. The right to sue the crown is not, after all, of the essence of contitutional government; the English managed to get along without it until 1947.

One major source of McIlwain's difficulties was his assumption that, if a king's obedience to the law was self-imposed, it was therefore licit for him to disobey the law, an idea quite alien to Bracton's whole scheme of thought. This assumption led McIlwain to search in Bracton for a sphere of governmental authority that would correspond to the "absolutist" texts he had cited, a sphere in which the king really would be quite arbitrary and absolute, unbound by law or by the counsel of his magnates. He found such a doctrine in a passage that Schulz also cited at length. Schulz saw no great significance in it, but McIlwain found in it, not only an interpretation of Bracton, but a whole theory of the nature of mediaeval constitutionalism.

The passage occurred in a section of the *De Legibus* dealing with the acquisition of incorporeal possessions like "liberties." Bracton wanted to argue that liberties could only be acquired from the king and so introduced his argument with a description of the content of royal power.

Habet enim omnia iura in manu sua quae ad coronam et laicalem pertinent potestatem et materialem gladium qui pertinet ad regni gubernaculum. Habet etiam iustitiam et iudicium quae sunt iurisdictionis, ut ex iurisdictione sua sicut dei minister et vicarius tribuat unicuique quod suum fuerit. Habet etiam ea quae sunt pacis . . . Habet etiam coertionem ut delinquentes puniat et coercet. Item habet in potestate sua ut leges et

---

[27] *Op. cit.* p. 76.

[28] The complications concerning obligation to the law in the absence of coercive sanctions do not arise when one is considering, not some particular unjust act of the king, but an attempt on his part to promulgate general legislation. If a thirteenth-century English king — it is hard to imagine — had attempted to introduce some radical change in substantive law without counsel and consent the remedy was built into the situation. The element of consent was necessary in practice as well as in theory; without it the law would not have taken effect. In the case of a specific unjust act redress could normally be obtained by petition. Cf. H. S. Richardson and G. O. Sayles, *Select Cases of Procedure Without Writ*, Selden Society Publications, LX (London, 1941), pp. lxx, clxxxvi–clxxxviii.

constitutiones et assissas in regno suo provisas et approbatas et iuratas, ipse in propria persona sua observet et a subditis suis faciet observari. Nihil enim prodest iura condere, nisi sit qui iura tueatur. Habet igitur rex huiusmodi iura sive iurisdictiones in manu sua.[29]

McIlwain saw in this passage a clear-cut distinction between *gubernaculum* and *jurisdictio*. *Gubernaculum* defined a sphere within which the king's authority was "autocratic and irresponsible"; it included the formation of government policy and the issuing of administrative orders. *Jurisdictio*, on the other hand, related to the law defining the rights of subjects and, in that sphere, the king was limited by coercive law enforceable by his magnates.[30]

McIlwain's observations have an evident relevance to certain real problems of thirteenth-century government. Unhappily, there is no trace whatsoever of the doctrines he described in the text from which he attempted to illustrate them. The exposition was founded on a series of misinterpretations of Bracton.

There is not in the text any sharp distinction between *gubernaculum* and *jurisdictio*. The only use of the former word is in the phrase, "(Rex) habet . . . materialem gladium qui pertinet ad regni gubernaculum." But in the Roman and canon law sources from which Bracton drew his doctrines on public law the "material sword that pertained to government" often simply *meant* jurisdiction. The precise term *materialis gladius* does not occur in Roman law, but *ius gladii* or *potestas gladii* was used for the capital jurisdiction in criminal cases that in-hered in the *imperium* of the highest magistrates.[31] *Materialis gladius* was com-monly used by the canonists and, fortunately, we have a series of fine articles by A. Stickler explaining the various senses in which it was employed in their works.[32] It could mean again coercive jurisdiction involving the shedding of blood; it could mean the licit use of armed force as in a just war; most commonly of all, by the beginning of the thirteenth century, *materialis gladius* was used in arguments about church and state to designate secular authority as such in opposition to *spiritualis gladius* signifying ecclesiastical authority. In any case it did not define a sphere of governmental administrative activity separate from jurisdiction. Bracton's insertion of the word *laicalem* before *potestatem*, together with that of *materialem* before *gladium*, suggest rather clearly that the third meaning was the one uppermost in his mind. At the outset of his passage defining various forms of royal authority he was making the point that the king's author-

---

[29] Woodbine, II, 166 (f. 55b); Schulz, *art. cit.*, p. 143.

[30] *Op. cit.* pp. 76 ff.

[31] *Dig.* 2.1.3, "Merum est imperium habere gladii potestatem ad animadvertendum facinorosos homines." See H. F. Jolowicz, *Historical Introduction to the Study of Roman Law* (Cambridge, Eng-land, 1932), pp. 317–327, 407–409, citing earlier literature, and M. P. Gilmore, *The Argument from Roman Law* (Cambridge, Massachusetts, 1941) p. 22.

[32] A. M. Stickler, "De ecclesiae potestate coactiva materiali apud Magistrum Gratianum," *Salesi-anum*, IV (1942), 2–23, 97–119; "De potestate gladii materialis ecclesiae secundum 'Quaestiones Bam-bergenses ineditas'," *Salesianum*, VI (1944), 113–140; "Der Schwerterbegriff bei Huguccio," *Ephe-merides Iuris Canonici*, III (1947), 1–44; "Il potere coattivo materiale della Chiesa nella Riforma Gregoriana secondo Anselmo di Lucca," *Studi Gregoriani*, II (1947), 235–285; "Magistri Gratiani sententia de potestate ecclesiae in statum," *Apollinaris*, XXI (1948), 36–111. See also R. Castillo Lara, *Coacción Ecclesiastica y Sacro Romano Imperio* (Turin, 1956).

ity pertained to the temporal sphere. He would say the same thing explicitly later on in his treatise, explaining then that the king could not judge in spiritual cases because there he lacked coercive power, and using the term *gladius* in that context to designate the temporal and spiritual authorities.[33]

Moreover, our text makes no suggestion at all that the king's exercise of *gubernaculum* could or should be any more arbitrary and absolute than his exercise of *jurisdictio*. McIlwain made the point that the king was said to have *gubernaculum* "in his hand" and added, "The significant fact is that acts of government strictly defined are in the hands of the king alone. There he 'has no peer, much less a superior'." But the words he quoted from Bracton referred quite explicitly in their original context to *jurisdictio* in the strictest sense. "Parem autem habere non debet nec, multo fortius, superiorem *in iustitia exhibenda*."[34] McIlwain saw in Bracton a distinction "far sharper than we make in our modern times between government and law, between *gubernaculum* and *jurisdictio*." But surely just the reverse is true. Nowadays, in spite of disputes over borderline cases like the competence of administrative tribunals, we do have a rather clear-cut theoretical distinction between the executive and judicial sides of government. There was no such distinction in the Middle Ages. Administrative business was commonly transacted under judicial forms and before courts that were also courts of judicature. Bracton's work is soaked in the preconceptions of such a system. Over and over again he refers to the exercise of jurisdiction as the very essence of royal authority.[35]

There is no special significance in the fact that the king was said to have *gubernaculum* "in his hand," for just the same phrase was used a little further on of *jurisdictio*. "The king has therefore rights and jurisdictions of this kind in his hand." McIlwain explained this by pointing out that the words referred back to an earlier sentence. "He has it in his power to observe in his own person and to make his subjects observe the laws and decrees and assizes provided and approved and sworn to in his realm." On this McIlwain commented, "Note particularly that last phrase indicating the kinds of enactment which the king is free to observe or ignore at his pleasure . . . It is not by accident, I think, that an enactment defining *consuetudo* or custom does not accompany *constitutio* in this list." And so he felt able to conclude that the "laws, decrees and assizes" were mere administrative orders which pertained to the king's *gubernaculum* and

---

[33] Woodbine, II, 304 (f. 107), " . . . eorum iura sive iurisdictiones limitatae sint et separatae, nisi ita sit quod gladius iuvare debeat gladium." See also p. 32 (f. 5b) where "gladius" was used in the second sense given above, "Gladius autem significat defensionem regni et patriae."

[34] Woodbine, II, 305 (f. 107). McIlwain, *op. cit.* p. 79.

[35] Woodbine, II, 33 (f. 5b): "Igitur non debet esse maior eo in regni suo in exhibitione iuris. . . . ."; II, 167 (f. 55b): "Ea vero quae iurisdictionis sunt et pacis, et ea quae sunt iustitiae et paci annexa, ad nullum pertinent nisi tantum ad coronam et dignitatem regiam, nec a corona separari poterunt cum faciant ipsam coronam."; II, 305 (f. 107): "Ad hoc creatus est rex et electus, ut iustitiam faciat universis, . . . "; IV, 281 (f. 412): "Et imprimis quod sicut dominus papa in spiritualibus super omnes ordinariam habet iurisdictionem, ita habet rex in regno suo ordinariam in temporalibus, et pares non habent neque superiores."

which hence were "in his hand" in the sense that he could ignore them at will.[36]
This interpretation is, however, untenable. The phrase, "He has it in his power . . . to observe the laws," was simply a restatement of Bracton's consistently held view that the king's duty to obey the laws was to be fulfilled by his voluntary adherence to them.[37] Once again it must be insisted that, when Bracton used language stating that the king's obligation to observe the laws was not enforced by coercive sanctions, he never meant to imply that the king could licitly disobey the law whenever he felt so disposed. As for the argument concerning the omission of the word *consuetudo*, the really important thing here was the inclusion of *leges*. Bracton himself defined quite clearly his understanding of these terms at the beginning of his treatise. *Leges* constituted the body of laws common to the whole kingdom; *consuetudines* were local customs.[38] There is no reason at all to suppose that Bracton was using the word *leges* in some quite different sense in this particular passage (and, of course, the laws were "in the king's hand" in the sense that he was the supreme judge charged with upholding and enforcing them.)

It seems unnecessary to continue with a word by word analysis; inevitably the initial misreading of the text led on to further misunderstandings about topics like the binding force of oaths, the legal nature of Magna Carta and, of course, the legislative function of the king.

There is another side to all this that I would want to emphasize. To a historian of my generation McIlwain is a venerable figure. His insight into the essential problems of thirteenth-century government was always impressive and it remains so even in these few pages of his work that are open to attack on technical grounds. There really was taking place at the heart of thirteenth-century constitutional development, two processes that McIlwain, sensing their importance but not discriminating properly between them, fused together in the definition of *gubernaculum* that he mistakenly fathered on Bracton. First, and most obviously, there was a growing area of bureaucratic administration within which the king claimed freedom from any control by the *universitas regni*. In the second place there was a growing area of policy formation where the king (although normally bound by the law) claimed the right to initiate extra-legal actions affecting his subjects' rights and liberties, sometimes in association with, sometimes independently of, the spokesmen for the *universitas*. This second development was intimately linked to the growth of the ideas of the state and the public welfare in the thirteenth century. These ideas spread from Roman law first to canon law (where a complex doctrine on *status ecclesiae* had grown up by 1200), then slowly

---

[36] *Op. cit.*, pp. 78, 85.

[37] Cf. Schulz, *art. cit.*, p. 172: "[This passage] must not be misunderstood. It contains Bracton's opinion that the king is subjected to the law. This is the sense of 'habet in potestate sua, ut leges . . . in propria persona sua observet'."

[38] Woodbine, II, 22 (f. 2), under the rubric *Quid sit lex et quid sit consuetudo*: "Videndum est etiam quid sit lex. Et sciendum quod lex est commune praeceptum virorum consultum prudentium, delictorum quae sponte vel ignorantia contrahuntur coertio, rei publicae sponsio communis . . . Consuetudo vero quandoque pro lege observatur in partibus ubi fuerit more utentium approbata, et vicem legis obtinet."

into the law and constitutional theory of the various secular kingdoms. *Status regni* is a common expression by mid-thirteenth century, and from certain mediaeval usages of the term there developed eventually the Renaissance "reason of state." It is only quite recently that studies on mediaeval public law have begun to illuminate the details of this process.[39] In his later works McIlwain repeatedly stressed that further advances in Roman law studies were essential for a proper understanding of mediaeval constitutionalism. It was an unhappy chance that the needed studies on Roman law, and on canon law too, that would have permitted him to clarify his insights and to document them adequately came just too late for their results to be incorporated in his own survey.

THE *"ADDICIO DE CARTIS"*

Item factum regis nec cartam potest quis iudicare, ita quod factum regis irritetur. Sed dicere poterit quis quod rex iustitiam fecerit, et bene, et si hoc eadem ratione quod male, et ita imponere ei quod iniuriam emendet, ne incidat rex et iustitiarii in iudicium viventis dei propter iniuriam. Rex habet superiorem, deum scilicet. Item legem per quam factus est rex. Item curiam suam, videlicet comites et barones, quia comites dicuntur quasi socii regis, et qui socium habet, habet magistrum. Et ideo si rex fuerit sine fraeno, id est sine lege, debent ei fraenum apponere nisi ipsimet fuerint cum rege sine fraeno. Et tunc clamabunt subditi et dicent *Domine Ihesus in chamo et fraeno maxillas eorum constringe.* Ad quos dominus. *Vocabo super eos gentem robustam et longinquam et ignotam, cuius linguam ignorabunt, quae destruet eos et evellet radices eorum de terra, et a talibus iudicabuntur, quia subditos noluerunt iuste iudicare.* Et in fine ligatis pedibus eorum et manibus, mittet eos in caminum ignis et tenebras exteriores, ubi erit fletus et stridor dentium.[40]

It is generally agreed, on the basis of the manuscript evidence, that the passage above formed no part of the original draft of Bracton's treatise; there has been

[39] Several articles by Gaines Post are especially relevant here: "Roman Law and Early Representation in Spain and Italy," SPECULUM, XVIII (1943), 211–232; "Plena Potestas and Consent in Medieval Assemblies," *Traditio*, I (1943), 355–408; "A Romano-Canonical Maxim, 'quod omnes tangit' in Bracton," *Traditio*, IV (1946), 197–251; "The Theory of Public Law and the State in the Thirteenth Century," *Seminar* (annual extraordinary number of *The Jurist*), VI (1948), 42–59; "The Two Laws and the Statute of York," SPECULUM, XXIX (1954), 417–432; "Ratio publicae utilitatis, ratio status und Staatsräson (1100–1300)," *Welt als Geschichte*, XXI (1961), 8–28, 71–99. Post's earlier articles and a number of other relevant works were discussed in the review article, "Some Recent Works on the Political Theories of the Medieval Canonists," *Traditio*, X (1954), 594–625. Since then several books dealing with problems of mediaeval public law have appeared. Besides the works of Ernst Kantorowicz, David, Gagnér, and Lara (cited *supra*, n. 3, n. 25, n. 32), see L. Buisson, *König Ludwig IX. der Heilige und das Recht* (Freiburg, 1954) and *Potestas und Caritas* (Cologne, 1958); P. N. Riesenberg, *Inalienability of Sovereignty in Medieval Political Thought* (New York, 1956). My criticism of McIlwain's position was written before I had seen Dr. Fesefeldt's thesis (n. 3 above). She also questioned his argument on the ground that Bracton repeatedly emphasized the king's supremacy precisely in the sphere of jurisdiction (*op. cit.*, Ch. ii, n. 86). Dissatisfied with McIlwain's interpretation that limited the king's absolute power solely to the sphere of *gubernaculum* and also with Schulz's view that Bracton's ruler was unqualifiedly "under the law," Dr. Fesefeldt found in Bracton's claims for the king a close approach to the modern theory of the state. "One may say that already reason of state in a very modern sense was concealed in the garb of Fürstenspiegelethik" (p. 61). The difficulty here is that the concept "status" itself was so ambiguous in the thirteenth century. Mediaeval jurists readily thought of a *status* that could be defended *against* the ruler as well as *by* the ruler. The barons of 1258 claimed claimed to be defending the *status regni*.

[40] Woodbine, II, 110 (f. 34). Cf. Woodbine, I, 124–125, 252–253, 332–333, 378.

much controversy, however, as to whether it was an afterthought by Bracton himself or the work of some anonymous interpolator. The theory of Bracton's authorship has found few defenders in modern times, the notable exceptions being Erlich and Hermann Kantorowicz (the latter arguing mainly on grounds of literary style).[41] The stylistic argument, so far as it goes, seems to me persuasive. The image of law as a bridle on the king was a favorite one with Bracton, and the recoil from a contemplation of perverted justice into a cocoon of doom-laden scriptural quotations and allusions precisely reproduces the structure of a genuinely Bractonian passage at fol. 2.[42] It might indeed seem that the *addicio*, if it was not written by Bracton, was a deliberate pastiche.

In a matter like this, however, no scholar is likely to be convinced by another person's subjective impressions. (Schulz thought that, "The style is unusually clumsy and not at all like Bracton's usual style"). It is not our purpose, therefore, to argue that Bracton did write the *addicio*; the point does not seem capable of proof one way or the other. We do hope to show that certain arguments against the authenticity of the text, especially those adduced by Lapsley which were based on assertions of its intrinsic improbability, are quite without foundation; and, above all, we shall try to offer a rational explanation of the most puzzling words in the *addicio*, "qui socium habet, habet magistrum."

Lapsley's paper[43] began in a fashion that seems quaintly old-fashioned only fifteeen years later. He cheerfully announced his lack of any techncial competence in Roman and canon law as well as in English law but, none the less, felt quite qualified to resolve a difficult Bractonian problem on the basis of his expertise in thirteenth-century political theory. We now know that most of the explicit political theory of the early thirteenth century was contained precisely in the works of Roman and canon lawyers and that Bracton often turned to such writings in formulating his own ideas. Lapsley went on to present a whole group of arguments against the authenticity of the *addicio* based on "antecedent probability" and he conveniently summarized them at the end of his paper.[44] In the first place, he could not believe that a learned and responsible judge would have given free rein to his "religious, moral and political passions" in writing a treatise on the laws of England. But, in fact, thirteenth-century jurists very commonly did give sharp expression to their moral and political convictions in the course of their technical treatises. It is useless to expect a mediaeval law commentary to be similar in content to a modern legal textbook and then to base a judgment as to the authenticity of this or that passage on such a pre-

---

[41] L. Ehrlich, *op. cit.*, pp. 47–49, 202–206; H. Kantorowicz, *Bractonian Problems*, pp. 49–52. Schulz criticized and corrected Kantorowicz's reading of the text (*art. cit.*, pp. 174–175). Sir Maurice Powicke, *King Henry III and the Lord Edward*, i (Oxford, 1947), 390, n. 2, accepted Schulz's textual criticisms but observed, "I see no reason why Bracton, at the time of his co-operation with the baronial council in 1258–60, should not have developed his thought in this way. It should not be read in any anti-royalist sense."

[42] Woodbine, ii, 21–22. Cf. Ehrlich, *op. cit.*, p. 205.

[43] *Art. cit.*, *supra*, n. 2.

[44] *Art. cit.*, pp. 17–18.

supposition. If we were to turn to the vast commentary on the laws of the church by Bracton's precise contemporary, that learned and responsible cardinal, Hostiensis, we should find, buried away among the intricate discussions on private law, views on political theory much more provocative than anything in Bracton's treatise (even if the *addicio* did form part of it).[45] Both the two great *Corpora iuris* of the thirteenth century, civil and canon, contained public as well as private law and, in commenting on the public law sections, the glossators were often led to write on matters that we would classify as political theory; and, naturally, their own convictions as well as their legal learning were reflected in such discussions. In treating similar topics in his own work Bracton was simply following the example of his sources.

To Lapsley it seemed in any case impossible that the doctrine of the *addicio* could be a reflection of Bracton's political views because of its crude radicalism. For me it is hard to understand why the *addicio* has so often been described as "fiery" or "crude" or "radical." Its only specific constitutional proposal, that the magnates should seek to restrain the king from perpetrating injustices in his curia, seems a modest proposal indeed by mid-thirteenth century standards. (In 1245 an incompetent king of Portugal was stripped of his powers of government altogether at the instance of his magnates and with the co-operation of the pope.)[46] In the *addicio* it was only the scriptural quotations that were "fiery," and Bracton had a taste for fiery scriptural texts, as is apparent in the passage on fol. 2 already mentioned. Lapsley maintained that the Biblical sentences of the *addicio* must be taken as an incitement to popular rebellion (though he conceded that "in form" the text says just the opposite, that the people had to await the vengeance of God); for, he wrote, the authors of the *addicio* could never "have been content in fact with an appeal to an inattentive deity busy perhaps with slumber or pursuit." This is more silly than cynical. Is it really necessary to insist that many men of the thirteenth century believed most sincerely in the reality of divine retribution, that they expected it to be quite hellish in nature, and that they did not suppose that it would necessarily be deferred until the next world? If we had to take every mediaeval prophecy of doom directed against wicked kings as an expression of crude and violent political theory we should indeed be floundering in a morass. But of course, as Schulz wrote, "All this is mere fancy."[47]

[45] There is a good article on the life and works of Hostiensis in *Dictionnaire de droit canonique,* v (1953), 1211–1227.

[46] The circumstances are set out in Innocent IV's decretal *Grandi* included in the *Liber Sextus* at 1.8.2. Cf. Riesenberg, *op. cit.,* pp. 167–169.

[47] *Art. cit.,* p. 174, n. 2. Schulz was criticizing H. Kantorowicz's view that the text was an incitement to rebellion. Lapsley was apparently anxious to disagree with Kantorowicz on every possible point; but Kantorowicz's view that the *addicio* had revolutionary implications fitted in very well with his own argument that it could not have been written by a moderate like Bracton. Lapsley therefore argued that the *addicio* was revolutionary "in substance" but not "in form." This enabled him to chide Kantorowicz for misreading the text while at the same time chiding the author of the *addicio* for its "extreme doctrine and excited language." To me it seems that the author did not intend either to incite or to justify acts of rebellion, but he did intend to warn the king that abuses of royal power

As to the doctrine which is generally accepted as that of the *addicio* — the doctrine that a king could be judged by his own court — Lapsley found this "repugnant to the notions of the nature of kingship current in western Europe in the thirteenth century" and more radical than most of the surviving radical writings themselves. He concluded that it was logically impossible to elaborate a juristic basis for a right of rebellion and that, in any case, a discussion of the *necessitas rebellionis* had no proper place in a practical treatise on law. Once again this betrays an unawareness of what practical treatises on law were often like in the thirteenth century. The truth is that every major commentary on the *Decretum* of Gratian written in the half century before Bracton's own work contained a detailed treatment of the right of resistance to an unjust ruler, and the canonists were thinking of resistance not only against a king but against a much more exalted figure, the pope himself (and this in spite of the fact that the *Decretum* contained texts asserting the pope to be above all human judgment since he had no superior on earth).[48] We need only quote the *Glossa Ordinaria* to the *Decretum* by Johannes Teutonicus, a work that Bracton certainly knew. At C.2 q.5 c.10 Johannes wrote, "The pope can be judged by no one, not even by a general council"; at D.40 c.6 he maintained that a pope could be deposed for any notorious crime.[49] If indeed there did exist in Bracton's text a conflict of utterances on this point (though that is not what I want to argue) it would only reflect a conflict in one of his sources. As for the deposition of mere kings and emperors, the canonists of the generation before Bracton took this for granted as an expedient that might be mildly regrettable but was obviously necessary from time to time in the conduct of political affairs.[50] There is evidently no substance in the view that the authenticity of the *addicio* is disproved by the antecedent improbability of such radical sentiments ever finding their way into a respectable law book. Let us turn to the text itself.

---

might very well be followed by such disastrous consequences. His meaning would then correspond to Bracton's view, "Non est enim rex ubi dominatur voluntas et non lex" (Woodbine, II, 33 (f. 5b)) or " . . . rex sapiens iudicabit populum suum; is autem insipiens perdet illum" (Woodbine, II, 306 (f. 107b). This was again a scriptural quotation, as Schulz noted; cf. Ecclesiasticus, ix, 17–18.

[48] *Dist.* 17 c.5, *Dist.* 17 *dictum post* c.6, *Dist.* 79 *dictum post* c.10, C.9 q.3 c.10–c.17, C.17 q.14 c.30.

[49] *Decretum Gratiani . . . una cum glossis* (Paris, 1601). Gloss ad C.2 q.5. c.10: "Quia papa a nullo potest iudicari . . . Nec etiam ab universali concilio. . . . " Gloss *ad Dist.* 40 c.6: "Certe credo quod si notorium est crimen eius quandocunque et inde scandalizatur ecclesia et incorrigibilis sit, quod inde possit accusari." In the argument that follows there has been no attempt to multiply quotations from canonistc sources. Many relevant texts are printed and discussed in my *Foundations of the Conciliar Theory* (Cambridge, England, 1955); "Grosseteste and the Theory of Papal Sovereignty," *Journal of Ecclesiastical History*, VI (1955), 1–17; "Pope and Council: Some New Decretist Texts," *Mediaeval Studies*, XIX (1957), 197–218. There is no reason to suppose that Bracton was familiar with all the intricacies of the canonists' arguments, though he can hardly have been unaware of their existence. Disputes about the extent of papal power were matters of practical politics as well as of abstruse theory in the days of Innocent IV. In any case Bracton did know the *Glossa Ordinaria* to the *Decretum* (Schulz, *art. cit.*, p. 176, referring to his other textual studies). We have therefore limited our references to that source.

[50] Thus Johannes Teutonicus continued his gloss on *Dist.* 40 c.6 in this fashion: "Sed pro quo peccato potest imperator deponi? Pro quolibet si est incorrigibilis, unde deponitur si est minus utilis."

It began with a statement that acts and charters of the king could not be invalidated, which is good Bractonian doctrine.[51] The next sentence is obviously corrupt, but the opening words "Sed dicere poterit . . . " correspond to a phrase that Bracton used elsewhere when he wished to introduce an opinion without committing himself to it, "Nisi sit qui dicat. . . . " It seems clear that the meaning of the *addicio* must be that given by Schulz, "It may, however, be said: 'it is the king's duty to maintain justice and this entails his duty to correct an unjust action'." Moreover, this corresponds precisely to a genuine text of Bracton at fol. 171b where, having explained that no suit could be brought to annul an unjust act of the king, he added, "nisi sit qui dicat quod universitas regni et baronagium suum hoc facere possit et debeat in curia ipsius regis.[52] In short, there is no serious problem (apart from the textual problem of tidying up the syntax) in this part of the *addicio*. If the text had gone straight from the end of this sentence to the beginning of the scriptural allusions, I do not think it would ever have been suspected on doctrinal grounds. All the real difficulties lie in the intervening words;

The king has a superior, namely God. Also the law by which he was made king. Also his court, namely the earls and barons because earls (*comes*) are so-called as being companions of the king, and who has a companion has a master. And therefore if the king shall be without a bridle, that is without law, they ought to put a bridle on him, unless they themselves are without a bridle with the king.

The claim that the king had a superior in his curia seems flatly opposed to Bracton's clearly asserted view that there was no superior who could invalidate the acts of the king. As Maitland crisply observed, "The statement that the king has fellows and masters is contradicted by at least five statements found in all parts of the book."[53] This is the one essential argument against the authenticity of the *addicio*. It may rest on a misunderstanding of the text, for no one seems to have attempted to attach a rational meaning to the words "qui socium habet, habet magistrum." On the face of it they are nonsense; a *socius* is not a *magister*; Schulz found the argument unintelligible.

One thing that does seem to be generally agreed is that the political sections of Bracton's treatise were based on Roman and canon law sources rather than on feudal law. If we approach the *addicio* with this in mind, a relevant canonistic parallel does present itself, We have in mind the principle that one could appeal from a prelate to the same prelate with counsel as to a higher authority. To

---

[51] Schulz's emendation of this passage (omitting "nec cartam") depends on his suggested emendation of the preceding sentence (where he would omit "nec factis regum"); but this has been criticized by Ernst Kantorowicz, *op. cit.*, p. 158, n. 209.

[52] Woodbine, III, 43 (f. 171b). The parallel was pointed out long ago by Maitland, *Bracton's Note-Book*, I (London, 1887), 32–33, then again by Ehrlich, *op. cit.*, p. 203, and by Schulz, *art. cit.*, p. 174. Maitland indeed pointed to the difference in emphasis between the two passages and Lapsley quoted him in that sense, *art. cit.*, p. 2. But, as indicated above, it was not this particular sentence of the *addicio* that caused Maitland's difficulties but rather the ensuing ones. Ehrlich suggested that the whole passage from "Sed dicere poterit . . . " to the very end might be regarded merely as the adumbration of a possible counter-argument. This seems an unnecessary hypothesis.

[53] *Op. cit.*, p. 32, citing f. 5b, f. 52, f. 107, f. 368, f. 412 (Woodbine, II, 33, 157, 305; IV, 159, 281).

quote Johannes Teutonicus again: "Item hic appellatur a metropolitano ad concilium metropolitanum . . . et sic concilium est maius ipso metropolitano, et sic appellatur ab aliquo ad seipsum cum aliis. . . . "[54] Our argument is not that the writer of the *addicio* was necessarily inspired by this particular text of canon law, but rather that it typified a widely applied principle of ecclesiastical administration that could not have been unfamiliar to any thirteenth-century cleric. The argument was not that the suffragan bishops who participated in the council were collectively greater than the metropolitan who presided over it but that metropolitan and bishops together constituted a tribunal superior to the metropolitan alone. Any prelate who had *socii* could be said to have a *magister* in this particular sense. A bishop had no ecclesiastical equal or superior in his diocese; he was superior to the canons of his cathedral church; but bishop and canons together had more authority than the bishop alone. They could do things that the bishop alone could not do — alienate church property, for instance.

Now the *addicio* refers to the king's court as "curiam suam videlicet comites et barones," but no thirteenth-century writer could have forgotten, or intended to deny, that the king was a part of his own curia, indeed its very head and center. The view that the curia was superior to the king did not necessarily contradict the view that the king had no superior judge set over him precisely because the judgments of the curia were the judgments of the king and derived their authority from the fact. In the same way the canonists would often write that a general council was superior to the pope, meaning only that pope and bishops together carried more weight than the pope alone.[55] This way of thinking was certainly familiar to Bracton, for at the outset of his work he pointed out that king and magnates together could change old laws and frame new ones but that the king alone did not have this authority.

The essential problem of the *addicio* lies in the fact that it envisaged a situation where the king's own acts were to be considered and judged in his curia. Whose judgment then would prevail in the last resort — that of the king or that of the magnates? The canonistic parallel is especially interesting here, for the Decretists sometimes advanced beyond the fairly simple proposition that pope and council together were of greater authority than the pope alone to consider explicitly the precise problem that the *addicio* raised in the secular sphere. Where did ultimate authority reside if a pope was in dispute with the members of a council? On this there were two clearly defined and mutually exclusive canonistic points of view. Some writers held that the judgment of the bishops in council outweighed that of the pope; others taught that, in the final analysis, if a pope adhered to one judgment and all the members of the council opposed it, the judgment of the pope had legal validity. Bracton could have read both

---

[54] Gloss *ad Dist.* 17 c.5 s.v. *Ad maiorem.*

[55] For example, Johannes Teutonicus, gloss *ad Dist.* 19 c.9 s.v. *Concilio*: "Videtur ergo quod papa tenetur requirere concilium episcoporum, quod verum est ubi de fide agitur, et tunc synodus maior est papa." Bracton compared the authority of the king in the secular sphere with that of the pope in the ecclesiastical sphere explicitly at Woodbine, II, 32 (f. 5b) and IV, 281 (f. 412).

opinions in the gloss of Johannes Teutonicus, though Johannes did not decide between them:

Sed nunquid potius stabitur sententiae Apostolicae vel omnium episcoporum. Videtur quod omnium episcoporum quia orbis maior est urbe ut 93 dist. legimus (c. 24).Arg. quod sententia Papae praevalet, 35 q.9. veniam (c.5). Nam etiam error principis ius facit.[56]

If we were to suppose that Bracton wrote the *addicio,* and that he was being entirely and literally consistent, we would have to assume that he adhered to the second view. The magnates could oppose the king's judgments in his curia, and they had a duty to do so when those judgments were unjust, but if the king persisted in upholding a royal act that was unjust, his judgment had legal validity. In this interpretation the legalities are preserved and the principle "parem autem habere non debet, nec multo fortius superiorem" remains unbreached. But, none the less, the restraints that could be imposed on a king by the magnates of his curia would not have been merely illusory. In real life it could scarcely have been possible for a king to uphold acts of flagrant injustice in his court in defiance of the considered judgment of his assembled earls and barons; in actual practice no pope ever has found it expedient to promulgate a decision in opposition to the unanimous opinion of the bishops in council.

In a genuine passage of the *De Legibus* which considered the possibilities of obtaining redress against the king Bracton showed how, by a suit against a third party who had acted with royal authority, the king might be virtually forced to revoke an unjust charter. He could not indeed be legally compelled to do so but he could be manoeuvred into a position where his charter would only stand if the king, in effect, publicly asserted his intention of upholding an unjust act that would not stand scrutiny in the courts — and that was scarcely thinkable.[57] The ventilation of complaints of injustice by the magnates in curia, which the author of the *addicio* advocated, would have had the same effect.

Our interpretation of the *addicio de cartis* takes us far from the views of those who have found radical or even revolutionary doctrines in it. There is one final point to be made that seems to me of decisive importance. The first words of the *addicio* itself are, "No one can judge the charter or act of the king so as to invalidate the king's act." The radical interpretations not only make the *addicio* disagree with Bracton; they make it disagree with itself. Any exegesis which is to make sense of the passage as a whole has to show that the implications of the later sentences are consistent with that clear opening statement; and any interpretation which shows the *addicio* to be self-consistent will probably also show that it is consistent with Bracton.

To sum up: Are we after all to say that Bracton was a constitutionalist or that he was an absolutist? A constitutionalist by temperament we may surely affirm, but one who was working with intractable materials. His work was es-

---

[56] Gloss *ad Dist.* 4 c. 3 s.v. *Iudicent,* see also "Pope and Council: Some New Decretist Texts," pp. 203–209.

[57] Woodbine, III, 43 (f. 171b). Lapsley discussed this passage (*art. cit.,* p. 12) but naturally found it entirely contrary to his own reading of the *addicio.*

sentially an attempt to fit a massive structure of English private law into a rather flimsy framework of Romanesque public law and naturally there are signs of strain. The figure of a king, half feudal lord half divine ruler, that he found in his plea rolls could not easily have been transformed into the first magistrate of a constitutional government even if Bracton had had any such conscious intention. It was indeed impossible to extract a theory of the constitutional state from the English materials because they simply lacked the idea of a state in the classical or modern sense. The writings of contemporary Roman and canon lawyers could have supplied that idea, but, while Bracton could deploy quotations from the more elementary Roman and canon law treatises competently enough, he had no sophisticated knowledge of contemporary jurisprudence in the two laws. His mind was formed by the law of England. The theories of western constitutionalism did indeed eventually grow out of the encounter of minds shaped by a feudal age with classical and early Christian ideas of society and government that in the nature of things they could only half-understand. By the middle of the thirteenth century the materials were already at hand from which some genius — he would have had to be a polymath — might have constructed a theory of the constitutional state. Bracton was not sufficiently learned in the two laws, nor sufficiently imaginative nor, I am sure, sufficiently interested in this kind of problem, to achieve such a synthesis.

CORNELL UNIVERSITY AND INSTITUTE FOR ADVANCED STUDY

V

The Continuity of Papal Political Theory
in the Thirteenth Century.

Some Methodological Considerations

THE transmission of political concepts in the Middle Ages provides a complex but rewarding theme of study for the historian of ideas. Some of the major problems in the field are semantic ones for, very often, words and phrases remained the same for century after century while the concepts that they signified changed radically. To take a particularly familiar example, the scriptural allegory of the "two swords" was used in an anti-papal sense by King Henry IV and his partisans in the eleventh century but it meant something quite different to St. Bernard of Clairvaux in the twelfth. The words of St. Bernard in turn were repeated by a whole line of popes and eventually were incorporated into *Unam Sanctam* by Boniface VIII. But in the process of transmission their meaning had changed yet again.[1] It is the same with many of the key phrases of medieval political discourse — Gelasius's *auctoritas sacrata pontificum et regalis potestas* for instance or *plenitudo potestatis* or *consilium et consensus*. They meant different things at different times and were exploited in different ways by opposing theorists. The task of analyzing them is further complicated by the fact that, often enough, the process of transmission has continued down to our own day. The medieval "advice and consent" recurs in modern constitutional documents. The problems of church and state are still very much with us. Hence there is a constant danger of distorting medieval concepts by defining them in language that is overladen with specifically modern connotations.

---

[1] The changing significance of the sword imagery has been discussed in a series of articles by A. Stickler. See his, "De potestate gladii materialis ecclesiae secundum 'Quaestiones Bambergenses ineditas'," *Salesianum*, 6 (1944), 113-140; "Der Schwerterbegriff bei Huguccio," *Ephemerides Juris Canonici*, 3 (1947), 1-44: "Il 'gladius' nel Registro di Gregorio VII," *Studi Gregoriani*, 3 (1948), 89-103; "Il 'gladius' negli Atti dei Concilii e dei RR. Pontefici fino a Graziano e Bernardo di Clairvaux," *Salesianum*, 13 (1951), 414-445. See also H. Hoffmann, "Die beiden Schwerter im hohen Mittelalter," *Deutsches Archiv*, 20 (1964), 78-114. Hoffman discusses Innocent III's contribution to the growth of a "hierocratic" doctrine of the two swords.

Given this whole situation it is not surprising that much of the recent controversy about the political theory of the medieval popes — whether it was essentially "dualistic" or "hierocratic" in orientation — has turned on problems of continuity and discontinuity. In particular a major dispute has arisen concerning the relationship between the teachings of Pope Innocent III (1198-1216) and those of Pope Innocent IV (1243-1254).[2] An older point of view saw both pontiffs as crudely ambitious pretenders to a universal temporal lordship and this interpretation has been given a more sophisticated formulation by Walter Ullmann who finds in the pontificate of Innocent III a decisive re-affirmation of an older monistic tradition of the papacy at a time when some leading canonists were beginning to defend the autonomy of the secular power.[3] According to this argument Innocent IV was merely a faithful follower of the theocratic doctrines expounded by his great predecessor. This whole approach has been challenged by an eminent group of modern historians — prominent among them Maccarrone, Mochi Onory, Kempf and Tillmann — who maintain that the political theory of Innocent III was based on a cautious discrimination between the spheres of action of spiritual and secular rulers.[4] If, then, Innocent IV was an out-and-out proponent of papal theocracy as has been very commonly assumed, it becomes necessary on this view to postulate a sharp change in the political theory of the medieval papacy between 1200 and 1250.

[2] The dispute involves more than a mere point of chronology. If we assume that the views of Innocent IV were much more theocratic than those of Innocent III then, given the extreme peril to the Roman church from the activities of Frederick II in the 1240s, it becomes relatively easy to dismiss all claims of the medieval papacy to universal temporal power as a mere passing aberration induced by a very abnormal political situation.

[3] W. Ullmann, *Medieval Papalism* (London, 1949), 146, "The vigorous pontificate of Innocent III exercised a decisive influence on the shaping of curialist theory. Huguccio and his English and Spanish followers were to sink into oblivion." The author's interpretation of papal political thought in the centuries before Innocent III is set out in his *Growth of Papal Government in the Middle Ages* (London, 1955).

[4] M. Maccarone, *Chiesa e Stato nella Dottrina di Innocenzo III* (Rome, 1940); S. Mochi Onory, *Fonti Canonistiche dell' Idea Moderna dello Stato* (Milan, 1951); F. Kempf, *Papsttum und Kaisertum bei Innocenz III* (Rome, 1954); H. Tillmann, *Papst Innocenz III* (Bonn, 1954). Several different interpretations of Innocent III's claims in the temporal sphere are discussed by A. Walz, "'Papstkaiser' Innocenz III. Stimmen zur Deutung, " *Miscellanea Historiae Pontificiae*, 18 (Rome, 1954), 127-138. See also A. Hof, "'Plenitudo potestatis' und 'Imitatio imperii' zur Zeit Innocenz III," *Zeitschrift für Kirchengeschichte*, 66 (1954-55), 39-71: O. Hageneder, "Das Sonne-Mond-Gleichnis bei Innocenz III," *Mitteilungen des Instituts für Österreichische Geschichtsforschung*, 65 (1957), 340-368; idem, "Exkommunikation und Thronfolgeverlust bei Innozenz III, "*Römische Historische Mitteilungen*, 2 (1959), 9-50; "Das päpstliche Recht der Furstenabsetzung (1150-1250)," *Archivum Historiae Pontificiae*, 1 (1963), 53-95.

A new twist to the whole discussion has been given by one of the most recent contributors to it, Joannes Cantini. He accepts the major conclusions of the second group of historians mentioned above but carries their arguments a step further. Cantini carefully combed through the writings of Innocent IV (the great canonical commentary on the *Decretales* as well as Innocent's own decretal letters) and for the first time brought together in a single work all the texts of this pope that bear on problems of church-state relations. His conclusion is startling. Innocent IV, Cantini claims, was a dualist too. We thus have a third position in the general debate, one which maintains that there was an essential continuity between the doctrines of Innocent III and those of Innocent IV but which reaches this conclusion by a line of argument diametrically opposed to that of the other scholars who have upheld it.[5]

The very fact that the political pronouncements of the two pontiffs have given rise to such very different interpretations raises two possibilities for consideration. The first is that both popes may simply have fallen into self-contradictions. In that case the very nature of the source material will probably ensure that conflicting interpretations of their ideas continue to appear. The other possibility is that modern criticism has not yet penetrated deeply enough into the texture of thirteenth century thought to discern an underlying coherence of argument that really existed below the surface of apparently conflicting texts. Our main concern is with this second possibility. In particular we hope to identify certain methodological difficulties which are currently impeding the development of any agreed interpretation of the political theories of the medieval popes.

There seem to be four such outstanding "difficulties". The first lies in the employment of an inadequate modern terminology to characterize medieval ideas, and especially in the abuse of the current jargon words "dualistic" and "hierocratic". The second difficulty is one of thought rather than language. It consists in anachronistic attempts to force medieval thought into the mould of modern concepts of sovereignty. The third difficulty arises from a widespread disposition to treat the various papal pronouncements as mere attempts to define a static existing structure of public law whereas they become intelligible and can be seen as self-con-

---

[5] J. Cantini, "De autonomia judicis saecularis et de Romani pontificis plenitudine potestatis in temporalibus secundum Innocentium IV, " *Salesianum*, 23 (1961), 407-480. Cantini provides a good bibliography of earlier work on the political theory of Innocent IV. At p. 416-417 he lists some forty authors who have treated the pope as an extreme exponent of papal theocracy. The most recent survey of the question, that of John Watt, "The Theory of Papal Monarchy in the Thirteenth Century: The Contribution of the Canonists," *Traditio*, 20 (1964), 179-317, presents a more nuanced and balanced account with which I am in general agreement.

sistent only when they are understood as dynamic attempts to bring about change in an existing system, to initiate processes of historical development that the popes regarded as desirable. Finally, and associated with this last point, there has been inadequate emphasis in modern interpretations of thirteenth century papal thought on the medieval doctrine that general consent was necessary to bring about licit and effective changes in an existing structure of laws and rights. If we approach the political thought of the thirteenth century popes with these considerations in mind it may be possible to show that the doctrines of Innocent III and Innocent IV were both self-consistent and consistent with one another and that, if the popes did indeed uphold a medieval ideal of papal world-monarchy, that ideal was far removed from any modern theory of Austinian sovereignty.

Let us begin with the difficulties posed by the conflicting texts of Innocent III. At the very outset of his pontificate Innocent issued a series of pronouncements that seem at first glance to be uninhibited assertions of an extreme theocratic doctrine. He described himself as a ruler "set between God and man, below God but above man, who judges all and is judged by no-one". He congratulated the king of Armenia for having appealed to the pope on a purely temporal issue. He declared to the Tuscan noble Acerbus that "just as the moon derives its light from the sun... so too the royal power derives the splendor of its dignity from the pontifical authority". He explained to the Greek patriarch that Peter had been given "not only the universal church but the whole world to govern," and to the Greek emperor that the priesthood was as superior to the kingship as the soul to the body.[6] As for the western empire, Innocent summoned his cardinals to a secret consistory on Christmas Day, 1200 — just four centuries after the coronation of Charlemagne — and read to them a *Deliberatio* asserting that the empire pertained to the Roman see "first and last", "principally and finally" — principally because the empire had been translated to the west from Constantinople by the papacy and finally because the emperor was "anointed, crowned and invested with the empire by the pope".[7] Moreover, according to Innocent, the temporal jurisdiction of the pope was not restricted to the empire. In the decretal *Per Venerabilem* he maintained that the pope was a supreme judge to whom appeal could be made in every kind of case, whether ecclesiastical or

---

[6] Migne, *PL* 217, 658; 214, 813, 377, 759; 216, 1185.

[7] *PL* 216, 1025; F. Kempf, *Regestum Innocentii III papae super negotio Romani imperii, Miscellanea Historiae Pontificiae*, 12 (Rome, 1947), 75. Cf. P. A. Van den Baar, *Die kirchliche Lehre der Translatio Imperiii Romani* (Rome, 1956), 99-111.

secular, whether civil of criminal, whenever the matter was difficult and ambiguous so that lesser judges disagreed about it.[8] This claim was put forward in an involved exegesis of an obscure passage of Deuteronomy and it has puzzled some modern scholars. It did not puzzle thirteenth century canonists. They all interpreted it in the sense just given and Innocent — a brilliant canonist himself — must surely have known that they would so interpret it when he included *Per Venerabilem* in an official collection of papal decretals which he promulgated in 1210.[9] Before that he had explained to the bishop of Vercelli (an imperial city outside the papal states) that, although secular cases there were normally to be heard by the consuls of the city, an appeal could be made to the bishop or to the pope whenever it was alleged that the consuls had failed to do justice, and this especially when the empire was vacant.[10]

Many historians have found in Innocent's numerous interventions in the secular politics of his age ample evidence that he was guided throughout his pontificate by the theocratic principles that seem so evident in his early decretals. The difficulties of interpretation arise from the fact that, in no really important political crisis, did Innocent ever assert simply and lucidly that he was acting by virtue of a supreme temporal authority that inhered in his office. In the decretal *Novit* which asserted the pope's right to mediate in a feudal dispute between King Philip of France and King John of England Innocent maintained that the dispute involved a question of sin and also a breach of a solemn oath and also a threat to the peace of Christendom. All of these matters, he insisted, were the proper concern of the pope as head of the church. But he also stated quite explicitly, "We do not intend to judge concerning a fief, judgment on which belongs to (King Philip)."[11] Again, in the disputed imperial election of 1202, Innocent asserted an effective right of choice between the two candidates by insisting on the powers inherent in his ecclesiastical role as consecrator of the emperor-to-be; but, in a spirit rather different from that of the *Deliberatio* of 1200, he conceded that in principle the right of electing an emperor belonged to the German princes.[12] Again, Innocent several times acknowledged — in letters to the rulers of Hungary and of France for'instance[13] —

---

[8] *PL* 214, 1133.

[9] *Quinque Compilationes Antiquae*, ed. E. Friedbreg (Leipzig, 1882), 128. The significance of the decretal is discussed in my article "'Tria quippe distinguit iudicia...' A Note on Innocent III's Decretal *Per Venerabilem*," *Speculum*, 37 (1962), 48-59.

[10] *PL* 215, 892.

[11] *PL* 215, 326.

[12] *PL* 216, 1065 (Kempf, *Regestum*, 168).

[13] *PL* 214, 871: 215, 526. These and other examples are cited by R. Castillo Lara, *Coaccion Ecclesiastica y Sacro Romano Imperio* (Turin, 1956), 168.

that the powers of kings came from God and he repeatedly declared that he did not wish to usurp the rights of secular rulers. Even in the decretal *Per Venerabilem* which contained Innocent's most extreme claim to universal temporal jurisdiction he began by asserting that he was well aware of Christ's saying "Render to Caesar the things that are Caesar's" and that, accordingly, he did not want "to prejudice the rights of any one else or to usurp any power that is not ours." Similarly he wrote to the bishops of France, "Let no-one suppose that we wish to diminish or disturb the jurisdiction and power of the king," and to the princes of Germany, "Just as we do not want our own justice to be usurped by others so too we do not want to claim for ourselves the rights of the princes."[14]

There is an evident conflict of utterances between the rhetoric of Innocent III's more general pronouncements on papal power and the legalistic caution of his specific claims to intervene in particular cases. If, now, we wish to argue that there was an essential continuity between his thought and that of Innocent IV it is necessary to show, firstly, that the more extreme claims which have sometimes been regarded as especially characteristic of the later pope were in fact anticipated by his predecessor and, secondly, that the qualifications and reservations which can be found in the writings of Innocent III occur also in those of Innocent IV.

We shall discuss below Innocent IV's interpretation of the Donation of Constantine. For the rest, his view that the word *Quodcumque* (in the famous phrase, "Whatsoever thou shalt bind on earth...") was used by Christ to confer on Peter jurisdiction over all kinds of affairs as well as over all classes of persons echoed faithfully a doctrine that Innocent III had enunciated both in the decretal *Solitae* and in a sermon composed for the feast of St. Sylvester.[15] Innocent IV's further explanation in the same context that this universal authority of the papacy could also be proved from

---

[14] *PL* 214, 1132: 215, 326: 216, 1065 (Kempf, *Regestum* 168).

[15] Innocent IV's claim was set out in the encyclical letter *Eger cui levia* ed. E. Winkelmann, *Acta imperii inedita seculi XIII et XIV* (Innsbruck, 1885), 697, "Generali namque legatione in terris fungimur regis regum, qui non solum quemcumque, sed ne quid de rebus aut negociis intelligeretur exceptum, sub neutro genere generalius universa complectens, etiam quodcumque ligandi super terram pariter et solvendi apostolorum principi nobisque in ipso plenitudinem tribuit potestatis..." Cf. Innocent III, *PL* 216, 1185, "Nobis enim in beato Petro sunt oves Christi commissae, dicente domino, 'Pasce oves meas,' non distinguens inter has oves et alias... Ut illud tanquam notissimum omittamus quod Dominus inquit ad Petrum et in Petro dixit ad successores ipsius, 'Quodcumque ligaveris super terram' etc., nil excipiens qui dixit 'Quodcumque'"; *PL* 217, 482, "Nihil excepit qui dixit 'Quodcumque'." Cantini does not regard *Eger cui levia* as an authentic work of Innocent IV. His arguments (*art. cit.*, 410-416) seem to me not altogether convincing and I hope to discuss the question on another occasion.

Paul's words at 1 Corinthians 6.3 seems borrowed directly from Innocent III's *Per Venerabilem* where the same text was used for the same purpose.[16] The claim of the later pope that the apostolic see possessed a supreme appellate jurisdiction whenever there was "a necessity of law because the judge is doubtful or a necessity of fact because there is no superior judge" was a conflation of the doctrines set out in Innocent III's *Per Venerabilem* and *Licet* (his letter to the bishop of Vercelli).[17] Finally, Innocent IV's view that the pope conferred the power of the sword on the emperor seems a mere re-statement of the view that Innocent III had adopted when he declared that the emperor was "invested with the empire by the pope."[18]

If we turn now to the "dualistic" texts emphasized by Cantini we find precisely the same tensions in the writings of Innocent IV that we encounter in the decretals of Innocent III. Innocent IV too referred several times to the divine origin of royal power. He stated explicitly that there were kings who did not "hold" their kingdoms from the pope (though he found other grounds for asserting jurisdiction over them);[19] and he insisted, in letters to the kings of France, of Castille and of Portugal, that he did not wish to diminish royal rights but to augment them.[20] In discussing Innocent III's statement that he did not intend to judge concerning a fief Innocent IV not only agreed that the pope ought not to judge in such a matter "directly" but added that a litigant who brought a feudal issue before the papal curia on the ground that sin was involved would probably have a hard time proving his case.[21] Over and over again Innocent IV

---

[16] Innocent IV, *loc. cit.*, "...etiam ut doctor gentium huiusmodi plenitudinem non restingendam ostenderet, dicens, 'An nescitis quoniam angelos iudicabimus. Quanto magis secularia?'" Innocent III, *PL* 214, 1133, "Paulus etiam, ut plenitudinem potestatis exponeret, ad Corinthios scribens ait, 'Nescitis quoniam angelos judicabimus. Quanto magis saecularia?'"

[17] *Innocentii IV Pontificis Maximi in quinque libros decretalium commentaria* (Venice, 1570) ad X. 2.2.10, fol. 121va (Cantini, 460), "Licet in multis distincta sunt officia et regimina mundi, tamen quandocumque necesse est, ad Papam recurrendum est, sive sit necessitas juris, quia judex dubius est quam sententiam de jure ferri debeat; vel necessitas facti, quia alius non sit judex superior .." Cf. Innocent III, *PL* 214, 1133, "...cum aliquid fuerit difficile vel ambiguum ad judicium est sedis apostolicae recurrendum"; *PL* 215, 892, "Licet tamen ipsis... ad nostrum si maluerint audientiam appellare, hoc praesertim tempore quo, vacante imperio, ad judicem saecularem recurrere nequeunt..."

[18] Winkelmann, *op. cit.* 698; PL 216, 1025.

[19] *Commentaria ad* X. 2.2.10, fol. 121rb, "Sed quid si alius rex est negligens vel alius princeps qui superiorem non habet? Dicimus idem, scilicet quod succedit (papa) in jurisdictionem eius... Sed hoc non facit quod ab eo teneat regnum sed de plenitudine potestatis quam habet quia vicarius est Christi."

[20] Cantini, *art. cit.*, 422-423, citing E. Berger, *Les Registres d'Innocent IV* (Paris, 1884-1911), 5211, 6247, 1932.

[21] *Commentaria ad* X. 2.1.13, fol. 119ra. Cf. Cantini, 430.

expressed the view that, in the ordinary course of events, secular cases were to be tried before secular courts, and Cantini finds especially convincing evidence of this "dualistic" conviction of the pope in the fact that Innocent thought it necessary to compile a list of special cases in which, by way of exception, an ecclesiastical judge could intervene in a secular suit — thus conceding the general principle that normally such intervention was not justified. These "exceptions", which are of considerable importance for understanding thirteenth century papal thought were based in large part on the decretals of Innocent III with supplementary material drawn from the texts of Gratian's *Decretum*. They fell into three classes. (1) Secular cases involving certain classes of persons who were especially entitled to the protection of the church — e.g. clerics, orphans, widows and *miserabiles personae* in general. (2) Secular cases related in any way to spiritual affairs. This category included all legal issues where sin was involved. (3) Secular cases where there was a failure of justice in the lay courts. This could come about because no superior judge was available as when the empire was vacant, or because the lay judge was negligent or biased, or because the case was so difficult and ambiguous as to cause disagreement among the lay judges.[22]

After Cantini's work there is no great difficulty in showing that Innocent III and Innocent IV expressed substantially the same opinions on problems of church and state. It is more difficult to decide whether those opinions were consistent ones. At any rate, it seems to me that merely to set out the views of the two popes is sufficient to establish that their positions cannot be adequately characterized by either of the two currently fashionable terms, "dualistic" and "hierocratic." Both words are too vague. If "dualistic" implies, as it well might, an attitude favoring, "a wall of separation between church and state," then obviously no medieval pope was a dualist. If, on the other hand, anyone was a dualist who acknowledged that two orders of jurisdiction were needed for the governance of human affairs, a secular one and a spiritual one, and that normally each order ought to judge according to its own laws through its own courts in the cases appropriate to its own jurisdiction — then all the medieval popes were dualists. Cantini goes to great lengths to prove that Innocent IV was indeed a dualist in this latter sense but the effort seems superfluous. No one, so far as I know, has ever denied the fact. The disputed question is this. Granted that the popes acknowledged the need for two orders of jurisdiction, how did they conceive of the relationship between those two orders ? Above all did they regard the secular order as so subordinated

---

[22] *Commentaria ad* X. 2.2.10, fol. 121rb. Cf. Cantini, 428-432.

to the spiritual that the head of the ecclesiastical hierarchy could, in the last resort take cognizance of any kind of case and so control the whole range of human activity?

In discussing this question the word "hierocratic" is no more helpful than the word "dualistic." Presumably a starkly simple, unqualified "hierocratic" doctrine would have asserted that the pope, as God's vicar on earth, possessed an absolute and unlimited authority over all men and all their affairs. It would follow then that all legitimate authority was derived from the pope, that he could appoint and depose secular kings or their subordinate governors at will, hear appeals from their courts, enact secular legislation, settle disputes between temporal princes as a superior lord set over them or even, in the last resort, abolish the structure of secular offices altogether and govern the world through clerical delegates. The truth is that the popes claimed some of these rights but not others. Moreover this fact is not really a matter of dispute. The historians who insist most vehemently that the medieval pontiffs were "hierocrats" have to concede that, since it was illicit for priests to shed blood, the popes always had to recognize the need for a permanently enduring order of temporal rulers who could actually exercise the "power of the sword." And the historians who maintian most emphatically that the popes were "dualists" have to concede, since the relevant texts are quite explicit on the point, that medieval pontiffs did on occasion claim to depose temporal rulers and to exercise secular jurisdiction. Even on points of detail, if we were to ask precise, specific questions instead of vague, general ones — e.g. did Innocent III or Innocent IV maintain that the papal curia was the proper court to hear such-and-such a case in such-and-such a defined set of circumstances — probably still we should find very little disagreement. Once again the texts are explicit and usually they leave no great room for argument. The dispute therefore seems to be less and less about what the popes' claims actually were and more and more about which label — "dualistic" or "hierocratic" — we ought to pin on them. Cantini indulges in this kind of argumentation to an extraordinary degree. He concedes that Innocent IV claimed a supreme appellate jurisdiction in temporal affairs; he then adds that the pope claimed this authority as a spiritual privilege divinely conferred on the apostolic see; but, finally, concluding his argument with a most improbable twist, he alleges that this makes Innocent IV a dualist after all since all his claims were spiritual ones.[23] A historian of the opposing school would use exactly the same argument to prove that Innocent was a "hierocrat" in that he regarded his spiritual

[23] Cantini, 431-432.

authority as being so all-embracing as to include jurisdiction over temporal cases.

To sum up then. The words "dualistic" and "hierocratic" served a useful purpose in the earlier stages of the modern debate in pointing up genuine divergencies of approach among different schools of historians. I have used them often enough myself. But their continued employment is serving only to conceal the fact that a considerable area of agreement has emerged out of all the recent controversies. If it is impossible to abandon them altogether they ought at any rate to be subjected to rigorous definition in future work.

Even if we succeed in avoiding mere pseudo-problems of language in investigating the ideas of the thirteenth century popes we are left with many real problems of thought to unravel. For instance, if the pope inherited the fulness of the power of Christ who had been both priest and king, as Innocent III liked to maintain, how could any assertion of political authority on his part possibly constitute a usurpation? More specifically, if the pope was empowered to judge everyone and everything, as Innocent IV maintained in one context, how could it be improper for him to judge directly concerning a fief as the same pope declared elsewhere?

These questions are related to our second "methodological difficulty," the tendency to read into medieval definitions of papal authority modern concepts of sovereignty that are not really contained in them. When we encounter a claim to "plenitude of power" it is perhaps natural to think at once of contemporary theories of despotism or positivism, to relate such a claim to patterns of thought in which all law is conceived of as the arbitrary will of a sovereign legislator and all rights as derived from him and revocable at his pleasure. If we next go on to ask whether the medieval popes claimed such sovereign power it becomes impossible to extract a coherent answer from their writings. Some texts seem to support such pretensions: others clearly repudiate them. But we should encounter just the same difficulty if we asked our question of any thirteenth century ruler. The very way of posing the question makes it impossible to find a satisfactory answer, for medieval men simply did not think in Austinian categories. It seemed to them perfectly consistent to assert that a king was the supreme lord in his own realm while at the same'time maintaining that his legislative and judicial authority were limited by divine and natural law, by the need to obtain counsel and consent in the conduct of arduous affairs and by the licit rights of his subjects, among which were rights of jurisdiction that some of them held. A king who attempted to swallow up all the jurisdiction of inferior lords would be denounced as a tyrant.

In this world of thought the papal texts which disclaimed any intention of usurping the rights of jurisdiction inhering in secular princes would not

V

have seemed inconsistent with the other texts which asserted the supreme temporal jurisdiction of the papacy. The co-existence of both sets of texts merely demonstrates that the popes were claiming the powers of a thirteenth century temporal ruler, not those of a nineteenth century Austinian sovereign. Their declarations that they did not intend to judge certain types of cases illustrate the same point. Even in England, the country where royal jurisdiction had developed most fully in the days of Innocent III, it was not assumed that royal courts could hear any and every case as a matter of right. Royal justice extended directly to certain classes of persons who were immediately subordinate to the king and to certain classes of cases in which the rights of the crown were in some way involved while, in addition, the king possessed a vaguely defined appellate jurisdiction based on his duty to redress wrongs in cases where there had been defect or denial of justice in any lower court. That is to say the categories of cases in which royal jurisdiction was normally exercised corresponded closely to those mentioned by the popes as appropriate for the exercise of the temporal jurisdiction of the papacy. Again, it is well known that Innocent III distinguished between his temporal power over the papal states and the authority which he possessed in other lands. ("Not only in the patrimony of the church where we wield full power in temporal affairs but also in other regions we may exercise temporal jurisdiction occasionally, having examined certain causes"[24]); and the text has sometimes been taken to mean that any temporal interventions of the papacy outside Central Italy must be regarded as merely "indirect" consequences of its spiritual authority. But any thirteenth century king could have defined the nature of his temporal power in much the same words that the pope used. Philip Augustus of France might well have said, "Not only in the royal demesne where we wield full power in temporal affairs but also in other parts of the realm we can exercise temporal jurisdiction occasionally, having examined certain causes."

If it is necessary at all to define the claims of the medieval papacy to temporal power in terms of modern political experience — and it may be unavoidable to some extent since modern experience shaped our own thought and language — the model of Austinian sovereignty is the very last one that we should choose. A much more appropriate analogy could be made with the pluralistic, federally organized societies which are as characteristic of the modern world as unitary centralized states. The

---

[24] *PL* 214, 1132. In all the subsequent argument we are concerned solely with the papal claim to temporal power. It is possible to make a case for the view that, in the spiritual sphere, the papal claims did approximate to a modern theory of absolute sovereignty. The question is discussed at length in M. J. Wilks, *The Problem of Sovereignty in the Later Middle Ages* (Cambridge, 1963).

functions that the medieval papacy claimed for itself correspond fairly closely to those of a supreme court of judicature in such a society. Any supreme court would be abusing its functions if it "usurped" the jurisdiction of lower courts by persistently meddling in matters that those courts could deal with satisfactorily. The judges necessarily have to define limited classes of cases that properly pertain to their jurisdiction. Such cases will normally include ones where there is a disputed point of law to be settled, or where there appears to have been a failure of justice in a lower court, or where the litigants are such that no other court is competent to judge them. It was in just such cases that Innocent III and Innocent IV proposed to exercise the temporal jurisdiction that they believed to be inherent in their office.

There remains to be considered yet one further matter in which the two popes seem to have fallen into inconsistencies of thought. Both of them declared repeatedly that a regal as well as a sacerdotal power had been implanted in the papacy from its very first foundation. This view was based on the assumption that Peter, the first pope, had received the full powers on earth of a Lord who was "a priest after the order of Melchisedech," that is to say both priest and king. Since Christ's kingship was conceived of as universal the argument would seem to imply that all earthly kings could possess only a derivative authority bestowed on them by the pope. Yet in fact Innocent III and Innocent IV seem clearly to have recognized the autonomy of certain secular kings although they insisted that the empire was held from the pope. To complicate matters further Innocent IV introduced a distinction between *de iure* and *de facto* power, maintaining that the pope was *de iure* (though not *de facto*) the temporal overlord of the king of France and indeed of all other kings.[25] This problem is related to our third "methodological difficulty" which arises from the widespread neglect of a central element in the political thought of the medieval popes, their conception of a "potential" power inherent in the apostolic see that became explicit only through the unfolding of a long historical process in which the popes themselves were involved as active participants.

The idea of the divine will shaping the destiny of the human race through a series of political structures succeeding one another in time was of course a common-place one at the beginning of the thirteenth century. It found expression, for instance, both in the eccentric speculations of a Joachim of

---

[25] Where Innocent III described the king of France as a ruler who recognized no temporal superior Innocent IV commented tersely, "De facto. Nam de iure subest imperatori Romanae ut quidam dicunt. Nos contra. Imo papae." *Commentaria ad* X. 4.17.13, fol. 285rb. For other kings cf. *infra* n. 27.

Flora and in the more conventional description of a succession of empires presented by a chronicler like Otto of Freising. Innocent III very frequently appealed to Old Testament history in the course of his political argumentation and Innocent IV described explicitly the sequence of governments that God had provided for His people. In the beginning, Innocent wrote, God had ruled all things directly, without intermediaries. Then, from the time of Noah, he began to govern the world through human agents, and subsequently patriarchs, kings and judges succeeded to the office of rulership. This lasted down until the time of Christ "who was our natural Lord and King." Christ in turn established Peter and the successors to Peter as his vicars on earth. It was for this reason Innocent IV argued, that the pope could claim a supreme appellate jurisdiction in temporal cases.[26] In another passage the same pope turned his attention away from the Christian world altogether and discussed the question whether licit governments could exist among infidels. He argued, with more magnanimity than some of his contemporaries, that, since all men were children of God and some sort of government was a necessity for "rational creatures," legitimate rulers could arise among all peoples. But, he concluded, Christ had possessed power over all men and so even infidel kings were subject to the jurisdiction of Christ's vicar, the pope. In practice of course infidel rulers did not recognize papal jurisdiction and so, in describing their position, Innocent applied to them the same terminology that he used to define his temporal power over the Christian king of France. "The pope has jurisdiction and power over them all *de iure* though not *de facto*."[27] There was, that is to say, a sharp divergence between the theological doctrine of pontifical power that the popes propounded and the actual structure of public law that existed in their own day. The two could be brought into accord only if the regal authority that Christ had bestowed on the papacy came to be acknowledged by all the princes of the earth as a genuine *de facto* power.

It was in this connection, and with especial reference to the Donation of Constantine, that Innocent IV referred to a "potential" authority inherent in the papacy:

> "They do not discern shrewdly or know how to investigate the origins of things who think that the apostolic see first received rule over the empire from the prince Constantine, for this rule is known to have been inherent in the

---

[26] *Commentaria ad* X. 2.2.10, fol. 121va. Cf. Cantini, 466. On the historical dimension in Innocent IV's thought see J. Watt, *art. cit. supra* n. 5, 244-245.

[27] *Commentaria ad* X. 3.34.8, fol. 255vb. Cf Cantini, 467, "Omnes autem tam fideles quam infideles oves sunt Christi per creationem licet non sint de ovili ecclesiae... Et sic per praedicta apparet quod Papa super omnes habet jurisdictionem et potestatem de iure licet non de facto."

apostolic see naturally and potentially beforehand; for our Lord Jesus Christ, the son of God, was a true king and true priest after the order of Melchisedech... and he established not only a pontifical but a regal monarchy in the apostolic see."[28]

These words have often been regarded as marking a radical advance in papal claims to temporal power. But, in fact, the doctrine is essentially similar to that which Innocent III had proclaimed half a century earlier in his own comment on the Donation. Innocent III did not find it necessary explicitly to deny that papal temporal power was derived from Constantine's grant because in his day the papacy had never countenanced the idea that this might indeed be the case.[29] He did, however, assert very plainly that the regal power of the papacy came directly from Christ and he affirmed this in language very similar to that of Innocent IV:

[28] Winkelmann, *op. cit.*, 698, "Minus igitur acute perspiciunt, nescientes rerum investigare primordia, qui apostolicam sedem autumant a Constantino principe primitus habuisse imperii principatum, qui prius naturaliter et potencialiter fuisse dinoscitur apud eam. Dominus enim Ihesus Christus, dei filius, sicut verus homo verusque deus, sic secundum ordinem Melchisedech verus rex et verus sacerdos existens... in apostolica sede non solum pontificalem sed et regalem constituit monarchatum..." Cantini tried to use the concept of "potential" power to prove that Innocent IV was a dualist even though he claimed to be *de iure* overlord of the king of France. He argued that, since the pope proposed to exercise his temporal jurisdiction only in certain special cases, he was claiming only a "potential" power, leaving the king's "actual" power untouched. Cantini then equated this claim to potential power with the claim to *de iure* lordship. But, when Innocent wrote that he was *de iure* but not *de facto* overlord of the king of France, he did not mean that he intended to exercise his power only in certain cases. He meant quite obviously that the king of France did not recognize him as a temporal overlord at all although he ought to have done so. Cantini's misunderstanding of the concept of "potential" power was perhaps inevitable, for he denied the authenticity of the one document of Innocent IV in which the term was used, i.e. *Eger cui levia*. In this letter the term "potential" was used in two senses, neither of them consistent with Cantini's interpretation. Firstly, the word referred to a regal power implicit in the papacy which became actual only when it was recognized by temporal rulers. This is the sense discussed above. Secondly, it referred to the familiar doctrine that there were certain powers inherent in the church — notably the power to shed blood — which could never be exercised by the pope (or any priest) and which became actual only when the church's material sword was conferred on a lay ruler.

[29] In 1236 Gregory IX relied heavily on the Donation of Constantine to prove both his right to rule in the papal states and his right to depose the emperor. But the Donation provided a very weak foundation for such claims since the validity of Constantine's grant could be attacked on legal grounds even if the authenticity of the document describing it was accepted. It became necessary, therefore, for subsequent papal publicists to point out that the political claims of the papacy were not based solely on the Donation. On the one occasion when Innocent III appealed to an imperial grant of power in order to justify papal intervention in a political dispute he added at once, "...illud humiliter omittamus... cum non humanae constitutioni sed divinae legi potius innitamur, quia nostra potestas non est ex homine sed ex Deo." *PL* 215, 326).

"Blessed Sylvester was not only a great priest, but the greatest, sublime with pontifical and regal power, truly the vicar of Him who is King of kings and Lord of lords, a priest for ever after the order of Melchisedech..."[30]

Innocent III, like Innocent IV, never based his claims to "regal" power on any merely human concession of authority to the apostolic see but always insisted on the powers that Christ Himself had conferred on Peter. His attitude is especially evident in the letter which he sent to King John of England accepting the king's offer to become a vassal of the papacy. For a pontiff who believed that the powers originally conferred on the papacy by divine grant were limited to the spiritual sphere there would have been no difficulty in acknowledging that, by this transaction, the apostolic see was acquiring for the first time a temporal jurisdiction to which it had had no valid claim before. Innocent did nothing of the sort. He preferred instead to deploy the same scriptural imagery that he had used in describing the Donation of Constantine.

"The King of kings and Lord of lords, Jesus Christ, a priest for ever after the order of Melchisedech, has so established in the church the priesthood and the kingship that the kingship is priestly and the priesthood is royal... and he has set over all one whom He appointed to be his vicar on earth..."[31]

Innocent most certainly did not intend to state that John's kingship had a priestly character. His words were rather a repetition of the claim that Christ had conferred regal as well as sacerdotal powers on his own office. The pope continued:

"Prudently heeding this, beloved son, and mercifully inspired by Him in whose hand are the hearts of kings, and who sways them as He wishes, you have decreed that your person and your kingdom should be temporally subject to the one to whom you knew them to be spiritually subject so that kingship and

---

[30] PL 217, 481, "Fuit ergo B. Silvester sacerdos, non solum magnus sed maximus, pontificali et regali potestate sublimis. Il ius quidem vicarius qui est Rex regum et Dominus dominantium, Sacerdos in aeternum secundum ordinem Melchisedech..." Innocent very frequently mentioned that he was the vicar of "a priest after the order of Melchisedech," of a lord who had been priest and king, e.g. in the decretals Per Venerabilem and Solitae and in the letter to King John cited below. The doctrine of a regal authority inherent in the apostolic see could evidently have referred simply to papal sovereignty in Central Italy. The point is that Innocent III brought in the reference to Melchisedech over and over again when he was quite clearly discussing his powers over other regions.

[31] PL 216, 923, "Rex regum et Dominus dominantium Jesus Christus, sacerdos in aeternum secundum ordinem Melchisedech, ita regnum et sacerdotium in Ecclesia stabilavit ut sacerdotale sit regnum et sacerdotium sit regale... unum praeficiens universis, quem suum in terris vicarium ordinavit." The letter is also printed from the original charter that survives in the British Museum by C. R. Cheney and W. H. Semple, Selected Letters of Pope Innocent III (London, 1953), 177-183.

priesthood, like body and soul, should be united in the one person of the vicar of Christ..."[32]

Finally Innocent re-stated his conviction that the acknowledgment by contemporary kings of the temporal power of the papacy would mark the historical climax of a divinely guided process that had begun with the first foundation of the church:

> "He has deigned to bring this about who, being alpha and omega, related the end to the beginning and the beginning to the end, so that those provinces which formerly had the holy Roman church as their proper teacher in spiritual affairs now have her as their special lord in temporal matters also..."[33]

Innocent III and Innocent IV did not then regard the papacy as actually possessed of all temporal power but as in a state of evolution toward that position. Its achievement, they believed, would mark the fulfilment of a divine plan for the governance of mankind. They taught, as a matter of theological doctrine, that Christ had conferred on Peter His own royal and priestly powers, but they realised that, in the sphere of law, the regal power remained merely "potential" until civil rulers were willing to recognize it. Thus, when Innocent III wrote of John's surrender and Innocent IV of Constantine's Donation, both pontiffs were maintaining that a temporal prince who submitted himself to the pope was merely consenting to acknowledge a regal power already inherent in the apostolic see, but neither was denying that a new legal relationship had indeed been created by the act of the ruler in so consenting.

This brings us to our final point, the very great influence of the medieval doctrine of consent on the formation of papal political theory. There was a lively debate among the canonists of the thirteenth century on the question whether a ruler could licitly make new laws at all without the consent of his subjects and all agreed that consent was necessary for laws that were to be both licit and effective.[34] Moreover, as we have noted, the power of any temporal ruler in the thirteenth century was conceived of as

---

[32] *PL* 216, 924. "Quod tu, fili charissime, prudenter attendens, illo misericorditer inspirante in cujus manu sunt corda regum, et quo voluerit vertit illa, teipsum et regna tua etiam temporaliter ei subjicere decrevisti cui noveras spiritualiter esse subjecta; ut in unam vicarii Christi personam, quasi corpus et anima, regnum et sacerdotium uniantur..."

[33] *PL* 216, 924, "Ille utique hoc dignatus est operari qui cum sit alpha et omega finem retulit ad principium, et principium protraxit ad finem; ut illae provinciae quae olim sacrosanctam Romanam ecclesiam propriam in spiritualibus habuere magistram, hunc etiam in temporalibus dominam habeant specialem."

[34] Luigi de Luca, "L'Accetazione Popolare della Legge Canonica nel Pensiero di Graziano e dei suoi Interpreti," *Studia Gratiana*, 3 (Bologna, 1955), 193-276.

limited by a whole complex of rights inhering in his subjects. The popes themselves acknowledged, not only that they could not in practice, but that they ought not in principle to deprive lay rulers of long established rights without their consent. As Innocent III wrote to Count William of Montpellier, "You know that you are subject to other (lords) and so you cannot submit yourself to us in this matter without injuring them *unless they give consent...*" And, to the princes of Germany, "We do not wish to claim for ourselves the rights of the princes. We acknowledge, *as we ought*, that the princes... have the right and power to elect a king."[35]

In a later age Pope Pius IX pointed out that the temporal power of the medieval popes rested solely on general consent. "Its source was not the Infallibility but the authority of the pope. The latter, according to the public law then in force and by the consent of the Christian nations... extended to judging, even in the temporal field, both Princes and States."[36] In a sense the words are obviously true. Medieval popes had no armies or police power to enforce their commands throughout Europe and the sword of excommunication often proved a blunt weapon when it was used in the political arena. Evidently enough, in practice, the popes could exercise jurisdiction in temporal affairs only in so far as lay rulers consented to their doing so. But Pius IX greatly over-estimated the degree of consent that actually existed in the Middle Ages. For a more sceptical discussion on that point we might turn to a contemporary canonist. Bazianus, who was writing at the end of the twelfth century, asked in one of his *Quaestiones* whether the pope, by virtue of his *plenitudo potestatis*, could enact a law decreeing that the Roman curia should henceforth be a general forum for all cases, spiritual and secular. He concluded that the pope could not do this without the direct inspiration of the Holy Spirit and he added, not without irony, that he would believe in such inspiration only if everyone, clergy and princes alike, consented to the new ordering of things. Bazianus evidently believed that, short of a miracle indeed such consent would never be forthcoming.[37]

---

[35] *PL* 214, 1132; 216, 1065 (Kempf, *Regestum*, 168).

[36] "Questo diritto (di deporre i sovrani e liberare i popoli dall' obbligo di fedeltà) essersi talvolta, in supreme circostanze esercitato dai Pontefici; ma nulla aver esso che fare coll' *infal'ibilità pontificia*. La di lui fonte però non essere stata la *infallibilità*, ma si l'*autorità* pontificia. Questa, secondo il diritto pubblico allora vigente, e per l'accordo delle nazioni cristiani, che nel Papa riverivano il supremo giudice della cristianità, stendeasi a giudicare anche civilmente dei Principi e dei singoli Stati." *Civiltà Cattolica*, series VIII, vol. 3 (1871), 485.

[37] "Quod tunc esse credimus si omnes tam clerici quam principes ad hoc consentirent et hoc vellent." The *Quaestio* is printed in A Stickler, "Sacerdotium et Regnum nei Decretisti e Primi Decretalisti," *Salesianum*, 15 (1953), 607-608. The discrepancy between existing secular law and the popes' conception of divine law extended to innumerable points of detail apart from the

If we bear in mind that a major task for the thirteenth century popes was to maximize consent to a temporal jurisdiction which they believed was inherent in their office but which the society of their age was extremely reluctant to acknowledge it becomes much easier to discern the orderly pattern of thought that runs through their various pronouncements. This is especially true of Innocent III. The language in which he set out the papal claim to universal temporal jurisdiction was abstract, symbolical, sometimes deliberately ambiguous; the letters containing the claim were always addressed either to remote potentates abroad or to much lesser figures closer to home. When Innocent sought to intervene in the disputes of the great princes of the western world he never relied on a claim to general overlordship for he knew that any such pretension would have been angrily and publicly rejected by the lay rulers. Rather he always found some "exceptional" reason, which the princes themselves might be persuaded to accept, in order to justify his action. The king of France would have indignantly denied that the pope was his temporal overlord but there was a chance at least that he would heed Innocent's claim to judge a matter of sin. The princes of Germany would never have conceded that the pope could appoint emperors at his own will but they might have been persuaded, especially the ecclesiastical ones, by a careful exposition of the canonical rights of a consecrator.

An important stage in the development of Innocent III's political policy came with his promulgation of the official collection of papal decretals known as the *Compilatio Tertia* in 1210. When Innocent commanded that these decretals, which contained many of his most important political pronouncements, were henceforth to be used "in the schools and in the courts"[38] he ensured that neither his general claims nor his specific reasons for intervening in particular cases would be lost sight of in the subsequent development of medieval canon law. If all had gone well the intellectuals in the schools would have been won over to a theory of universal papal sovereignty while an accretion of precedents in the courts would have shown that virtually any case of major political significance could be included in one or another of the "exceptional" categories that justified the exercise of papal jurisdiction; and, eventually, the theories of the schools and the practice of the courts might have fused into an unchallengeable complex

---

general reluctance to accept the full claims of the papacy to temporal jurisdiction. In England, for instance, the laws of advowson, of testamentary dispositions and of bastardy were all out of accord with ecclesiastical teaching. Here again effective change could come about only through consent. When the barons of England were urged by the English bishops to reform the law of bastardy they replied, "Nolumus leges Angliae mutare" — and the law was not changed.

[38] *Quinque Compilationes Antiquae*, 105.

of papal power. It was in just such a fashion that papal control over the internal machinery of church government grew up between the twelfth century and the fourteenth. It was in this way too that decentralized feudal kingdoms grew into ordered national monarchies — that is to say by the growth of theories of royal supremacy side by side with small, step by step extensions of the jurisdiction of the kings' courts. The process could take place, however, only in so far as there was widespread consent to the extension of royal jurisdiction expressed in a general willingness of litigants to take advantage of new procedures that kings made available. So too, in the ecclesiastical sphere, there was no question of the popes asserting judicial supremacy over an unwilling church. It was rather the eagerness of bishops, abbots and other litigants to appeal to Rome that stimulated the process of judicial centralization. On the other hand, Innocent III's evident willingness to do justice in various kinds of secular cases evoked no such response.

The medieval popes sought to actualize all the potentialities of the regal power that had been implanted in their office — so they believed — by Christ Himself. The complexity of their statements merely reflects the complexity of the task they set themselves. As theologians they could deploy every resource of Scriptural allegory and symbolism to proclaim all the heighth and breadth and depth of papal power. As politicians and diplomats they had to work within the framework of public law that existed in their own day. As legislators they could bring about effective changes in that law only by winning general consent for their proposals. As it turned out the temporal power of the papacy never did become firmly established outside Italy precisely because the necessary consent was never forthcoming from the Christian princes and prelates and peoples of Europe.

Cornell University.

VI

Grosseteste and the Theory of Papal Sovereignty

'**B**ecause of the obedience by which I am bound to the Apostolic
See . . . filially and obediently, I do not obey, I oppose, I rebel.'[1]
The more we learn of Robert Grosseteste's achievements as theologian and scientist[2] the less likely does it seem that he will be remembered
in the future—as he used to be in the past[3]—principally for this letter of
defiance concerning papal provisions in the diocese of Lincoln. Yet the
letter itself remains something of an enigma in spite of all the attention it
has received from a long line of scholars. It may seem an unprofitable
task to go gleaning in a field where workers like Maitland and Sir Maurice
Powicke have helped with the harvest, but we would suggest that
Grosseteste's direct refusal to obey an unambiguous papal command has
never been adequately analysed from one obvious point of view—as an
extreme instance of a classical problem of political theory, the right to
resist an unjust command of a divinely ordained power.

The case can be called an extreme one both because of the status of the
parties involved and because of the nature of the correspondence that
passed between them. The pope was acknowledged to be Vicar of Christ,
head of the Church on earth, and though there did exist, already by this
time, trends of thought which sought to limit his absolute power by associat-
ing the cardinals with him in the exercise of *plenitudo potestatis* or by alleging
the superior authority of a General Council,[4] Grosseteste's writings display

---

[1] *Roberti Grosseteste Episcopi Quondam Lincolniensis Epistolae*, ed. H. R. Luard (Rolls
Series 1861), Ep. 128, 436.

[2] For recent work on Grosseteste's life and thought see the bibliography of A. C.
Crombie, *Robert Grosseteste and the origins of experimental science*, Oxford 1953, 320–52.

[3] So, at least, we are often told. E.g. Luard referred to the clash with Innocent IV as
'the transaction which has done more to make Grosseteste's name known and popular
than any other in his long and active life' (*Epistolae*, lxxix). Similarly, Mandell Creighton
(*Historical Lectures and Addresses*, London 1903) '. . . the event that made Grosseteste
most famous . . .' (145); Abbot Gasquet (*King Henry III and the Church*, London 1905)
'. . . the most serious as it is perhaps the best known incident in his whole career . . .'
(337).

[4] B. Tierney, 'A conciliar theory of the thirteenth century,' in *Catholic Historical
Review*, xxxvi (1951), 415–40; 'Ockham, the conciliar theory, and the canonists,' in
Journal of the History of Ideas, xv (1954), 40–70.

no sympathy with such ideas. On the contrary, he accepted whole-heartedly and expressed in language that reflects his own metaphysical pre-occupations, the high doctrine of papal authority propounded by Innocent III, that the pope received plenitude of power directly from God, and was himself the source of all other authority in the Church. Grosseteste even admitted that the authority he exercised as bishop came to him through the pope.[1]

Again, there existed already an elaborate jurisprudence concerning the validity of papal rescripts. Not every papal command imposed an immediate obligation of obedience on the recipient; the principle laid down in the Decretals was, 'Papal commands are to be obeyed or letters sent explaining why they cannot be obeyed.'[2] We are no longer accustomed to think of papal provisions in general as acts of arbitrary despotism but rather, in Powicke's phrase, as 'a reflection, a symbol, of the complicated texture of ecclesiastical life.' The law of the Church took heed of the 'complicated texture' by providing numerous grounds for contesting the validity of a papal rescript. The pope's letter might conflict with another papal command, it might not reflect accurately the pope's intention, it might have been obtained by misrepresentation, it might conflict with the common law of the Church concerning 'idoneity' of clerks for benefices.[3] Only when all previous privileges and all canonical impediments were explicitly abrogated by a *non obstante* clause, and when the pope affirmed that he was acting *ex certa scientia*, was his mandate to be regarded as an incontestable expression of the *plenitudo potestatis*. But that was precisely the sort of letter that Grosseteste had to deal with; it was indeed the use of the *non obstante* clause in such a fashion as to bar any appeal to the common law that drove him to the point of rebellion. From any point of view the central issue stands out simply and starkly. The pope was the supreme embodi-

---

[1] For Innocent III's doctrine see, e.g. Migne, P.L., ccxv, col. 279 (Ep. 1), 'Petrum caput ecclesiae ... qui ... in membra diffunderet ut nihil sibi penitus deperiret, quoniam in capite viget sensuum plenitudo, ad membra vero pars eorum aliqua derivatur.' (Cf. J. Rivière, 'In partem sollicitudinis ... évolution d'une formule pontificale,' *Revue des Sciences Religieuses*, v (1925), 210–31.) Grosseteste's very high conception of the papal authority is in evidence all through his letters. See especially Ep. 127, 364, '... sicut autem dominus Papa se habet ad universalem ecclesiam in potestatis plenitudine, sic se habet episcopus in potestate accepta a potestate apostolica ad suam diocesim ....' 389–90, 'Quemadmodum igitur sol, quia non potest ubique super terram simul et semel praesentialiter lucere ... de plenitudine luminis sui, nullo per hoc sibi diminuto, lunam et stellas illuminat ... Ita dominus Papa, respectu cujus omnes alii praelati sunt sicut luna et stellae, suscipientes ab ipso quicquid habent potestatis ad illuminationem et vegetationem ecclesiae, suam exhibit praesentiam ....' The image of the Holy See as a sun radiating light and life throughout the Church also occurs in the exhortation read at the papal curia in 1250, see Edward Brown, *Fasciculus Rerum Expetendarum et Fugiendarum*, London 1690, ii. 254. Mr. W. A. Pantin's translation of the relevant passage is quoted by Sir Maurice Powicke, 'Robert Grosseteste, Bishop of Lincoln,' *Bulletin of the John Rylands Library*, xxxv (1953), 482–507 at 505.

[2] I. iii. 5, 'Qualitatem negotii pro quo tibi scribitur, diligenter considerans, aut mandatum nostrum reverenter adimpleas aut per litteras tuas, quare adimplere non possis rationabilem causam praetendas.'

[3] Such points were discussed at length in the Gregorian Decretals, especially in the title, *De Rescriptis*, and in the glosses and *summae* on this title.

THEORY OF PAPAL SOVEREIGNTY

ment of God's authority on earth; his command was explicit, its rejection uncompromising.[1]

These circumstances have led some critics to deny either the reality of Grosseteste's devotion to the papacy or the authenticity of his letter of defiance. While archdeacon Perry was devoting himself to the fashionable sport of discovering premature Protestants among the leaders of medieval Catholicism, Charles Jourdain was arguing that a bishop of Grosseteste's Catholic convictions could never have written such a letter to a reigning pope.[2] The first position need not be taken seriously and the arguments advanced by Jourdain based on the manuscript tradition of the crucial letter seem untenable in the light of subsequent research.[3] If the authenticity of Grosseteste's letter is to be called into question it must be because of the inherent improbability of its contents.[4] The attitude it displays is indeed so different from that expressed in other writings of Grosseteste that commentators who have accepted it as genuine have usually been compelled either to postulate a radical change in Grosseteste's attitude to the papacy in the last years of his life,[5] or, granted that he retained to the end his high conception of papal *plenitudo potestatis*, to charge him with a logical inconsistency in committing an act of disobedience. This latter view was forcefully expressed by Maitland. 'The more we make of Grosseteste's heroism in withstanding Innocent IV the worse we think of his logical position. And bad enough it was. He had conceded to the apostolic see a power of freely dealing out ecclesiastical benefices all the world over and then had to contend that this power should be used, but not abused. Instead of the simple statement that the pope cannot lawfully provide

---

[1] The fact that Grosseteste's letter was addressed to the pope's notary, Master Innocent, not to the pope himself, does not seem materially to affect the issue. The pope sent his command through this agent; Grosseteste replied through the same man.

[2] G. G. Perry, *The Life and Times of Robert Grosseteste*, London 1871. Jourdain's criticisms were originally published in 1868 in the *Bulletin de l'Académie des Inscriptions et Belles-Lettres* and were reprinted in his *Excursions Historiques à travers le Moyen Âge*, Paris 1888, 147–71.

[3] S. Harrison Thomson, *The Writings of Robert Grosseteste*, Cambridge 1940, 171, 193, 212–3. Jourdain's arguments were criticised by J. Fehlten, *Robert Grosseteste, Bischof von Lincoln*, Freiburg 1887, 109–12. See also F. S. Stevenson, *Robert Grosseteste, Bishop of Lincoln*, London 1899, 315, 316, 319 ff.; F. M. Powicke, *King Henry III and the Lord Edward*, Oxford 1947, i. 285, n. 3.

[4] This was, indeed, Jourdain's principal argument, *Excursions Historiques*, 170–1, 'Un point demeure constant, c'est que les écrits contre la cour de Rome, attribués à Robert Grosse-Tête aussi bien que les faits correspondants, racontés dans l'*Historia major* et dans l'*Historia minor* sont en contradiction manifeste avec les opinions qui se font jour à chaque page de la correspondance authentique de l'évêque de Lincoln. La critique est donc en droit de rejeter ces écrits commes apocryphes . . . .' This conclusion was accepted and vigorously re-stated by A. L. Smith, *Church and State in the Middle Ages* (Ford Lectures delivered in 1905), Oxford 1913, 101–37. H. K. Mann took note of these criticisms, but did not commit himself concerning the authenticity of Ep. 128, *Lives of the Popes*, xiv, London 1928, 262–3.

[5] L. Dehio, *Innocenz IV. und England*, Berlin-Leipzig 1914, 75–81. Cf. W. Stubbs, *Constitutional History of England*, 3rd ed. Oxford 1887, ii. 314, 'Certainly as he grew older his attitude to the pope became more hostile.' Mandell Creighton, *Historical Lectures*, 148, 'Grosseteste, devoted to the existing ecclesiastical system as he was, an absolutely devout son of the pope, yet was driven in spite of himself into antagonism to that system . . . .'

clerks with English benefices . . . we find this indefensible distinction between use and abuse. . . . The bishop who makes a stand against the pope at the line between use and abuse is indeed heroic; but his is the heroism of despair.'[1]

In more recent years this presentation of Grosseteste's attitude has been sharply criticised by Professor Barraclough. He observes that 'Grosseteste was a bishop and administrator: he was not concerned with logical attitudinizing, but with the good government of the Church. If the effects of papal intervention in the distribution of benefices were wholesome, he had no quarrel with the system of provisions as such. The question was simply one of ways and means.'[2] Barraclough, it will be seen, does not attempt to refute Maitland's charge that Grosseteste was illogical; rather he seems to magnify it by suggesting that the great bishop would have regarded logic as irrelevant in a matter of this sort. It is certainly true that Grosseteste was primarily concerned with the good government of the Church, and any useful discussion of his attitude must insist on that fact; but the famed *Lincolniensis* did after all possess one of the most subtle and searching intellects of the thirteenth century, and it seems an oversimplification to suggest that his acknowledgment of the pope's normal right to make provisions was based solely on considerations of administrative expediency. It was rather a logical corollary of a theological proposition, which Grosseteste whole-heartedly accepted, concerning the origin and nature of papal authority. To make Grosseteste a premature pragmatist is worse than making him a premature Protestant.

The most recent writer on the problem, Professor Powicke, if we have understood him rightly, takes up a position that does not differ essentially from that of Maitland, though it is expressed in language more sympathetic to Grosseteste. With his gift for writing thirteenth-century history 'from the inside', Professor Powicke enables us to see how Grosseteste's protest was in accordance with all his moral convictions on the episcopal duty of pastoral care, and how his very exaltation of the papal dignity led him to react with unusual vehemence when confronted with abuses of papal power. But Powicke seems concerned to show that Grosseteste's attitude was psychologically comprehensible rather than that it was logically consistent. He point out that, in the thirteenth century, 'Orthodox minds

---

[1] F. W. Maitland, *Roman Canon Law in the Church of England*, London 1898, 66–7. Cf. Stevenson, *Robert Grosseteste*, 312, 'Although the language of the letter is full of vigour, the sequence of the thoughts is less logical than when Grosseteste's faculties were in their prime.'

[2] *Papal Provisions*, Oxford 1935, 169. And again, 'Maitland himself was one of the first to protest against reading the history of the mediaeval Church through Protestant spectacles; but the mere application to Grosseteste of "the simple statement that the pope cannot lawfully provide clerks with English benefices", is anachronous . . . It was an attitude impossible for a churchman in the thirteenth century.' It is hard to see the point of this criticism. Maitland's whole argument was designed to establish the fact that Professor Barraclough himself seems concerned to emphasise—that Grosseteste could not have relied on a 'simple statement' of the ancient practice of the Church, because neither he, nor any other English bishop of the time, denied the validity of the contemporary decretals which claimed universal authority for the pope.

were more outspoken than they were in post-Tridentian times in their criticism of papal behaviour.'[1] This is very true and very relevant. It explains Grosseteste's 'sermon' to the papal curia; it would explain a vigorous protest against any specific papal action of which he disapproved; but it does not seem adequately to explain an act of direct disobedience to an authority whose divinely conferred power to command Grosseteste had acknowledged over and over again. And, in the matter of Frederick de Lavagna, he did not merely protest; he flatly refused to obey. One is still left with the problem that Mandell Creighton formulated in discussing Grosseteste's position. 'If we grant spiritual supremacy and unlimited power, is it possible to define either the contents or the limits and restrictions of that power?'[2]

One might observe at this point that, if the question at issue were one of disobedience to the unjust command of a temporal ruler, it would present no great problem or paradox, at least to the historian of political theory. We have been told so often and so emphatically—perhaps too emphatically —that the Middle Ages had no true conception of secular sovereignty, that the authority of a king was limited by custom and natural law, that the ruler who governed unjustly became a tyrant whose commands carried no obligation of obedience. Such limitations on kingship are familiar enough; but there has been no comparable enquiry into the influence of these medieval preconceptions on the theory of papal authority that was built up by Grosseteste's contemporaries in the first half of the thirteenth century. It has usually been vaguely assumed that the powers attributed to the pope as Vicar of God were such as to exclude any possibility of legitimate disobedience to a papal command. As Fritz Kern put it, '. . . on the whole, the contrast between the ecclesiastical and the secular authorities was considered to lie in the fact that the former, being in the last resort infallible, was worthy of unconditional obedience, whilst the latter, being fallible, was not to be accepted without conditions.'[3] It is this under-

---

[1] F. M. Powicke, art. cit., 503.   [2] *Historical Lectures*, 148.

[3] F. Kern, *Gottesgnadentum und Widerstandsrecht im früheren Mittelalter*, Leipzig 1914, 183. The translation is that of S. B. Chrimes, *Kingship and Law*, Oxford 1939, 89. See also Chrimes, 112: 'In the Church papal infallibility and exemption from every jurisdiction were claimed and unconditional obedience was demanded from the laity.' In a note to the first quotation (*Gottesgnadentum*, 183, n. 337) Kern pointed out that the infallibility (*Unfehlbarkeit*) of the Church was not held necessarily to reside in the person of the pope. Perhaps the use of the word infallibility at all, with its overtones of modern controversies, is unfortunate; the doctrine concerning the indefectibility of the whole Church, which was commonly held in the early Middle Ages, had little to do with the question at issue. See A. Van Leeuwen, 'L'Église, règle de foi chez Occam,' *Ephemerides Theologiae Lovanienses*, xi (1934), 249–88, A. M. Landgraf, 'Scattered remarks on the development of dogma and on papal infallibility,' *Theological Studies*, vii (1946), 577 ff. The question of the right to resist a tyrannical pope was also raised briefly by Gierke, but he referred only to the doctrines of fourteenth- and fifteenth-century conciliarists on this point, see Gierke-Maitland, *Political Theories of the Middle Age*, Cambridge 1900, 36: 'Gradually also the doctrines of Conditional Obedience, of a right of resistance against Tyranny, of a right of revolution conferred by necessity were imported into the domain of ecclesiastical polity' (referring to the works of Ockham, Gerson, Dietrich of Niem, Andreas Randulf, Antonius de Rosellis, Nicholas of Cues).

lying assumption that has made Grosseteste's letter seem illogical to some critics and unauthentic to others; some further enquiry into its validity may help to explain both the position that Grosseteste adopted and the arguments by which he defended it.

It is to the canon lawyers that we must turn for the most penetrating discussions on problems of papal authority in the age of Innocent III and Innocent IV. Grosseteste himself was no professional lawyer indeed (and he had hard things to say about the canonists on occasion) but we may be sure that, as an active administrator, frequently immersed in legal business, he was familiar with the basic principles of ecclesiastical law.[1] Nor need we doubt that, in his younger days, as a brilliant scholar and teacher with an exceptionally enquiring mind, he would have been familiar with at least the major controversies concerning the right government of the Church that were being vigorously pursued in the law schools of Paris and Oxford as well as at Bologna around the turn of the twelfth and thirteenth centuries.[2] The canonists of that period were putting forward ever more extreme claims for the papacy, especially in the realm of temporal affairs, but they never altogether lost sight of the possible dangers to the Church that could arise from abuse of the great powers they conceded to the pope. They did, in fact, think it possible to develop a most exalted doctrine of papal *plenitudo potestatis*, but still to 'define the contents' and even the 'limits and restrictions' of that power.

Although the precise issue of resistance to papal commands has attracted little attention, it has sometimes been pointed out in standard histories of political theory that the authority attributed to medieval popes, even by their most enthusiastic supporters, was never wholly irresponsible nor wholly arbitrary.[3] A pope could be deposed, at least in the one case of

[1] The letter of Giraldus Cambrensis to the bishop of Hereford on behalf of the young Grosseteste referred not only to his skill in the liberal arts but also to his usefulness 'in the decision of cases', *Giraldi Cambrensis Opera*, ed. J. S. Brewer (Rolls Series 1861), i. 249. Grosseteste's familiarity with *Decretum* and Decretals is especially in evidence in Ep. 72 (Luard, 205–34).

[2] On the French school of canonists see Stephan Kuttner, 'Les débuts de l'école canoniste française,' *Studia et Documenta Historia et Iuris*, iv (1938), 193–204; and on the English school, Stephan Kuttner and Eleanor Rathbone, 'Anglo-Norman canonists of the twelfth century,' *Traditio*, vii (1949–51), 279–358. For information concerning the various canonists mentioned in the text see J. F. v. Schulte, *Die Geschichte der Quellen und Literatur des canonischen Rechts*, i, Stuttgart 1875; S. Kuttner, *Repertorium der Kanonistik*, i, Città del Vaticano 1937, and *idem*, 'Bernardus Compostellanus Antiquus,' *Traditio*, i (1943), 277–340; A. Van Hove, *Prolegomena* (Commentarium Lovaniense in Codicem Iuris Canonici, I, i, Malines-Rome 1945).

[3] A. J. Carlyle, *A History of Mediaeval Political Theory in the West*, London 1928, ii. 164–78, provides a discerning analysis of Gratian's views on the pope's authority in relation to existing canon law. Carlyle's discussion of the Decretists' treatment of the question (178–94) is interesting but based on a very narrow selection of texts. C. H. McIlwain also discussed the theoretical limits to the pope's competence in *The Growth of Political Thought in the West*, New York 1932, 279, 283–4. His illustrations were taken from the works of fourteenth-century papal publicists but their arguments in turn were usually borrowed from thirteenth-century canonistic sources. See also Maitland, *Canon Law in England*, 11–12; A. L. Smith, *Church and State*, 85–91; F. Gillmann, 'Romanus pontifex iura omnia in scrinio pectoris sui censetur habere,' in *Archiv für katholisches Kirchenrecht*, xcii (1912), 3–17.

heresy,[1] and he was bound by the ancient law of the Church, at least in two defined spheres of activity. Gratian wrote at one point of the *Decretum* that only those papal decretals were binding 'in quibus nec praecedentium patrum decretis nec Evangelicis praeceptis aliquid contrarium invenitur',[2] and went on to cite the case of a pope who was punished by God and repudiated by the Church because he acted 'against the decrees of God and of his predecessors and successors.' But, in a later, more detailed discussion, Gratian maintained that the Roman church was not bound by the earlier canons since it was the source of their authority: 'Sacrosancta Romana ecclesia ius et auctoritatem sacris canonibus impertitur, sed non eis alligatur.'[3] The commentators on the *Decretum*, faced with these apparently contradictory opinions, evolved a doctrine that became generally accepted in the early thirteenth century. They held that, although the pope was not bound by every detail of the early canons and could normally grant special dispensations contrary to their general provisions, nevertheless he was bound by them in matters touching the Christian faith and also in matters touching the 'general state of the Church'. 'Nec a papa quidem canones possunt abrogari, puta de articulis fidei vel de generali statu ecclesiae.'[4] There was also much elaborate discussion concerning possible limitations on papal authority by the precepts of Scripture and by natural law (especially in the matter of oaths and vows). The tendency was to concede to the pope the maximum freedom of action in such matters, but some limits were always recognised, at least in theory. It was usually held, for instance, that a pope could not dissolve a consummated marriage nor dispense from a vow of chastity, and that the pope's powers did not license him to sin or to lead others into sin.[5] Such specific limitations were recognised even by a canonist like Tancred who, when indulging in

---

[1] This was universally acknowledged in the Middle Ages. A selection of canonistic texts illustrating the point was printed by J. F. v. Schulte, *Die Stellung der Concilien, Päpste und Bischöfe*, Prague 1871, 253–69. For further references see Gierke-Maitland, *Political Theories*, 154, n. 176.

[2] *Dist.* 19 *dictum Gratiani post* c. 8.

[3] 25 q. 1 *dictum Gratiani post* c. 16.

[4] Huguccio, *Summa ad Dist.* 4 *post* c. 3, MS. 72 of Pembroke College, Cambridge, fol. 119ra, and again *ad Dist.* 15 c. 2, fol. 125vb, *ad Dist.* 16 c. 9, fol. 126rb, *Dist.* 40 c. 6, fol. 147vb. These limitations on the pope's authority were commonly recognised, e.g. by Rufinus, *Summa* (ed. Singer, Paderborn 1902) *ad Dist.* 4; *Glossa Palatina ad* 25 q. 1 c. 3 and 25 q. 2 c. 17, MS. O.10.2 of Trinity College, Cambridge, fol. 35vb and fol. 37va; Joannes Teutonicus, *Glossa Ordinaria ad* 25 q. 1 c. 3, 25 q. 2 c. 17; Tancred, Gloss *ad Comp. III*, II. vi. 3, MS. 17 of Gonville and Caius College, Cambridge, fol. 197vb; Bernardus Parmensis, *Glossa Ordinaria ad Decretales*, II. xiii. 13, III. viii. 4; Hostiensis, *Summa Aurea*, Venetiis 1570, *De Constitutionibus*, fol. 7vb.

[5] For typical discussions of such questions see Bernardus Parmensis, *Glossa Ordinaria ad* I. vii. 2, I. ix. 11, II. xiii. 13, II. xxiv. 18, III. viii. 4, III. xxxv. 6. It was often held that the pope could not annul natural law or divine law but that he could interpret them: e.g. Raymundus de Pennaforte, *Summa Iuris*, ed. J. R. Serra, Barcelona 1945, 38, 'Licet autem dixerim nullam dispensationem admittendam contra ius naturale tamen papa potest ipsum interpretari. . . .' The power to 'interpret' might in practice prove very elastic, as was emphasised by W. Ullmann, *Medieval Papalism*, London 1949, 50–75, but it was never altogether limitless. On the bounds of the pope's dispensatory authority see J. Brys, *De dispensatione in iure canonico praesertim apud Decretistas et Decretalistas usque ad medium saeculum decimum quartum*, Bruges 1925.

rhetorical generalities, carried the exaltation of papal *plenitudo potestatis* to the utmost peak in phrases that passed into the *Glossa Ordinaria* on the Gregorian Decretals, and subsequently became a part of the standard equipment of the fourteenth-century papal publicists: 'In is gerit vicem dei quia sedet in loco Jesu Christi qui est verus deus et verus homo . . . item de nichilo facit aliquid. . . . Item in is gerit vicem dei quia plenitudinem potestatis habet in rebus ecclesiasticis. . . . Item quia dispensare potest supra ius et contra ius. . . . Nec est qui dicat ei, cur ita facis.'[1] In spite of such sentiments Tancred thought that the pope could not dispense *contra articulos fidei vel generale statutum ecclesiae*, nor in questions of monastic poverty and chastity.[2]

All this is relatively straight-forward. Maitland observed that, 'As a matter of fact, popes do not attempt to repeal the ten commandments'; and we need not be surprised to find even the medieval canonists pointing out that it was improper for them to do so. Of course a pope was not expected to teach heresy or to issue unjust commands or to bring ruin on the Church. But what if he did? There is the crux of our problem—and Grosseteste's; and it was a problem quite familiar to the medieval canonists as well. The whole question of unjust decisions by ecclesiastical superiors was raised by Gratian in the third *Quaestio* of *Causa* 11 of the *Decretum*. He first cited some forty texts tending to prove that even unjust sentences were to be respected and unjust commands obeyed; but then, following his normal dialectical technique, he went on to argue the other and stronger side of the case. 'Quod autem iniustae sententiae parendum non sit, multis auctoritatibus probatur';[3] and there were even more texts cited in support of this point of view. Perhaps the one that expresses the essence of the argument most succinctly is c. 92: 'Non semper malum est non obedire praecepto, cum enim Dominus iubet ea quae sunt contraria Deo, tunc ei obediendum non est.' However, all this argumentation dealt with obedience in general, not with the specific issue of disobedience to papal commands. If the question had been simply whether one should obey God or man, no medieval lawyer or theologian would have hesitated; the problem of disobedience to a pope was so difficult precisely because the pope was said to 'stand in place of Jesus Christ who is true God and true man', because, as the canonists were fond of pointing out, his edicts were promulgated not by human but by divine authority. If that dictum had been applied to every papal command, there could evidently have been no basis for licit disobedience in any circumstances, but the canonists did not in practice press it so rigorously. The *Glossa Ordinaria* to the Decretals, for instance, declared that, 'quod fit auctoritate Papae dicitur fieri

---

[1] Gloss *ad Comp. III*, I. v.3, Caius MS. 17, fol. 147va. Repeated by Bernardus Parmensis, *Glossa Ordinaria ad* I. vii. 3.

[2] Gloss *ad Comp. III*, II. vi. 3, Caius MS. 17, fol. 197vb, 'Dominus papa potest dispensare in omnibus quae non sunt contra articulos fidei vel generale statutum ecclesiae . . . nec in his quae sunt contra substantiam monachatus ut monachus haberet uxorem vel proprium . . . nec in his quae in sui natura sunt mala ut quis sine peccato posset adulterari.'

[3] 11 q. 3 *dictum Gratiani post* c. 43.

auctoritate Dei,' but added at once, 'et est verum, *si iusta causa hoc faciat.*'[1]

Grosseteste based his whole case on the assertion that not every command emanating from the pope was supported by the divine authority of the Apostolic See: '. . . contra Ipsum autem nec est nec esse potest Apostolicae sedis sanctitas divinissima. Non est igitur praedictae literae, tenor Apostolicae sanctitati consonus . . . .'[2] And this led him to his concluding declaration that, precisely in order to remain loyal and obedient to the Apostolic See, it was necessary for him to disobey that particular command of the pope. One might have expected that this sharp distinction between the person of a ruler and the institution that he represented would have attracted the attention of constitutional historians, coming as it does from a most influential bishop about half a century before the English barons declared that their allegiance was owed to the Crown, not to the person of the king, and that, in defence of the Crown, they might lawfully take up arms against the king. But Grosseteste's argument has usually been passed over as a piece of 'epigrammatic and paradoxical language', 'a strange form of words', 'a curious formula'. The distinction between the pope and the Apostolic See upon which he relied was in fact no invention of Grosseteste but was well established in the glosses of the preceding half century. Huguccio, commenting on an assertion that all the decrees of the Apostolic See were to be obeyed, put the point quite explicitly. 'Hoc non fit ratione papae sed propter auctoritatem sedis, unde caute dixit apostolicae sedis et non dixit apostolici.'[3] Laurentius, approaching the question from a different angle, explained that it was possible to distinguish between the source of authority of an office and that of the individual who occupied the office.[4] There is, moreover, an interesting English gloss written in the last years of the twelfth century which seems precisely to anticipate Grosseteste's argument that one could resist the pope while remaining in communion with the see of Peter. The author was considering the case of the Roman clergy who deserted the erring pope Anastasius, and suggested that they sinned in doing so since all Catholics were required to remain in communion with the Apostle Peter or with 'eo qui sedet pro Petro'. His reply was that, in this case, 'Anastasius non fuit de societate Petri, sed cardinales erant . . . .'[5] Finally, Joannes Teutonicus, in his *Glossa*

---

[1] Bernardus Parmensis, *Glossa Ordinaria ad* I. vii. 2.

[2] Luard, Ep. 128, 434.

[3] *Summa ad Dist.* 19 c. 2, Pembroke MS. 72, fol. 128rb.

[4] His view was cited by S. Mochi Onory, *Fonti canonistiche dell' idea moderna dello stato*, Milano 1951, 196, '. . . set dic quod aliud est ipsa iurisdictio per se inspecta, que a Deo processit, et aliud, quod ipsius iurisdictionis executionem consequatur aliquis per populum . . . Nam populus per electionem facit imperatorem, set non imperium, sicut cardinales per electionem preferunt aliquem sibi ad iurisdictionem, que a Deo data est, exercendam.'

[5] The gloss was commenting on 24 q. 1 c. 27, 'Quicunque ab unitate fidei vel societatis Petri Apostoli quolibet modo semetipsos segregant, tales nec vinculi peccati absolvi. . . .' It runs, '*societatis*, i.e. ab eo qui sedet pro Petro sed tunc 19 *dist. Anastasius* contra. Solutio, Anastasius non fuit de societate Petri sed cardinales erant.' Caius MS. 676, fol. 166ra. On the date and provenance of this work see S. Kuttner and E. Rathbone, art. cit., 317–21.

Ordinaria to the *Decretum*, maintained that, in promulgating a law that endangered the Church, a pope stripped himself of the authority pertaining to the head of the Church, so that the law was of no effect.[1] A good deal of the 'illogicality' of Grosseteste's attitude disappears when one realises that, according to the prevailing opinion of the time, there was no certain presumption that every papal command was consistent with the divine will nor supported by divine authority. After all, the crimes and errors of several popes had been described in the *Decretum*; there were elaborate discussions concerning the steps to be taken against a pope who fell into heresy; and, though one text of the *Decretum* declared that the pope was to be presumed holy, the *Glossa Ordinaria* rather drily commented, 'It does not say that he is holy but only that he is to be presumed holy until the contrary is established.'[2]

One is left with the problem of whether, and in what circumstances, a subject could take it upon himself to assume that the pope was so grievously at fault that there was a duty to disobey his command. Once again, if one looks only at the canonistic generalities—'Nemo iudicabit primam sedem', 'Papa a nemine potest iudicari'—it would seem that there could be no such right or duty; but, again, one finds that the generalities were considerably modified in discussions on particular cases. The issue was posed for the Decretists by two consecutive chapters which Gratian cited in support of the proposition, 'Quod absque discretione iustitiae nulli agere licet.' The first declared,

'Quidquid ergo sine discretione iustitiae contra huius (Romanae ecclesiae) disciplinam actum fuerit, ratum habere ratio nulla permittit.'[3]

The second, in the same strain, laid down that,

'Praeceptis Apostolicis non dura superbia resistatur sed . . . quae . . . Apostolica auctoritate iussa sunt salutifere impleantur.'

Having regard to the context it would seem that Gratian meant to suggest that *cum discretione* or *sine dura superbia* it might be permissible to resist, and this was assumed without question by earlier commentators like Rufinus and Stephanus Tornacensis.[4] Huguccio, however, would have none of this. No one could judge the act of the pope, he argued, and so it was impossible to act *cum discretione* against the discipline of the Roman church,

---

[1] *Glossa Ordinaria ad Dist.* 40 c. 6. After setting out the usual doctrine that a pope could be deposed for heresy Joannes Teutonicus went on, 'Item nunquid papa posset statuere quod non posset accusari de haeresi. Respondeo quod non, quia ex hoc periclitaretur tota ecclesia quod non licet . . . quia hoc fit in eo casu quo desinit esse caput ecclesiae et ita non tenet constitutio.'

[2] *Glossa Ordinaria ad Dist.* 40 c. 1, 'Sed non dicitur hic quod sancti sunt sed quod sancti praesumuntur donec contrarium constet.'

[3] *Dist.* 12 c. 1.

[4] Rufinus, ed. cit., *ad Dist.* 12, 'Dictum erat quod nulli preter consuetudinem romane ecclesie faciendum est; sed ne hoc omnino absolute intelligeretur, determinat quod cum discretione iustitie aliquando secus licet.' Stephanus Tornacensis, *Summa* (ed. Schulte, Giessen 1891) *ad Dist.* 12 c. 1, '*Sine discretione*. Alterum cum discretione fieri. . . .'

and Gratian was wrong to envisage such a situation.[1] The suggestion that one might resist the pope, not with pride but with humility, evoked the same comment from Huguccio.

'. . . non esset humilitas sed superbia, non esset discretio sed indiscretio si ei resistatur, et sic non facit ad propositionum Gratiani.'[2]

Yet, when he came to consider the words *iussa sunt salutifere*, Huguccio did acknowledge the possibility of licit resistance in some circumstances.

'*Salutifere*. Si contra salutem aliquid praecipitur non est parendum, et est argumentum quod non omnia statuta a praelatis sunt observanda sed tantum illa quae statuenda sunt salutifere.'[3]

Commenting on these passages a century later, Guido de Baysio observed that Huguccio first contradicted Gratian and then contradicted himself.[4] It would seem more correct to suggest that he was shifting the emphasis from the subjective disposition of the recipient of a command to the objective nature of the command itself. In all these discussions one is aware of the intense medieval conviction of an objective moral law whose tenets were accessible to a man of good will and good sense, and whose precepts were to be obeyed in preference to those of any human superior, whether prince or pope.

In the next generation the *Glossa Ordinaria* sharply denied any right to disobey.

'Nunquid ergo cum discretione iustum est contra illam agere? Certe non . . . unde vacet hic argumentum a contrario sensu.'[5]

This view was also held by Joannes Faventinus,[6] but it does not reflect a general consensus of opinion. The *Glossa Palatina* repeated Huguccio's argument that a command *contra salutem* was not to be obeyed, and added the suggestion that a papal command *contra ius* should not be obeyed at once, but a second message awaited;[7] Goffredus Tranensis returned to the

---

[1] *Summa ad Dist.* 12 c. 1, Pembroke MS. 72, fol. 124ra. Huguccio drew a distinction between following a local practice different from that of the Roman church, but not forbidden by it, and acting against the discipline of Rome. 'Sed nunquid cum discretione licet agere contra disciplinam romanae ecclesiae, nunquid licet alicui judicare de facto papae? . . . Dico ergo vacat argumentum a sensu contrario nec facit ad propositum magistri . . . licet ergo cum discretione aliter agere quam romana ecclesia teneat, sed nec cum discretione nec sine discretione licet agere contra disciplinam eius.'

[2] *Summa ad Dist.* 12 c. 2, Pembroke MS. 72, fol. 124ra.

[3] Ibid. The argument recurred in very similar form in Ockham's *Breviloquium* (ed. L. Baudry, Paris 1937), II. xxi, 61. See 'Ockham, the conciliar theory, and the canonists,' 45–6.

[4] *Rosarium seu in Decretorum Volumen Commentaria*, Venetiis 1577, *Dist.* 12 cc. 1, 2, fol. 15ra–15rb.

[5] *Glossa Ordinaria ad Dist.* 12 c. 1.

[6] For his view and that of Goffredus Tranensis see *Rosarium ad Dist.* 12, fol. 15ra.

[7] Vatican MS. Pal. Lat. 658, fol. 3rb, Gloss *ad Dist.* 12 c. 1; 'Quid ergo quod romana ecclesia aliquid praecipit contra ius. Dico quod non statim est faciendum sed secunda responsio est expectanda.' Gloss *ad Dist.* 12 c. 2; '*Salutifere impleantur* . . . et est argumentum quod non quaecumque a praelatis statuuntur observare tenemur, nisi salutifere sint statuta.'

old point of view that *cum discretione* resistance was permissible. The discussion was continued in glosses on the Gregorian Decretals with special emphasis on the proper attitude to a papal rescript *contra ius*. Raymundus de Pennaforte, the compiler of the Decretals and, incidentally, a correspondent of Grosseteste,[1] wrote in his early *Summa Iuris* that such a rescript should be rejected,[2] and Goffredus Tranensis expressed the same opinion, taking up a similar position in his *Summa* on the Decretals to that expressed in his gloss on *Dist.* 12 of the *Decretum*.[3] Hostiensis held that a rescript destructive of divine law should be utterly rejected. 'Si sit destructivum iuris Evangelici vel Apostolici omnino respuitur.'[4] (One is reminded of Grosseteste's '. . . his quoque quae mandatis Apostolicis adversantur, parentalem zelans honorem, adversor et obsto.') Hostiensis also, in his discussion on the title, *De Maioritate et Obedientia*, provided a brief treatise on the whole principle of canonical obedience which included a discussion on the proper limits of that obedience. An evil command was not to be obeyed, he wrote, provided that there was no doubt whatsoever as to its injustice; if there was any doubt it was better for the subject to obey.[5] The same reservation was put forward by Bernardus Parmensis in his *Glossa Ordinaria* on the Decretals. He was discussing the text, 'Qui non obedierit principi morte moriatur', and, after explaining that *princeps* in this context could be taken to mean the pope, he went on,

'Vel dic qui non obedierit iusto praecepto, 11 q. 3 *si dominus*. Si est iniustum et hoc manifestum, non obediat ut ibi et c. *Iulianus*. Si dubium esset praeceptum principis, propter bonum obedientiae, quod sibi praecipit, faciat . . .'[6]

These texts suggest that, according to canonistic doctrine, the obedience due to the pope was subject to qualifications and limitations. How-

---

[1] Luard, Ep. 37, 128.

[2] *Summa Iuris*, ed. cit., 28; 'Si dubitatur utrum rescriptum habeat vim constitutionis, videas utrum sit secundum ius, aut preter ius, aut contra ius. In primo et secundo casu est epistola decretalis, et habet auctoritatem canonis in causis definiendis. . . . In tertio casu, scilicet cum est contra ius, reiciendum est.'

[3] *Summa super titulos Decretalium*, Venetiis 1601, fol. 4, n. 6.

[4] *Summa Aurea*, Venetiis 1570, *De Rescriptis*, fol. 11va.

[5] *Summa Aurea, De Maioritate et Obedientia*, fol. 90vb–fol. 93ra, '. . . secularis vero et regularis consequenter obedire debet preceptis maioris in his quae pertinent ad divinum cultum, vel respiciunt utilitatem communem . . . ideo si quid precipiat maior quod canonicis obviet institutis servandum non est . . . hoc si certum est quod iniustum sive iniquum sit . . . nunquam enim propter obedientiam malum committendum, licet bonum aliquando debeat intermitti . . . alias in dubio obediendum est . . .' (fol. 92rb). Hostiensis, one of the most eminent jurists of the thirteenth century, lived for several years in England in the service of Henry III. The most recent survey of his life and thought is that of C. Lefebvre, *Dictionnaire de Droit Canonique* (1953), s.v. Hostiensis. On his stay in England see F. M. Powicke, *King Henry III and the Lord Edward*, i, 272–3; N. Didier, 'Henri de Suse en Angleterre,' *Studi in Onore di Vincenzo Arangio-Ruiz*, Napoli 1953, 333–51.

[6] *Glossa Ordinaria ad* I. xxxiii. 2. Bernardus expressed himself more ambiguously in his gloss *ad* I. xiv. 4: 'Si enim ex certa scientia scriberet papa pro minori eius mandato esset obediendum quia sacrilegii instar obtinet, dubitare an is sit dignus quem Princeps eligit. . . . Praeterea contra ius et contra publicam utilitatem est tale rescriptum et ideo non valet. . . . Item est hic argumentum quod non est obediendum semper mandato Papae . . . sed non dicitur mandatum, quando ignoranter mandat.'

ever, we have not so far mentioned the canonist whose views on the whole question must seem most interesting and relevant in the present context— that is, of course, Grosseteste's adversary, pope Innocent IV himself. Matthew Paris has left us a vivid if not wholly reliable account of the great pontiff's angry reaction when he learned of Grosseteste's defiance; there is a certain piquancy in investigating his treatment of the question at issue when, as one of the greatest lawyers of his age, he reviewed it dispassionately in the calm of the study. Needless to say, Innocent was, in theory as well as in practice, an extreme exponent of the theory of papal *plenitudo potestatis*. Even if one sets aside the difficult question of his conception of the temporal power of the papacy, it is still clear that he pressed the papal claims beyond all previous bounds. In his *Commentaria* the limits of the pope's dispensatory authority were stretched further than ever before;[1] the pope's immunity from all human judgment was vigorously reemphasised; and, characteristically, Innocent showed himself less willing than his predecessors to condone resistance to papal commands even when there was just cause for disobedience. Even then, he held, it was sinful for the subject to disobey unless he was permitted to do so by the author of the command,[2] and, apparently, papal rescripts *contra ius vel publicam utilitatem* were to be held valid provided only that they were issued *ex certa scientia*.[3]

But even Innocent IV found it necessary to admit certain exceptions to this general rule. For instance, he acknowledged that monks who were commanded to act in violation of their monastic vows ought not to obey even if the command came from the pope: 'Quia etiam si papa mandaret eis aliquid, quod esset contra substantiam ordinis, vel peccatum, non deberent obedire.'[4] There was an interesting discussion too concerning the pope's authority in relation to episcopal rights. Innocent raised the question whether a pope could take away a bishop's power to administer the sacrament of confirmation, and argued that, while the pope could not abolish the sacrament itself, he could make such regulations concerning its administration as to exclude any particular bishop from conferring it. But he went on,

'Tamen si papa talia faceret sine causa magna et aliis nota non debet sustineri tanquam faciens contra generalem statum ecclesiae.'[5]

---

[1] E.g., in the matter of monastic poverty and celibacy. *In Quinque Libros Decretalium Commentaria*, Venetiis 1570, 517, ad III. xxxv. 6.

[2] *Commentaria ad* I. iv, *Rubrica*, 40: 'Vel dicas et melius quod contra iura et contra praecepta venire licet his, quibus licitum est novam legem et specialem introducere contra illud ius vel praeceptum similiter, et novam consuetudinem. Sed si tale esset, quod contra illud ius vel praeceptum non licet sine peccato legem specialem statuere; et ad hoc, ut non peccet ille qui contra ius vel praeceptum domini papae facit, opportet quod ex aliqua iusta causa faciat, et volens consuetudinem introducere, et superiore consentiente, scilicet eo qui legem fecit, vel qui potestatem habet condendi legem contra illud ius, vel mandatum.'

[3] *Commentaria ad* I. xiv. 4, 125: 'Non enim semper literis papae obediendum est, quia decipi potest papa . . . sunt enim literae aliquando contra ius vel publicam utilitatem, unde non valent, nisi ex certa scientia facta inde mentione quod pro minus literato vel minore scriberet.'

[4] *Commentaria ad* V. iii. 34, 601.   [5] *Commentaria ad* I. iv. 4, 41.

The words *non debet sustineri* seem to imply a right of resistance, but Innocent did not pursue the question further at this point. His most detailed treatment of the whole problem was reserved for the last pages of his treatise. C. 44 of the title, *De Sententia Excommunicationis* in the Decretals dealt with the case of a man who, after his marriage, discovered the existence of an impediment which rendered the marriage invalid. The decretal laid down that it was then his duty, under pain of mortal sin, to abstain from conjugal relations with his wife, and—provided he was acting with certain knowledge—he was required to do so in the face of any ecclesiastical sentence to the contrary, even to the point of undergoing excommunication if necessary.[1] As the *Glossa Ordinaria* commented, 'potius debet omnia mala pati quam contra conscientiam peccatum operari mortale.'[2] Innocent took this case, which so clearly raised the issue of the subject's conscience, as the basis for further enquiries into the limits of the obedience due to an ecclesiastical superior. What if a bishop issued, under pain of excommunication, an unjust command whose fulfilment did not actually involve the subject in mortal sin? He need not obey, wrote Innocent, but should appeal to a superior for absolution from the sentence. That led inevitably to the next question. What if the command came from the pope who had no superior?

'Sed quid si papa iniustum praecipiat qui superiorem non habet cum quo agi possit. Potest dici quod si de spiritualibus vel ecclesiasticis personis aliquid praecipit, etiam iniustum, illud servandum est quia nemini licet de eius factis iudicare 40 *dist. si papa*, 9 q. 3 c. *cuncta* et multis aliis cc . . .'

So far it was merely a re-assertion of the claim that even unjust commands of the pope were to be obeyed; but the conclusion of the passage introduced very significant reservations.

---

[1] V. xxxix. 44: 'In primo casu debet potius excommunicationis sententiam humiliter sustinere, quam per carnale commercium peccatum operari mortale.' It is interesting to note that this authoritative decretal of Innocent III directly contradicts a twelfth-century opinion quoted by A. L. Smith, *Church and State*, 54–5: 'A *Summa Quaestionum*, a book of problems more than thirty years before the Lateran Council, had put the case of a man bound to adhere to a wife whom he knows to be not really his wife. "Yet he sins not if he is obeying a command of the Church. . . . If the objection be raised that he is acting against his conscience and therefore sins, we answer he must let conscience go".'

[2] *Glossa Ordinaria ad* V. xxxix. 44. Grosseteste, indeed, did not profess himself willing to undergo punishment for his disobedience, but rather declared in advance that no action could be taken against him for his conduct. Luard, Ep. 128, 437: 'Nec ob hoc potest inde vestra discretio quicquam durum contra me statuere, quia omnis mea in hac parte et dictio et actio, nec contradictio est nec rebellio, sed filialis divino mandato debita patri et matri honoratio.' But the whole issue of 'passive resistance' as against 'active resistance' assumed a different form when the penalty involved was a spiritual one whose main sanction was its effect on the soul of the excommunicated party; for the question naturally arose whether an unjust sentence of excommunication could be binding in the eyes of God even though promulgated by the pope. The point was often discussed by the canonists in connection with the words, 'Quodcumque ligaveris super terram erit ligatum et in caelis.' The more common opinion held that an unjust papal excommunication might bind as regards the Church Militant, but not as regards the Church Triumphant. This was the view, e.g. of Joannes Teutonicus, *Glossa Ordinaria ad* 11 q. 3 c. 48, 24 q. 1 c. 5, c. 6.

THEORY OF PAPAL SOVEREIGNTY

'. . . nemini licet de eius factis iudicare . . . nisi mandatum haeresim contineret, quia tunc esset peccatum, vel nisi ex praecepto iniusto vehementer praesumeretur statum ecclesiae turbari, vel etiam forte alia mala ventura esse, quia tunc peccant obediendo . . .'[1]

Nisi . . . vehementer praesumeretur statum ecclesiae turbari. That is exactly what Grosseteste did presume! *Quia tunc peccant obediendo.* That was the whole substance of Grosseteste's protest. One is faced with the irony that his conduct can be justified out of the writings of Innocent IV himself, for Grosseteste defended his 'rebellion' on precisely the grounds that Innocent conceded as justifying disobedience to a papal command. He was vehemently convinced that the pope's policy was disrupting the peace and order of the Church.

'. . . primo, quia de illius literae et aliarum ei consimilium longe lateque dispersarum superaccumulato *Non obstante* . . . scatet cataclysmus inconstantiae, audaciae, et procacitatis etiam inverecundae mentiendi et fallendi, diffidentiae cuiquam credendi vel fidem adhibendi, et ex his consequentium vitiorum, quorum non est numerus, Christianae religionis puritatem et socialis conversationis hominum tranquillitatem commovens et perturbans.'[2]

And, accordingly, he argued that obedience to the pope's command would involve mortal sin, and, moreover, a sin more damnable and detestable than any since Lucifer's.

'Praeterea, post peccatum Luciferi . . . non est nec esse potest alterum genus peccati tam adversum et contrarium Apostolorum doctrinae et Evangelicae . . . quam animas curae pastoralis officio et ministerio vivificandas et salvandas, pastoralis officii et ministerii defraudatione mortificare et perdere.'[3]

Even a brief survey of contemporary opinions on the limits of the obedience due to the pope makes it possible to re-consider some of the arguments that have been advanced against the authenticity of Grosseteste's letter. Some critics have emphasised the 'general' language in which it was written, and have suggested that, if Grosseteste wrote it at all, it was intended as a protest against the papal policy as a whole, not as a direct refusal to a specific command.[4] It seems more probable that Grosseteste, taking the extreme step of resisting the pope, was couching his letter in the language best calculated to justify such resistance. Like

---

[1] *Commentaria ad* V. xxxix. 44, 661. The edition cited has 'nisi ex praecepto *iusto* vehementer praesumeretur'. *Iniusto* is given in the edition of Frankfürt 1570 and seems obviously preferable in this context. There is no critical edition of Innocent's work.
[2] Luard, Ep. 128, 434.   [3] Ibid.
[4] This argument was advanced by H. K. Mann, *Lives of the Popes*, xiv, 263: 'This language, which under the circumstances must be set down as too general, has led some authors to regard the letter as a forgery, or at least as a mere literary exercise. It may perhaps with more justice be said to be a letter in which Grosseteste was dealing, not with the particular case of Frederick, but with the whole method of procedure of the papal commissioners.'

most of his contemporaries, he had conceded that the pope normally possessed the right of distributing ecclesiastical benefices; but he also followed the common opinion of the time in holding that no exercise of papal power should be endured which threatened the well-being of the Church, which was, as the canonists put it, 'contra generalem statum ecclesiae', or, in Grosseteste's words (borrowed from St. Paul), 'non in aedificationem sed in destructionem'. The specific act of disobedience could be most effectively defended by an emphasis on the injury to the Church as a whole arising from the papal policy.

The comment that, 'It is unlike Grosseteste to lay down, with no philosophical and scriptural arguments to back it up, so new a proposition . . .'[1] is evidently wide of the mark. There was no new proposition in Grosseteste's letter. But A. L. Smith's further argument that Grosseteste's defiance of the pope reflects an attitude of mind radically different from that implied by his other, more deferential, letters of protest concerning papal appointments does present a serious difficulty. Once again, however, the problem can be resolved by reference to the contemporary doctrine on canonical obedience. The prevailing opinion held that resistance to an ecclesiastical superior could be justified only by certain knowledge that he had commanded something evil; there was a strong presumption in favour of the superior, and if there was any trace of doubt in the mind of the subject it was his duty to obey. Grosseteste, one may suppose, was driven only very slowly and reluctantly to the conclusion that God's own Vicar was using his plenitude of power for the 'destruction' of the Church. It is not quite accurate to say that he based his disobedience on an 'indefensible distinction between use and abuse'. The line at which disobedience became a duty was drawn by the law and doctrine of the Church; the burden that lay on Grosseteste's conscience was to determine whether the pope had crossed that line. As long as the pope's demands seemed merely inconvenient and inconsiderate Grosseteste felt bound to obey. It was only when submissively worded letters of protest had been brushed aside, when even personal exhortation at the papal curia had proved ineffective, that he was forced to the certain conviction that further compliance would actually endanger the Church. But once Grosseteste was so convinced his proper course of action was clear; according to the common doctrine of the time—according to the teaching of Innocent IV himself—it was his duty to disobey the pope. We need not wonder that the letter recording his outraged decision was filled with a grief and bitterness that set it apart from the rest of his correspondence.

These observations suggest two main conclusions. In the first place we ought not to accept without reservations the platitude that medieval canonistic theories of papal *plenitudo potestatis* provided an 'archetype' for later ideas of royal absolutism. A doctrine which sought to define in some detail the proper limits of a ruler's authority (even though those limits were broad indeed), and which also imposed on subjects a duty of dis-

---

[1] A. L. Smith, *Church and State*, 104–5.

obedience in certain circumstances when those limits were transgressed, was by no means identical with either Renaissance despotism or Stuart divine right. The more obvious conclusion is that, in disobeying the pope, bishop Grosseteste was neither rejecting his own inner convictions in a moment of anger nor formulating a novel principle of resistance to papal authority. He was acting in accordance with a widely accepted and well developed theory which could find support even in the writings of pope Innocent himself. It is rare indeed to find the theory so uncompromisingly put into practice by a medieval bishop—but then Grosseteste was a man of rare courage. Perhaps one day he will be canonised after all.

Reprinted from
The Journal of Ecclesiastical History VI/1
by permission of Cambridge University Press

VII

NATURA ID EST DEUS: A CASE OF JURISTIC PANTHEISM?

In several juristic discussions on natural law written around 1200 A.D. one encounters the phrase "natura id est deus." It has attracted little attention in all the very extensive modern literature about mediaeval theories of natural law,[1] and the two scholars who have considered it reached diametrically opposed conclusions as to its significance. Walter Ullmann, writing about the canonists, was concerned to emphasize the identification of natural law with divine law in their works. He suggested that they explained the agreement between the two laws by reference to "the Stoic and pantheistic idea that 'nature is God,' " and, without pursuing the matter in detail, he was inclined to think that there was indeed "a sort of Christian pantheism which permeated the canonistic conception of the divine (natural) law."[2] Ugo Gualazzini discussed the occurrences of "natura id est deus" in the civilian

* The author wishes to thank the American Council of Learned Societies for a grant which was helpful in writing this article.

[1] The best introduction to the subject, with extensive literature, is provided by Ch. Lefebvre and G. Simon, "Naturel (Droit)," *Dictionnaire de droit canonique*, VI (Paris, 1957), cols. 966–990. For a good selection of canonistic and theological texts on natural law see O. Lottin, *Le droit naturel chez Saint Thomas d'Aquin et ses prédécesseurs*, 2nd ed. (Bruges, 1931). Ph. Delhaye has recently discussed our particular formula from a theologian's point of view, but without detailed exegesis of the legal texts, *Permanence du droit naturel* (*Analecta Mediaevalia Namurcencia*, X, 1961), 66–72 and 120–127. He expressed some doubts as to its propriety. "Demandons-nous tout d'abord de quelle nature on parle lorsqu'on traite du droit naturel . . . Une première réponse historique dit: la nature qui fonde la loi, c'est Dieu, *Natura, id est Deus*. En un sens c'est vrai, car l'être premier est Dieu, il nous a fait à son image et à sa ressemblance . . . Cependant, il faut le remarquer, cette expression n'est pas sans danger ou tout au moins sans ambiguité. Elle est dangereuse parce qu'elle ouvre la porte au panthéisme."

[2] W. Ullmann, *Medieval Papalism* (London, 1949), 40–41, 46, citing Huguccio, "Dicitur ius naturale ius divinum quod continet lex Moysaica et evangelia; sic accipitur in principio et dicitur hoc ius naturale quoniam summa natura, id est Deus nobis illud tradidit . . . ." Also similar texts from the anonymous author of the *Summa Oxoniensis* and from Guido de Baysio. On these writers and other canonists mentioned in the text see S. Kuttner, *Repertorium der Kanonistik* (Vatican City, 1937) and A. Van Hove, *Prolegomena* (Commentarium Lovaniense in Codicem Iuris Canonici, I, i, Malines-Rome, 1945). For the civilians it is still necessary to consult F. von Savigny, *Geschichte des römischen Rechts im Mittelalter* (Heidelberg, 1834–1851). A guide to the more important modern work on mediaeval Roman law is provided by F. Calasso, *Medio evo del diritto I. Le fonti* (Milan, 1954). In subsequent references to the *Corpus Iuris Canonici* we have used the edition of Lyons, 1624 (which includes the *Glossae Ordinariae* to the various books) and, for the *Corpus Iuris Civilis* that of Lyons, 1635 (with the *Glossa Ordinaria* of Accursius).

gloss of Accursius, where one might more readily expect to find Stoic and pantheistic influence, but he was quite unprepared to admit that there were any such implications in the texts he considered.[3] Their ambiguous wording, he thought, could be explained by the fact that the jurists were "unaccustomed to theological subtleties." The whole problem is of interest in that it provides a particularly good example of the interplay between theology, philosophy, and jurisprudence that was of such decisive importance in shaping mediaeval conceptions of law and government.[4]

The idea of pantheistic influence on legal thought at this time is not on the face of it absurd. Some of the Roman law texts, which were drawn into the discussions of canonists as well as civilians, did spring from a background of Stoic pantheism. Moreover, the translations of neo-Platonic and Aristotelian works from the Arabic provided a new stimulus to pantheistic speculations, and the concern of the ecclesiastical authorities about the spread of such notions is indicated by the condemnations of David de Dinant and Amaury de Bène in 1210.[5] It would not be surprising in these circumstances to find some minor legist whose thought did flow in unorthodox channels or whose modes of expression displayed a dangerous ambiguity. But it seems most improbable that a whole series of distinguished canonists and civilians could have fallen into a crude pantheistic heresy. On the other hand, if the usage of Accursius in particular arose from mere clumsiness of expression and lack of familiarity with the subtleties of theological terminology, it is hard to understand how it could have held its place in the *Glossa Ordinaria,* a work studied as a standard text in every school of Roman law throughout Christendom, without evoking a

[3] U. Gualazzini, "Natura id est Deus," *Studia Gratiana,* III (1955), 413–424. He discussed the comments of Accursius on Ulpian's words, "Ius naturale est quod natura omnia animalia docuit . . . Hinc descendit maris atque feminae coniunctio." The relevant glosses occur at *Dig.* 1.1.1.3, *"Quod natura,* id est Deus . . ."; *Inst.* 1.2, *"Ius naturale est quod natura,* id est Deus . . ."; *Inst.* 1.2, *"Hinc,* id est ab hoc iure naturali scilicet Deo qui primo Adam Evae coniunxit et in paradiso deliciarum posuit."

[4] Much of the most stimulating recent work on mediaeval government has been concerned with this borderland where different disciplines meet. We may mention especially the books of Ernst H. Kantorowicz, *The King's Two Bodies* (Princeton, 1957) and of Walter Ullmann, *Principles of Government and Politics in the Middle Ages* (London, 1961). In this latter work Dr. Ullmann has reconsidered on a broad front the whole question of the impact of Aristotelian naturalism on the theocratic society of the earlier Middle Ages.

[5] See especially E. Gilson, "Le moyen âge et le naturalisme antique," *Archives d'histoire doctrinale et littéraire du moyen âge,* VII (1932), 5–37; and, on the condemnation of 1210, G. Théry, *Autour du décret de 1210: I, David de Dinant, Etude sur son panthéisme matérialiste* (Paris, 1925); *Autour du décret de 1210: II, Alexandre d'Aphrodise* (Paris, 1926); C. Capelle, *Autour du Décret de 1210: III, Amaury de Bène, étude sur son panthéisme formel* (Paris, 1932).

challenge from the theologians. It would seem then that the texts in question might repay some further study.

It is clear at the outset that much of the complexity in mediaeval discussions on natural law arose simply from the fact that the term *ius naturale* was used in different senses in different contexts of the legal collections that the jurists had to interpret. The first definition given in the Digest came from Ulpian. "Natural law is what nature has taught all animals. For this law is not peculiar to the human race but common to all animals that are born on land or sea and to birds. From this comes the union of man and woman that we call matrimony, from this the procreation and upbringing of children." The text continued with an explanation that this natural law, since it applied to all living creatures, was different from the *ius gentium* which pertained only to men. The *ius gentium* itself was defined in a phrase of Gaius as "what natural reason has established among men." But then, almost at once, natural law was re-defined as an ethical norm, evidently relevant only for human beings, the definition this time being taken from Paulus. *"Ius* is defined in several ways. In one way what is always equitable and just is called *ius,* as is *ius naturale."* [6]

The same dichotomy was repeated in the Institutes. First Ulpian's definition of the *ius naturale* and Gaius's of the *ius gentium* were given again. Then natural law was distinguished from the *ius gentium* in another way, as referring to a primordial state of existence before human laws had arisen at all. "By natural law all men were free from the beginning." Next, the idea of natural law as an ethical norm common to all men was re-stated, and its existence this time attributed to the workings of divine providence. Finally, yet another text suggested that the terms *ius naturale* and *ius gentium* could sometimes be used interchangeably. [7]

The glossators thus had to deal with several different and really irreconcilable definitions. The term *ius naturale* could refer to the instinctive modes of behavior of all living creatures. It could describe a primordial state of human existence before the growth of any laws. It could, on the other hand, designate certain enduring rules of equity which were believed to have been common to all men before the enactment of the codes of civil law that varied from people to people. In the first two senses natural law had to be distinguished from the *ius gentium;* in the third sense the two kinds of law could be equated with one another.

[6] *Dig.* 1.1.1.3, 1.1.1.4 (Ulpian); 1.1.9 (Gaius); 1.1.11 (Paulus). The different definitions were discussed (but without reference to the formula *natura id est deus*) by W. Onclin, "Le droit naturel chez les Romanistes des XIIᵉ et XIIIᵉ siècles." *Miscellanea Moralia Arthur Janssen* (Louvain-Gembloux, 1949), II, 329–337.

[7] *Inst.* 1.2.pr., 1.2.1, 1.2.2, 1.2.11, 2.1.11.

310

To all these definitions of the civilians Gratian added yet another
for the canonists which became the usual starting-point for their discussions. The very first words of the *Decretum* were these. "The
human race is ruled by two (laws), namely by natural law and by
custom. Natural law is what is contained in the Law and the Gospel,
by which each man is commanded to do to others what he wishes done
to himself and is forbidden to do to others what he does not wish done
to himself." [8] The Roman corpus had already provided texts from
which it might be argued that natural law proceeded either from
human reason or from divine providence. This further identification
(or apparent identification) of natural law with the divine revelation
of Scripture is at the root of the problem of terminology that we have
to consider. Gratian's own position was more complicated than his
opening remark suggested. Natural law, he explained, did not really
begin with the divine revelation recorded in the Old and New Testaments, but originated "from the beginning of the rational creature"
and remained always immutable.[9] His natural law then corresponded
to the Roman category of equitable and just rules that men, as distinct from other creatures, recognized as binding through their inherent rationality. Gratian pointed out that these basic rules of conduct
were also defined for Christians in the Scriptures and that accordingly
one could say that natural law was divine, but he also indicated that
not everything contained in the Scriptures constituted natural law.[10]
The ceremonial observances and various other rules laid down for the
Jews in the Old Testament were divinely promulgated but they were
not natural law. Rather they were a kind of positive legislation (*constitutio*) and were neither universal in scope nor immutable in time.[11]

[8] *Dist.* 1 *dictum ante* c. 1. Cf. *Dist.* 1 c. 1, "Omnes leges aut divinae sunt aut
humanae. Divinae natura, humanae moribus constant . . . "

[9] *Dist.* 5 *dictum ante* c. 1. "Naturale ius inter omnia primatum obtinet tempore
et dignitate. Coepit enim ab exordio rationalis creaturae, nec variatur tempore sed
immutabile permanet."

[10] *Dist.* 6 *dictum post* c. 3, "His itaque respondetur. In Lege et in Evangelio
naturale ius continetur; non tamen quaecunque in Lege et Evangelio inveniuntur
naturali iuri cohaerere probantur. Sunt enim in Lege quaedam moralia praecepta,
ut Non occides: quaedam mystica utpote sacrificiorum praecepta . . . Moralia man-
data ad naturale ius spectant, atque ideo nullam mutabilitatem recepisse monstran-
tur. Mystica vero, quantum ad superficiem, a naturali iure probantur aliena . . . "
On this question see, F. Arnold, "Die Rechtslehre des Magister Gratianus," *Studia
Gratiana*, I (1953), 451–482 at 460–465; A. Wegner, "Ueber positives göttliches
Recht und naturliches göttliches Recht bei Gratian," *Studia Gratiana*, I (1953),
503–518; D. Composta, "Il diritto naturale in Graziano," *Studia Gratiana*, II
(1954), 151–210.

[11] *Dist.* 7 *dictum ante* c. 1, "Ius autem constitutionis coepit a iustificationibus
quas Dominus tradidit Moysi dicens: Si emeris servum Hebraeum etc."

Natural law and divine law were not then really identical in Gratian's thought; rather the two categories overlapped.

Among the texts which Gratian cited to illustrate his argument the most important by far for the commentators was one from Isidore of Seville which began, "Natural law is common to all nations in that it is held everywhere by instinct of nature, not by any constitution."

Ius naturale est commune omnium nationum eo quod ubique instinctu naturae, non constitutione aliqua habetur: ut viri et foeminae coniunctio, liberorum successio et educatio, communis omnium possessio et omnium una libertas, acquisitio eorum quae coelo, terra marique capiuntur; item depositae rei vel commendatae pecuniae restitutio, violentiae per vim repulsio. Nam hoc, aut si quid huic simile est, nunquam iniustum, sed naturale aequumque habetur.[12]

Isidore did not consider natural law as applicable to all animals but apart from that he ran together in this one passage all the different meanings of natural law that occur separately in the Roman corpus—natural law as the instinct of nature, as a primordial state of things (the one liberty of all), and as the basic rules of equity.

Faced with so many different meanings of natural law the canonists produced interpretive glosses that were necessarily complex, but they were not merely muddled. The greater jurists, civilians and canonists alike, did not attempt to lay down one definition of natural law as the "right" one and then misinterpret all the other texts so as to produce an artificial and spurious agreement among them. Rather they began their discussions by defining all the different senses in which *ius naturale* was used in their legal sources.[13] Once it was clearly established that the term did have several different connotations further analysis became possible. It was necessary to explain when *ius divinum* was used as a synonym for *ius naturale,* and when not; when the term *ius naturale* itself was being used to describe immutable rules of morality and when it referred merely to a primordial state of things; when, and in what senses, the canon law could be called *ius divinum.* There then arose a host of subsidiary questions concerning the limitations on the right of pope or emperor to legislate against or dispense from the rules of divine and natural law in all the different connotations of those terms.[14] It is unnecessary to pursue the ramifications of these arguments here, though a detailed re-assessment of all this material will be necessary before we can understand fully the con-

---

[12] *Dist.* 1 c. 7.

[13] For typical examples of such lists see Accursius, *Glossa Ordinaria ad Inst.* 1.2.pr. and Johannes Teutonicus, *Glossa Ordinaria ad Dist.* 1 c. 7.

[14] The kinds of difficulties that arose are illustrated admirably by Stephan Kuttner, "Pope Lucius III and the Bigamous Archbishop of Palermo," *Medieval Studies Presented to Aubrey Gwynn, S.J.* (Dublin, 1961), 409–453.

tributions of the canonists and civilians to mediaeval political theory or give a final answer to the question, much debated in recent years, whether their doctrines of natural law were compatible with modern conceptions of sovereignty and the state.[15] The immediate point is that, against this background of multiple meanings, nearly all the canonistic usages that seem at first sight to confuse nature and God find a ready explanation.

Among the numerous meanings of the word nature there are two that are of special relevance here. The word can mean the whole complex of existent phenomena or it can mean the intrinsic essence of a particular being, that which is proper to it, not merely accidental. It was relatively easy for the canonists to make the point that the term *ius naturale* was used with different meanings in different contexts, but an adequate treatment of the matter required that they also explain how in fact the same word *naturalis* could be significantly posited of widely different kinds of law. The usual explanation was that, whenever the term *ius naturale* was used, it referred to a law that flowed from the intrinsic nature of some class of being, though the content of the law might vary according to the being involved. The point was put succinctly by Sicardus:

Ius naturale dicitur a divina natura, hoc est quo quisque iubetur, etc.; a communi natura, hoc est quod natura docuit omnia animalia; ab humana natura, hoc est quedam vis et potentia homini naturaliter insita ad faciendum bonum et vitandum contrariam.[16]

The lists of the connotations of the term *ius naturale,* that occur in nearly all the major *summae* and glosses on the *Decretum* from the mid-twelfth century onwards, regularly explained the description of divine law as natural, not by confusing God with created nature, but by explaining that this law proceeded from the *summa natura* that was God himself. The classification of Stephanus Tornacensis (c. 1160) was repeated by several later authors with only minor modifications:

Et notandum ius naturale quatuor modis dicitur. Dicitur enim ius naturale quod ab ipsa natura est introductum et non solum homini sed etiam ceteris animalibus insitum . . . Dicitur et ius naturale ius gentium quod ab humana solum natura quasi cum ea incipiens traxit exordium. Ius etiam divinum dicitur naturale quod summa natura nostra, id est Deus, nos docuit et per legem et prophetas et evangelium nobis obtulit. Dicitur etiam ius naturale quod simul comprehendit humanum et divinum et illud quod a natura

---

[15] On this controversy see most recently G. Post, *"Ratio publicae utilitatis, ratio status* und 'Staatsräson,' " *Die Welt als Geschichte,* XXI (1961), 8–28, 71–99.

[16] MS Bamberg, Staatsbibl. can. 38, fol. 57r, cited Lottin, *op. cit.* 19–20.

omnibus animalibus est insitum . . . Vel si quintam iuris naturalis acep-
tionem non abhorreas, intellige hic dici ius naturale quod hominibus tantum
et non aliis animalibus a natura est insitum, scilicet ad faciendum bonum
vitandumque contrarium. Que quasi pars divini iuris est.[17]

According to Stephanus the ability to distinguish between right and
wrong was an intrinsic quality of human nature which set man apart
from the animals, but since man was a creature of God, the dictates
of man's conscience necessarily coincided with the divine law proclaimed by God himself. Some canonists, pursuing further this line of
argument, explained that the divine law of the Scriptures could be
called natural either because it proceeded from God, the *summa
natura,* or alternatively because the natural reason of man impelled
him to observe this same code. Thus Huguccio wrote:

Item quarto modo dicitur ius naturale ius divinum . . . et dicitur hoc ius naturale quia summa natura, id est deus nobis illud tradidit et docuit per legem
et prophetas et evangelium, vel quia ad ea que iure divino continentur, naturalis ratio etiam in extrinseca erudicione ducit et impellit.[18]

But this recognition that human conscience impelled men to follow
God's law did not involve any confusion between creator and creatures. Indeed, in all the texts that referred to God as the *summa
natura,* the whole point of the usage was to distinguish between this
supreme nature which promulgated divine law and the human nature
or mere "common nature" or even animal nature, all of which could
give rise to natural law in some other accepted sense of the term. It
must be added that the term *summa natura* itself was of course not a
canonistic coinage but an accepted theological expression that was
used to designate God and that had been especially favored by St.
Anselm.[19]

So far no great difficulty arises. There is, however, another canonistic gloss, not hitherto noticed, which does not fit into the pattern we
have been describing. The *Glossa Palatina* (1210–1215), commenting
on Isidore's text, "Ius naturale est . . . quod ubique instinctu naturae

---

[17] F. von Schulte, *Die Summa des Stephanus Tornacensis über das Decretum
Gratiani* (Giessen, 1891), 7. For other passages using *summa natura* in the same
sense see the texts of Johannes Faventinus and of the *Summa Coloniensis* cited by
Lottin, *op. cit.* 17, 106–107, and, on the doctrine of Stephanus, Ph. Delhaye, "Morale
et droit canonique dans le 'Summa' d'Etienne de Tournai," *Studia Gratiana,* I
(1953), 435–449.

[18] MS Munich, Staatsbibl. Clm 10247, fol. 1r, cited by Lottin, 109–110. Similarly
the *Summa Lipsiensis,* cited Lottin, 108.

[19] It will suffice to refer to the index volume of Anselm's collected works, *S. An-
selmi Cantuariensis Opera Omnia,* VI (Edinburgh, 1961). There are five columns of
references to *summa natura* at pp. 244–246.

314

... habetur," declared simply *"Nature, id est dei."* [20] There seems to be no question here of a distinction between the *summa natura* which is God and the nature of creatures; rather it is the instinctual nature of creatures that is treated as divine. Moreover it is a precisely similar usage that occurs in the civilian gloss of Accursius. Where Ulpian wrote, "Ius naturale est quod natura omnia animalia docuit," the Gloss explained, "Natura, id est Deus." Gualazzini suggested that this might not be a genuine Accursian gloss but a later addition.[21] However, the suggestion, which finds some support in the manuscript tradition of the Gloss, is undermined by the fact that the crucial phrase had already appeared in Azo's *Summa* on the Institutes.

Ius naturale est quod natura id est ipse deus docuit omnia animalia: et ita istud pronomen "quod" erit accusativi casus et hoc nomen "natura" erit casus nominativi. Vel dic quod nomen istud "quod" sit casus nominativi: ut sic dicat quod docuit omnia animalia natura id est per instinctum naturae et ita hoc nomen "natura" erit casus ablatavi.[22]

Here again the author seems to be asserting that the nature which inheres in all creatures and determines their characteristic activities

[20] MS Vatican, Pal. Lat. 658, fol. 1rb. The author understandably found difficulty in defining a sense of the term natural law that would embrace all the examples given by Isidore of Seville whose text he was glossing. *"Ius naturale etc.* Quod ius naturale hic accipiatur pro instinctu nature innuit id quod sequitur, *eo quod etc.* Set si hoc dicatur non competunt exempla. Supponat ergo pro instinctu rationis. Hoc enim innuitur in fine cum dicitur *nam hoc etc. . . . Nature,* id est dei." The passage was quoted in 1300 by Guido de Baysio in his *Rosarium super Decreto* (Lyons, 1516) ad Dist. 1 c. 7, fol. 4ra, and there attributed to Laurentius Hispanus. Recent research by A. M. Stickler (not yet published) tends to confirm that the *Glossa Palatina* was indeed the work of Laurentius. On this canonist see Fr. Stickler's article, "Laurent d'Espagne," *Dictionnaire de droit canonique,* VI (Paris, 1957), cols. 361–364.

[21] Gualazzini, *art. cit.* 414–415, referring to P. Torelli's edition of the Accursian gloss on the Institutes where it was pointed out that the comment, "Natura id est deus" at *Inst.* 1.2 does not occur in the earliest versions of the work. The first recension of the *Glossa Ordinaria* was probably completed by 1228, but Accursius continued to work on it until his death between 1259 and 1263. On the chronology of his life and work see H. Kantorowicz, "Accursio e la sua biblioteca," *Rivista di storia del diritto italiano,* II (1929), 35–62, 193–212; P. Torelli, *Per l'edizione critica della Glossa Accursiana alle Istituzioni* (Bologna, 1935); E. Genzmer, "Zur Lebensgeschichte des Accursius," *Festschrift für Leopold Wenger,* II, 223–241 (Münchener Beiträge zur Papyrusforschung und antiken Rechtsgeschichte, XXXV, 1945), (criticizing H. Kantorowicz).

[22] *Summa Azonis* (Basel, 1563) *ad Inst.* 1,2, col. 1071. The same comment occurs in Azo's unpublished apparatus on the *Digestum Vetus,* MS Paris BN 4459, fol. 1ra *ad Dig.* 1.1.1.3, *"Natura,* id est Deus, et ita 'quod' erit accusativi casus, vel dic nominativi et 'natura' sic ablativi. Az."

can be identified with God, on the face of it a thoroughly pantheistic position.

In discussing the Accursian texts Gualazzini provided an interesting essay on the interplay of classical and Christian influences in the thought of the glossators at the beginning of the XIIIth century. He called attention to the difficulty that faced all the jurists at that time of reconciling Gratian's definition with Ulpian's and observed that the glossators were compelled to expound scattered texts without possessing the philosophical equipment for a systematic investigation of the concept of natural law. He emphasized the importance of Christian equity, its close relationship with natural law, and the dependence of both on God in mediaeval thought. But he did not explain how the actual words used by Accursius are to be understood in an orthodox sense, though he insisted that they are not to be taken in a pantheistic one. Perhaps, he suggested, the gloss meant to say, not, "Nature, that is God . . ." but rather, "It is not nature but God himself that has taught all animals natural law." One can only say that Accursius did not in fact write this. Moreover, as Gualazzini noted, the explanation fails to account for the other gloss of Accursius which referred to "the natural law, namely God, that first joined Adam to Eve." [23] In the end he abandoned the attempt at exegesis and turned to rhetoric. "Equity is applied in the moment when conscience speaks, in which the facts of the case are considered in a more organic vision of human phenomena, in which all is raised to the sphere of the highest understanding. We are at the limits of God." [24]

This is all very well, but in fact the places where Accursius chose to deploy his phrase, "Natura, id est Deus," had nothing to do with equity and, in any case, we are left with the original problem. If Accursius wished to make an orthodox statement, but, through lack of philosophical equipment, stumbled into one that was technically heretical his comment could not have held its place in the *Glossa Ordinaria* throughout the Middle Ages. Since his statement was accepted as orthodox in expression as well as in intention we still have to explain how the word *natura* in this context could have been taken by contemporary theologians as a synonym for *Deus*.

[23] *Art. cit.* 419–420. Cf. *supra* n. 3.

[24] *Art. cit.* 424. The passage continued, "Per tutte queste considerazioni, io penso che i nostri glossatori . . . pensassero piu al Vangelo che al Digesto, più a Christo che a Giustiniano, anche perchè essi, poco o punto abituati alle sottigliezze teologiche . . . pensavano utile considerare come fonte del diritto e dell' equità, che ne è quasi l'espressione ultima, la sintesi, non tanto la natura, realtà tangibile ma transeunte, quanto Dio stesso, realtà incorporea, ma immanente."

To understand this it is helpful to go back to the grammatical analysis that Azo provided in the original comment that lies behind the gloss of Accursius. Nature could only mean God, Azo explained, if the word stood in the nominative case, as the subject of the sentence. This explanation was evidently regarded as an essential element in his exposition of the text for it was repeated in both the relevant glosses of Accursius. The implication was that the word *natura* could stand for God provided that it was understood as referring to an active agent, the creative force that implanted in each creature its own proper mode of activity. (Accursius explained that natural law in Ulpian's sense did not refer merely to the instinct for procreation but to the *regimen* established in all creatures according to which birds fly, fish swim, and so on.) For a complete explanation of the language of the Gloss it would be necessary to show that the word *natura* was used in orthodox theology to designate God conceived of as a creative being as well as the whole complex of created things, and that Accursius was merely indicating that the former accepted sense of the word was the more appropriate one in this particular context.

There were indeed several ways in which the word nature could be posited of God in XIIIth-century thought. Since the early Christological controversies it had been said that Christ united two natures in one person, and, in a different sense, the same word nature was used to describe the unity of the three persons of the Trinity. Both doctrines had been a matter of renewed controversy at the end of the XIIth-century, the first because of the adoptionist dispute at Paris, the second because of Joachim of Flora's attack on the Trinitarian doctrine of Peter Lombard; and in both cases the decrees defining the orthodox faith had passed into the collections of the canon lawyers. Accursius must certainly have known of the definition of the Fourth Lateran Council, " . . . quaelibet trium personarum est illa res, videlicet substantia, essentia seu natura divina . . ." [25] but it does not really explain his own comment. To say that there is one nature in God is quite different from saying that God is Nature. Nor, for this particular problem, can we find any help in the usage that described Christ as God "by nature" to distinguish his true divinity from the attributes of human rulers who might be called "gods by grace." [26]

[25] H. Denzinger and C. Rahner, *Enchiridion Symbolorum*, 28th ed. (Barcelona, 1952), 200–203. The canon was included in the Gregorian decretals at X.1.1.2. The adoptionist controversy was settled by the decretal *Cum Christus* which restated the doctrine of the two natures of Christ (X.5.7.7). On the canonistic implications of this decretal see "Pope and Council: Some New Decretist Texts," *Mediaeval Studies*, XIX (1957), 197–218 at 204.

[26] Ernst H. Kantorowicz, "Deus per naturam, Deus per Gratiam," *Harvard Theological Review*, XLV (1952), 253–277.

There was, however, yet another use of the word nature in XIIIth-century scholasticism that does fit in perfectly with the Accursian gloss. That was the distinction between nature as *natura naturans* on the one hand, a creative first cause that could be identified with God, and nature as *natura naturata* on the other, signifying the world of created beings. The idea of God as a creative "nature" is at least as old as St. Augustine [27] but this particular terminology seems to have originated in the first Latin translations of Averroes' commentaries on the scientific works of Aristotle.[28] Other sections of Averroes' work would raise severe problems for Christian philosophers, but this particular phrase could be accepted without difficulty. It did not confuse creator and creatures but rather emphasized the distinction between them; and so the term *natura naturans* came to be used in the writings of several orthodox theologians of the thirteenth century as a designation for God. It occurs in this sense in the writings of St. Bonaventure and St. Thomas,[29] but the passage that most closely parallels those of the jurists is in the *Speculum Maius* of Vincent of Beauvais:

In summa vero nota quod natura primo dicitur dupliciter. Uno modo natura naturans, id est ipsa summa lex naturae quae Deus est . . . Aliter vero dicitur natura naturata et haec multipliciter.[30]

This brings together in one passage the two usages that we have encountered in Accursius. God is equated with nature understood as *natura naturans* and also with the "supreme law of nature."

[27] *Ep.* I, 18.2, Migne *PL* XXXIII, col. 85, "Est natura per locos et tempora mutabilis ut corpus. Et est natura per locos nullo modo, sed tantum per tempora etiam ipsa mutabilis, ut anima. Et est natura quae nec per locos, nec per tempora mutari potest; hoc Deus est. Quod hic insinuavi quoquo modo mutabile, creatura dicitur; quod immutabile, creator." *De Trinitate* XV.1.1, *PL* XL, col. 1057, "Supra hanc ergo naturam, si quaerimus aliquid, et verum quaerimus, Deus est, natura scilicet non creata, sed creatrix."

[28] H. Siebeck, "Ueber die Entstehung der Termini natura naturans und natura naturata," *Archiv für Geschichte der Philosophie*, III (1890), 370–378; H. A. Lucks, "Natura naturans—Natura naturata," *The New Scholasticism*, IX (1935), 1–24.

[29] Bonaventure, *Commentaria in Quatuor Libros Sententiarum*, L. III, *Dist.* 8, *dub.* 2, *Opera Omnia*, III (Quaracchi, 1887) 197, "Dicendum quod *natura* non accipitur ita communiter, sed pro natura *creata:* unde non vult dicere quod generatio Filii sit supra naturam aeternam, quae est natura *naturans*, sed super naturam creatam, quae consuevit dici natura *naturata*." Thomas, *Summa Theol.* 1–2ae, Q. 85, art. 6 (Turin-Rome, 1948) 397, "Natura vero universalis est virtus activa in aliquo universali principio naturae, puta in aliquo caelestium corporum; vel alicuius superioris substantiae, secundum quod etiam Deus a quibusdam dicitur *natura naturans*." *De Divinis Nominibus*, IV, *lect.* 21 (Turin-Rome, 1950) p. 206, "Est autem Deus universalis causa omnium quae naturaliter fiunt; unde et quidam Ipsum nominant naturam naturantem."

[30] *Speculi Maioris Vincentii Burgundii . . . Tomus Secundus* (Venice, 1591) XV. 4, fol. 257ra.

318

If we assume that Accursius had the term *natura naturans* in mind when he wrote, "Natura, id est Deus," the problem of his orthodoxy disappears, but we must then suppose that, far from being ignorant of all that was going on in the schools of philosophy and theology, he was rather keenly alert to the latest trends of scholarship in those fields. We can be certain that he was not ignorant of the particular phrase under discussion for an explicit distinction between *natura naturata* and *natura naturans id est deus* occurs in two other passages of his Gloss where he was contrasting the limitations of man's natural knowledge with the omniscience of God.[31] We must still establish that a XIIIth-century glossator could readily have assumed that this same distinction was applicable to the legal doctrine of natural law. It often happens that the voluminous writings of the mid-XIIIth-century jurists provide expanded explanations of glosses that were so brief as to be ambiguous in the works of their predecessors. In this case Odofredus settles the matter for us. Commenting on Dig. 1.1.1.3 he repeated and expanded the comment of Accursius thus:

Ius naturale est quod natura omnia animalia docuit. Or, signori, hec littera legitur duobus modis et uno modo quod hec dictio natura sit nominativi casus et sic tunc exponatis litteram: ius naturale est quod natura, id est deus, quia deus est natura naturans et docuit omnia animalia.[32]

At about the same time the great canonist Hostiensis introduced similar terminology in his *Summa Aurea* on the Decretals. He was considering the circumstances in which a custom contrary to natural law was invalid and explained:

... non valet si sit contraria iuri naturali id est naturae naturanti id est deo, quasi dicat si consuetudo contradicat iuri quo non servato animus periclitaretur, reprobanda est.[33]

The terms *natura naturans* and *natura naturata* have attracted the attention of historians of philosophy mainly because they were eventually adopted (and adapted) by Spinoza.[34] Their use has accordingly

[31] Gloss *ad Dig.* 12.1.38, "*Hominum.* Est ergo natura naturans id est Deus et ille omnia scit . . . Alia est natura naturata, scilicet hominis quae praeterita et praesentia tantum scit." Gloss *ad Inst.* 3.16.6 "*Naturam* . . . Sed dic quod aliud est esse certum per rerum naturam, i.e. per naturalem cursum naturae . . . Et aliud est in natura rerum, id est in scientia Dei . . . et dicitur prima natura naturata sed secunda natura naturans quod idem est quod ipse Deus." It will be remembered that the mediaeval pattern of education normally required all students to spend several years in philosophical studies before proceeding to the higher faculties of theology, law or medicine.

[32] *Odofredus super Digesto Veteri* (Paris, 1604) ad 1.1.1.3 (no foliation).

[33] Hostiensis, *Summa Aurea* (Venice, 1605), *De consuetudine*, col. 81.

[34] *Ethices* I, *Prop.* 29, *Spinoza Opera*, ed. Gebhardt II (Heidelberg, 1926), 71.

been traced from the great scholastics of the XIIIth-century through the less orthodox writings of Eckhardt and Giordano Bruno to the world of the Renaissance.[35] It has apparently never been noticed, however, that there was a parallel juristic transmission of the same terminology from the middle of the XIIIth-century to the end of the Middle Ages and beyond.[36] It may be useful therefore to conclude with a few examples of this transmission in the works of the Roman and canon lawyers.

At the beginning of the XIVth-century Cynus of Pistoia (citing Jacobus de Arena) distinguished between the source of justice and the source of law (*ius*). The author of justice was God himself, "qui est natura naturans," but the author of law was the emperor "qui est natura naturata."[37] Albericus de Rosate, a little later, repeated the view of Odofredus that natural instinct was implanted by the *natura naturans id est deus* and added references to the places in the Ordinary Gloss where Accursius himself had distinguished between *naturans* and *naturata*.[38] Baldus offered a slight variation of terminology:

[35] The history of the term is outlined briefly in the standard encyclopedias of philosophy, e.g. R. Eisler, *Wörterbuch der philosophischen Begriffe*, 4th ed. II (Berlin, 1929), 205–206; *Encyclopedia Filosofica*, III (Venice-Rome, 1957), col. 820–821; A. Lalande, *Vocabulaire technique et critique de la philosophie*, 8th ed. (Paris, 1960), 673. The mediaeval background of Spinoza's doctrine was discussed perceptively by A. O. Lovejoy, "The Dialectic of Bruno and Spinoza," *Univ. of California Publications: Philosophy* I (Berkeley, 1904), 125–174. See also A. O. Lovejoy and G. Boas, *A Documentary History of Primitivism and Related Ideas*, I (Baltimore, 1935), 448, where the term *'natura naturans'* is listed and defined along with sixty-five other meanings of the word 'nature.'

[36] H. Kämpf discussed Siger of Brabant's use of *natura naturans* as an influence on the growth of the naturalistic theory of the state propounded by Pierre Dubois, but ignored both the scholastic and juristic backgrounds of the term, *Pierre Dubois und die geistigen Grundlagen des französischen Nationalbewussteins um 1300* (Leipzig-Berlin, 1935), 65.

[37] *Cyni Pistorensis . . . in Digesti Veteris libros commentaria* (Frankfurt, 1578), fol. 3rb. "Vel potest responderi, secundum Ia. de Aren. quod ius et Iustitia differunt authore et substantia. Authore differunt: quia Iustitiae author est Deus, ut hic not. qui est natura naturans. Iuris author est homo, ut Imperator, qui est natura naturata." Later in the same passage Cynus used the phrase, "natura, id est deus," in discussing the question whether marriage was according to natural law (fol. 4ra).

[38] *Prima Alberici super Digesto Veteri* (Lyons, 1534) *ad Dig.* 1.1.1, fol. 11rb, "Sed prout convenit (ius naturale) cuilibet animali est quoddam ius nature sensibilis in eius productione a natura inserta, quod natura naturans id est Deus docuit inserendo habeat, sive habitum eius nature naturate in eius productione. Et de ista natura naturante que est Deus habetur infra de iudi. l. sed et si restituatur in fine (*Dig.* 5.1.28), de natura naturata, inst. de ver. ob § conditiones (*Inst.* 3.16.6)." Angelus de Perusio, commenting on Accursius's "Natura id est Deus," was content to explain the matter by giving a reference to the context of the Digest where the Gloss distinguished between *naturans* and *naturata*, *Angelus de Perusio super prima*

Ius naturale. Quod a divina procedit seu descendit providentia est commune omnibus animalibus naturatis naturatione perfecta et non orbatis. Hinc descendit maris et femine coniunctio.[39]

Around 1400 the canonist Aegidius de Bellamera deployed the two meanings of *natura* in a different context. In his commentary on the Proemium of the Clementines he discussed the need for new promulgations of positive law from time to time to meet new needs and changing circumstances. He referred to the discussion of the same point in the Code and, where Justinian had written that "nature hastens to bring forth new forms," Aegidius explained this as a result of the creative activity of the *natura naturans.*[40]

The use of the term *natura naturans* to explain how divine law could properly be called natural continued into the XVth-century. In a discussion on the limits to the pope's dispensatory powers Antonius de Rosellis repeated Huguccio's doctrine that natural law could be so-called either because it sprang from the natural human reason or because its source was God himself, but he preferred to use *natura naturans* in place of Huguccio's *summa natura.*[41] His contemporary, Dominicus de Sancto Gemignano, employed both expressions in commenting on the first Distinction of the *Decretum.*[42] Some writers of

---

parte Digesti Veteris (Lyons, 1534) *ad Dig.* 1.1.1.3, fol. 3vb, "De duplici natura nota hic in glossa et clarius infra, si cer. per. l. respiciendum (*Dig.* 12.1.38)." Martinus de Azpilcueta referred to the same gloss in his commentary on Innocent III's decretal, *Novit, Martini Azpilcuetae . . . Tomus Secundus* (Lyons, 1589) 121. "Paulus . . . ait in natura omnia certa esse: naturam autem, de qua ille agit, dicebat glo. l. respiciendum, ff si cer. per. esse naturam naturantem, hoc est Deum ipsum."

[39] *Baldus Ubaldi . . . in primam Digesti Veteris* (Venice, 1616) *ad Dig.* 1.1.1.3, fol. 8vb.

[40] *Repetitionum in universas fere Iuris Canonici partes . . . Volumina Sex* (Venice, 1587) VI, fol. 5ra, "Caeterum enim natura naturata ex virtute naturae naturantis, quae est prima causa sine qua secunda non agit, laetatur novas et dissimiles formas iam creatas in posterum edere . . . ut C. De vet. iur. enuc. 1.2 Sed quia . . . "

[41] Antonius de Rosellis, *De Conciliis, Volumen II Tractatum ex variis iuris civilis interpretibus collectorum* (Lyons, 1549), fol. 39ra, " . . . natura sumitur multis modis. Nam legiste dicunt quod est natura naturans et hec est deus ut no. glo. in l.i § ius naturale, ff de iustitia et iure (*Dig.* 1.1.1.3)." Fol. 39va, "Et ideo dicitur etiam hoc ius naturale vel quia a natura naturante que est deus . . . promulgatum sit in naturam naturatam; sive quia hoc ius est commune omnibus fere gentibus et nationibus in instinctu rationabili nature non constitutione aliqua ut dicitur in hoc c. ius naturale (*Dig.* 1.1.1.3)."

[42] *Commentaria in Decretum* (Venice, 1504) *ad Dist.* 1 c. 7, fol. 7ra, "Et dicitur naturale eo quia instinctu nature id est dei non constitutione alique habetur . . . Ibi instinctu nature, i.e. inspiratione summe nature, id est dei." Fol. 7rb, "Quandoque sumitur ius naturale pro quodam instinctu naturali regulato tamen ratione anime rationalis infuse. Alio modo dicitur natura naturans."

the early XVIth-century indulged in lavish displays of classical erudition in their remarks on natural law. Fortunius Garcia, for instance was especially anxious to defend the orthodoxy of the Accursian gloss:

... exponit verbum "natura" in diffinitione iuris naturalis positum, et interpretatur "natura" id est deus, et quidem iusta est et sancta interpretatio.[43]

To prove his point he cited Plato and Aristotle, then Vergil, Lucan, Seneca, and Pliny, not to mention Thomas Aquinas. Fortunius rejected the view of the Stoics that nature itself was God and argued that Accursius' gloss was compatible with the view that the natural world was divine only in the sense of being an instrument of divine providence.[44] He concluded with the usual explanation that the *natura* identified with the deity by Accursius was the *natura naturans* which was commonly understood to be God.

Tertio ex his colligemus ratione eius, quod vulgo dicitur aliam naturam naturantem, id est deum, nam natura id est instrumentum quandoque sumitur pro deo, tanquam pro agente principale. Ut in glossa nostra.[45]

In a quite different spirit the great humanist jurist, Cujas, was disposed to commend Accursius for his gloss, "Natura id est Deus," in that it had correctly presented the Stoic conception lying behind Ulpian's text:

Utemur Accursio in hoc uno solum, *Natura,* id est Deus; non displicet haec oratio, imo admodum placet; quia Stoicis, quos semper fere sequuntur Iureconsulti idem est Deus et natura ...[46]

This takes us into a different world of thought. It would be interesting to trace the changing conception of nature from the works of the late scholastics to those of the humanist lawyers, but the task would be a complex one and beyond the scope of this paper. For us the main conclusion is that the mediaeval jurists were neither pantheists nor so ignorant of accepted theological terminology as to stumble into a doctrinal error through mere inadvertence. Even before the new Aristotle

---

[43] *Repetitionum seu commentariorum ... volumen primum* (Lyons, 1553), fol. 35rb.

[44] *Ibid.,* "Natura igitur serva est, nec aliud est quam divine providentie instrumentum ... Hinc abiicienda est Stoicorum sententia qua tradebatur mundum ipsum animantem et sapientem esse; ipsumque cognoscebant vel potius ignorabant deus."

[45] *Op. cit.,* fol. 39va. Fortunius went on to cite the places where Accursius distinguished between *naturans* and *naturata.* Franciscus Herculanus also discussed these places with a rather ponderous attempt at philosophic exegesis in his treatise, *De negativa probanda, Tractatus Illustrium ... Iurisconsultorum,* IV (Venice, 1634), fol. 19rb.

[46] *Iacobi Cuiacii ... Operum Tomus Secundus* (Lyons, 1606) *ad Dig.* 1.1.1.3, col. 101.

322

began to influence their thought the canonists were able to assimilate from the Digest (and without undue strain) the classical idea of natural law as flowing from the intrinsic nature of things—and men—as they actually were, a break with the earlier Augustinian tradition that had considered only the state of primal innocence as truly natural.[47] Aristotelian terminology itself was adopted earlier than has been supposed but it served only to buttress a position already arrived at in the process of reconciling the texts of Roman and canon law. Since several of the passages that we have considered dealt explicitly with natural law as a factor limiting human government, the pattern of doctrinal development is of some interest to the student of mediaeval political and constitutional theory. In modern treatments of those subjects it is usual to emphasize the influence of Aristotle and Aquinas. We should not forget that Ulpian and Accursius were just as important.

Cornell University.

[47] It is quite exceptional by the end of the XIIth century to find a canonist stating the old position with no hesitations or reservations. The English *Summa Prima Primi* provides such an example, but the author indicates that his viewpoint had been widely rejected by contemporaries, "Hic notandum quod multi multas circa ius naturale inutiles posuerunt distinctiones, plures uocabuli significationes assignando. Sufficit enim hec unica acceptio ut dicatur ius naturale quod procedit ex prima natura sine corruptione, secundum quod scilicet homo uiueret si Adam non pecasset . . . Si hanc acceptionem semper tenueris ab intelligentia non deuiabis." MS London, BM Royal 11 D. II, fol. 321ra, cited in "Two Anglo-Norman Summae," *Traditio*, XV (1959), 483–491 at 485.

VIII

THE DECRETISTS AND THE "DESERVING POOR"

In spite of all the complex controversies concerning the interplay of religious ideas and economic forces at the end of the Middle Ages the investigation of the pre-existing medieval poor law has been rather neglected by modern scholars. Evidently enough attitudes toward the relief of poverty are as significant as attitudes toward the acquisition of wealth in gauging the climate of economic thought in any given age. Yet, apart from studies on hospital administration, little has been done in this field of medieval research since the pioneering works of Ratzinger, Emminghaus, Ehrle, Uhlhorn and Ashley in the nineteenth century.[1] Since then the attitudes of social welfare experts to the problems of poor relief have radically changed and a great mass of source material unknown to the earlier writers, notably the work of the medieval canonists, has come to the attention of historians.[2] Both these facts suggest a need for some reconsideration of medieval attitudes to the poor and to the relief of poverty.

The writings of the canonists did not of course deal only with technicalities of ecclesiastical administration. The law of the medieval church was far-reaching in content and the great commentaries on it ranged often into the fields of sociology, economics and political theory.[3] On the subject of poor

---

[1] Georg Ratzinger, *Geschichte der kirchlichen Armenpflege* (Freiburg im Breisgau, 1868); Albert Emminghaus, *Das Armenwesen und die Armengesetzgebung in Europäischen Staaten* (Berlin, 1870); Franz Ehrle, *Beiträge zur Geschichte und Reform der Armenpflege* (Freiburg im Breisgau, 1881); G. G. W. Uhlhorn, *Die Christliche Liebestätigkeit in der alten Kirche* (Stuttgart, 1882-90); W. J. Ashley, *An Introduction to English Economic History and Theory*, I, ii (London, 1893). For bibliography of modern works on medieval hospitals see Jean Imbert, *Les hôpitaux en droit canonique* (Paris, 1947).

[2] The records of manorial law constitute another type of source material that has been little used by historians of poor relief. The value of this material was pointed out by F. M. Page, "The Customary Poor Law of Three Cambridgeshire Manors," *Cambridge Historical Journal*, III (1929-31), 125-133.

[3] In recent years a whole spate of books and articles has appeared on the political theories of the canonists. Some of this work is discussed in the article, "Some Recent Works on the Political Theories of the Medieval Canonists," *Traditio*, X (1954), 594-625. Their social and economic theories have not attracted so much attention except as regards the doctrine of usury. On this see T. P. McLaughlin, "The Teaching of the Canonists on Usury," *Mediaeval Studies*, I (1939), 81-147; II (1940), 1-22; and B. N. Nelson, *The Idea of Usury* (Princeton 1949).

relief it is possible to extract from the canonistic works a whole legal philosophy which related the claims of the poor to a coherent theory of natural law and property, and against that background discussed the legal status of the poor, the obligations of public authorities and private individuals and the regulation of the administrative agencies through which relief was distributed.[4]

Much of this material, it seems to me, can be discussed intelligibly only when it is related to the social and economic environment of medieval men. Too often in the earlier writings on medieval charity one encounters a sort of unconscious comparative method. Medieval principles were evaluated in accordance with standards based on experience of a radically different kind of society without any awareness that the standards employed were not themselves absolute. It remains true though that some of the major questions relating to the administration of poor relief that the canonists discussed were not concerned with specifically medieval problems but with ones that recur in all ages and all cultures. In such cases a comparative approach seems legitimate and can be very rewarding. The purpose of this article then is to present the arguments of a group of canonists on one such question in order to illustrate the potentialities of canonistic research in this field and to provide material for a comparative study of the problem they discussed.

The canonists to be considered are the Decretists who produced their *summae* and glosses on the *Decretum* of Gratian in the first half century after its publication (c. 1140-1190), whose arguments on the point at issue were to be decisive for the rest of the Middle Ages.[5] The problem is the perennial one of discrimination in poor relief – whether eligibility for relief should be determined by need alone or by other considerations, whether there should be any fixed order of preference among eligible applicants, whether the principles of selection should be conditioned by a desire to reform, or alternatively to punish, the paupers seeking relief.

The most common criticism of medieval charity is that it hardly concerned itself with this question at all. As far back as 1870 Emminghaus argued that the whole orientation of medieval ethics, with their emphasis on almsgiving as atonement for sin and as a way of winning a reward in the next world, militated against any serious consideration of the real needs and deserts of the beggar. The medieval system, he maintained, was not really aiming at the alleviation of want; rather it encouraged idleness and pauperism.[6] In 1881 Franz Ehrle

---

[4] A sketch of this "legal philosophy" is attempted in the book *Medieval Poor Law* (Berkeley and Los Angeles, 1959). Ermenegildo Lio has recently been investigating the nature and extent of a man's obligation to contribute to the support of the poor in the works of the scholastic theologians. See especiall: his article, "Le obligazioni verso i poveri in un testo di S. Cesario riportato da Graziano," *Studia Gratiana*, III (Bologna, 1955), 51-81, which gives references to Fr. Lio's earlier studies on this theme.

[5] The basic reference work on the canonists and canonistic manuscripts of this period is Stephan Kuttner, *Repertorium der Kanonistik* (Città del Vaticano, 1937).

[6] Emminghaus, *op. cit.*, 6.

replied with a substantial list of scriptural and patristic texts which insisted that alms were to be given only in cases of genuine need,[7] but it was the views of Emminghaus that found more general acceptance. In England, for instance, they were taken over with little qualification by the Webbs in their *English Poor Law History*, though the authors did give a passing nod of recognition to the "isolated sentences" from the church fathers adduced by Ehrle.[8]

The issue is really one that cannot be decided by the mere citation of texts for the simple reason that there is an abundance of texts that can be quoted on both sides of the question. The point that the earlier controversialists missed was that medieval men themselves were quite well aware of this fact and often set themselves to explain the dichotomy in the source material available to them. Indeed, for some historians of scholastic thought, the principal interest of this question might be that it provides a very good example of twelfth century dialectical technique in action.

In spite of his own title for his work, *Concordia Discordantium Canonum*, Gratian himself did not harmonize all the "discordances" in the great collection of texts that he assembled, and our problem of discrimination in charity is a case in point. Gratian presented an excellent selection of texts bearing on the subject but did not explain how they were to be reconciled with one another. At one point in his work he wrote, *In hospitalitate autem non est habendus delectus personarum, sed indifferenter quibuscumque sufficimus hospitales nos exhibere debemus*;[9] and in support of this doctrine of "indiscriminate charity" he cited a passage of St. John Chrysostom which began with the trenchant words, *Quiescamus ab hac absurda curiositate et diabolica et peremptoria*. The passage went on to explain that if a stranger presented himself as a priest he was to be examined, but that normally a man who simply asked for food was to be helped without question, for it was not the deserts of the recipient but the generosity and goodwill of the giver that counted in the sight of God.

Further on in the *Decretum* Gratian wrote of the quality of generosity to the poor which he held to be essential in a good bishop, and here he observed, *In ipsa autem liberalitate modus adhibendus est rerum et personarum*.[10] Gratian illustrated this requirement with a series of texts taken from the *De Officiis* of St. Ambrose, which specified the classes of persons who were to receive preferential treatment in the administration of ecclesiastical charity. Faithful Christians had a prior claim on the resources of the church, and also those

[7] Ehrle, *op. cit.*, 10-24.

[8] Sidney and Beatrice Webb, *English Poor Law History*, I (London, 1927), 4-5, "The diligent student can pick out all down the centuries, from the more statesmanlike Catholic writers, isolated sentences pointing to the duty of practical wisdom in almsgiving... But the overwhelming tendency of regarding alms as an act of piety, like fasting and prayer principally from the standpoint of the state of mind of the giver was in the direction of dismissing all considerations with regard to the character of the recipient."

[9] D. 42 *post* c. 1.

[10] D. 86 *post* c. 6.

who were unable to work through age or sickness and those who were victims of misfortune. The administrator of charity was also to concern himself specially with those needy persons who were ashamed to beg publicly for alms.[11] In this same context Gratian also quoted St. Augustine who had held that no alms were to be given to followers of infamous professions such as actors, prostitutes, gladiators.[12] There was also another text of Augustine, cited twice in the *Decretum*, that could have formed the basis for a severely punitive system of poor relief, "It is more useful to take bread away from a hungry man than to break bread for him if, being sure of his food, he neglected righteousness."[13]

C. R. Cheney, commenting on the common medieval gibes against those who studied the profitable science of law instead of the more spiritually rewarding discipline of theology, has recently observed that, "so long as they read their Gratian they would absorb the right ideas about the priestly office and the pastoral care – largely indeed in the very words of the early Fathers." This is true enough as regards the administration of charity, but Gratian's texts only served to illustrate the divergence of opinion that existed among the fathers themselves. It was for the canonists to make what they could out of the materials provided.

The first of the Decretists, Paucapalea, was content to repeat in different contexts the two contrasting points of view put forward by Gratian himself, and none of the works of the next decade, the *Summa Rolandi, Summa Ius aliud divinum* or *Summa Sicut vetus testamentum* addressed themselves to the problems of poor relief implicit in Gratian's comments and quotations. Rufinus, however, whose important *Summa* on the *Decretum* was completed at Bologna in the years 1157-59, did undertake a detailed discussion of the need for discrimination in almsgiving.[14] Commenting on Gratian's words, *In hospitalitate autem non est habendus delectus personarum*, Rufinus first pointed out that there were many texts expressing a contrary point of view, and he went on to quote several of them. The first, *Desudet elemosina in manu tua donec invenies iustum cui des* seems to have been a kind of proverbial saying in the Middle Ages.[15] Next, Rufinus cited the Canticle of Canticles, *Ordinavit in me caritatem*[16] together with the interpretation of St. Ambrose who had taught

---

[11]   D. 86 cc. 14-18.

[12]   D. 86 cc. 7-9.

[13]   C. 5 q. 5 c. 2 and C. 23 q. 4 c. 37, "Melius est cum severitate diligere quam lenitate decipere. Utilius esurienti panis tollitur, si de cibo securus iustitiam negligebat quam esurienti panis frangitur ut iniustitiae seductus acquiescat."

[14]   *Die Summa Decretorum des Magister Rufinus*, ed. H. Singer (Paderborn, 1902), *Summa ad* D. 42 *post* c. 1, pp. 100-101. See infra, Appendix A.

[15]   Rufinus did not give any reference for this text, but later canonists often quoted it as being *in scripturis* or in *evangelio*. It does not in fact occur in the Scriptures, though it might have been suggested by Eccles XII. 2, "Benefac iusto et invenies retributionem magnam."

[16]   *Cant. Canticorum* II. 4.

that *caritas ordinata* required a man to love first God, then his parents, then his children, then those of his own household and finally strangers. This text became as important in subsequent canonistic discussion as the passages of St. Ambrose that were incorporated in the *Decretum* itself; the canonists always strongly emphasized the duty of a man to provide for any member of his own family who fell into want. Finally Rufinus quoted the *Glossa Ordinaria* to Matthew V.42, *Da ei ita scilicet ut nec tibi nec alii noceat; pensanda enim est iustitia.*

Rufinus then set himself to reconcile these texts with the passage of the *Decretum* under discussion by a series of distinctions. In almsgiving, he suggested, four factors were to be considered – the quality of the person seeking alms, the resources of the giver, the cause of the petition and the amount requested. In the first place the beggar was either *honestus* or *inhonestus*. If he was *inhonestus* and especially if he was a man capable of working who preferred rather to beg and steal, certainly nothing was to be given to him but he was to be corrected (unless he was actually dying of hunger). If the resources available were sufficient then all the *honesti* could be helped, but if there was not enough for all then the rules of St. Ambrose regarding discrimination in charity were to be adopted. These distinctions applied when the applicant was known. All those who were unknown and who asked only for food were to be helped, but an unknown man who claimed support on the ground that he was sent as a preacher was to be examined. Demands for excessive sums were to be refused.

These distinctions and categories of Rufinus eventually proved very influential but they were not at once generally accepted. Three major *summae* of the French school written in the 1160's put forward alternative approaches to the problem of discrimination. The *Summa Parisiensis* (c. 1160) suggested tersely that the texts in favor of indiscriminate giving meant that all were to be helped while those in favor of discrimination meant that there could be some differentiation in the treatment of the persons who received help according to their status.[17]

Stephanus Tornacensis offered still another solution. Gratian had written, *In hospitalitate autem non est habendus delectus personarum*, but then again, *In ipsa autem liberalitate modus adhibendus est rerum et personarum*. Stephanus called attention to the difference in terminology. Evidently "hospitality" was one thing, "liberality" or almsgiving something different.

Nota aliud esse in eleemosyna danda, aliud in hospitalitate sectanda. In eleemosyna danda habendus est delectus personarum, ut si viderit quis iustum et iniustum pauperem, prius detur iusto, et secundum ordinatam caritatem prius suis egentibus quam alienis, prius infirmo quam sano, prius seni quam iuveni, prius erubescenti mendicare quam effronti. In hospitalitate non est delectus habendus, sed, cum hospitium a

[17] The *Summa Parisiensis on the Decretum Gratiani*, ed. T. P. McLaughlin (Toronto, 1952), *Summa ad* D. 42 c. 2, p. 38. "Non debet esse delectus quin omnibus subveniatur quibus potest, et erit delectus et in dispersione et in distinctione honoris personarum."

nobis petitur, omnes quos possumus recipere recipiamus, nec dicamus: reciperem te si esses clericus, si esses illius aut illius conditionis.[18]

Stephanus here seems to have touched on a topic that was to become a major theme of controversy in later poor law history, the distinction between indoor and outdoor relief. It is possible to think of a number of reasons to justify the view that hospitality, indoor relief, could be offered to all who applied, while almsgiving had to be more strictly regulated. In some later systems, for instance, it proved possible to make the "hospitality" so extremely unattractive that only the really desperate would apply for it.

One does not, however, have the impression that Stephanus had reflected on these matters, but rather that he had merely seized on a verbal discrepancy in order to resolve a dialectical tension. The more common tradition among the canonists was to take the word *hospitalitas* as a generic term that included all forms of poor relief, but Stephanus' solution did find some support among canonists of the French school.

The next major work of that school expressly rejected it however. The *Summa Elegantius in iure divino* (c. 1169) opened its discussion thus:

Sextum apostolice regule capitulum est hospitalem esse. In quo utrum delectus habendus sit queri potest. Videtur quod sic, inde quia species est elemosine.[19]

This author pointed out that according to St. Ambrose we ought to help our own before strangers, the sick before the well, the just before the unjust and so on, and that according to St. Augustine it was a sin to give to members of infamous professions, but that, on the other hand, St. John Chrysostom would have us aid all indiscriminately. His solution was based on the donor's knowledge of the applicants or lack of it. If he did not know anything about their way of life he was to give to all provided that his resources sufficed; if he did know them and he had not enough for all, then the usual system of preferences was to be applied. This conclusion seems substantially similar to that of Rufinus, but the author of the *Summa Elegantius* did not refer to any class of *inhonesti* who were to be excluded from relief even when ample resources were available.

Meanwhile the arguments of Rufinus which had begun the whole discussion seem to have been accepted for the time being at Bologna. Johannes Faventinus in his *Summa*, written shortly after 1171, was content to repeat Rufinus verbatim without taking any note of the intervening discussions. A number of French

---

[18]   *Die Summa der Stephanus Tornacensis über das Decretum Gratiani*, ed. J. F. v. Schulte (Giessen, 1891), *Summa ad* D. 42 c. 2, p. 62.

[19]   MS Paris BN 14997, fol. 15 v. The passage continued, "In elemosina autem delectus est habendus personarum ut potius suis quam alienis, infirmis quam sanis, mendicare erubescenti quam effronti, egenti quam habenti et inter egentes prius iusto quam iniusto des. Hec est caritas ordinata, unde Dominus, 'Desudet', inquit 'elemosina in manu tua....' Item Augustinus, 'Donare histrionibus vitium immane est non virtus....' E contra Iohannes Chrisostomus, 'Si quis sacerdotem se nominat, scrutare. Si pro nutrimento postulat non examines.' Verum hec sibi non contradicunt, ut si postulantium vita nescitur et omnibus sufficimus omni petenti tribuatur. Cesset examinatio unde non agnoscitur petentis persona. Si vita cognoscitur delectus habeatur."

works of the 1170's also made use of the distinctions and categories proposed by Rufinus without, however, accepting all his conclusions. The *Summa Inperatorie maiestati* held that both the receiving of guests and the dispensing of alms were included in the term *hospitalitas,* and discussed the second meaning under the headings, *qualitas petentis, facultas tribuentis, res petita* and *modus petitionis.* The author was especially insistent that only common foodstuffs should be given to the poor, not rich delicacies, a point often repeated by later canonists.[20] (Simon de Bisignano quoted an anecdote from Galen to prove that luxurious foods were bad for the poor just as coarse foods were bad for the rich.[21]) The author of the *Inperatorie Maiestati* added that demands accompanied by force or threats were to be refused. The *Summa Tractaturus magister* presented a discussion that consisted in the main of an elaborate structure of cross-references, the argument closely following that of Rufinus.[22]

About 1180 Sicardus undertook an unusually lengthy review of various problems involved in the administration of charity, resting his discussion, as Stephanus had done, on a distinction between hospitality and almsgiving. He

---

[20] *Summa ad* D. 42, MS Munich, Staatsbibliothek 16084, fol. 6 rb, "Hospitalitas in duobus consistit, in hospitis receptione et elemosine largitione. Circa elemosinam ista considerari solent, qualitas petentis, facultas tribuentis, res petita et modus petitionis. In prima discretio est habenda. Primo subveniendum est parentibus, deinde filiis, deinde familie, deinde aliis notis, deinde omnibus, set prius christianis, deinde infidelibus, quia dicit apostolus, "Operantes bonum ad omnes, maxime tamen ad domesticos fidei" (Gal. VI. 10). Facultas eius qui dare debet, an dives sit an pauper. Res petita consideranda est, an pretiosa sit an minus bona, an delitiosa sint fercula an rusticana, quia vero peccare dicitur qui delitiosa et voluptuosiora fercula pauperibus prestat. Modus petitionis; refert enim an solius Dei intuitu requirat an vi vel more mimico velit extorquere. Pro Deo petenti non denegatur, secundo denegari debet, quia quod ioculatoribus datur demonibus immolatur."

[21] *Summa ad* D. 25 *post* c. 3 MS Bamberg, Staatsbibliothek Can. 38, p. 7, "Huius prohibitionis ratio potuit esse huiusmodi. Ex eo enim pretio quo quis emit lautos cibos qui sufficiant tribus pauperibus poterant emi tot de communibus qui sufficiant forte x, et melius est pluribus dare modicum quam uni totum. ... Vel ideo quia sicut infirmatur dives si utatur vilibus ut infra d. xli *Non cogantur* (c. 3) sic infirmantur pauperes si utantur preciosis. Sicut de quodam Galienus narrat qui de arato ad regnum est vocatus et dum uteretur preciosis cepit deficere nisi ad consueta nature transmitteretur." Huguccio added a third reason why delicacies were not to be given to the poor, "Scilicet quia inde pauperes provocantur ad libidinem et excitatur irritamentum gule." (*Summa ad* D. 25 *post* c. 3, MS Admont, Stiftsbibliothek 7, fol. 36 vb.)

[22] *Summa ad* D. 42 *post* c. 1, MS Paris BN 15994, fol. 13 ra, "*In hospitalitate autem non est habendus delectus personarum*: d. lxxxvi *Non satis* (c. 14) contra. Et in evangelio, 'Desudet elemosina in manu tua' etc. contra. In canticum canticorum, ibi 'Ordinavit in me caritatem' glossa 'Primo Deus diligendus est, secundo parentes, inde filii, postea propinqui, qui si boni sunt malis filiis sunt preferendi'. In evangelio mathei, ibi, 'Omni petenti te tribue', glossa 'Si non das rem da vel benedictionem vel correctionem' contra. Solvo. Consideranda est persona petentis ut non detur nisi honestis et illis potius qui ministrant spiritualia secundum verbum evangelii, d. lxxxvi *Donare* (c. 7), v q. v *Non omnis* (c. 2), in quo casu locuta prima duo contra. Facultas dantis, etiam ubi persona petentis est honesta ut d. lxxxvi *Non satis* (c. 14) ibi *Est* et *alia,* quo casu intelliguntur iii contra. Causa petendi ut in sequenti capitulo, *Quiescamus* (c. 2), d. lxxxvi *Qui venatoribus* (c. 8). ... Quantitas petiti ut di. lxxxvi *Non satis* ibi *misericordia tamen,* quibus casibus iiii contra. Excepta ubique ultima necessitate ut d. lxxxvi *Non satis* ibi *Pasce* (c. 21). Vel aliud est in helemosina ut in predictis contra, aliud in hospitalitate ut hic.

discussed the position of a man charged with the administration of another's property (whether he could give alms from it) and struck an unusual note in discussing the quality of food to be distributed to the poor when, instead of declaring like everybody else that it should not be *deliciosa*, he wrote that it should not be *vitiosa*. Sicardus also enlarged the textual basis of the discussion by throwing in quotations from Seneca along with the usual scriptural and patristic passages. But there was nothing really original in his discussion on discrimination among applicants for relief. His gloss was essentially a synthesis and amplification of points of view developed in the *Summa Stephani*, the *Summa Parisiensis* and the *Summa Elegantius*.[23]

Hitherto we have considered works of the Bolognese and French schools of canonists. Another particularly interesting and thoughtful contribution to the discussion came from the Anglo-Norman school in the *Summa Omnis qui iuste* probably written at Oxford in about 1186.[24] In this work, as in the *Summa Elegantius*, the primary distinction was between those poor who were known to the administrator of charity and those who were strangers. Among those who were known the more deserving cases were to be preferred to the less deserving. As for the strangers, a man claiming support as a priest was to be examined, while any who asked only food for the love of God were to be helped. But the author made one significant exception to this rule. A man who was capable of working with his hands was not to be given anything but was to be corrected and told to go to work. This reservation was common enough in the glosses dependent on Rufinus, but the English canonist was unusual in suggesting that the test of ability to work was one that could be applied even to strangers. He showed another unusual insight when, having declared that an able-bodied pauper should be refused alms and corrected, he added, "These things are true provided that he can find someone to employ him" (*Hec ita vera sunt si possit repperire cui serviat*.)

The author next introduced Stephanus' distinction between hospitality and almsgiving, and here again he had something original to contribute for he seems to have been the first to have suggested any specific reason for the distinction.

Vel forte aliud est in hospitalitate aliud in elemosinis quia durum est viatori respondere scrutanti.

If we bear in mind that the man seeking hospitality would commonly be a traveller, a stranger, who could not easily prove his identity or his deserts, then Stephanus' doctrine that there should be no discrimination in hospitality seems complementary to Rufinus' view that all petitioners who were unknown should be regarded as eligible for help. After these very pertinent observations the author of the *Summa Omnis qui iuste* continued, "This is a brief and useful distinction. Others distinguish more fully and better thus...." And he went

---

[23] *Infra*, Appendix B.
[24] *Infra*, Appendix C.

on with a conventional analysis in terms of the cause of the petition, person of the applicant and resources of the giver. In another context this canonist pointed to some problems posed by St. Ambrose's suggested order of preference among applicants for relief. It might be that a close relative who was a very bad man and an outsider who was a very good man were both in need. Who should then have first claim on a man's resources? Or again, what was to be done if two men, one very righteous and the other very unrighteous, were both in danger of death and only one could be saved? According to St. Ambrose we ought to help the just before the unjust, but in this case if the unjust man was allowed to die he would go straight to Hell, whereas if he was saved he might repent. On the other hand, if the just man died he would go to Heaven. It would seem therefore that we ought to give preference to the unjust. The glossator concluded doubtfully, "But this is not exactly true," and left this knotty problem unsolved.[25]

There are certain elements common to all the glosses considered so far. In the first place there was no disposition at all to regard a state of poverty as itself implying a moral defect in the individual concerned. On the other hand it was always recognized that, among the poor, some cases were more deserving than others and that, when the resources available did not suffice for all, the more deserving cases were to be helped first. Also, it was very generally agreed that when funds were adequate strangers should be given the benefit of the doubt, should be helped without prior inquisition as to their merits. Finally, all the canonists held that if a man was actually near death from starvation then he was to be helped regardless of all other considerations.

But on one important point there was a sharp cleavage of opinion. Some canonists held that there was a class of undeserving poor who were to be denied alms on principle even when ample resources were available; others held that the only ground for excluding a needy applicant was inadequacy of funds. Rufinus and the authors of the *Summa Tractaturus magister* and the *Summa Omnis qui iuste*, for instance, held the first view. Sicardus and the authors of the *Summa Parisiensis*, the *Summa Elegantius* and the *Summa Inperatorie maiestati* held the second.

The first position was commonly supported by the citation of St. Augustine's words, "It is more useful to take bread away from a hungry man if, being sure of his food, he neglected righteousness." As for the types of undeserving to be

---

[25] *Summa ad* D. 86 C. 14, MS Rouen, Bibliothèque muncipale 743, fol. 40 r, "Set quero utri citius subveniendum esset, vel patri qui iniustus est vel alii qui iustus est. Item si iudeus ad fidem conversus videret patrem suum adhuc iudeum et obstinatum indigentem utrum citius deberet dare et illi subvenire quam christiano et iusto. Item ubi concurrunt duo istorum, puto conditio, etas. Quid in hoc casu faciendum est? Utrum citius deberet dare nobili indigenti vel seni. Sic potest queri in aliis duobus concurrentibus. Item si teneantur duo ab hostibus, alter iustissimus, alter iniustissimus et nisi statim redimantur, interficiantur, uter est redimendus? Et videtur quod iniustissimus quia si redimatur adhuc poterit corrigi. Si autem interficiatur statim transit ad gehennam. Iustus autem statim ad gloriam. Unde non videtur quod ita necessarium sit eum redimere sicut et alium. Hoc autem non est precise verum.

excluded, Rufinus mentioned that alms were to be refused "especially to a man who can seek food by his own work", but the use of the word "especially" implies that he had others in mind as well. Rufinus' successors who discussed this point brought into play the other texts of Augustine which condemned giving to those who followed an evil way of life. The canonists who taught that all *inhonesti* were to be refused alms commonly cited adherents of infamous professions, prostitutes and *ioculatores* for instance, as examples of persons who were ineligible for help unless they were actually *in extremis*. The other group of canonists taught that there was nothing wrong in helping such people whenever they were in need; the only sin was to give to them "for the exercise of their evil arts", and this they took to be the meaning of St. Augustine.[26]

The problem here is a central one for all poor relief systems. The issue involved is whether administrators of relief should aim simply at alleviating want or should also seek, by withholding relief, to punish (or reform) those among the needy whose way of life seems morally objectionable. The decisive treatment of this question came from the great canonist Huguccio whose *Summa*, completed towards 1190, is generally reckoned as the greatest achievement of the Bolognese school of Decretists. The views of Huguccio were accepted in the *Glossa Ordinaria* of Johannes Teutonicus, written a generation later, and so continued to be studied all through the Middle Ages as the standard exposition of the problem.

After citing an ample selection of texts for and against indiscriminate charity, Huguccio put forward the by then conventional distinction between the poor who were known and those who were strangers. The stranger was to be helped without examination unless he claimed to be a priest. Among those who were known all were eligible for help, according to Huguccio, except only "one who, being sure of his food, neglects righteousness". This seems an evasion. We are told in effect that all should be helped except those who would be morally injured by freely available charity, but we are not told who these people are.[27] Huguccio, however, was quoting the familiar text of St. Augustine, so we can turn to his gloss on that passage of the *Decretum* for further information. There his position was made clear.

---

[26] *Summa Parisiensis* ad D. 86 *post* c. 6, ed. cit. p. 67, "In subveniendo, si omnibus potest, non debet esse delectus. Sed in modo subveniendi, quod hic dicit quibusdam sicut mimis et joculatoribus, *prohibemur* dare eo respectu quia sunt joculatores, cum alias non essemus daturi." *Summa Elegantius* ad D. 86, MS Paris BN 14997, fol. 41 r, "Histrioni quia membrorum et vultus transformatione corporis sui ludibrium exhibet dare vitandum est, sed si arta necessitate laboret et huic et venatori subvenire officii est. (Ubi ergo legitur talibus dandum non esse, subintelligendum est ob causam professionis sue.)" The words *Ubi ergo ... professionis sue*, lacking in the Paris MS, are supplied from MS Bamberg Can. 39; they also occur in MS Vienna, Staatsbibl. 2125. Sicardus, *Summa ad* D. 42, MS Bamberg Can. 38, p. 125, "Histrionibus aut meretricibus, venatoribus non est dandum quia qui donat istis non donat homini set arti nequissime ... nisi in necessitate; tunc enim das homini non arti." (cf. *infra* Appendix B).

[27] *Infra*, Appendix D.

Set hic intelligitur in eo casu cum quis potest laborare et suo labore sibi victum querere et non vult, set tota die ludit in alea vel taxillis.[28]

The class of poor who would be encouraged in their evil ways by receiving assistance was thus defined as the able-bodied who were able to work but chose rather to idle their time away. Consistently with this position Huguccio held that followers of vile professions were eligible for help whenever they were in need.[29]

These arguments applied when sufficient funds were available for all applicants. If there was not enough for all the usual rules of preference derived from St. Ambrose were to be applied, with the proviso that cases of severe need were to be helped first.[30] The canonistic discussions thus issued in a doctrine which did regard one category of undeserving poor as ineligible for assistance, but limited that category to the wilfully idle. Those whose way of life was objectionable on other grounds were not ineligible. There remained a certain ambivalence in the canonistic position, however, since, if the charitable funds available were not sufficient for everyone, which must after all have been a common situation, then, other things being equal, a good man was to be helped before a wicked one.

Some of the preoccupations of the canonists will seem very remote from those of modern social workers and public assistance administrators. For instance, the distinction which they always made and which was evidently very important to them, between a stranger who claimed to be a priest and one who asked alms only for charity's sake, is meaningful only in the context of medieval life. On the other hand, some of the canonists' insights and arguments retain their relevance. The public assistance worker who has had the task of interviewing the relatives of an applicant for relief to determine whether they can contribute to his support will find a familiar ring in the canonists' insistence that a man's first charitable obligation was to provide for members of his own family. (One text of the *Decretum* laid down that a widow was not to be maintained out of church funds if her parents were capable of supporting her.[31]) Again, many a modern social worker will have found herself trying to reform the way of life of a client to whom she is administering assistance and will have wondered how far her responsibilities in this direction extend or ought to extend. But the most perennially relevant of all the canonists' considerations is surely the

[28] *Summa ad* C. 5 q. 5 c. 2, MS Admont, Stiftsbibliothek 7, fol. 191 vb.
[29] *Summa ad* D. 86 c. 7, MS Admont 7, fol. 110 va, "*Dare ystrionibus* . . . Istis dare causa inanis glorie pro exercitio sui vitii peccatum est. Set in necessitate dare eis intuitu pietatis peccatum non est . . . nam vitium in talibus non est fovendum, set natura substentanda est."
[30] On this, besides the passage quoted in Appendix D, see *Summa ad* D. 86 c. 14, MS Admont 7, fol. 111 rb, "Primo enim debemus subvenire domesticis fidei et postea alienis a fide, et intelliguntur ea que hic dicuntur cum equaliter indigent domestici et alii vel plus domestici, set si alii plus indigeant, puta ad mortem, primo eis subveniendum est, ut infra eadem, *Pasce* (c. 21). Item quod hic dicitur intelligitur cum extraneus a fide (non est nobis pater vel filius vel consanguineus. Tunc enim extraneus a fide) preponi debet alii, scilicet domestico fidei." (Words *non est* . . . *a fide* supplied from MS Vatican lat. 2280.)
[31] C. 1 q. 2 c. 5.

distinction which they so often drew between the situation that existed when funds were ample and that which obtained when the resources available were insufficient to provide for all the needy. For it seems to be almost a law of nature that poor relief agencies that are sympathetically administered operate with less funds than the administrators themselves regard as necessary.

Even in the context of modern public assistance it can happen that a legislature defines standards of eligibility but fails to appropriate sufficient funds to provide adequately for all who qualify for relief according to the standards laid down. The situation does indeed arise in practice. It arose in Washington D.C. during 1957. The modern public assistance worker thinks of his case work as being concerned with the establishment of "eligibility" or "non-eligibility" rather than with the old-fashioned discrimination between the "deserving" and the "undeserving" poor. And yet, both in public assistance and private charities, if there is simply not enough money available to supply all those in need, then presumably in practice some principles of discrimination must be applied. It would be interesting to know whether such principles bear any resemblance to those that the canonists advocated in the twelfth century, or St. Ambrose in the fourth.

Washington, D.C.

APPENDIX

A. Rufinus, *Summa ad* D. 42 *dictum Gratiani post* c. 1.

In hospitalitate autem non est habendus delectus personarum. . . . Hoc multis contrarietatibus patet. Et primum, quia dicitur "Desudet elemosina in manu tua, donec invenies iustum cui des". Post, quia differenter quibusdam dare debemus, unde in canticis, "Ordinavit in me caritatem". Caritas debet esse ordinata ut post Deum parentes, deinde filii, post domestici, ad ultimum extranei diligantur. Infra dist. lxxxvi c. *Non satis* (c. 14) habetur, quanta sit habenda differentia in impendenda misericordia. Invenitur quoque super illum locum in Matheo, "Qui petit a te da ei", (Mat. V. 42) invenitur hoc, "Da ei, ita scilicet ut nec tibi nec alii noceat; pensanda enim est iustitia". Itaque enim dabis omni petenti, etsi non id, quod petit, sed melius, cum iuste petentem correxeris. Per hec omnia claret quia non omni ad nos venienti debemus indifferenter nos exibere largificos. Sed sciendum quod in suscipientibus hospitis hec quattuor attendenda sunt, qualitas petentis alimoniam et facultas dantis, causa petitionis et quantitas petiti. Qualitas, utrum honestus vel inhonestus, facultas dantis, utrum omnibus possit sufficere vel tantum aliquibus, causa petitionis, scilicet an pro alimento tantum postulet pro amore Dei, an quia dicat se tibi missum ad predicandum et ideo pro debitis sibi stipendiis a te petat, quantitas petiti, utrum nimis vel modestum petatur. Si ergo inhonestus sit qui petit, et maxime cum possit suo opere victum querere et negligit, ita etiam ut magis eligat mendicare vel furari, procul dubio tunc ei dandum non est, sed corripiendus, in quo casu intelligitur illud predictum super Matheum, nisi forte ad mortem indigeat; tunc enim omnibus, si habemus, indifferenter dare debemus. Unde Ambrosius, "Pasce fame morientem" etc.; require in dist. lxxxvi *Non satis* (c. 14). Si autem honestus est ille, qui petit, debes omni huiusmodi dare, si facultas dandi suppetat, licet plus et melius dandum sit domesticis quam extraneis. Si autem omnibus talibus te petentibus dare non poteris, proximioribus primum dabis, in quo casu intelligende sunt auctoritates de differenter dando. Pre omnibus autem dandum ei qui tibi spiritualia seminat predicando aut orando. . . . Et hec quidem omnia exaudienda sunt in his, qui solummodo pro nutrimento postulant et cogniti sunt. Si autem pro nutrimento alimonie tantum postulet incognitus, in tali casu omnes debes suscipere. Si autem querit vel vult a te suscipi causa eius, quod tibi predicaverit vel predicaturus adveniat, non statim debes suscipere, nisi prius probes, utrum sit talis, qualem se esse protestatur, quod habetur in presenti capitulo, *Quiescamus* (c. 2). In his omnibus quantitas petite rei attendenda est. Si enim nimis petat, non est ei dandum. (*Die Summa Decretorum des Magister Rufinus*, ed. H. Singer [Paderborn, 1902] pp. 100-101.)

B. Sicardus Cremonensis, *Summa ad* D. 42.

After listing authorities against indiscriminate charity Sicardus continues:

Contra, "Omni petenti dabis" (Luc. VI. 30). Item imitare deos ut philosophus ait quia sol oritur etiam sceleratis et piratis patent maria. Item si Abraham extitisset scrutator forsitan angelos hospitio non recepisset ut di. xlii *Quiescamus* (c. 2). Respondeo. Aliud est considerandum in hospitalitate, aliud in elemosina vel liberalitate. In hospitalitate namque non est personarum habendus delectus ad suscipiendum quin omnes suscipiamus quibuscumque sufficimus. Nec dicamus, 'Reciperem te si illius uel illius conditionis esses.' Si uero non sufficimus quicquid possumus faciamus sub spirituali iudicio conscientie et sine carnali personarum acceptione, unde Iacobus, "Nolite in personarum acceptione habere fidem domini nostri Iesu Christi" (Iac. II. 1). . . . Discretio namque secundum dignitatem, etatem, sexum et similia facta propter deum effectus est iusticie et dicitur iustificatio, facta propter seculum, effectus est vane glorie et dicitur personarum acceptio. . . .

In liberalitate consideranda sunt: Persona distribuentis, utrum sit sui iuris vel alterius. Alterius ut filius familias, servus, qui si habent peculium vel amministrationem pauperibus erogare poterunt. Similiter uxor. Alioquin non sine licentia viri. . . . Qualitas distribuendorum, utrum res sit vitiosa vel non. Nam de vitiosa non faciat elemosinam nisi vitio purgato. . . . Si vero non fuerit vitiosa attendatur quantitas distribuendorum, utrum omnibus sufficere valeant, ut non omnia simul effundantur, quia dicitur, "Dispersit et dedit pauperibus" (Psal. CXI. 9), nisi velit totum veterem hominem exuere ut Heliseus. Item attendatur causa distribuendi, utrum ex debito vel solius humanitatis officio. Ex debito ut si tibi spiritualia seminavit obligatus es ut a te carnalia metat, unde "Communicet autem is" etc. (Gal. VI. 6). Si tamen nondum predicavit set predicaturus advenit scrutare ut di. xlii *Quiescamus* (c. 2) quia circa maiora periculum vertitur. Si solius humanitatis officio tunc attendatur persona suscipientis, utrum fidelis vel infidelis nam "Operemur bonum ad omnes, maxime ad domesticos fidei" (Gal. VI. 10); utrum sit dives vel pauper nam divitibus dare quid aliud est quam perdere ut C. i Q. i *Pastor* (C. 1 q. 2(!) c. 7)? Propensior ergo benignitas debetur in pauperes et calamitosos nisi sint calamitate digni, ut qui latrocinio cecidit in egestatem ut di. lxxxvi *Non satis* (c. 14). "Viduas honora que vere vidue sunt" ut C. i Q. ii *Auctoritate* (post c. 4). Item utrum tibi sit natura vel beneficiorum collatione vel sola humanitate coniunctus. Est enim ordo caritatis ut prius tuis subvenias et beneficiis respondeas, non tamen ut illos divites facias. Causam enim prestat natura non gratia ut di. lxxxvi *Non satis* (c. 14). Utrum debilis vel etate vel infirmitate, utrum verecundus qui suos prodit natales ingenuos, utrum honestus vel inhonestus. Neminem puto negligendum in quo significatio virtutis apparet ut philosophus ait. Histrionibus aut meretricibus, venatoribus (non est dandum[1]) quia qui donat istis non donat homini set arti nequissime cui nichil donandum est, nisi in necessitate; tunc enim das homini non arti, unde "Pasce fame morientem" (D. 86 c. 21), alioquin si non paveris occidisti. Similiter de hereticis et anathematis sentiendum est ut C. xi Q. iii *Quoniam* (c. 103) (MS Bamberg, Staatsbibliothek Can. 38, p. 125.)

C. *Summa Omnis qui iuste ad* D. 42 c. 2.

Per hec omnia patet quod non omni ad nos venienti debemus indifferenter nos exibere largifi-

---

[1] The words *non est dandum*, lacking in the Bamberg ms., are supplied from MS Paris BN 4288.

cos, unde quidam sic distingunt. Aut est notus aut ignotus. Si notus dignior minus digno prefertur. Si ignotus aut petit pro amore Dei vel pro nutrimento, vel ex debito, ea ratione quia dicat se sacerdotem et velit seminare spiritualia, quia secundum apostolum parum est accipere temporalia ubi seminat spiritualia. Si pro nutrimento nulli est denegandum nisi talis sit qui possit querere victum ex labore, cui dabis correptionem dicens ei quod querat sibi victum manibus suis, cui nullo modo aliquid dandum est nisi fame vergat ad interitum vel forte ultra modum indigeat. Hec ita vera sunt si possit repperire cui serviat. Si vero pro debito predicationis tunc debes scrutari an sit fidelis et si dicat se esse sacerdotem an sit sacerdos et an sit hereticus. ... Set si petat pro nutrimento dandum est tali presbytero ignoto et cuilibet alii. Vel forte aliud est in hospitalitate aliud in elemosinis quia durum est viatori respondere scrutanti. Hec distinctio brevis et utilis. Alii sufficientius et melius sic distingunt. Circa elemosine distributionem attendendum est primo causa petitionis. Si enim ratione oficii petat indagine est opus ut hic dicitur. ... Si causa pietatis hic attendatur secundo qualitas persone petentis. Si ignota est sine delectu dandum ut hic ubi dicitur, *ne in hiis* Gra(tianus) et in principio. Si nota et inhonesta dandum non est iuxta illud evangelicum, "Tunc bene tribuere intelligeris cum inportune petentem corripis". Et hec elemosina spiritualis est, de qua habetur infra d. xıv *Tria* (c. 12). Talibus enim dandum non est, ut d. lxxxvi *Donare*, *Qui venatoribus* (cc. 7, 8) et infra v q. v *Non omnis* (c. 2), set hoc ita nisi fame periclitetur. Tunc enim omni subveniendum est ut d. lxxxvi *Pasce* (c. 21). Si honesta est et abundans non est dandum ei quia ideo petit ut fiat ditior et ei dare nichil aliud est (quam) perdere ut d. lxxxvi *Non satis* (c. 14) et infra i q. ii *Clericos, Pastor* (cc. 6, 7). Si vero eget tunc consideranda est facultas eius a quo petitur. Si nulla pia intentio sufficit ut d. xlv *Due* (c. 13). Si modica sit quod potest faciat et pro magno Deus computabit ut xxiiii q. 1 *Odi* (c. 28). Si vero ampla est et non sufficit omnibus ordinatam caritatem distribuat iuxta illud "Ordinavit in me" etc. (Cantic. II. 4) et d. lxxxvi *Non satis* (c. 14). Si sufficiat omnibus et omnibus debet ut i q. ii *Quam pio* (c. 2) et xvi q. i *Si cupis* (c. 5), ne ut raptor iudicetur ut supra d. eadem § i (D. 42 dictum ante c. 1). (MS Rouen, Bibliothèque municipale 743, fol. 19 vb-20 ra).

D. Huguccio, *Summa ad* D. 42, *dictum Gratiani post* c. 1.

Eorum qui petunt eleemosinam alii sunt cogniti alii incogniti. Item alii petunt quasi ex debito ut predicatores et prelati, alii pro nutrimento et substentatione corporis. Si ergo quis petit ex debito et ratione sui officii, scilicet quia dicat se esse missum ut sit tibi prelatus et debeat tibi predicare, si cognitus est et constat tale officium esse se commisum recipiendus est et dandum est ei. Si vero est incognitus non est statim suscipiendus set premittenda est examinatio utrum ita sit sicut dicit ut infra prox. c. (c. 2). (Si vero quis petit tantum pro nutrimento et substentatione corporis et est incognitus indifferenter omnibus est dandum si omnibus dare sufficimus ut infra c. prox. (c. 2)[1]) et i q. ii *Quam pio* (c. 2) et xi q. iii *Quoniam* (c. 103) et xvi q. 1 *Si cupis* (c. 5) et xxiii q. iiii *Duo* (c. 35). Similiter si est cognitus et omnibus dare sufficimus idem est faciendum, scilicet omnibus indistincte est dandum ut in premissis capitulis, nisi quis propter securitatem cibi negligat iustitiam. Tunc subtrahendum est ei et non dandum ut v q. v *Non Omnis* (c. 2) et xxiii q. iiii *Nimium* (c. 37), nisi ad mortem indigeat. Tunc enim dandum ei ut di. lxxxvi *Pasce* (c. 21). Si vero non omnibus sufficere possumus tunc potius dandum est iusto quam iniusto, bono quam malo, consanguineo quam extraneo, religioso quam non religioso, meliori vel propinquiori vel religiosori quam minus bono vel minus propinquo vel minus religioso, ut illud "Desudet" etc. ... nisi illud (!) malus vel iniustus vel extraneus vel non religiosus vel minus bonus vel minus propinquus vel minus religiosus magis indigeat, ita quod deficiat nisi ei subveniatur. Tunc potius illi subveniendum est ut d. lxxxvi *Pasce* (c. 21), et sic plane placuntur omnes auctoritates que loquuntur de indifferenter vel differenter dando vel hospitando. (MS Admont, Stiftsbibliothek 7, fol. 59 ra.)

Reprinted by permission of Cambridge University Press

[1] The words *Si vero* ... *c. prox.*, lacking in the Admont MS, are supplied from MS Biblioteca Vaticana, Vat. Lat. 2280.

IX

"SOLA SCRIPTURA" AND THE CANONISTS

Catholic theologians agree that revealed truth is known to us through Scripture and Tradition. There are, however, various ways of understanding this duality. It is possible to assert that all the essential truths of faith are contained in the Old and New Testaments and that Tradition is, so to speak, a perpetual meditation of the church on Scripture, a continuing activity that makes ever more explicit the implicit truths of Holy Writ. Since the Council of Trent Catholic theologians have more commonly maintained that truths of faith exist which are not to be found in Scripture at all, but which were transmitted orally by Christ to the Apostles and by the Apostles to the church. An extreme and distorted form of this second doctrine would identify Tradition solely and simply with the teaching of the magisterium — or even of the pope alone — at any given moment and so would open the way to a possibility of unbridled innovation in the sphere of church doctrine; for each new declaration could be presented, without reference to Scripture, as an implicit, even if hitherto unheard-of, part of the body of undefined doctrine enshrined in the Tradition of the church. The leaders of the Protestant Reformation accused their Catholic adversaries of defending just such a conception of Tradition.

A vast new literature on these questions has appeared during the past decade (1). Our own aim is a limited one. Out of all the current argumentation we wish to isolate and criticise only one particular strand of thought, the assertion — made in several recent works — that the medieval canonists first formulated the position which we have called « extreme and distorted » and that their doctrines exercised a corrupting influence on the theology of the church in the fourteenth and fifteenth centuries.

The starting point of this modern misunderstanding can be identified clearly enough. In presenting Scripture as the sole necessary guide to Christian life John Wyclif was concerned especially to attack those *traditiones humanae* of his own day that he regarded as abuses. But, as De Vooght pointed out, these « human traditions » that Wyclif complained about were typically formulated in recent papal legislation in " Les bulles papales, les chartes de privilèges, les décrets, les décrétales... " (2). Since it was the business of the canonists to interpret and expound this material Wyclif was naturally hostile to them and he was particularly hostile to any suggestion that their decrees and decretals might be regarded as equal to the Scriptures in authority.

De Vooght noted this point without discussing it at length, but G. H. Tavard carried the argument a considerable step further. He seems to have simply taken at face value the complaints of Wyclif (and Hus) and to have assumed that the canonistic tradition of the Middle Ages did indeed tend to equate papal decretals with Holy Scripture as a source of Christian faith. " ... The most extreme instances of devaluation of Scripture are culled from the writings of canon-lawyers ", he observed; and again, " We can hardly imagine nowadays to what an extent this could reach " (3). In support of these assertions Tavard quoted the following passage from an anonymous writer of the fourteenth century:

> He, the Pope, is above all Council and all statute; he it is who has no superior on earth; he, the Pope gives dispensations

---

(1) See GULIELMUS BARAUNA, *Bibliographia traditionem eiusque habitudinem ad S. Scripturam respiciens* in CAROLUS BALIC (ed.), *De scriptura ett raditione*, Romae, 1963, pp. 85-112.

(2) PAUL DE VOOGHT, *Les sources de la doctrine chrétienne*, Bruges, 1954, p. 186.

(3) G. H. TAVARD, *Holy Writ or Holy Church*, London, 1959, pp. 38, 39.

from every Law... He it is who holds the plenitude of power
on earth and takes the place and seat of the Most High...
He it is who changes the substance of a thing, making legitimate what was illegitimate... and making a monk into a canon
regular... He it is who absolves in heaven what he absolves
on earth... over whose binding nobody trespasses, for it is
not a man, but God, who binds by giving that power to a man...
He it is who in his absolute knowledge strengthens and heals
what is sick, who supplies what is defective... To him nobody
may say: why do you do that?... He it is in whom the will
is sufficient reason, for what pleases him has the strength
of Law... he is not bound by laws... He, the Pope is the Law
itself and the living rule, opposition to which is illegitimate (4).

We shall return to this passage, but we may note at the outset
that, for all its extravagant language, it does not say anything specifically about the authority of Scripture or about the pope as a source
of divine revelation.

Heiko A. Oberman, in his brilliant and perceptive book on late
medieval nominalism, has offered a different interpretation of medieval
canonistic thought. He called attention to a passage of St. Basil
which traced certain liturgical practices back to an unwritten apostolic
tradition and to the fact that this passage was incorporated in
Gratian's *Decretum* at Dist. 11. c. 5. Oberman commented on this,
" For the canon lawyer, then, the two-sources theory has been accepted: canon law stands on the two pillars of Scripture and Tradition ".
He added that, in the fourteenth century, when the canonists stood
at the height of their prestige, " the canon-law tradition started to
feed into the major theological stream... " (5). On this we may make
the preliminary remark that Gratian incorporated very many texts
into the *Decretum* with which he himself did not wholly agree and
that, to understand the significance of any particular one of them
in the growth of canonistic thought, a careful study of the exegetical
tradition of the glossators is needed. Since we are concerned mainly
with the impact of Decretist thought on the later Middle Ages we

---

(4) *op. cit.*, p. 39, citing R. Scholz, *Unbekannte kirchenpolitische Streitschriften aus der Zeit Ludwigs des Bayern*, II, Rome, 1914, p. 544.

(5) Heiko A. Oberman, *The Harvest of Medieval Theology*, Cambridge, Mass., 1963, pp. 369, 372.

shall rely especially on the *Glossa Ordinaria* of Johannes Teutonicus and on the *Rosarium* of Guido de Baysio, for, taken together, these two works contain almost all that was living of the Decretist tradition at the beginning of the fourteenth century.

There are thus two modern arguments to be considered. One asserts that the canonists favored a " two-sources theory " of divine revelation because of their excessive regard for the innovative powers of the pope, the other that they favored this same theory because of an excessive regard for ancient tradition. The two arguments are hardly compatible with one another and, in fact, they are both mistaken. Canonistic teaching throughout the twelfth and thirteenth centuries was entirely consistent with the doctrine commonly taught by the theologians of that age — that Holy Scripture contained, implicitly or explicitly, all the revealed truths of Christian faith. We use the words " consistent with " because the precise issue of the relationship between Scripture and Tradition was not extensively discussed by the earlier canonists. But, when the problem did arise as a matter of overt controversy at the beginning of the fourteenth century, the definitive canonical solution of it took the form of a strong affirmation of the " single-source theory ", if we may adapt Oberman's terminology. (We shall use the term " single-source theory " to describe the view that all necessary truths of Christian faith are contained in the Scriptures as interpreted by the Tradition of the church). This canonical decision was handed down to the later Middle Ages in the *Extravagantes Johannis XXII* and no major canonist of the fourteenth century dissented from it. In view of these facts the modern argument that, at just this point in time, the canonists began to influence medieval ecclesiology in the direction of a " two-sources theory " of revelation seems highly paradoxical.

* * *

We can perhaps best explain the paradox and show how the texts cited by Tavard and Oberman fit into the real canonical tradition of the Middle Ages if we first discuss some aspects of medieval canonical jurisprudence in general, then analyse the account of the sources of canon law given in the first twenty *Distinctiones* of Gratian's *Decretum* and, finally, consider Decretalist developments of doctrine against this background of thought.

Oberman was entirely correct when he wrote that " canon law stands on the two pillars of Scripture and Tradition ". But this does not in the least imply that the canonists believed in two sources of divine revelation.   The essential point is that the great bulk of medieval canon law was not, and did not purport to be, divinely revealed truth.   On the contrary, the task of distinguishing what was divine and permanent in the life of the church from what was human and transitory lay at the very heart of the whole medieval enterprise of constructing a science of canon law separate from the science of theology.   Unless this is grasped at the outset the whole structure of canonistic claims on behalf of the papacy will indeed seem extravagant, paradoxical, hardly intelligible.   We should not be misled by the canonists' frequent assertions that the whole of their jurisprudence constituted a sacred science.   Canon law could be called sacred in that it regulated the life of holy church.   It was sacred again in that the popes and bishops who administered it held divinely ordained offices.   Moreover, every kind of law, including secular human law, was conceived of as divine in the sense that " the powers that be are ordained of God ' (6).   In such a climate of thought it was easy for the canonists to call all their laws " sacred " while maintaining a sharp and clear distinction between those that were of merely human origin, and so subject to change, and those that were truly divine, and hence immutable.   The immutable divine laws included those rules of morality that Gratian called natural law and also the supernatural truths of Christian faith.   The statements on papal power which have led some modern scholars to treat the canonists as proponents of a " two-sources theory " of divine revelation simply did not apply to these areas of Christian life and thought.

---

(6) On the " divinity " of human law see *Dist.* 8, *c.* 1 *...iura humana per imperatores et reges saeculi Deus distribuit generi humano* and *Dig.* 1. 2. 2, *...omnis lex inventum et munus deorum est...* Similarly HOSTIENSIS, *Lectura ad X.* 1. 14. 4, *...ars artium est divina lex a qua non est excludenda canonica nec humana...* On the high claims of Hostiensis and other canonists for the dignity of their own science see especially STEPHAN KUTTNER, *Harmony from Dissonance*, Latrobe, 1960, pp. 48-50, 62-64. The distinction between canon law which could be called divine because founded *by* God and canon law that could be called divine because founded by men *for* God was brought out clearly in an anonymous gloss of the twelfth century cited by WALTER ULLMANN, *Medieval Papalism*, London, 1949, p. 42, (Jus divinum est) *a Deo insitum menti, ut lex naturalis; a Deo traditum: lex Mosaica; a Deo editum: evangelicum; pro Deo conditum: canones.* Similarly GUIDO DE BAYSIO, *Rosarium Decretorum*, Strassburg, 1473, *ad Dist.* 1, c. 1, *Divine* (leges), *i. e. a Deo per ministros suos late vel de divinis rebus late.*

352

The idea of a ruler set above human law but below divine and natural law is of course a commonplace of medieval political theory. The point we wish to emphasize is that the intrinsic nature of the doctrine of sovereignty that the canonists were operating with rendered virtually unthinkable any application of that doctrine to the sphere of divine revelation. In developing their doctrine of papal *plenitudo potestatis* the canonists, as is well known, were much influenced by the Roman law theory of imperial power. They very often applied to the pope phrases that the classical jurists had used of the emperor and, indeed, it is precisely such usages that tend to offend modern scholars who find the canonistic claims for the papacy excessive. Now an essential element in the Roman law theory of sovereignty was the doctrine that the Prince was not bound by existing laws. If such laws had been enacted by any inferior authority the Prince stood above them; if they had been enacted by the Prince's own predecessor then he was not bound by an equal (7). The Decretists and Decretalists enthusiastically accepted this argument. It was of the essence of their doctrine that the pope could repeal old laws and make new ones. But it was also evident to the medieval canonists — if not to their modern critics — that a doctrine of sovereignty conceived in such terms could not possibly apply to the permanent, revealed truths of the Christian faith. By definition a permanent truth cannot be subject to repeal. Hence the canonists were able to apply the Roman law doctrine of sovereignty to the pope only by carefully delimiting the sphere within which juridical sovereignty could be exercised — and this sphere was, in essence, all that was of human origin in the life of the church.

The problems that concern us arose at the beginning of Gratian's *Decretum*. It's very first words were these:

> *Humanum genus duobus regitur, naturali videlicet iure et moribus. Ius naturale est quod in lege et Evangelio continetur...* (8).

---

(7) *Dig.* 1. 3. 31, *Princeps legibus solutus est.* The Ordinary Gloss of Accursius commented, " *Princeps legibus,* ab alio conditis ut infra *de. arbit.* 1. *nam et magistratus* vel a seipso ut infra *de arbit.* l. penultim. " in *Corpus Iuris Civilis,* Lugduni, 1627, I, col. 80. At *Dig.* 4. 8. 4, col. 626 Accursius cited the familiar maxim: *par parem cogere non potest.*

(8) *Dist.* 1 *ante* c. 1. The word *moribus* can be taken here, as the Ordinary Gloss pointed out (in *Decretum Gratiani,* Venetiis, 1600), to mean human law in general, " *Moribus, i. e. consuetudinario iure, vel etiam iure humano sive scripto sive non scripto*".

There are two sources, it should be noted, natural law contained in Scripture and human law. Gratian had no idea that there might be three sources — Scripture, extra-Scriptural revelation and man-made law.

The first six *Distinctiones* of the *Decretum* defined the various types of human law and explained that the term " natural law " was being used to mean, not the whole content of Scripture in general, but the permanent principles of morality revealed in it. Having made this clear, Gratian could next describe the degree of authority of the various kinds of law he had mentioned. In *Distinctio* 9 it was made plain that human *constitutiones* were not only a part of the whole complex of laws governing the human race but also that they constituted a part of canon law in particular. In case of conflict, however, they always had to give way to natural law:

> *Constitutiones ergo vel ecclesiasticae vel seculares, si naturali iuri contrariae probantur, penitus sunt excludendae* (9).

Distinctio 10 stated that canon law was of higher authority than civil law and *Distinctio* 11 that statute law was superior to custom. Gratian next wished to point out that custom was not altogether lacking in authority even though it stood below statute law and, *a fortiori*, below natural law and Scripture. It was to make this point that he introduced the crucial text of St. Basil with its assertion that some established liturgical practices were based on Scripture and some on apostolic tradition. The text was cited in support of the proposition that, " When a custom is not opposed to sacred canons or human law it is to be kept unchanged " (10). Gratian was quite

---

(9) *Disı. 9, dici. post* c. 11. Some confusion has arisen because the term " natural law " had many other connotations in medieval jurisprudence. When the words referred merely to a supposed primitive condition of mankind then papal legislation could over-ride " natural law ". But no legislation could change " natural law " understood as Gratian himself understood the term at this point of the *Decretum*. On natural law as divine see GUIDO FASSO, *Dio e la natura presso i Decretisti ed i Glossatori* in: *Il diritto ecclesiastico*, 67 (1956), pp. 3-10 and my, *Natura id est deus: A Case of Juristic Pantheism?* in: *Journal of the History of Ideas*, 24 (1963), pp. 307-322. Earlier volumes of *Studia Gratiana* contain several relevant articles on Decretist concepts of natural law. See the contributions of DELHAYE, ARNOLD and WEGNER in: *Studia Gratiana*, I (1953), of COMPOSTA and ROTA in: *Studia Gratiana* II (1954), of VILLEY and GUALAZZINI in: *Studia Gratiana*, III (1955).

(10) *Dist.* 11, *post* c. 4. St. Basil's text follows at *Dist.* 11, c. 5, *Ecclesiasticarum institutionum quasdam scripturis, quasdam vero apostolica traditione per successiones in ministerio confirmatas accepimus, quasdam vero consuetudine roboratas approbavit usus, quibus par ritus*

prepared to admit that certain ecclesiastical practices were deserving of respect simply because they could be traced back to the time of the apostles but, far from regarding such traditions as a second source of divine revelation, he presented them as merely one form of the least authoritative branch of the man-made law that constituted one province of ecclesiastical jurisprudence (11).

Distinctio 15 considered the authority of General Councils and quoted the famous words of Gregory I asserting that the first four Councils were to be venerated " like the four Gospels ". However, neither the text itself nor any of the glosses on it suggested that the Councils were a source of revelation separate from and independent of Scripture (12).

Distinctio 17 dealt with the origins of papal power and the Decretists' comments on it provide an excellent illustration of their attitude to Scripture and Tradition. One of Gratian's texts suggested that the authority of the Holy See might be based in part on the decrees of church councils and some of the canonists, fascinated as always by a possible analogy with Roman law, played with the idea that, just as the *populus* had conferred authority on the emperor, so too councils might have conferred authority on the pope. They always pointed out, however, that such a theory could not be accepted without major qualifications. Papal primacy, they acknowledged, was established in the first place by Christ himself so that subsequent councils could only have conferred authority "secondarily' or have made manifest an authority that already existed (13). Indeed there could hardly be a better example of the " single-source theory " of divine revelation than the canonists' treatment of the origins of papal power. They regarded the primacy as a doctrine divinely

---

et idem utrisque pietatis debetur affectus. It seems most improbable that Basil intended to propound a theory of the sources of divine revelation in this text, for he put post-Apostolic custom on the same level as Scripture and Apostolic tradition. On the misuse of the text by William of Waterford see DE VOOGHT, *op. cit.*, p. 204.

(11) This is not to deny that the canonists regarded custom as a valid source of law. But it was always held to be invalid if opposed to natural law. Hence it was evidently inferior to Scripture, not a co-equal source of revelation. On the whole question of custom in canonical jurisprudence see O. WEHRLE, *De la coutume dans le droit canonique*, Paris, 1928.

(12) TAVARD, *op. cit.*, p. 8, commented on Gregory's words, " Yet there is no equation in this text, between the Gospels and the Councils. The former serve as a common measure to which the latter are assimilated. Through them it is still the Word who determines the value of ' other scriptures ' ".

(13) On this point see my *Foundations of the Conciliar Theory*, Cambridge, 1955, pp. 55-56.

revealed in the New Testament which was affirmed and interpreted by subsequent ecclesiastical Tradition. The first medieval thinker of major importance who suggested that the pope's power was based only on Tradition, considered as a source separate from Scripture, was Marsilius of Padua. The popes did not like the idea at all. In considering the argument that papal claims tended to " devalue " Scripture, it is important always to bear in mind the scriptural basis of those claims themselves.

With *Distinctio* 19, which dealt with the relationship between papal decretals on the one hand and evangelical or patristic precepts on the other, we begin to approach the issues raised by Tavard. Gratian considered this problem in two widely separated contexts of the *Decretum,* here at *Distinctio* 19 and then again, towards the end of the work, at *Causa* 25 q. 1, and it is necessary to consider the two discussions together if we are to understand Gratian's thought correctly. In *Causa* 25 he produced an impressive series of texts asserting that the pope could not depart from rules laid down by the Gospels, the Apostles and the Fathers; but, at the end of the discussion Gratian apparently rejected all these arguments.

> *His ita respondetur. Sacrosancta Romana ecclesia ius et auctoritatem sacris canonibus impertitur, sed non eis alligatur* (14)

This seems an extreme example of exaggerated canonistic claims for the papacy. It is interesting to note, however, that at *Distinctio* 19 *post* c. 7 Gratian had already committed himself to an apparently quite different point of view. There, after emphasizing the high authority of papal decretals, he wrote:

> *Hoc autem intelligendum est de illis sanctionibus vel decretalibus epistolis in quibus nec praecedentium patrum decretis, nec Evangelicis praeceptis aliquid contrarium invenitur.*

Gratian did not attempt any reconciliation of these two discordant texts but the Decretists were in no doubt as to his true meaning and they all offered substantially the same explanation. *Causa* 25, they pointed out, referred to church discipline; *Distinctio* 19 referred to church doctrine. In glossing *Causa* 25 the Decretists explained that the discretionary power there attributed to the pope did not extend to matters of faith; in glossing *Distinctio* 19 they explained that the

---

(14) C. 25, q. 1 *post* c. 16.

356

limitation on his authority imposed by preceding legislation did not extend to matters of discipline. Huguccio stated the two parts of the argument neatly in a single gloss which was transmitted to the fourteenth century by Guido de Baysio

> *Videtur dicere quod papa contra bona statuta suorum prae-decessorum non possit aliquid statuere, quod non puto verum, nam eciam bona statuta potest revocare, inspecta causa, dum-modo non tangat praecepta veteris vel novi testamenti vel arti-culos (fidei) vel ea quae sunt necessaria ad salutem vel quae per-tinent ad generalem statum ecclesiae...* (15).

That Gratian himself had in mind a distinction between doctrine and discipline is made clear by the further development of his argument. Having insisted on the doctrinal authority of the Scriptures and Fathers at the end of *Distinctio* 19 he went on to affirm the juridical authority of papal decretals at the beginning of *Distinctio* 20. Here he wrote:

> *Sed aliud est causis terminum imponere, aliud sacras scrip-turas diligenter exponere. In negotiis definiendis non solum est necessaria scientia sed etiam potestas... apparet quod divina-rum tractatores scripturarum et si scientia pontificibus prae-mineant, tamen, quia dignitatis eorum apicem non sunt adepti, in sacrarum quidam scripturarum expositionibus eis praepo-nuntur, in causis vero definiendis secundum post eos locum me-rentur* (16).

Gratian's meaning seems clear enough. An exegete, seeking to understand all the theological significance of St. Paul's words, " The husband is the head of the wife as Christ is the head of the church ", would do well to turn to the writings of the Fathers. A judge, concerned to settle a matrimonial dispute between husband and wife, would need to consult the appropriate decretals and canons. But Gratian's text had further implications which he himself did not explore. Theology and law could not be separated quite so neatly as he suggested at this point for many of the pope's judicial decisions, most obviously in cases of heresy, would have doctrinal implications, and the pope was universally accepted as supreme judge in cases involving disputed

---

(15) *Rosarium ad Dist.* 19 *dict. post* c. 7. See also *Pope and Council: Some New Decretist Texts* in: *Mediaeval Studies*, 19 (1957), pp. 197-218 at pp. 201. 210-212.

(16) *Dist.* 20, *dict. ante* c. 1.

articles of faith. The canonists' discussions on this point provide important evidence about their conception of the relationship between papal power and revealed truth.

Oberman called attention to a late fifteenth century text which explained Gratian's words thus:

> *Et huic responsioni adde unum granum salis quod hoc verum est, sive quod in expositione scripturarum standum est dictis sanctorum patrum; supple: nisi tractaretur de expositione super sacramentis vel articulis fidei quia tunc standum est pape quia pape et non sanctis data fuit potestas interpretandi legem dubiam* (17).

For Oberman these words constituted " a very sharp and most succint formulation " of the " two sources theory ". But the text has no such implications. The doctrine contained in it was not a fifteenth century development but a commonplace of twelfth century Decretist thought, and the Decretist texts make it quite plain that, for a medieval canonist, to insist on the pope's role as judge in disputed matters of faith was by no means to make him a second fount of divine revelation, co-equal with Scripture. The author of the *Summa Antiquitate et Tempore*, for instance, gave equal emphasis to the supreme anthority of Scripture and to the Pope's role in interpreting it. He first wrote:

> *... primum locum et principale obtineat lex naturalis, vetus testamentum et novum...*

and then added:

> *... in obscuris scripturis et maxime circa articulos fidei maioris auctoritatis esset interpretatio papae quam Augustini* (18).

Huguccio, while of course upholding the pope's position as supreme judge, strongly emphasized the binding force of patristic tradition in the interpretation of Scripture:

> *Proponuntur, adeo etiam quod summis pontificibus non licet recedere ab eorum expositionibus... sunt enim huiusmodi vocati in partem sollicitudinis non in plenitudinem potestatis* (19).

---

(17) H. A. OBERMAN, *op. cit.*, pp. 373-374, quoting Ambrosius of Speier.

(18) MS Göttingen, Universitätsbibliothek iur. 159 fol. 25vb. Cf. TIERNEY, *art. cit.* (n. 15), p. 201, n. 20.

(19) MS Pembroke College, Cambridge 72, fol. 129rb.

358

The main point is that, whatever nuance of thought a particular canonist presented, the Decretist arguments in general always dealt with the relative authority of the popes and the Fathers *within* the sphere of Scriptural exegesis and did not allude at all to any extra-Scriptural realm of revealed truth. In commenting on *Distinctio* 20 some of the Decretists referred to Alexander III's decretal, *Cum Christus* to explain the nature of a papal judicial ruling on a matter of faith and, again, their remarks are entirely consistent with a " single-source theory " (20). *Cum Christus* was directed against a peculiar recrudescence of the Adoptionist heresy among the theologians of the University of Paris which took the form of affirming the proposition, " *Christum non esse aliquid secundum quod homo* ". Against this Alexander quoted the ancient formula declaring that Christ was " *verus deus et verus homo* ". Here the pope, as supreme judge, was evidently not acting as a source of new revelation. He was re-affirming the doctrine of the Council of Chalcedon which itself was rooted in the Scriptural accounts of the Incarnation. The English canonist, Alanus, did indeed maintain that Alexander created a new article of faith with *Cum Christus* in the sense that a theological expression which had been permissible before the decretal, became heretical after it. But, when this gloss came to the attention of Pope John XXII at the beginning of the fourteenth century, he refused to countenance this form of words and insisted on a more careful and nuanced explanation of the papal authority (21).

---

(20) For a group of Decretist texts discussing *Cum Christus* see TIERNEY, *art. cit.* p. 204, n. 28.

(21) Alanus's comment was contained in his Gloss *ad Comp. I*, 5. 6. 5 (MS Karlsruhe Aug. XL, fol. 68ra). It was repeated in the following form by GUIDO DE BAYSIO, *Rosarium ad. Dist.* 15, c. 1, *Notat Alanus quod ante illam diffinicionem de qua loquitur ipsa decreta contrarium dicere licebat cum prohibitum non esset. Sed post nequaquam. Ergo quod prius non fuit fidei articulus post consecrationem* [MS — *constitutionem*] *factus est fidei articulus. Et ita papa potest facere novos articulos fidei, quod verum est in una accepcione huius vocabuli " fidei articulus "*, i. e. *tale quod credi opporteat cum prius non opporteret*. Zenzelinus de Cassanis quoted the whole of this passage approvingly in the first draft of his gloss on the *Extravagantes Joannis XXII*, but he came under papal censure for this and was required to compose another version of the gloss which is given below (n. 39). Both versions are printed together in G. MOLLAT (ed.), *Jean XXII. Lettres Communes*, VI (Paris, 1912). The most important revision was the change from " *cum prius non opporteret* " to " *cum prius ex precepto ecclesie necessario credere non opporteret* ". John XXII wanted to make it quite clear that his predecessor had not created a new obligation in a matter of faith but had merely issued a command concerning a pre-existing obligation. The doctrine of Alanus himself was by no means extreme. After the words quoted his gloss continued: *Set secundum quod dicitur " articulus "*,

There is one final point to be made about the Decretist comment on Gratian's *Distinctio* 20. Several canonists undertook at this point to give a list of all the sources of ecclesiastical authority arranged in order of dignity. Invariably the Scriptures were given first place. Never were papal decretals put on the same level as Scripture. And we are not dealing here with a twelfth century tradition that was forgotten by the curialist canonists of the fourteenth century for Guido de Baysio chose to incorporate just such a list into his Rosarium:

> *Nam primo recurrendum est ad rescripti novi et veteris testamenti. Secundo ad canones apostolorum et conciliorum. Tertio ad decreta vel decretalia romanorum pontificum. Quarto ad scripta graeca. Postea ad scripta sanctorum patrum latinorum* (22).

In the Decretist tradition then there is little or no trace of a " two-sources theory " of divine revelation. If we turn now to the Decretalists we shall find the same situation.

The letters of promulgation preceding the *Decretales* and the *Liber Sextus* state explicitly that the main concern of the papal legislators was with the changing structure of human law needed to regulate the life of the church. Gregory IX referred to the *nova litigia* which necessitated new juridical rulings from the papacy and the *Glossa Ordinaria* quoted in explanation the famous words from Justinian's *Proemium* to the Code, *" natura semper novas deproperat edere formas"* (23). In the *Liber Sextus* these words of Roman law were incorporated into the papal letter of promulgation itself. But, in emphasizing the changing character of human affairs as the justification of their own legislative activity, the popes were by no means denying the existence of a sphere of divine revelation whose truths lay outside the scope of papal sovereignty. Innocent III insisted on his right to revoke the decrees of his predecessors in accordance with the Roman law theory of sovereignty and he once declared that

---

i. e. *tale quod credi debebat, quicquid semel fuit articulus semper fuit et semper erit articulus. Nota tamen quod stricte appellantur articuli hoc nomine, illi soli qui in simbolo apostolorum continentur...*

(22) *Rosarium ad Dist.* 20, c. 3, quoting Huguccio. For other similar lists see C. MUNIER, *Les sources patristiques du droit de l'église*, Mulhouse, 1957, p. 200.

(23) *Proemium ad Liber Extra*, gloss s. v. *Nova litigia: Hoc dicit quia humana natura prona est ad dissentiendum... et semper novas deproperat edere formas. C. de veter. iur. enuc. I. secunda § sed quia divinae.*

he stood between man and God, " Higher than man but lower than God ". But, in the same sermon in which he used those audacious words, Innocent also declared, " For a sin against the faith I may be judged by the church " (24).

These considerations may help us to understand that fourteenth century litany of texts in praise of the pope that Tavard found so diconcerting. The anonymous author did not invent this list of papal prerogatives. He followed closely a similar list given by Gulielmus Durandus (the *Speculator*). Durandus apparently based himself on the *Glossa Ordinaria* of Bernardus Parmensis and Bernardus in turn was amplifying a gloss of Tancred. The original form of the passage, as set down in Tancred's gloss on the Comp. III, written c. 1219 was as follows:

> Vices. *In is gerit vicem dei quia sedet in loco Jesu Christi qui est verus deus et verus homo ut in constitutione* In nomine, Firmiter credimus. *Item de nichilo facit aliquid ut deus, arg. III q. vi,* Haec quippe *et C.* De rei uxo. art. 1. *unico in prin. Item in is gerit vicem dei quia plenitudinem potestatis habet in rebus ecclesiasticis ut II q. vii,* Decreto, De usu pallii, c. ii. *Item quia potest dispensare supra ius et contra ius ut infra,* De concessione preb. et ecc. non vac., c. 1. *Item quia de iusticia potest facere iniusticiam, corrigendo ius et mutando ut in constitutione Innocentii III, Ut debitus et extra III.* De consang. et affin., c. Non debet. *Nec est qui dicat ei: cur ita facies? ut* De pen., dist. *III ex persona. T.* (25).

As Tavard observed, canon law could be cited to support every one of these " wondrous claims " — and sometimes Roman law too it will be noticed. But that is the whole point. The claims were juridical ones. They referred to the legislative and dispensatory powers of the pope within the framework of positive ecclesiastical law. The whole passage was a sustained rhetorical analogy. Just as God exercised a creative power in the universe as a whole so too the pope could create and innovate in the sphere of positive canon law. This was

---

(24) MIGNE *PL* 216, col. 656: *Propter solum peccatum quod in fide committitur possem ab ecclesia judicari. Nam qui non credit jam judicatus est.* Professor ULLMANN has recently emphasized the sharp distinction in medieval thought between " inessential " matters in which the pope enjoyed unlimited authority, and " essential " ones, in which his power was sharply limited. See *Studies in Church History*, II (1965) pp. 88-89.

(25) MS Caius College, Cambridge 17, fol. 147va.

admirably brought out by the *correctores Romani* in a comment on Bernardus Parmensis's *Glossa Ordinaria.* " This gloss expounds hardly anything in proper language, though if it is understood correctly it affirms things that are true. For to make something out of nothing is to establish a new law and to make justice out of injustice means through the constitution of law, and to change the substance of things has to be understood as referring to matters of positive law " (26). A check of Tancred's legal references makes it clear that this was indeed precisely what he meant.

Can we not say, even so, that the language that Tancred chose to use was highly misleading? The answer must be that it might have been misleading to a Wyclif or Hus but was not in the least so to the professional canonists for whom the passage was written. The whole meaning of the text was conveyed by its citations of Roman and canon law and, in reading it, we must remember that medieval jurists knew by heart the content of the texts they cited by *incipit* in a way that no modern scholar does. The misleading thing is to quote the text without the Roman and canon law references which alone make it intelligible (27). In fact, the language was tiresome but the actual claims were ones that could readily be accepted by anyone who believed in the pope's primacy of jurisdiction. Let us add finally that Tancred, who in this passage so boldly compared the pope's power with God's, maintained quite explicitly in other contexts that the pope could not go against articles of faith in his decisions nor against the general state of the church, that he could not dissolve a consummated marriage or dispense from a monk's vows of poverty and chastity (28).

---

(26) *Decretales D. Gregorii IX cum glossis* (Lugduni, 1624), col. 217, " *Tota haec glossa vix aliquid explicat propriis verbis: quod si bene intelligatur vera astruit. Nam de nihilo aliquid facere est ius novum condere et de iniustitia iustitiam intellige per constitutionem iuris et immutare substantiam rerum accipi debet in his quae sunt iuris positivi...* ". On Tancred's text see John A. Watt, *The Theory of Papal Monarchy in the Thirteenth Century* (New York, 1965), p. 81.

(27) In this matter, to be sure, Tavard was merely following Scholz.

(28) Gloss *ad Comp.* III, MS Caius College, Cambridge 17, fol. 147ra: *...carnale* (vinculum) *in veritate fortius es ;quia dissolvi non potest etiam si interveniat consensus papae et ipsorum coniugium.* Gloss *ad Comp.* III, 2. 6. 3, fol. 197vb: *Papa potest dispensare in omnibus quae non sunt contra articulos fidei vel generale statutum ecclesiae... Nec in his quae sunt contra substantiam monachatus, scilicet ut monachus haberet uxorem vel proprium... nec in his quae in sua natura sunt mala...* In referring to a *generale statutum*, Tancred, I think, must have had in mind general statutes defining the intrinsic structure of the church itself. On *status ecclesiae* and *statutum ecclesiae* see J. H. Hackett, *State of the Church: A Concept of the Medieval Canonists* in: *The Jurist,* 23 (1963), pp. 259-290.

362

The Decretalists' habit of expressing claims that were not intrinsically unreasonable in language that is often disconcerting must be taken into account in considering their treatment of the pope's relationship to Holy Scripture. There is certainly a persistent claim in their works that the pope could dispense against the words of the Bible — "against the words but not against the intention" as Innocent IV wrote. But only the most primitive Biblical literalist would maintain that every precept to be found anywhere in the Bible is to be followed to the letter without any modifying interpretation. No Christian sect, so far as I know, purports to do this. And no Catholic need be shocked at the suggestion that the authority of the Roman See may be invoked when it is a question of deciding whether a given text was intended to establish an absolute law binding for all time or merely to define for the ancient Israelites or the church of the apostles a point of discipline that was subject to change in the future.

When we turn to the actual contexts within which the canonists discussed the pope's power to " dispense from Scripture " we find that they were concerned with precisely this kind of question. The main issue that arose was the extent of the pope's power to grant dispensations from Scriptural impediments to the promotion of candidates for the priesthood. One such dispute has been studied in illuminating detail by Stephan Kuttner. The question at issue was whether the pope could permit a man who had been twice married and twice widowed to be ordained as a bishop. The canonists disagreed about this but they all acknowledged that, if such an action was possible at all, it lay at the extreme limit of the pope's dispensatory authority (29). And this is hardly a fundamental issue of the Christian faith. To concede to the pope such a power is not really to set him up as a second source of divine revelation. The Decretists and Decretalists indeed had no such intention. It would be hard to find in their works any evidence to support Yves Congar's suggestion that they regarded the pope as simply " au-dessous de l'Ecriture " (30). There was always present in their minds a sharp and clear distinction between the changing rules of church discipline,

---

(29) S. KUTTNER, *Pope Lucius III and the Bigamous Archbishop of Palermo* in: *Medieval Studies Presented to Aubrey Gwynn S. J.*, ed. J. WATT etc., Dublin, 1961, pp. 409-453. This paper provides an abundance of Decretist texts on the limits to the pope's dispensatory authority and references to the modern literature on the question.

(30) Y. CONGAR, *La tradition et les traditions*, I, Paris, 1960, p. 236.

where the pope might grant dispensations even against the letter of the Bible, and the eternal truths of Christian faith, where he was absolutely bound by Scriptural revelation like all other Catholics (31).

Such was the doctrinal situation when Pope John XXII's dispute with the Franciscans over evangelical poverty led to a definitive canonical pronouncement on the primary authority of Scripture in matters of faith. In 1322 John promulgated the bull *Cum inter non-nullos* which denounced as heretical the view that Christ and the Apostles had never owned anything, either individually or in common. A group of dissident Franciscans, of whom Ockham eventually became the principal spokesman, maintained that John's bull contradicted an earlier decree of Pope Nicholas IV which, they said, had established the contrary doctrine as an inviolable rule of faith, and that John XXII was accordingly a heretic.

Several modern scholars have emphasized the importance of William of Ockham in the development of the " two-sources theory " of divine revelation but none has called attention to the specifically Franciscan background of his thought on this question. In fact the tendency to treat the church (and particularly the pope) as a source of divine revelation separate from and co-equal with Scripture was already apparent in the works of St. Bonaventura. For him the revelation of the Holy Spirit, expressed in the consensus of the church, was of the same authority as the words of Christ recorded in Scripture. In discussing the verbal formula used in baptism, he wrote:

> ... *si Christus non instituit, instituit Ecclesia instinctu Spiritus sancti, et hoc tantum est ac si ipse proprio ore dixisset. Tota enim Trinitas approbat quod ipse Spiritus sanctus inspiret fieri, sicut illud quod Christus instituit* (32).

Bonaventura also professed his complete confidence in the pope's power to give expression to the inspired faith of the church. In disussing

---

(31) One could construct an almost endless catena of canonistic texts to illustrate this point. See є. g. *Summa Omnis qui iuste*, Huguccio, Johannes de Deo in: KUTTNER, *art. cit.*, pp. 441, 443, 450: *Summa Parisiensis, Summa Reginensis, Glossa Palatina* in: CONGAR, *op. cit.* p. 212; Innocent IV, Johannes Teutonicus in: TIERNEY, *Foundations*, pp. 89, 254. The same position was upheld by the later Decretalists. On the persistent tension in their works between the *blenitudo potestatis* of the pope and the inviolability of Christian doctrine see L. BUISSON, *Potestas und Caritas*, Köln-Graz, 1958.

(32) *Commentaria in Quatuor Libros Sententiarum*, IV Dist. 3 p. 1. art. 2 q. 2 in *S. Bonaventura Opera Omnia*, IV, Quaracchi, 1889, p. 71. DE VOOGHT, who presented Bonaventura as a zealous exponent of the " single-source theory " did not discuss this text.

the *Filioque* clause he first argued, quite moderately, that the Latin formula was a " perfection " not a corruption of the Greek one. But then he added that the pope could in fact replace ancient formulas of faith with new ones if he saw fit to do so:

> *Vel potest dici, sicut dicit Anselmus, quod novum edidimus: et hoc quidem facere potuimus quia Romana ecclesia plenitudinem potestatis a Petro, Apostolorum principe, acceperat in qua nulla Patrum sententia nec interdictum potuit nec arctare nec ei praeiudicare nec ligare eam ad aliquid* (33).

The phrase *sententia Patrum* as used in this context referred plainly to the decrees of early General Councils; Bonaventura's claim went far beyond anything that the contemporary canonists were teaching.

In this same tradition Duns Scotus held that there were truths of faith which were not expressed in Scripture but revealed by Christ to the Apostles and handed on by them to the church (34); and Pietro Olivi emphasized the need for a papacy authorized to make new explications of divine truth in each succeeding century (35). Ockham inherited such ideas from his Franciscan predecessors and ingeniously turned them against the contemporary pope, John XXII (36). He pointed out that, if the pope was a source of divine revelation, and if a previous pope had promulgated a particular doctrine, then any subsequent pope who disagreed with it was a heretic and as such automatically ceased to be pope. The whole of the ensuing controversy is of the highest importance in the development of medieval ecclesiology, but the point that immediately concerns us is that, in defending his position, John XXII was led to state explicitly that Scripture was the one essential foundation on which all articles of faith were based. The Franciscan claim that Christ and the Apostles had only a " bare use of fact " in the goods they held was subversive of the whole Christian faith, he argued, for it was contrary to the

---

(33) *In Sent.* I, Dist. 11, art. 1 q. 1, *Opera*, I, Quaracchi, 1882, p. 212.

(34) J. FINKENZELLER, *Offenbarung und Theologie nach der Lehre des Johannes Duns Skotus* in: *Beiträge zur Geschichte der Philosophie und Theologie des Mittelalters*, Münster, 1961, pp. 37-80; L. ROSATO, *Ioannis Duns Scoti doctrina de scriptura et traditione* in: *De scriptura et traditione*, Rome, 1963, pp. 233-252.

(35) L. OLIGER, *Petri Iohannis Olivi de renuntiatione papae* in: *Archivum Franciscanum Historicum*, 11 (1918), pp. 309-373 at pp. 361-362.

(36) Ockham's views and their relationship to the preceding tradition of Franciscan ecclesiology are discussed in detail in my forthcoming article: *From Thomas of York to William of Ockham.*

plain words of Scripture, and, by casting doubt on Scripture, it cast doubt on the articles of faith since they had to be proved (*probari*) by Scripture (37). If there was any lingering ambiguity in the pope's words the *Glossa Ordinaria* of Zenzellinus de Cassanis removed it. Zenzellinus declared explicitly:

> *... fides nisi per scripturam sacram probari penes homines non possit* (38).

In another gloss, which was explicitly approved by John XXII, Zenzellinus de Cassanis explained that the pope had no power to innovate in matters of faith:

> *Per iam dicta vero non credas papam posse facere articulum per quem nova fides inducatur aut veritai fidei detrahatur aliquid vel accrescat quo ad substantiam* (39).

All this is far removed from a " two-sources theory " of divine revelation. As to the sources of that theory there seems to be a need for still more research. It may well prove that the true line of development flows from Bonaventura through Pietro Olivi to William of Ockham and from him through Pierre d'Ailly, William of Waterford

---

(37) *Extravagantes Johannis XXII*, Antverpiae, 1572, *Tit.* 14, c. 5: *Profecto hoc ad fidem non pertinet, cum de hoc articulus non sit aliquis, nec sub quo valeat comprehendi, ut patet in symbolis in quibus articuli fidei continentur, nec etiam reducte, ne quasi hoc sacra scriptura contineat, quo negato tota scriptura sacra redditur dubia, et per consequens articuli fidei, qui habent per scripturam sacram probari, redduntur dubii et incerti.* Hoc enim in scriptura sacra *non poterit, sed contrarium reperiri.* John XXII had used a similar form of words in the bull *Cum inter* which precipitated the controversy, *Extrav. Jo. XXII, Tit.* 14, c. 4, *...ipsamque scripturam sacram, per quam utique fidei orthodoxae probantur articuli...*

(38) Gloss ad *Extrav. Jo. XXII, Tit.* 14, c. 4, s. v. *Per consequens: Dicas quod cum scriptura sacra asserat Christum et apostolos aliqua habuisse assertio contrarium astruens, ex se dicit scripturam sanctam mentiri... et sic fidei (si negaretur) probationem reddit dubiam, cum fides nisi per scripturam sacram probari penes homines non possit.*

(39) Gloss ad *Extrav. Jo XXII, Tit.* 14, c. 4, s. v. *Declaramus: Collige hic principem ecclesiae Christique vicarium posse etiam super fide catholica declarationem facere... Potest etiam articulum fidei facere si sumatur articulus non proprie sed large pro illo quod credere opporteat cum prius ex praecepto ecclesiae necessario non opporteret. Patet exemplum in hac decre... Et per aliquos inducitur in exemplum, licet non videatur mihi proprium: extra De haer. Cum Christus, ubi papa interdici mandat ne quis de cetero audeat dicere Christum non esse aliquid secundum quod homo, cuius contrarium ante dicere licebat cum non esset prohibitum secundum aliquorum opinionem quae per dictum capitulum confunditur. Sic Alanus notasse ibidem recitat Guido, xv di. c. i. Per iam dicta vero non credas papam posse facere novum articulum per quem nova fides inducatur aut veritati fidei detrahatur aliquid vel accrescat quo ad substantiam xxv q. i c. sunt quidam et c. seq. et c. si eam destruerem et c. quae ad perpetuum.* See above n. 21.

and Gabriel Biel to the theologians of Trent (40). In any case it was a specifically theological development. The canonists had little or nothing to do with it.

* * *

Wyclif argued that papal decretals could not have the same authority as Holy Scripture because any particular decretal could be revoked by the pope who promulgated it or by any subsequent pope (41). We have tried to show that any competent medieval canonist, any sound scholar who knew his *Decretum* and *Decretales* would have agreed with this argument insofar as it referred to the mass of positive canon law that Wyclif had in mind. As regards dogmatic decrees, which the pope could not set aside, they derived binding force from their relationship to Scripture — *per quam utique fidei orthodoxae probantur articuli* — and not from any alleged power of the pope to expound an extra-Scriptural Tradition. It is important to distinguish between administrative abuse and doctrinal corruption. Wyclif certainly had much to complain about. There were too many abuses in the fourteenth century church and too many canonists who devoted themselves to defending abuses instead of correcting them. But the canonists never ceased to affirm the principles that the primary guide to the truths of Christian faith was Holy Scripture and that no structure of church law could endure if it stood in opposition to those truths. If canon law was corrupt it contained within itself the seeds of its own regeneration. This never ceased to be true in the Middle Ages. It remains true today.

---

(40) A major contribution of OBERMAN's work (*supra* n. 5) was to show the relationship between late medieval nominalism and the Tridentine theology of Scripture and Tradition.

(41) For this argument of Wyclif see DE VOOGHT, *op. cit.*, p. 186 n. 4.

X

A SCRIPTURAL TEXT IN THE DECRETALES AND IN ST. THOMAS: CANONISTIC EXEGESIS OF LUKE 22-32

In the writings of the church fathers we find several interpretations of Christ's words at Luke 22.32, "I have prayed for you Peter that your faith shall not fail. . ." The text could be taken as referring to Peter alone or to the church in general. In the first sense it was sometimes seen as a reference to Peter's role as head of the apostles (since Christ also said, "Strengthen thy brethren"). Much more commonly the text was interpreted as simply a prayer for Peter's final perseverance in the faith. Christ, foreseeing Peter's coming denial, prayed that, after his lapse, Peter would recover his faith and remain steadfast in it. When the text was understood in a broader sense it could be seen as a prayer for the indefectibility in the faith of the universal church or of the Roman church over which Peter and his successors presided. More commonly it was interpreted as a prayer for final perseverance in the faith of all Christ's followers as individuals, addressed to them all through Peter. In this sense the text was sometimes associated with John 17.9, "I pray for them that thou hast given me" (1).

Gratian mentioned Luke 22.32 in the *Decretum* as one of the texts that had established papal headship in the church (2). Then in his Decretal *Majores* (X.3.42.3), Innocent III went a step fur-

---

(1) On patristic exegesis of Luke 22.32 see J. LANGEN, *Das Vaticanische Dogma*, t. 1 (Bonn 1871) 70-9.

(2) *Dist.*21 *ante* c.1.

ther. He associated Christ's prayer for Peter's faith with the old claim—Pseudo-Isidorian in form but more ancient in substance—that the greater causes of the church, especially those involving matters of faith, were to be referred to the apostolic see for decision.

> Majores ecclesiae causas, praesertim articulos fidei continentes, ad Petri sedem referendas intelliget, qui eum quaerenti Domino quem discipuli dicerent ipsum esse, respondidisse notabit, 'Tu es Christus filius Dei vivi' et pro eo Dominum exorasse ne deficiat fides eius.

The same sequence of argument is found in Thomas Aquinas' *Summa Theologiae* at 2a 2ae q.1 art. 10 where Thomas discussed the authority of the pope in determining matters of faith

> Hoc autem pertinet ad auctoritatem summi pontificis, ad quem majores et difficiliores ecclesiae quaestiones referuntur, ut dicitur in Decretalibus, extra, de baptismo, cap. Majores. Unde et Dominus (Luc. XXII, 32) Petro dicit: Ego rogavi pro te Petre ut non deficiat fides tua, et tu aliquando conveisus confirma fratres tuos (3).

Thomas may have cited *Majores* directly as in the version given above. In any case it seems likely that he had Innocent's text in mind since his own argument closely followed that of the pope (4).

In the debates stimulated by Vatican Council I the issue arose whether Thomas intended to assert a doctrine of papal infallibility when he cited Luke 22.32 here and at other points in his work; and recently the question has been re-opened. F.X. Leitner, writing in 1872, saw a clear affirmation of the pope's infallibility in Thomas' commentary on the Sentences:

---

(3) *Divi Thomae Aquinatis Opera Omnia*, ed. L. Vivès, t. 3 (Paris 1889) 86.

(4) The reading given above is in the Vivès edition just cited and in the Migne edition (Paris 1859). But the Leonine edition and the Piana edition give another canonical reference, "... ut dicitur in Decretis, Dist. 17 ..." Dist. 17 c.5 stated the principle that "greater causes" were to be referred to the apostolic see but without reference to Luke 22. It may be that Thomas gave only a vague reference to canon law and that the precise citations were supplied by later redactors of the text. Before Innocent III, Alexander III had associated Luke 22.32 with the pope's right to decide disputed questions of faith. See his *Ep.* 1447, P.L. 200, 1259. But Alexander's letter did not find a place in the *Decretales* and could hardly have been known to Thomas.

> Praeterea ecclesia universalis non potest errare quia ille, qui in omnibus exauditus est pro sua reverentia, dixit Petro, super cujus confessione ecclesia fundata est, 'Ego rogavi pro te ut non deficiat fides tua' (5).

On this Leitner commented, "Thomas adhered so firmly to the doctrine of papal infallibility that without further discussion he based the infallibility of the church on that of the pope" (6). This is evidently an oversimplification. Very recently Yves Congar has reconsidered the whole question in a typically learned and moderate fashion. Luke 22.32, he notes, was commonly cited "in favor of the indefectibility of the *universal church.*" But Christ's words were addressed to Peter and were sometimes taken to apply to Peter's successors in the papacy. Hence "the passage was thus very easy from the inerrancy or indefectibility *of the church* to the expression of the church's faith by the universal and supreme public authority that presides over the church." After a detailed consideration of the whole of Thomas's argument at 2a 2ae q.1 art. 10, Congar concludes, "Thus, it is legitimate to see, here in article 10, a first statement of what would soon become the theological idea and, six centuries later, the dogma, of the infallibility of the pontifical *magisterium*" (7).

In the present brief study we shall consider only the significance of Thomas' citation of Luke 22.32 in this connection. The question to be pursued is this. What were the implications—for medieval thinkers as distinct from modern theologians—of the universally accepted doctrine that "greater causes" involving matters of faith were to be referred to the apostolic see for decision? Specifically, did the association of this doctrine with the words of Luke 22.32 "I have prayed for you Peter that your faith shall not fail" carry any implication of papal infallibility in the days of Thomas Aqui-

---

(5) *Commentum in Lib. IV Sententiarum, Opera Omnia,* t. 10 (Paris 1889) 574.

(6) F.X. LEITNER, *Der hl Thomas von Aquin über das unfehlbare Lehramt des Papstes* (Freiburg-im-Breisgau 1872) 42 n. 1.

(7) Y. CONGAR, *Saint Thomas Aquinas and the Infallibility of the Papal Magisterium. Sum. Theol. IIa-IIae, q.1, a.10,* in *The Thomist* 38 (1974). Through the kindness of the author and the editor of *The Thomist* I was able to see the manuscript of this article before publication. See also E. MÉNARD, *La tradition. Révélation, écriture, église selon Saint Thomas Aquinas* (Bruges-Paris 1964); U. BETTI, *Assenza dell'autorità di S. Tommaso nel Decreto Vaticano sull'Infallibilità Pontificia,* in *Divinitas* 6 (1962) 407-22.

nas? Since the major passage in which the two texts were associated before Thomas is the decretal *Majores*—and since Thomas relied heavily on canonistic doctrine in shaping his theories of papal authority—an investigation of the canonistic interpretations of *Majores* may help us to understand the background of his thought.

* * *

As noted above, Gratian included Luke 22.32 among the Petrine texts which established papal headship in the church. He also several times presented the doctrine that the greater causes were to be referred to the apostolic see for decision (8). We have considered the Decretist commentaries on these texts elsewhere (9) and the briefest summary will suffice here. The Decretists all held, and insisted very strongly, that normally the pope was the supreme judge in matters of faith. But they had one reservation. The pope was supreme judge so long as he himself did not stray from the faith. The Decretists acknowledged a theoretical possibility—they must have thought of it as a very remote possibility in real life—that a pope might publicly teach heresy. In that case, if he persisted in his error, he had to be deposed from the apostolic see. The Decretists interpreted Luke 22.32 in accordance with this doctrine. They gave very little emphasis to the text in presenting scriptural arguments for papal primacy. (All the emphasis fell on Matt. 16.19 and John 21.15.) The Decretists regarded Luke 22.32 as primarily a prayer for Peter personally, for his final perseverance in the faith. When the text was given a more general significance it was understood as a prayer for the indefectibility of the church. There was no disposition to associate the text with any doctrine of papal infallibility. On the contrary the Decretists sometimes used Luke 22.32 specifically to distinguish between the proneness to error of particular popes and the indefectibility of the universal church. Thus Johannes Teutonicus wrote in the *glossa ordinaria*:

> Quaero de qua ecclesia dicitur quod hic dicitur, quod non potest errare ... certum est quod papa errare potest ...

---

(8) Dist. 17 c.5, C.2 q.6 c.3, C.24 q.1 c.12.

(9) *Foundations of the Conciliar Theory* (Cambridge 1955) 23-67; *Origins of Papal Infallibility, 1150-1350* (Leiden 1972) 14-57.

Respondeo, ipsa congregatio fidelium hic dicitur ecclesia
... et talis ecclesia non potest non esse ... nam ipse dominus orat pro ecclesia 21 dist. § 1, vers. "Ego pro te (rogavi ut non deficiat fides tua)" (10).

But, in the decretal *Majores*, Pope Innocent III based the
pope's claim to decide disputed matters of doctrine precisely on
Christ's prayer that Peter's faith should not fail. We need to consider therefore whether this argument led to any re-appraisal by
the Decretalists of the earlier Decretist teachings. At first the comments of the Decretalists were brief and uninformative. None of
the earlier commentators on the text seems to have seen any great
significance in it. The *glossa ordinaria* of Bernardus Parmensis
referred only to the common Decretist interpretation.

> *Ne deficiat.* Ex hoc patet quod ecclesia non potest
> esse nulla, 24 q.1 c. *pudenda* in fin. ubi Augustus hoc pro-
> bat. Ad idem 21 dist. c.1 ad fin. in vers. *ego rogavi pro*
> *te* (11).

Abbas Antiquus merely paraphrased Innocent's words (12). Gulielmus Naso took the opportunity provided by Innocent's text
to list thirty different kinds of cases which it was proper for the
pope to decide (13). Several canonists glossed *Majores* simply by
giving citations to two relevant sections of the *Decretum*—Dist. 17
c.3 and C.24 q.1 c.12—which dealt with the judicial authority of
the Roman see in cases involving matters of faith (14). Innocent IV,
Bernardus Compostellanus and Goffredus Tranensis made no comment at all on the opening words of *Majores*.

This general indifference to the ecclesiological implications of

---

(10) *Gl. ord.* ad C.24 q.1 c.9.

(11) *Gl. ord.* ad X.3.42.3.

(12) Abbas Antiquus, *Lectura Aurea* (Venetiis 1638) fol. 121vb. "Papa commendat
hic eum in principio quia in hoc quod ad fidem pertinet apostolicam sedem consuluit, pro-
bans quod ita debet fieri ex eo quod beatus Petrus cuius vicem gerit papa, querenti de se Domino, quem discipuli dicerent ipsum esse, respondit, Tu es etc.".

(13) Vienna, Ö.N.B., 2083, fol. 68ra. "Nota xxx casus in quibus papa se debet in-
tromittere. In articulis fidei, xxiiii q.1, quoties ...".

(14) Tancred, Florence, B.Laur., S. Croce 4 sin 2, fol. 215cb (citing Johannes Teutonicus). Similarly Vincentius, Melk, 333, fol. 247v.

Innocent's decretal ended with the great commentary of Hostiensis on the Decretals. In this matter, as in so many others, Hostiensis far surpassed his contemporaries in insight and vigor of thought. He began his discussion with the usual two references to the *Decretum* but then moved on to a long, subtle and intricate explication of all the ways in which Christ's prayer for Peter's faith could be understood as applying to Peter's successors in the papacy. (It is interesting that Hostiensis was serving the Roman see as a cardinal in the same years that Thomas Aquinas was teaching at the papal curia or in the immediate vicinity of the curia at Orvieto, Rome, and Viterbo.)

Hostiensis began by observing that it was indeed proper for matters of faith to be referred to the see of Peter for, although Christ said to all the apostles, "Lower your nets" and also said to all of them "Whatsoever you shall bind on earth it shall be bound in heaven," he said to Peter alone, "Put forth into the deep"; and this referred to the consideration of profound matters. (Hostiensis was here following a text of Ambrose referring to Luke 5.4 which had been included in the *Decretum*.) (15) Moreover, Christ wished that matters of faith should be referred to Peter and his successors because Peter had spoken with such constancy, truth and fidelity when he said "Thou art Christ, the son of the living God." In these words Peter, in effect, acknowledged the divinity and humanity of Christ. When Christ replied "Thou art Peter..." he approved the headship of Peter and his successors in the church (16).

All this was standard exegesis of well-known Petrine texts. Everyone agreed that Peter's profession of faith was followed by his designation as head of the church and that this role was inherited by Peter's successors in the papacy. Hostiensis next moved on to the point that especially concerns us, the significance of the words, *ne deficiat fides tua*. The main purpose of the intricate argumentation that followed was to explore all the ways in which Christ's words to Peter applied to future popes and to the church as a whole. In considering these questions Hostiensis discussed in turn Peter's

---

(15) C.24 q.1 c.7.

(16) Hostiensis, *Commentaria in Tertium Decretalium Librum* (Venetiis 1581) fol. 168vb, "Sed et ex responsione quam Christus fecit ibidem, 'et ego dico tibi quod tu es Petrus etc.' Petri et successorum praelatio comprobatur...".

final perseverance in the faith, the indefectibility of the universal church, and the pope's role as head of the church.

He began by observing that the words *ne deficiat fides tua* had three implications. (1) From them it was presumed that the church could not err in faith. (2) The words also proved that the church was indefectible, that it could not cease to exist. (3) Finally, they proved that a doubt concerning the faith was to be referred to the apostolic see (17). Hostiensis continued his commentary with an inquiry as to how these propositions could be deduced from the Scriptural text. If the faith of Peter never failed, he suggested, the church could never cease to be. Rather, Peter or his successor, when consulted, would respond by declaring the true faith. Just as Christ conferred power not only on Peter but also on his successors, so too he prayed not only for Peter but for his successors; and Christ's prayer was certainly heard (18). This is perhaps the closest that any thirteenth century canonist came to asserting a doctrine of papal inerrancy. If Hostiensis had defended all these propositions and they had found general acceptance, we should be justified in seeing an evolution toward the later doctrine of papal infallibility in the works of the medieval canonists and of theologians like Thomas Aquinas whose theories of papal authority reflected the canonists' teachings. But the truth is just the opposite. Hostiensis immediately rejected as obviously untenable the argument he had put forward. If Christ's prayer for Peter's faith applied to all future popes then it would follow that every pope would enjoy the grace of final perseverance in the faith and so no pope could ever be damned—which was false. Hostiensis solved the problem thus. As regards final perseverance and the attainment of eternal salvation, Christ's prayer applied to those who succeeded Peter not only in his see but in his way of life. "In order that the

---

(17) *"Nec deficiat fides eius*, xxi dist. §1, et propterea ecclesia non praesumitur posse errare. Ecclesia nempe nunquam a tramite apostolicae traditionis errasse probatur, xxiiii q.1 *a recta* (c.7) Per hoc etiam probatur quod ecclesia non potest deficere, quia nec potest esse nulla ... Per hoc etiam probatur quod super dubio fidei sit ad sedem apostolicam recurrendum."

(18) "Haec autem sic eliciuntur ex hoc. Si enim Petri fides non deficit, ergo ecclesia numquam nulla erit, ergo ipse et successor consultus veritatem fidei respondebit. Nam sicut potestas non solum sibi sed et successoribus data intelligitur, sic oratio non solum pro ipso, sed pro successoribus effusa videtur."

faith shall not fail in the person of a pope, it is necessary that he live faithfully as a Catholic, and honorably" (19). Here Hostiensis seems to confuse two concepts that modern theologians are careful to separate — impeccability and infallibility. But, for Hostiensis, the pope was prone to err precisely because he was prone to sin (i.e. he might sinfully choose to promulgate a heretical doctrine as the true faith). Moreover, Hostiensis simply ignored a possibility that would occur at once to a modern scholar—that a pope might err in his private capacity and so merit damnation while being preserved from error in his definitive pronouncements as pope.

Hostiensis next turned to the second stage of his argument— the words *ne deficiat fides tua* understood as applying to the faith of the universal church. Considered as a prayer for final perseverance, Christ's words were not addressed to Peter alone, Hostiensis noted, but to all Christ's followers. Considered as a prayer for the indefectibility of the church, however, the words were addressed very specifically to Peter.

> Quantum autem ad duo prima, scilicet quod ecclesia universalis non erret nec deficiat, intelligitur in persona tantum Petri facta oratio indistincte, ut et patet in eo quod leg. et no. extra d.n. *de homocidio, pro humani.*

These words might be misleading at first glance. Hostiensis did not mean that the guarantee of unfailing faith applied to Peter alone or only to his successors. Rather he had in mind the words of Augustine (often cited by earlier canonists), "in persona Petri ecclesia significatur." Christ prayed for the faith of the whole church *in persona tantum Petri*, because it was specifically Peter's faith —i.e., the faith Peter had declared—which would never become extinct in the church according to Christ's prayer. As Hostiensis wrote at the beginning of this passage, *"Ecclesia* non praesumitur posse errare."

Hostiensis finally considered Luke 22.32 as a text referring

---

(19) "Sed contra, quia secundum hoc sequeretur quod nullus papa damnaretur quod tamen non sequitur ut probatur ix q.iii *aliorum* (c.14). Sol. Dic quod quantum ad salutem consequendam rogavit pro Petro et successoribus suis non solum in sede sed et in conversatione ... Ergo quantum ad hoc ne fides personae papae deficiat necesse est quod fideliter, i.e. catholice et honeste vivat. Et hoc est quod probatur per glo. super illo verbo Luc. xxii "Ego rogavi pro te," glo. "Immo pro omnibus, Io. xvii."

to the continuing role of Peter's successors as heads of the church. In his gloss on the decretal, *Pro humani* (referred to at the end of the preceding quotation) he wrote that the power originally conferred on Peter and the apostles descended to their successors (20). But Hostiensis had argued that only a pope who imitated Peter's way of life would share in Christ's promise to Peter of final perseverance in the faith. This might have been taken to mean that a pope who did not imitate the holiness of Peter's life could not be a true pope at all. Hostiensis did not intend to assert this of course and he made the point clear at the end of his argument. Even a sinful pope could exercise valid jurisdiction in the church so long as he did not fall into heresy.

> Quantumcumque ergo papa peccator sit, dum tamen in haeresim non labatur, regere potest. Et ea quae gerit, quantum ad ecclesiam tenent, ut patet in eo quod no. s. *de voto, magnae.* . .(21)

Thus the text at Luke 22.32 had several meanings for Hostiensis. It was a prayer for final perseverance in the faith addressed to Peter and all Christ's followers. It also guaranteed that the faith Peter had declared would never become extinct in the church. It also designated Peter and his successors as supreme judges in the church. The one interpretation Hostiensis specifically excluded was one holding that all Peter's successors inherited Peter's unfailing faith. Indeed, Hostiensis' whole argument was based on an essential distinction between the possession of infallibility and the exercise of supreme jurisdiction. Christ's prayer did not guarantee that every future pope would remain true to the faith of Peter; but it did ensure that each pope would hold supreme jurisdiction in the church, including jurisdiction in the *causae fidei* unless and until he actually became a heretic. To all this we must finally add that, in the common opinion of the canonists, a pope did not become a heretic simply because he made an error in pronouncing

---

(20) *Commentaria,* fol. 28rb *"Absque pastore.* Per hoc patet potestatem concessam Petro beato apostolo non solum ipsi sed et ceteris apostolis et successoribus perpetuo concessam fuisse . . ."

(21) In his commentary on c. *Magnae* (X.3.34.7) Hostiensis wrote, "Papa, dummodo a fide non deviet per neminem poterit condemnari."

on a *causae fidei*—a contingency that was always recognized as being theoretically possible. It was assumed that a pope would normally correct his mistake after due admonition by the church. Heresy—with a consequent loss of papal jurisdiction—was incurred only by obstinate persistence in error.

It is not our purpose to explore in detail the late medieval exegesis of *Majores* but a few examples will show the persistence of Hostiensis' views. The only significant development was a simplification of Hostiensis' argument leading to a sharper emphasis on the contrast between the faith of individual popes (who might become heretics) and the faith of the universal church (which could never fail). Johannes Andreae posed the same problem as Hostiensis in these words.

> *Exorasse.* Luc. 22. Debemus autem presumere quod Christi oratio fuerit exaudita; ergo ecclesia vel eius caput non potest errare. Ergo super dubio fidei ad illud recurrendum . . . Secundum hoc sequeretur quod nullus papa damnaretur quod tamen est falsum, 9. q.3. Aliorum, et potest hereticus esse, 40 di. si papa (22).

The response of Johannes was simply a paraphrase of Hostiensis

> Dicit Host. quod quo ad salutem consequendam rogavit pro Petro et successoribus non solum in sede sed in conversatione vitae . . . Quantum ad hoc quod dixi papam esse posse haereticum, dicimus orationem factam pro Petro et in eius persona pro ecclesia universali, ne erret vel deficiat.

This gloss of Johannes Andreae seems to have been decisive for the future. Petrus de Ancharano reproduced it with only minor changes of wording (23) and Antonius de Butrio in turn copied the gloss of his master Petrus. Cardinal Zabarella also reproduced the substance of the gloss, ending his comment with a sharp contrast between the inerrant church and the possibly erring pope.

---

(22) *In Tertium Decretalium Librum Novella Commentaria* (Venetiis 1581) ad X.3. 42.3, fol. 226va.

(23) *Super Tertio Decretalium Commentaria* (Bononiae 1581) ad X.3.42.3, 473.

> Christus oravit pro Petro et eius persona et pro ec-
> clesia universaliter ne erret vel deficiat. Stat ergo quod
> papa singulariter consideratus posset esse hereticus (24).

For the medieval canonists the outstanding example of a Roman pontiff who had actually fallen into heresy was the fifth-century pope Anastasius. According to a text of the *Decretum* (Dist.19
c.9) Anastasius was smitten by God because he entered into communion with the heretic Acacius "without a council of bishops."
The *glossa ordinaria* to the *Decretum*, commenting on this caes,
observed "Where matters of faith are concerned . . . then a council
is greater than a pope." In the last gloss on *Majores* to be considered here, Panormitanus explicitly cited these texts. Panormitanus is known as one of the leading conciliarists of Basel. It is interesting therefore that he did not introduce the case of Anastasius in order to undermine the pope's normal jurisdiction over cases
involving matters of faith. On the contrary he rebuked those radi-
cals who wanted to argue that, because a pope might possibly err
in his judgments and be subject to a general council, therefore the
whole principle of *Majores* was invalidated.

> Et ex hoc et ex tex. infero solum papam posse cogno-
> scere et decidere causas fidei. In contrarium tamen facit
> gl. in c. Anastasius, xix di. que videtur velle quod papa
> in causa fidei debet congregare concilium et in tali causa
> concilium est supra papam, et sic aliqui ruditer intelligen-
> tes illam gl. aperte veniunt contra ipsum tex (25).

Panormitanus explained that in the ordinary course of events (*regulariter*) the pope alone could decide a dispute concerning the faith.
The case of Anastasius was exceptional in that this pope sought
to violate a teaching established by the church. It was only in such
emergency cases that a council was needed to correct the pope.

> Unde dic quod regulariter solus papa potest decidere
> causas concernentem fidem . . . Ad c. Anastasius dic quod
> ibi papa voluit decidere contra aliquod institutum per ec-
> clesiam quod non poterit sine concilio . . . quia posset papa

---

(24) *Super Tertio Decretalium Lectura* (Lugduni 1557) ad X.3.42.3, fol. 231va.
(25) *Commentaria in Tertium Decretalium* (Lugduni 1531) ad X.3.42.3, fol. 214rb.

374

esse hereticus et sic errare in fide xl di. si papa, sed tota
ecclesia errare non potest ut infra c. a recta et ibi bo. glo.,
xxiv q. 1. (26)

Panormitanus was especially insistent that the pope's jurisdictional authority should not be considered dependent on the possession of a personal charism of inerrancy or infallibility. He returned to the point later in his gloss. It was evidently false, he
wrote, to argue that Christ's words to Peter ensured that all Peter's
successors would be unerring in faith. A pope could be a sinner
or a heretic or a fool. It might seem then that Luke 22.32 could
provide no support for the claim that recourse should be had to
the pope *in causis arduis* (27).

But, again, Panormitanus rejected this line of argument. In
replying to it he quoted the common opinion of the doctors that
Christ's prayer for Peter's perseverance in the faith applied only
to those popes who imitated Peter in holiness of life. But he did
not find this wholly satisfactory. The crucial point, he held, was
this. All the powers conferred on Peter were conferred on him *in
persona ecclesiae*, but they were conferred specifically on Peter as
head of the church. Likewise when Christ prayed for Peter's faith
he prayed for the universal church but also *principaliter* for Peter
as head of the church. From this two consequences followed. Firstly,
the faith declared by Peter could never become extinct in the church
even if it survived only in one faithful Christian. Secondly the pope
was divinely established as head of the church and so could judge
the *causae arduae* (even though an individual pope might err). Moreover he could do this without necessarily summoning a general
council (since this was not always practicable) (28).

---

(26) *Commentaria*, fol. 214va. The *bona glossa* mentioned by Panormitanus is the
text of Johannes Teutonicus cited above p. 366f.

(27) *Loc. cit.*, "Ergo sequitur quod successores Petri non possent errare, quod tamen
est falsus, nam papa potest peccare ... et potest esse hereticus ... Item potest esse igna-
rus ... Ergo ratio litere non concludit ut propter orationem Christi factam in persona Petri
sit recurrendum ad papam in causis arduis."

(28) *Loc. cit.*, "Sol. Dicunt hic doctores quod Christus oravit pro Petro et successoribus suis ut non deficerent tam in fide quam in moribus. Nam successores in fide et moribus erunt salvi nec errabunt in fide. Ad id quod dicitur de heresi respondent quod oravit
pro Petro et ecclesia. Ego aliter dicerem quod quemadmodum potestas tradita Petro fuit
sibi tradita in persona ecclesie sed sibi tamquam capite ... Ita Christus oravit pro Petro

In essence these arguments were an elaboration of the doctrine presented by Hostiensis two centuries earlier. Indeed the comments of Panormitanus that we have outlined can be seen as a recapitulation of the whole medieval canonistic tradition in this area of thought. The central point to be noted is the constant distinction in canonistic writings between the idea of juridical headship in the church and the idea of inerrancy in the faith. None of the canonists taught that the pope was, in any definable circumstances, inerrant or infallible. But they all affirmed most strongly that the pope was head of the church and that, as such, he could judge the greater causes, including those that involved matters of faith. In the normal course of events he could do this without summoning a general council. (Thomas Aquinas, following the earlier canonistic teaching made this same claim for the popes.) But if a pope violated the faith of the church in his pronouncements—and this was always considered a possibility—then the ultimate authority of the general council could be invoked in order to correct him. In any case all Christians could be certain that, even if a pope erred, his error could not infect the whole church, for Christ had prayed that the faith of the church would never fail. At the end of his discussion, Panormitanus re-emphasized this point with a reminiscence of Huguccio that carries us full-circle back to the beginnings of the Decretist tradition in the twelfth century.

> ...Ubi sunt boni Christiani est Romana ecclesia, unde post mortem Christi fides remansit solum apud beatam virginem. Sic potest contigere quod absit, quod apud unum solum dumtaxat fidelem, licet feminam, possit consistere recta fides (29).

---

id est pro tota ecclesia in persona Petri sed pro Petro principaliter tamquam pro capite ut non deficeret fides Petri. Fides autem Petri est fides universalis ecclesie et ideo directe concluditur quod ecclesia tota errare non potest quia saltem remaneat in uno et ita probatur per Aug. et est textus cum glo. notabilis in d.c. a recta, xxiiii q.1. Sed quia papa est caput huius ecclesie et presumitur omnibus sanctior et doctior, xl di. c.1, ideo ad ipsum est recurrendum in causis maxime arduis, quia de facili non potest totam ecclesiam congregare dubio maxime existente.

(29) *Loc. cit.* On the phrase "Ubi sunt boni Christiani est Romana ecclesia" in Huguccio and William of Ockham see *Ockham, the Conciliar Theory and the Canonists* in *Journal of the History of Ideas* 15 (1954) 40-70. On Panormitanus' use of this doctrine see K. Nörr, *Kirche und Konzil bei Nicolaus de Tudeschis* (Köln 1964) 131-3.

* * *

In commenting on the decretal *Majores* the canonists were dealing with the precise point emphasized by Congar in his recent study on Thomas Aquinas—"the passage . . . from the inerrancy or indefectibility of the church to the expression of the church's faith by the universal and supreme public authority that presides over the church." We have seen that, in considering this question, the canonists saw no reason to assert that the indefectibility of the church implied the inerrancy of its "supreme public authority." In particular they did not see in Innocent III's application of Luke 22.32 to the pope's role as supreme judge any implication of papal infallibility.

We may add that the theologians who commented on Luke 22.32 down to the time of Thomas Aquinas also saw no such implication. The earlier authorities collected by Thomas in his *Catena Aurea* on Luke 22.32 did not refer to papal authority at all. Nor did the twelfth century *glossa ordinaria*. Hugh of St. Cher raised the question why Christ's prayer was addressed to Peter alone but he did not reply by referring to any gift of inerrancy conferred on Peter or his successors. Rather (following John Chrysostom) he merely observed "Ostendens quod difficilior est casus ei, i.e. prelati" (30). Bonaventure offered the two standard interpretations. Christ prayed either for Peter's final perseverance in the faith or for the indefectibility of the universal church (31). Albertus Magnus observed that Christ's prayer applied to Peter's successors and to his see, but again he was dealing with the grace of final perseverance. Peter erred, but later he recovered his faith. So too Albert implied, particular popes might err but the faith would not become totally extinct in the Roman see (32).

---

(30) *Postilla super Quattuor Evangelia*, t. 5 (Parisiis 1506) fol. 238ra.

(31) *Commentarius in Evangelium Lucae, Opera Omnia*, t. 7 (Quaracchi 1882-1902) 552.

(32) *Commentarii in Lucam, Opera Omnia*, t. 10 (Lugduni 1651) 326 "*Ut non*, finaliter. *Deficiat fides tua*. Hoc argumentum efficax est pro sede Petri et successore ipsius, quod fides eius non finaliter deficiat." The interpretation given above seems to me the only possible one. Albert cannot have intended to write that every pope, by the fact of being elected pope, was assured of eternal salvation. In any case his argument about final perseverance in the faith has nothing to do with the inerrancy of particular papal decisions.

As for Thomas Aquinas: It is true that we cannot reach definite conclusions about his work merely by exploring the canonistic and theological traditions that he inherited. But is is also true that we cannot even begin to understand Thomas' thought unless we familiarize ourselves with the every-day, taken-for-granted meanings of the texts he employed at the time he was writing. A full treatment of Thomas' theology of the papacy will require a detailed analysis of all the relevant texts scattered through the whole corpus of his work. We would suggest one guiding rule for scholars undertaking this work. In studying the world of medieval thought we must never assume that a strong—even extreme—affirmation of the pope's role as supreme judge in matters of faith necessarily implied any commitment to a doctrine of papal infallibility.

XI

OCKHAM, THE CONCILIAR THEORY,
AND THE CANONISTS

" In Conciliar studies . . . we are frequently told that this or that view ' is to be found in Ockham ' and there the matter is unsatisfactorily left." [1] Professor Jacob's complaint might be echoed by workers in half a dozen fields of medieval research, for in theology, logic, ecclesiology, political theory, the enigmatic figure of the English Franciscan dominates the intellectual life of the later Middle Ages; and, as studies multiply on particular aspects of his work,[2] it becomes increasingly evident that without a complete understanding of Ockham's doctrines there can be no adequate evaluation of that whole complex movement of destructive criticism which sapped the vitality of medieval thought and medieval institutions in the fourteenth century, which opened the way for the Conciliarist attack on the Papacy and, ultimately, for the Lutheran schism and the emergence of the modern state.

Yet in the present state of our knowledge any synthesis could only be an over-simplification, and one sympathizes with J. B. Morrall's recent remark that de Lagarde's attractive exposition of Ockham's thought arouses suspicions precisely because it is so lucid and coherent. " Can so complex a system of thought . . . be patient of quite so clear an explanation? " asks Morrall,[3] and, indeed, it may well prove, when the various branches of Ockham's intellectual achievement have been much more thoroughly investigated, that the only possible synthesis will have to be sought on the level of personality rather than in any formal interdependence between the different spheres of mental activity that Ockham himself so rigorously separated. In any case, such an attempt must await a more detailed exploration of the sources of Ockham's thought in each different department of his work.

---

[1] E. F. Jacob, " Ockham as a political thinker," *Essays in the Conciliar Epoch* (Manchester, 1943), 85–106 at 85.

[2] A list of works dealing with Ockham's political theory was given by P. A. Hamman, *La doctrine de l'église et de l'état chez Occam* (Paris, 1942). To this should now be added E. F. Jacob, *op. cit.*; the introduction of R. Scholz to Ockham's *De Principatu Tyranico*, Schriften des Reichsinstituts für ältere deutsche Geschichtskunde, VIII (1944); G. de Lagarde, *La naissance de l'esprit laïque au déclin du Moyen Age*, III–VI (Paris, 1942–46); C. C. Bayley, " Pivotal concepts in the political philosophy of William of Ockham," this *Journal*, X (1949), 199–218; J. B. Morrall, " Ockham's political philosophy," *Franciscan Studies*, IX (1949), 335–369. The most recent work on Ockham's life and on the chronology of his political works is that of L. Baudry, *Guillaume d'Occam*, I (Paris, 1949).   [3] J. B. Morrall, *art. cit.*, 336.

In the field of Conciliar studies the need for such research has long been apparent, for there can be no hope of assessing the importance of Ockham's contribution to future Conciliar theories until we have learned to understand the nature of his debt to the past. Accordingly much has been written concerning the relationship between Ockham and Marsilius of Padua,[4] and recently attempts have been made to provide a more respectable ancestry for some of his most influential doctrines.[5] There remains, however, one whole field of inquiry which has been almost entirely neglected and which we shall try tentatively to explore, the relationship between Ockham's theories on Church government and the doctrines of earlier canonistic writers.

The need for such a study is emphasized by the fact that several among the more discerning of Ockham's recent interpreters have called attention to the importance of the canonistic quotations which occur very frequently in all his political works. Hamman observed that Ockham's patristic quotations were taken " en majeure partie . . . du Décret de Gratien ou des Décretales." [6] C. K. Brampton pointed out that, " for support he relied on an extensive series of quotations from canon law—a strange but significant procedure." [7] A. Van Leeuwen too made the same observation, " . . . loin de nier l'autorité des décisions ecclésiastiques, il emprunte presque toutes ses preuves au *Corpus Iuris canonici.*" [8] Finally de Lagarde maintained that, " Toute sa théorie du droit naturel est notamment fondée sur la glose des premières distinctions du Décret," and added that one could not hope to understand Ockham's thought " si on ne la confronte pas constamment avec cette source." [9] It must be added, however, that the difficulties of interpretation arise, not when Ockham gives a series of canonistic references which can be verified easily enough, but when, as is often the case, he makes use of canonistic doctrines without giving any reference to his sources. Even de Lagarde himself has

---

[4] J. Sullivan, " Marsiglio of Padua and William of Occam," *American Historical Review,* II (1896), 593–610; J. Hofer, " Biographische Studien über Wilhelm von Ockham O.F.M." *Archivum Franciscanum Historicum,* VI (1913), 209–233, 439–465; R. Seeberg, *Dogmengeschichte,* III (Leipzig, 1930), 583–586; J. G. Sikes, " A possible Marsilian source in Ockham," *English Historical Review,* LI (1936), 496–504; G. de Lagarde, " Marsile de Padoue et Guillaume d'Ockham," *Revue des Sciences Religieuses,* XVII (1937), 168–185.

[5] C. C. Bayley, *art. cit.;* J. B. Morrall, *art. cit.;* especially valuable is the article of A. Van Leeuwen, " L'Église, règle de foi chez Occam," *Ephemerides Theologicæ Lovanienses,* XI (1934), 249–288. P. A. Hamman observed a close affinity between certain doctrines of Ockham and those of the Dominican, John of Paris, *op. cit.,* 183–188.   [6] *Op. cit.,* 29.

[7] Introduction to *De imperatorum et pontificum potestate,* ed. C. K. Brampton (Oxford, 1927), xxx.   [8] *Art. cit.,* 258.   [9] *Op. cit.,* VI, 109.

42

been misled on occasion by this deceptive reticence.[10]

Although Ockham's use of canonistic material has thus often been noticed it has usually been taken for granted that he displayed a profound originality in his handling of the legal texts that he cited so freely. He is said, for instance, to have shown " an almost terrifying efficiency " in " manipulating " the concepts of civil and canon law,[11] and the remark reflects an underlying assumption of nearly all his commentators, namely that Ockham, with remarkable ingenuity, succeeded in extracting from the canonistic texts a series of doctrines quite different from anything that the canonists themselves had ever envisaged. We would suggest that this may be a misunderstanding, arising partly perhaps from Ockham's own frequent and scathing references to the *canonistae,* but mainly from the general neglect of earlier canonistic theories of Church government,[12] and especially

[10] Cf. " L'idée de représentation dans les oeuvres de Guillaume d'Ockham," *Bulletin of the International Committee of Historical Sciences* IX (1937), 425–451 at 446. De Lagarde found it astonishing that Ockham should even have mentioned the idea that a General Council represented the whole Church, so that the decisions of a General Council could be regarded as established " by universal consent." " Mais voici le texte le plus intéressant, parce qu'il critique l'idée de représentation dans son acception la plus moderne. Qui a suggéré l'objection à Ockham? Nous l'ignorons, car elle semble dépasser la conception de ses contradicteurs eux-mêmes." And he went on to quote the relevant passage of the *Dialogus.* " Diffinitio autem et iudicium generalis concilii tanquam diffinitio universalis ecclesiae debet haberi, quia universali consensu constituta videtur." There is really no mystery about the source of Ockham's argument. The assertion that decrees of General Councils " universali sunt constituta consensu " is found in a very widely-quoted chapter of the *Decretum, Dist.* 15 c.2, which had been mentioned in numerous canonistic discussions on the authority of General Councils from the twelfth century onwards.

[11] C. C. Bayley, *art. cit.,* 199.

[12] This is the more surprising since the more purely political doctrines of the canonists, their theories on the relationship of Church and State, have recently attracted a great deal of attention. Cf. Gaines Post, " Some unpublished glosses on the Translatio Imperii and the two swords," *Archiv für katholisches Kirchenrecht* CXVII (1937), 403–429; M. Maccarrone, *Chiesa e Stato nella dottrina di papa Innocenzo III* (Rome, 1940), and *idem,* " Il Papa ' Vicarius Christi '," *Miscellanea Pio Paschini* (Rome, 1949), I, 429ff.; A. Stickler, " De ecclesiae potestate coactiva materiali apud Magistrum Gratianum," *Salesianum,* IV (1942), 2–119; *idem,* " De potestate gladii materialis ecclesiae secundum ' Quaestiones Bambergenses ' ineditas," *Salesianum,* VI (1944), 113–140; *idem,* " Der Schwerterbegriff bei Huguccio," *Ephemerides Iuris Canonici,* III (1947), 201–242; W. Ullmann, *Medieval Papalism* (London, 1949); S. Mochi Onory, *Fonti canonistiche dell'idea moderna dello Stato* (Milan, 1951). In 1924 Franz Gillmann announced that he was collecting material for a study on " die kirchenpolitischen Anschauungen der ältesten Dekretglossatoren," but the work was never completed, *Archiv für katholisches Kirchenrecht,* CIV (1924), 40.

from our inadequate knowledge of the various doctrines propounded in that most fruitful era of canonistic speculation, the years around the turn of twelfth and thirteenth centuries.[13]

The ferment of intellectual activity at Bologna during that period produced not only a juristic framework for Innocent III's policy of ecclesiastical centralization, but also in some quarters a perceptible reaction against that policy. Fundamental problems concerning the proper limits of papal authority, and the relationship between the Pope's powers and those of Cardinals and General Council appear in the glosses of the time as matters of ardent debate; and, in view of the general flux of opinion, it is not surprising that we find in the works of distinguished contemporary canonists like Huguccio and Joannes Teutonicus, as well as in various anonymous gloss compositions of the period, ideas concerning the structure of the Church and the nature of papal authority that are sharply at variance with the orthodoxies of a later age. Ockham, for his part, certainly saw in the canonists of his own day who supported the temporal claims of the Papacy his most dangerous enemies, but one should not assume on that account that he felt any disinclination to make use of earlier canonistic teachings when they happened to be in accordance with his own ideas. Moreover there is every reason to suppose that Ockham would have had his attention directed to the apparently somewhat recondite views of the early Decretists, for, at the beginning of the fourteenth century, Guido de Baysio, the erudite Archdeacon of Bologna, had assembled in his *Rosarium* a vast compendium of Decretist glosses; and, through the *Rosarium*, a very well-known and widely-quoted work, many early canonistic opinions that had been half-forgotten since the days of Innocent III acquired a new currency in the fourteenth century.[14]

---

[13] These years saw the production of the five very important " compilationes antiquae " which formed the basis of Gregory IX's official collection of Decretals, and also of numerous glosses on these compilations, and of a series of influential commentaries on the *Decretum*, culminating in the *Glossa Ordinaria* of Joannes Teutonicus. For general surveys of the canonistic literature of the period see J. F. Schulte, *Die Geschichte der Quellen und Literatur des canonischen Rechts*, I (Stuttgart, 1875); Stephan Kuttner, *Repertorium der Kanonistik*, I (Città del Vaticano, 1937); A. Van Hove, *Prolegomena* (Commentarium Lovaniense in Codicem Iuris Canonici, I, i, Malines-Rome, 1945).

[14] Guido de Baysio, a native of Bologna, was Archdeacon there from 1296. His *Rosarium*, " in quo numero immenso glossas aliorum compilavit," appeared in 1300. Guido also produced an apparatus on the *Liber Sextus* between 1306 and 1311. He died in 1313. See Schulte, *Quellen und Literatur*, II, 187–188; F. Gillmann, " Die Abfassungszeit der Dekretsumme Huguccios," *Archiv für katholisches Kirchenrecht* XCIV (1914), 246; A. Van Hove, *Prolegomena*, 475, 483.

44

In discussing Ockham's use of canonistic material there are two main topics to be considered, first, his technique in handling the legal sources, and secondly, the actual doctrines of Church government that he deduced from them.

We can gain some idea of Ockham's polemical versatility by comparing two recent views on the first point. C. C. Bayley emphasizes Ockham's appeal to the spirit of the law rather than the letter, his insistence on the need for equitable interpretation of the law in exceptional circumstances, his belief that necessity could justify extralegal actions in cases of emergency.[15] E. F. Jacob, on the other hand, maintains that it was characteristic of Ockham's adversary, Pope John XXII, to appeal to the spirit rather than the letter of the texts cited against him, and that Ockham preferred " to analyze with critical care and subtle distinctions the meaning of words and expressions dominant in the controversy." [16] The paradoxical fact is that both judgments are shrewd and sound appraisals of different aspects of Ockham's work, and one might add that both methods of argument were quite familiar to Ockham's canonistic predecessors.

In the first place, Professor Bayley himself has very properly pointed out that Ockham's technique of appealing to " necessity " and " the spirit of the law " did not originate with the Franciscan master himself but had roots deep in the theological and juristic traditions of the thirteenth century, and that, in particular, the principle, " Quod non est licitum lege necessitas facit licitum " had actually been incorporated in the *Decretales* of Gregory IX as a *regula iuris*.[17] It may be added that the same principle was invoked by Hostiensis in mid-thirteenth century to prove the well-known Conciliar doctrine that the Cardinals could exercise during a vacancy powers that normally belonged to the Pope alone,[18] that the " sollers et acutus indagator " so dear to the later Conciliarists was a very familiar figure in the canonistic glosses of the thirteenth century, and that the appeal from the letter of the law to the intention of the legislator and the principles of equity had already made its appearance in the *Glossa Ordinaria* to Gratian's *Decretum*.

Arg. quod non debemus inhaerere verbis sed potius menti . . . verba enim in rescriptis posita vel in lege conformare debemus aequitati . . . .[19]

---

[15] *Art. cit.*, 199.   [16] *Op. cit.*, 91.   [17] X. V.xli.4.

[18] *Lectura in quinque decretalium Gregorianarum libros* (Paris, 1512), fol 102ra, " necessitas legem non habet," with a reference to X. V.xli.4. On the views of Hostiensis see " A Conciliar theory of the thirteenth century," *Catholic Historical Review* XXXVI (1951), 415–440.

[19] Gloss *ad* 23 q.1 c.2. See also X. I.iii.38 and *Glossa Ordinaria ad* X. I.xxxviii.10, " Verba debent deservire intentioni, non intentio verbis."

It would therefore be quite incorrect to see in the application of such principles by Ockham and other fourteenth-century publicists any radical departure from the accepted canonistic tradition.

As for Ockham's "subtle distinctions," they were especially in evidence when he discussed the thorny problems of Franciscan poverty (and most of all in the *Opus Nonaginta Dierum*), but he would also on occasion apply the same technique of verbal analysis to canonistic quotations touching on the broader issues of Church government. In this again, however, he was merely following the example of the canonists themselves, for the innumerable glosses on the *Decretum* and *Decretales* had time and again subjected every significant word in those compilations to minute analysis. It would hardly have been possible for anyone in Ockham's day to have suggested any radically new interpretation of texts that had already been so exhaustively annotated; Ockham's task was rather to select from the works of previous expositors the interpretations that seemed most suitable for his own purposes and to present them as forcefully as possible. Even when he appears most perversely ingenious in extracting an anti-papal significance from a text clearly intended to emphasize the authority of the Holy See, he was almost invariably following faithfully in the footsteps of some canonistic predecessor. We may mention as an example his treatment in the *Breviloquium* of the Decretist text, *Dist.* 12 c.2, which was cited by Hamman as an example of Ockham's dexterity in adapting the canonistic texts to his own purposes. This canon of the *Decretum* laid down that,

> Praeceptis apostolicis non dura superbia resistatur, set ... quae ... apostolica auctoritate iussa sunt salutifere impleantur.

Ockham suggested that the word *salutifere* referred to *iussa sunt* rather than to *impleantur,* and concluded that the real sense of the passage was that there could be no obligation to obey papal commands that were not conducive to salvation. This certainly seems a typical example of Ockham's verbal subtlety, but in fact his interpretation followed very closely an explanation of the same passage put forward in Guido de Baysio's *Rosarium.*

Ockham [20]	*Guido de Baysio* [21]
... non dura superbia sed moderate resistere quandoque licet, quandoque vero necessarium est	... non dura superbia, quasi ex humilitate et discretione potest ei resisti ....
Similiter ... dicitur ... quae iussa sunt salutifere, impleantur ut punc-	Salutifere, id est ita ut proficiat ad salutem, vel puncta in verbo hoc

[20] *Breviloquium de Potestate Papae,* ed. L. Baudry (Paris, 1937), II.xxi.61.

[21] *Rosarium seu in Decretorum Volumen Commentaria* (Venice, 1577), *ad Dist.* 12 c.2, fol 15rb. Guido de Baysio presented arguments for and against this interpretation.

46

tus sit post hoc adverbium salutifere
et ideo si aliquid iussum fuerit . . .
non salutifere non est necesse implere.

salutifere. Et tunc est argumentum
quod non quecunque a prelatis statuuntur observare tenemur, nisi salutifere sint statuta . . . .

When Ockham was faced with a canonistic text which unambiguously repudiated the point of view that he wished to sustain, he appealed to equity, necessity, or the intention of the legislator; when the
wording of the decree provided any possibility of an interpretation
favorable to his own position, he resorted to the method of verbal
analysis. And that was exactly what the canonists themselves had
been doing for more than a century past. Ockham certainly exploited
both techniques with considerable virtuosity, but one would hesitate
to assert that he displayed any more dialectical subtlety in interpreting the texts of the *Decretum* and *Decretales* than had been shown
by, say, Huguccio or Hostiensis or Guido de Baysio.

In his methods of interpreting the canonistic texts, then, there
seems nothing that sharply distinguished Ockham's technique from
that of the great lawyers themselves. The more interesting problem
remains of whether the doctrines of Church government that Ockham
derived from those texts had also been anticipated by the canonists
who had analyzed them so meticulously.

It would be possible to go through a whole range of Ockham's
political and ecclesiological concepts, his theory of *dominium*,[22] his
doctrine of the *bonum commune*,[23] his views on the source of temporal

[22] In Ockham's view dominion of Church property rested with the whole *congregatio fidelium* and the Pope was a mere *dispensator*. *Breviloquium, ed. cit.*, II.vi,
26, and *Octo Quaestiones de Potestate Papae*, ed. J. G. Sikes in *Guillelmi de Ockham
Opera Politica* (Manchester, 1940), I, 65, " Vere enim denominatur ' ecclesiastica '
ab ecclesia, non quae est papa aut congregatio clericorum, sed ab ecclesia quae est
congregatio fidelium." Already in the twelfth century Huguccio had written, " Illa
bona (ecclesiastica) competant ecclesiae catholicorum, non enim parietibus sed con-
gregationi fidelium "—cited by P. Gillet, *La personnalité juridique en droit ecclésiasti-
que* (Malines, 1927), 101. Ockham's theory of dominion very closely resembles that
of John of Paris, *De Potestate Regia et Papali*, ed. J. Leclercq (Paris, 1942), 186;
but John of Paris in turn was much indebted to earlier canonistic theories. This was
pointed out long ago by Gierke, *Das Deutsche Genossenschraftsrecht*, III, 255 n.33,
and more recently by Gillet, *op. cit.*, 118 n.2.

[23] Ockham argued that since the Pope received spiritual power from God for the
good of the whole Church he was not empowered to act in any fashion prejudicial
to the *bonum commune*. (*Octo Quaestiones, ed. cit.*, I.vi, 31, *Breviloquium, ed. cit.*,
II.v, 22–25, II.xx, 60, *De imperatorum et pontificum potestate*, ed. C. K. Brampton
(Oxford, 1927), 12, 14, 19.) The canonists had put forward a similar point of view,
maintaining that the Pope had no authority to promulgate legislation or grant dispensations that endangered the *generalis status ecclesiae* (*Glossa Ordinaria ad* 25
q.2, c.17; *Glossa Ordinaria ad* X. II.xii.13 and X. III.viii.4; Innocentius, *Commen-*

authority,[24] and point to more or less exact parallels in the works of thirteenth-century canonists. In all these cases, however, it is certain that Ockham was influenced by several different traditions of thought. There may well have been canonistic influence on his doctrines, but recent work has made it clear that ideas derived from theology, philosophy, and Roman law played a major part in molding his thought on these important subjects. We shall prefer therefore to illustrate his use of canonistic theories by concentrating on two of Ockham's doctrines which were of central significance in his theory of ecclesiastical authority, which were very influential for later Conciliar theories, and which were firmly grounded on a canonistic tradition already ancient when Ockham wrote. These are Ockham's doctrine on the deposition of a heretical Pope and his discussion on the location of unerring authority within the Church.

Both problems had their roots in certain rather ambiguous doctrines of Gratian's *Decretum*. Gratian repeatedly stated that the Holy See was the supreme arbiter in matters of faith, the authority to which all doctrinal disputes were to be referred for final decision; [25] but these assertions were not reinforced by any claim that the Pope was necessarily unerring in the doctrinal decisions that he pronounced. Instead, Gratian emphasized that the Pope's decisions were only worthy of acceptance when they were in accordance with the existing tradition of faith,[26] and he further suggested that in the interpretation of Holy Scripture the Pope was not the most reliable authority—the

---

taria super libros quinque decretalium (Frankfurt, 1570), *ad* X. I.iv.4, X, V.xxxix.44; Hostiensis, *Summa Aurea super titulis decretalium* (Cologne, 1612), *De Constitutionibus*, fol 19ra.

[24] Ockham held that, whilst imperial authority came ultimately from God (like all lawful authority), the jurisdiction of any particular Emperor was derived directly from the act of election and not from subsequent papal coronation or confirmation. His views on the subject were expressed most clearly in the *Breviloquium, ed. cit.,* IV.i–viii, 101–118, and in the *Octo Quaestiones, ed. cit.,* IV.i–x, 126–157. Some of the earlier canonists were of the same opinion, *e.g.,* Huguccio, " Hinc aperte colligitur, quod utraque potestas, scilicet apostolica et imperialis, instituta sit a Deo et quod neutra pendeat ex altera . . . . Ar. contra XXII di. c.1 et Di. LXIII tibi domino (c.33), in synodo (c.23) . . . . Ex hiis omnibus contrariis introductis colligi videtur, quod imperator potestatem gladii et imperium habeat ab apostolico . . . . Ego autem credo quod imperator potestatem gladii et dignitatem imperialem habet non ab apostolico set a principibus et populo per electionem." (Cited by A. Stickler, " Der Schwerterbegriff bei Huguccio," 211 n.1.) Cf. W. Ullmann, *op. cit.,* 142–146, and S. Mochi Onory, *op. cit.,* 197, 222, 260.

[25] *Dist.* 17 c.5, 2 q.6 cc.4–10, 24 q.1 cc.9–14.

[26] *Dist.* 19, *dictum Gratiani post* c.8, " Hoc autem intelligendum est de illis sanctionibus vel decretalibus epistolis in quibus nec praecedentium Patrum decretis, nec Evangelicis praeceptis aliquid contrarium invenitur . . . . "

48

expositions of learned theologians were to be preferred to those of a Pope.[27] Thus the central paradox in early canonistic doctrine that Ockham was eventually to exploit lay in the fact that Gratian strongly affirmed the judicial authority of the Pope in doctrinal disputes without attributing to him that quality of unerringness that would have put his judgments beyond all possible challenge.[28] From this position arose quite naturally the two problems whose treatment by Ockham and some of his canonistic predecessors is to be considered. If the Pope, the supreme judge, could err in faith, how was the Church to be protected against the menace of a Pope who had become a heretic? And, again, if even a Pope could become a heretic, where could Christians find that unfailing guidance and authority that Christ had promised would always sustain His Church?

The existence of such problems was just as apparent to the great Decretists of the twelfth and early thirteenth centuries as to Ockham and the fourteenth-century Conciliarists, though the canonists' motives in discussing them were no doubt somewhat different. The Decretists envisaged only as a remote and theoretical possibility the advent of a heretical Pope whose behavior might endanger the well-being of the whole Church, while Ockham was entirely convinced that the Church in his own day was menaced by just such a tyrant in the person of John XXII. Ockham was therefore interested in the possibility of deposing a Pope very much as a matter of practical politics, but for the canonists the problem was essentially one of legal dialectics. Gratian had bequeathed to them a magnificent collection of authorities and had also provided a critical commentary on them which showed how many of his conflicting texts could be reconciled; but some problems he had left unresolved, and the need for a more adequate synthesis was especially apparent in those sections of the *Decretum* dealing with questions of Church government. When the

---

[27] *Dist.* 20, *dictum Gratiani ante* c.1, " Quo enim quisque magis ratione nititur, eo maioris auctoritatis eius verba esse videntur .... Unde nonnullorum Pontificum constitutis, Augustini, Hieronymi atque aliorum tractatorum dicta videntur esse praeferenda." Gratian went on to explain the apparent discrepancy between this opinion and his view of the Pope as supreme arbiter in doctrinal disputes by an analysis of the papal " power of the keys." According to Gratian there were two keys, a *clavis scientiae* and a *clavis potestatis*. In the decision of judicial cases " power " as well as " knowledge " was required, and only the Pope possessed both gifts; but others besides the Pope might possess the " key of knowledge " and might indeed possess it in greater degree.

[28] It should perhaps be emphasized at this point that the distinction between the Pope's private opinions and his public teaching as Head of the Church, which to a modern Catholic offers an obvious solution to many of the Decretists' difficulties, was never adequately formulated at this early period.

canonists considered such questions, therefore, they were mainly concerned to continue the process of harmonization that Gratian himself had begun. It is fascinating to observe how, influenced solely by the tensions inherent in the material they were expounding, they were led to consider the same problems as Ockham, and sometimes to propound the same solutions that he was to evolve in response to the external stresses and tensions of his stormy career.

The canonist whose views on these questions most closely anticipated those of Ockham was Huguccio of Pisa,[29] a master of the late twelfth century very well known to historians of canon law, but until recently somewhat neglected by students of medieval political theory. Huguccio's remarkable powers of synthetic reasoning, the originality and clarity of his thought on problems of Church government,[30] his very considerable influence on the next generation of canonists [31] (among them his own great pupil, Innocent III),[32] certainly entitle him to be ranked not only as a distinguished jurist but also as an important master in the broader fields of ecclesiology and political theory. Indeed, there are many trends of thirteenth-century thought that will never be fully understood until we have a definitive study of Huguccio's teachings and an edition of his great *Summa* on the *Decretum*.

Huguccio, moreover, was apparently the first of the Decretists to attempt a really detailed discussion of the first of our two problems, and his exposition formed the basis of a whole tradition of canonistic thought that Ockham was to inherit and exploit. The case of a hereti-

[29] Huguccio was a native of Pisa who lectured at Bologna and became Bishop of Ferrara in 1190. His great *Summa* on the *Decretum* was completed c. 1190 and certainly not before 1188. Schulte, *Quellen und Literatur*, I, 156–170; F. Gillmann, " Die Abfassungszeit der Dekretsumme Huguccios," *Archiv für katholisches Kirchenrecht* XCIV (1914), 233–251, *Catholic Encyclopedia*, s.v. Huguccio (A. Van Hove); S. Kuttner, *Repertorium*, 158 and *idem*, " Bernardus Compostellanum Antiquus," *Traditio* I (1943), 277–340 at 183–284.

[30] Huguccio of course owed much to the Bolognese tradition of Decretist scholarship that stretched back to the days of Gratian himself, but he was not always content to accept traditional patterns of thought. His independence of judgment is well illustrated in the collection of extracts presented by S. Mochi Onory, *op. cit.*, 145 n.1.

[31] Mochi Onory, *op. cit.*, 147, " il pensiero di Uguccio conquistò il mondo canonistico."

[32] Innocent studied under Huguccio at Bologna, Schulte, *Quellen und Literatur*, I, 156. The influence of Huguccio's doctrines on Innocent's political ideas is discussed by M. Maccarone, *Chiesa e Stato*, 79ff., 95ff., 108ff., and by Mochi Onory, *op. cit.*, 183ff.; Dr. Ullmann suggested that Huguccio's influence lay in supplying the future Pope with " juristic equipment " rather than in his " actual political arguments " (*Medieval Papalism*, 144 n.2).

cal Pope provides a typical example of an important problem posed by the texts of Gratian's compilation which the great master himself had made no attempt to resolve. The *Decretum* contained several very explicit assertions that the Pope was immune from all human judgment, even from that of a Council of " all the clergy."

Neque ab Augusto neque ab omni clero neque a regibus neque a populo iudex iudicatur.[33]

On the other hand another text of the *Decretum* implied quite clearly that a Pope could be brought to trial and deposed if he erred in faith.

[Papa] a nemine est iudicandus, *nisi deprehendatur a fide devius*.[34]

The juristic problem presented to the twelfth-century canonists was to reconcile these apparently conflicting texts, and further to explain why heresy was mentioned as the one offense for which a Pope might be brought to judgment.

In his long and complex gloss on the crucial text Huguccio first put forward the widely accepted view that a heretical Pope could be deposed since heresy in the Pope was peculiarly injurious to the Church as a whole.[35] But to Huguccio the argument did not appear altogether satisfactory. In his opinion heresy was not the only papal offence that might injure the whole Church. He maintained, on the contrary, that for a Pope to scandalize the Church by contumacious persistence in any notorious crime was tantamount to heresy and should be pun-

---

[33] 9 q.3 c.13. See also *Dist.* 17, *post* c.6, *Dist.* 21 c.4, c.7, 7 q.4 c.30, 9 q.3 cc.10–18.

[34] *Dist.* 40 c.6. This critical text was attributed to St. Boniface by Gratian. It really has its origin in a Symmachian forgery (E. Caspar, *Geschichte des Papsttums*, II, 109ff.), which was repeated in Pseudo-Isidore. It was apparently first formulated by Cardinal Humbert in the precise form given by Gratian. The text of the *Decretum* is in literal agreement with the *Fragmentum A* attributed to Humbert by A. Michel (cited by Percy Schramm, *Kaiser, Rom, und Renovatio* (Leipzig-Berlin, 1929), II, 128–129). The interpretation suggested by Michel (Schramm, II, 126–136) that " nisi deprehendatur devius " referred to the word " nemine " (so that the general sense would be, " no-one except a man erring in faith would presume to judge the Pope ") is ingenious but unconvincing, and was never put forward by the canonists themselves. Michel has since withdrawn it, *Die Sentenzen des Kardinals Humbert* (Leipzig, 1943), 32 n.1.

[35] *Summa ad Dist.* 40 c.6, MS 72 of Pembroke College, Cambridge, fol 147va, " si papa esset hereticus non sibi soli noceret sed toto mundo, presertim quia simplices et idiote facile sequerentur illam heresim cum credent non esse heresim . . . ." That a heretical Pope could be deposed was not a matter of controversy but was generally accepted by the canonists. A considerable number of texts illustrating their viewpoint was assembled by Schulte in his polemical work, *Die Stellung der Concilien, Päpste und Bischöfe* (Prague, 1871), *Anhang*, 253–269.

ished as such;[36] and he concluded that the statutes which declared
the Pope immune from all human judgment could never have been
intended to apply to such cases—no ecclesiastical statute was to be
interpreted in a sense that would endanger the well-being of the whole
Church.

... si papa esset hereticus publice et inde non posset accusari tota periclitaretur ecclesia et confunderetur generale statutum ecclesiae. Sed non credo
eum posse constituere aliquid in prejudicium generalis statuti ecclesiae ut
XV *Dist. Sicut* .... Item solent quidam quaerere qualiter papa potuit suis
successoribus hanc legem imponere ut possint accusari de heresi ... generale enim et regulare erat quod crimina punientur in quolibet, ergo in papa,
sed illam generalitatem circa papam restringit constituendo privilegium ut
non posset accusari de quolibet crimine, sed propter periculum ecclesiae
vitandum ... noluit per illud privilegium removere heresim vel notorium
crimen.[37]

A century and a half later Ockham was to put forward a very
similar point of view. He too maintained that a Pope could be tried
for any notorious crime,[38] and argued that the founders of the canons

[36] Pembroke MS 72, fol 147va. " Ego autem credo quod idem sit de quolibet
crimine notorio quod papa possit accusari et condemnari si admonitus non vult
cessare. Quod enim ecce, publice furatur, publice fornicatur, publice committit
simoniam, publice habet concubinam, publice eam cognoscit in ecclesia iuxta vel
supra altare, admonitus non vult cessare, nunquid non accusabitur ... nunquid sic
scandalizare ecclesiam non est quasi heresim committere? Praeterea contumacia est
crimen ydolitrae et quasi heresis ... unde et contumax dicitur infidelis ut Dist.
XXXVIII, *Nullus.* Et sic idem est in alio crimine notorio quam in heresi .... "

[37] Pembroke MS 72, fol 147vb. On this passage see W. Ullmann, *Medieval
Papalism,* 156.

[38] *Octo Quaestiones,* I, 60. " In tribus casibus tenetur papa humanum subire
iudicium secundum quosdam; primo in casu haeresis .... Secundo tenetur papa
humanum subire iudicium quandocunque crimen eius est notorium et inde scandalizatur ecclesia et ipse est incorrigibilis, ut dicit glossa di. xl, super c. *Si papa* ....
Tertio, ut dicunt quidam, tenetur papa humanum subire iudicium, si res vel iura
aliorum invadit vel detinet minus iuste." Ockham writes in a carefully non-commital style, but the editor of the *Octo Quaestiones* (following Haller) points out that
the chapters of *Responsiones* at the end of each *Quaestio* normally contain Ockham's
own opinions. (Introduction to *Octo Quaestiones,* ed. J. G. Sikes, 2–3.) Ockham's
third case in which a Pope may be subject to human judgment is hardly relevant
to our problem of the deposition of a Pope. It concerns rather the settlement of
civil suits between a Pope and an injured party. Ockham's suggestion that such a
case should ge to neutral arbitrators had been anticipated by Innocent IV himself.
Commentaria ad X. V.xl.23, fol 567rb, " ... si papa contra alium vel alius contra
papam movet quaestionem super rebus vel iuribus aliquibus eligantur arbitri utrin-
que, ut iudicium procedat sine suspicione." Innocent, however, regarded it as an act
of grace to submit the case to arbitrators in this way. Ockham regarded it as a
legal obligation, to which the Pope could be compelled, if necessary, by the Emperor.

relating to papal immunity could never have intended such immunity to extend to the case of a heretical Pope.

Sic in casu haeresis propter magnitudinem periculi quod imminet universali ecclesiae si papa efficiatur haereticus . . . rationabile videtur . . . quod de ipso in hoc casu canones non debent intelligi, et quod canonum conditores, si de hoc casu cogitassent et ipsum timuissent eventurum, ipsum excepissent omnino.[39]

However, these arguments in themselves would not suggest any especially close resemblance between Ockham's ideas and those of Huguccio, for Huguccio's opinions on these points found general acceptance among the Decretists of the early thirteenth century and were reproduced in Joannes Teutonicus' *Glossa Ordinaria* to the *Decretum* from which Ockham often quoted.[40] Even in Ockham's own day, although the prevailing canonistic opinion limited the charges admissible against a Pope to the single case of heresy, there were still distinguished canonists who adhered to the older point of view.[41]

Huguccio, however, had not been content to explain why a Pope could be brought to judgment in certain circumstances, but had also set himself to unravel all the intricate problems of legal procedure involved in the trial of a Pope, and it was in discussing these points that his views were most distinctive and controversial. *Dist.* 40 c.6 certainly withheld the privilege of immunity from a heretical Pope, but several other texts of the same compilation stated without any reservation that the Pope had no judicial superior, and hence that no court was competent to try him on any charge. It was also laid down in the *Decretum* that an inferior could not even bring an accusation against a superior [42]—and of course all men were held to be inferior to the Pope. Huguccio himself crisply stated the general difficulty, the lack of a judge competent to try a Pope, in considering the particular problem of why the normal canonistic procedure (which permitted denunciations for secret crimes) could not be applied in the case of a Pope.

. . . ecce ii vel iii vel iiii sciunt crimen papae occultum. Non possunt inde eum accusare? Non possunt post amonitionem denuntiare illud crimen iuxta regulam ecclesiasticam, *Si peccaverit etc?* Nunquid illa regula evangelica non habebit locum circa papam? . . . . Respondeo, videtur quod illa regula

[39] *Octo Quaestiones, ed. cit.,* I, 62.

[40] *Gloss ad Dist.* 40 c.6, cited by Ockham at 60 (*supra* n.38).

[41] *E.g.,* Henricus Bohic, *Distinctionum libri quinque ad decretales* (London, 1557) *ad* X. I.vi.6, fol 19va.

[42] The whole of c.2 q.7 of the *Decretum* was taken up with a discussion of this point.

non habet locum circa papam propter defectum iudicis coram quo conveniretur . . . . [43]

In attempting to meet this difficulty Huguccio was obliged to define the precise circumstances in which a charge of heresy could lawfully be brought against a Pope, and to recognize severe limitations to the exercise of this right. A Pope could only be accused, according to Huguccio, when he publicly announced his willful adherence to a known heresy and refused to abandon his heretical opinions after due admonition. If the Pope propounded a new doctrine which was suspected as heretical no action could be taken against him; if he held in secret a heresy that was already condemned but denied the fact, then again no accusation could be brought against him.[44] For a Pope to become liable to accusation it was necessary that his heresy should be " public " or any other crime " notorious "; he could never be accused for an " occult " crime.

. . . in eo est differentia inter heresim et alia crimina notoria, scilicet quod de crimine heresis potest papa accusari si heresim publice praedicat et non vult desistere quamvis talem crimen non sit notorium, sed de alio crimine non potest accusari nisi sit notorium. Ergo de occulto crimine non potest accusari.[45]

These rather elaborate reservations were of the essence of Huguccio's argument. He was attempting to meet the difficulty that no court was competent to try a Pope by eliminating the necessity for a trial of the Pope as such, and to achieve that result he was applying to the Papacy in meticulous detail a series of arguments that Gratian himself had formulated in considering the position of lesser prelates. Gratian held that no inferior could condemn a superior, but he also held that no formal condemnation was necessary in the case of a man who accepted a heresy already condemned, for such a one was regarded as having wilfully included himself in the previous condemnation [46]—

---

[43] Pembroke MS 72, fol 147vb. The normal canonistic doctrine held that a crime could be described as " occult " when it was known to as many as five people. Cf. 6 q.1 *dictum Gratiani post* c.21.

[44] " Sed ecce, papa fingit novam heresim, aliquis vult probare illam esse heresim, papa dicit non esse heresim, est ne recipienda eius probatio? Credo quod non. Item sequitur heresim dampnatam latenter. Aliqui tamen hoc sciunt et volunt probare papam sequi talem heresim. Ille tamen negat. Debet audiri? Credo quod non. Tunc enim demum accusari potest de heresi cum constat quod illud factum sit heresis et papa non negat se illud facere et admonitus non vult resipiscere sed errorem suum contumaciter defendit." Pembroke MS 72, fol 147va.

[45] Pembroke MS 72, fol 147vb.

[46] 24 q.1 *dictum Gratiani ante* c.1, " Qui vero heresim iam damnatam sequitur eius damnationis se particem facit."

hence Huguccio's careful distinction between a new heresy and an old one. Again, Gratian conceded that accusations by an inferior against a superior might be admitted in the one case of heresy,[47] but he added that this concession only applied in cases of self-evident heresy. A prelate of good repute who denied that he was a heretic was not subject to such accusations.[48] Huguccio, therefore, was following Gratian's doctrine with scrupulous fidelity when he asserted that a pope could not be accused of "occult" heresy, but only when he "publicly preached heresy." The deposition of any prelate, even a Pope, who was thus self-convicted of heresy would not involve any breach of the principle that a superior could not be condemned by an inferior, for, as Huguccio pointed out in another context, a pope who adhered to a condemned heresy became *ipso facto* inferior to any true Catholic.

Cum papa cadit in heresim non iam maior sed minor quolibet catholico intelligitur.[49]

Evidently Huguccio's argument did not rest on any alleged superiority of a General Council over a Pope and Huguccio indeed did not consider a Council necessary to condemn a Pope for heresy; he remarked that the Cardinals could depose a heretical Pope,[50] and the logic of his argument would seem to imply that no especially exalted tribunal was needed to deal with the case of a man who was "minor quolibet catholico."

Although the intricacies of Huguccio's argument have not been fully appreciated in modern works, both H.-X. Arquillière[51] and, following him, Mgr. Martin[52] have stressed the importance of his general conclusions in their discussions on the growth of Conciliar ideas. Both writers concluded that, since the individual brought to trial was assumed to be no longer a Pope before any legal process against him was instituted, the canonistic tradition of the thirteenth

[47] 2 q.7 *dictum Gratiani post* c.26, "In quo hereticus inferior est, videlicet in regula fidei, in eo a malo catholico accusari potest."

[48] 6 q.1 *dictum Gratiani post* c.21, "Verum hoc . . . de his intelligendum est quos constat esse hereticos, non de his qui se negant in heresim lapsos."

[49] *Summa ad Dist.* 21 c.4. Pembroke MS 72, fol 130va.

[50] *Summa ad Dist.* 63 c.22, MS 2 of Lincoln Cathedral Chapter Library, fol 121va. "Nam et cardinales possunt deponere papam pro heresi. Non tamen ipsi sunt maiores quam papa."

[51] H.-X. Arquillière, "L'origine des théories conciliaires," *Séances et travaux de l'Académie des Sciences Morales et Politiques* CLXXV (1911), 573–586, and *idem,* "L'appel au concile sous Philippe le Bel et la genèse des théories conciliaires," *Revue des questions historiques* XLV (1911), 23–55.

century concerning the deposition of a heretical Pope did not carry any implication of Conciliar supremacy; and Mgr. Martin was inclined to see in the works of Ockham the "solvent" of traditional ideas that prepared the way for the extreme Conciliar doctrines of the late fourteenth century.[53] However, in this particular matter of the trial of a heretical Pope, the truth would seem to be rather the reverse. Ockham did reproduce Huguccio's arguments faithfully enough, but no satisfactory evidence has been adduced to prove that the canonists themselves were equally scrupulous.

Instead, there appeared almost at once a tendency to simplify Huguccio's rather elaborate arguments and, in the process to compromise the central principle that they sought to defend. The *Glossa Palatina*,[54] for instance, in its discussions of *Dist.* 40 c.6 did not reproduce the distinction between new heresies and heresies already condemned which had seemed so important to Huguccio. Moreover its author cited another of Huguccio's reservations and then explicitly rejected it.

H(uguccio) dicit quod . . . alii prelati accusantur etiam de occultis, papa non, etiam de heresi nisi constaret prius id quod facit vel dicit heresim esse. Mihi videtur . . . quod de heresi accusari posset etiam si occulta sit, de aliis non nisi sint manifesta . . . . Sed nunquid illa regula, *Si peccaverit in te etc.*, habet locum in papa? Dicit H(uguccio) quod non propter iudicis defectum. Sed non credo hanc esse causam, nam credo papam iudicem habere, cetum cardinalium.[55]

Huguccio had maintained that no accusations could be brought against a Pope except when his own admissions provided a legal basis for presuming his guilt in accordance with Gratian's doctrines. The *Glossa Palatina* held that he could be accused without any such self-incriminating evidence and made no suggestion that the man brought to trial had ceased to be Pope before he was found guilty.

Joannes Teutonicus offered a development of Huguccio's thought which was less coherent than that of the *Glossa Palatina* but ultimately more influential, if only because in the fourteenth century the

[52] V. Martin, "Comment s'est formée la doctrine de la supériorité du concile sur le pape," *Revue des Sciences Religieuses*, XVII (1937), 121–143, 261–289, 405–407 at 121–143.   [53] *Ibid.*

[54] The *Glossa Palatina* was compiled between 1210 and 1215 (S. Kuttner, *Repertorium*, 81–92). The identity of the author is not known. Guido de Baysio, in his *Rosarium*, attributed all his quotations from the *Glossa Palatina* to Laurentius, but on this question see S. Kuttner, "Bernardus Compostellanus Antiquus," *Traditio* I (1943), 277–340 at 288–291, 309.

[55] *Glossa Palatina ad Dist.* 40 c.6, MS Pal. Lat. 658 of the Bibliotheca Vaticana, fol 10va.

56

Glossa Ordinaria was much the best known of the early Decretist commentaries.[56] He seems to have borrowed arguments from both the sources already mentioned. He followed Huguccio in stating that no Pope could establish a valid law exempting himself from future charges of heresy and went so far as to say that a Pope promulgating such a law would cease to be head of the Church.[57] He also pointed out, like Huguccio, that a heretical Pope was *minor quolibet catholico*, though in the *Glossa Ordinaria* the argument was used only to prove that a Pope might be bound by the decisions of a predecessor in matters of faith,[58] and was not cited in any discussion on the deposition of a Pope.

On the other hand Joannes Teutonicus followed the *Glossa Palatina* in maintaining that a pope could be brought to trial for even " occult " heresy,[59] and he made no attempt to restate Huguccio's cautious distinctions which had explained in detail how a heretical Pope could be condemned without any violation of the existing laws on the judgment of superiors by inferiors. On this point, however, Joannes had something of his own to contribute. He emphasized the close connection (inherent in Gratian's texts) between the Pope's immunity from judgment and the fact that his own judicial decisions were inviolable. In his view the fact that the Pope could not normally be judged even by a General Council proved that the Pope's decisions could stand against " the whole world."

Arguo quod concilium non potest papam iudicare . . . unde si totus mundus sententiaret in aliquo negotio contra Papam videtur quod sententiae papae standum essent.[60]

But in other contexts Joannes put forward the view that in one special case the Pope's decisions were not thus sacrosanct, that in the definition of articles of faith—and in that alone—the decisions of a General Council were to be preferred to those of a Pope.[61] There is an inter-

---

[56] The *Glossa Ordinaria* was completed after the Fourth Lateran Council and probably before the *Compilatio Quarta* (1217). Cf. S. Kuttner, *Repertorium*, 93–102 and *idem*, " Johannes Teutonicus, das vierte Laterankonzil, und die Compilatio Quarta," *Miscellanea Giovanni Mercati* V (Città del Vaticano, 1946), 608–634.

[57] *Glossa Ordinaria ad Dist.* 40 c.6, " Item nunquid papa posset statuere quod non posset accusari de heresi. Respondeo quod non quia ex hoc periclitaretur tota ecclesia quod non licet . . . quia hoc fit in eo casu quo desinit esse caput ecclesiae et ita non tenet constitutio." [58] Gloss *ad* 24 q.1 c.1.

[59] Gloss *ad* Dist. 40 c.6, " . . . et si occulta esset heresis de illa posset accusari. Sed de alio occulto crimine non posset."

[60] Gloss *ad* 9 q.3 c.13. [61] Gloss *ad* Dist. 19 c.9. " Videtur ergo quod papa teneatur requirere concilium episcoporum, quod verum est ubi de fide agitur et tunc

esting discussion of the point at *Dist.* 15 c.2, a text which dealt with the authority of the first four General Councils of the Church.

Praesumit. Videtur ergo quod Papa non possit destruere statuta concilii, quia orbis maior est urbe, 93 *Dist. Legimus,* unde et requirit Papa consensum concilii, 19 *Dist. Anastasius.* Arg. contra, 17 *Dist.* § *Hinc etiam* . . . . Sed intellige quod hic dicitur circa articulos fidei.

Now *Dist.* 17 § *Hinc etiam* referred to a case in which the Pope's immunity from judgment by a Council was upheld, and this was presented as an argument against the proposition that the Pope was bound by the decisions of previous General Councils. The argument of Joannes apparently ran thus. The person of a Pope was not normally subject to the judgment of a General Council; therefore the opinions of a Pope could stand against those of a previous Council. But at the end of the gloss it was conceded that where articles of faith were involved the Pope was in fact bound by the decisions of previous Councils. It would seem entirely consistent with this trend of thought to suppose, therefore, that in cases where articles of faith were involved the person of the Pope might also be subject to the judgment of a Council, that in this one case the Pope had a judicial superior.[62] This would explain satisfactorily why a Pope could be accused of even secret heresies, but not normally of other crimes; [63] and again, if Joannes Teutonicus supposed that the Pope's liability to judgment rested on the superior authority of a General Council (and not on any supposed self-condemnation or automatic degradation), there would be no need for him to reproduce all Huguccio's cautious reservations. Taking into account all the relevant glosses,[64] it seems probable that this was the real opinion of Joannes Teutonicus, but it must be

---

synodus maior est papa ut 15 *Dist. sicut* in fin. Arg. ad hoc 93 *Dist. legimus."* At *Dist.* 15 c.2 (cited in text) Joannes laid down that a Pope could not go against decisions of previous Councils in matters of faith. At *Dist* 93 c.24 he wrote, " Et est hic argumentum quod statutum concilii praeiudicat sententiae papae si contradicant," but went on to give a reference to another gloss in which he had expressed a contrary opinion (9 q.3 c.13), without making clear his real opinion.

[62] Ockham certainly understood Joannes Teutonicus in this sense. Cf. *infra* n.73.

[63] Joannes Teutonicus agreed with Huguccio that a Pope could be accused of any notorious crime, but, again like Huguccio, he based this view on the legal doctrine that contumacy was equivalent to heresy. Gloss *ad Dist.* 40 c.6, " Certe credo quod si notorium est crimen . . . et inde scandalizatur ecclesia et incorrigibilis sit, quod inde possit accusari. Nam contumacia dicitur heresis . . . ."

[64] *Dist.* 4 c.3, *Dist.* 15 c.2, *Dist.* 17 c.6, *Dist.* 19 c.9, *Dist.* 21 c.7, *Dist.* 40 c.6, *Dist.* 63 c.23, *Dist.* 79 c.9, *Dist.* 93 c.24, 2 q.5 c.10, 2 q.7 c.41, 9 q.3 c.13, 24 q.1 cc.6,9,12,14.

emphasized that he always expressed himself with studied ambiguity on such a delicate point, and it would be impossible to construct an entirely consistent doctrine from the mass of conflicting opinions that he presented. What is certain is that the *Glossa Ordinaria* to the *Decretum* provided a useful source of arguments for later thinkers whose views were more radical than those of Joannes himself.

After the appearance of the *Glossa Ordinaria*, there was little further Decretist activity for several generations, and the great Decretalist commentaries that were the outstanding achievements of thirteenth-century canonistic scholarship paid little attention to the problem of a heretical Pope. Goffredus Tranensis, Bernardus Parmensis, Innocentius IV, Hostiensis, Gulielmus Durandus all noted that the Pope's immunity from judgment did not extend to the case of heresy, but none of them attempted any detailed description of the procedure to be adopted in such a case. Nor, in their voluminous glosses, did they refer to such discussions in the works of their contemporaries.

The whole issue of a Pope's liability to judgment was brought into prominence again at the end of the thirteenth century by the disputes between Boniface VIII and Philip the Fair, and especially by the attempts of Nogaret to indict Boniface before a General Council. The glosses of canonists contemporary with Ockham himself, therefore, displayed a renewed interest in the subject, and this was especially true of Guido de Baysio, who of all the canonists of the period was most familiar with the early Decretist discussions. Although numerous quotations in his *Rosarium* show that he was thoroughly familiar with Huguccio's *Summa* he did not choose to reproduce the argument that a heretical Pope was *minor quolibet catholico* nor any of the reservations by which Huguccio had safeguarded the principle that no legal process could be initiated against a man who was presumably a true Pope. On the other hand he did call attention to a rather different doctrine which had found wide acceptance in the thirteenth century—that resistance to a heretical Pope could not take the form of an *exceptio* (an allegation that he had never been a true Pope or had ceased to be one because of heresy), but must be expressed in an *accusatio*, a form of action that would necessitate a subsequent trial of the Pope.[65] Again, Guido asserted, like Joannes Teutonicus

---

[65] *Rosarium ad Dist.* 40 c.6, fol 53ra, " Inn. dicit quod de hoc crimine bene potest accusari sed contra eum non potest excipi et hoc forte verius est . . . . " According to Henricus Bohic, *Distinctiones ad* X. I.vi.6, fol 19va, the opinion that an *accusatio* but not an *exceptio* could be brought against a Pope was upheld by Vincentius, Innocentius, Hostiensis, Bernardus Compostellanus, Abbas Antiquus, Alanus, Joannes Andreae as well as Guido de Baysio.

and the *Glossa Palatina*, that a Pope could be accused even of occult heresy, and he added unambiguously that the authority competent to judge such a case was a General Council.[66]   Joannes Andreae and Henricus de Bohic were of the same opinion.[67]   Finally Guido de Baysio rejected the opinion of those who held that, when a General Council found a Pope guilty of heresy, it should be left for the Pope to condemn himself; in Guido's view it was the duty of the Council to pronounce the sentence of deposition.[68]   Joannes Andreae repeated this view without comment.[69]

In the writings of these distinguished canonists there seems little trace left of the theories of Huguccio, but certain publicistic writings of the time did re-affirm Huguccio's main contention, that a heretic automatically ceased to be Pope before any legal action was taken against him, though they did not reproduce all the ingenious arguments with which Huguccio had buttressed that central assertion.[70]

It is evident that when Ockham approached the problem of a heretical Pope there was already in existence a rather rich background of speculation on the subject.   In his *Breviloquium* he announced that

[66] *In Sextum decretalium commentaria* (Venice, 1577), *ad Sext* V.ii.5, fol 114, " . . . tantus est favor fidei, quod de crimine haeresis etiam in occulto papa potest accusari . . . et hujus criminis iudex competens est concilium generale . . . . Scias tamen quod Huguccio scripsit . . . quod Cardinales possunt deponere Papam propter heresim. Sed hoc iure aliquo non probavit . . . . "

[67] Henricus Bohic *ad* X. I.vi.6, fol 19va, " Archidiaconus et Joannes Andreae [dicunt] quod criminis heresis pape iudex competens est concilium generale, quod verum est . . . . "

[68] Gloss *ad Sext* V.ii.5, " . . . quamvis tale crimen probetur in concilio contra papam, videtur quod concilium non debeat eum condemnare sed ipse papa contra se sententiam habeat promulgare . . . . Sed contra credo . . . . "

[69] *Novella in Sextum Decretalium* (London, 1550), *ad Sext* V.ii.5, fol 103. It should be noted that neither Guido de Baysio nor Joannes Andreae nor Henricus Bohic based their doctrines on any claim that the General Council was superior to the Pope in the decision of cases involving articles of faith and indeed none of them accepted that opinion; but since they chose to ignore the arguments of Huguccio which had shown how a Pope could be brought to trial without the need for any such assumption, their doctrines carried at least an implication of conciliar supremacy which was exploited by the publicists of the age of the Great Schism.

[70] V. Martin, *art. cit.*, 129–130, mentioned especially the Franciscan publicist, Pietro Olivi, whose views probably influenced Ockham directly. Olivi argued that since any heretic ceased to be a member of the Church, *a fortiori* a heretical Pope ceased to be head of the Church. (F. Ehrle, " Petrus Iohannis Olivi," *Archiv für Literatur und Kirche-geschichte* III, (1887), 524.) Van Leeuwen, *art. cit.*, 278, quoted a similar opinion put forward by Guillaume d'Amilani, " Si autem haereticus esset in fide tunc non deponitur sed sua depositio manifestatur. Nam eo ipso quod haereticus et praecisus ab ecclesia, ecclesiae caput desinit esse."

he proposed to discuss the problems of procedure involved in the trial of a Pope,[71] but unfortunately the promise was not fulfilled in that work in which Ockham's own opinions were expressed most unambiguously. Accordingly we must turn to the *Octo Quaestiones* for the clearest statement of his views on the question, and to the formidable *Dialogus* for a detailed discussion of all the problems involved.[72] It is natural that in such eclectic works one should find elements of thought derived from various preceding theories, both publicistic and canonistic, but the most interesting aspect of Ockham's treatment of the whole subject is his general conservatism. On the whole he neglected the opportunities which the existing canonistic tradition presented of building up a thorough-going Conciliar doctrine and preferred to re-state in detail the old arguments of Huguccio. Ockham, indeed, reproduced Huguccio's arguments more accurately than did any of the canonists whose views have been mentioned.

It is true that in his first great political treatise he cited Joannes Teutonicus to prove that the Council was a " superior judge " set over the Pope, and so a court to which a legitimate appeal from the Pope's decisions could be addressed; [73] but in his later works, when he was actually discussing the deposition of a Pope, there was a marked change of emphasis. In the *Opus Nonaginta Dierum* Ockham had appeared to favor the view, which was probably that of Joannes Teutonicus himself, that the jurisdiction of a Council over a Pope in cases of heresy was based on the Council's greater authority in the definition of articles of faith; in the *Octo Quaestiones* he distinguished clearly between the two functions, remarking that even the Universal Church did not provide a certain judge of a Pope's orthodoxy, for though it could not err in a matter of doctrine it might very well err

[71] *Breviloquium, ed. cit.*, V.iv, 136, " Judicare autem papam errare judicialiter per sentenciam, quomodo judicant judices potestatem habentes legittimam, spectaret ad illum qui esset judex pape: de quo postea apparebit."

[72] *Octo Quaestiones, ed. cit.*, I.xvii, 60–66, *Dialogus, ed. cit.*, I.v.cc.1–3, 467–473, I.vi.cc.83–100, 601–634.

[73] *Opus Nonaginta Dierum*, ed. R. F. Bennett and J. G. Sikes in *Guillelmi De Ockham Opera Politica* (Manchester, 1940), I, 295–296, " Primo quia ab omni habente superiorem in aliqua causa, licet pro eadem causa ad eundem superiorem iudicem appellare . . . sed papa in causa haeresis habet iudicem superiorem, nam papa potest pro haeresi iudicari, di. xl, c. *si papa.* Immo sicut notatur in glossa ibidem, *papa non posset statuere quod non posset de haeresi accusari, quia ex hoc periclitaretur tota ecclesia.* Qui autem potest de haeresi accusari et etiam iudicari, habet superiorem a quo poterit iudicari; ergo papa habet in causa haeresis superiorem, quod glossa di. xix, c. *Anastasius*, asserit manifeste, dicens quod *ubi de fide agitur, synodus maior est papa;* ergo a papa pro causa haeresis est licitum appellare."

in a matter of fact.[74] Ockham preferred therefore to emphasize the quite different argument of Huguccio that a heretical Pope was *ipso facto* deposed and so subject to the judgment of any Catholic.

. . . si est in rei veritate haereticus, ipso facto et iure scilicet tam divino quam humano, est papatu privatus . . . .

As for the authority competent to judge a heretical Pope, Ockham suggested that a group of bishops, or the individual bishop in whose diocese the Pope was resident, or any other Catholic (especially the Emperor) might exercise such jurisdiction.[75]

These views were stated in the *Octo Quaestiones,* but only defended at length in the *Dialogus,* and there, in introducing the whole topic of the authority competent to depose a heretical Pope, Ockham faithfully reproduced Huguccio's careful distinctions, which so many of the canonists themselves had ignored, between occult heresy, notorious heresy, and heresy that was public but not notorious.[76] In the ensuing maze of arguments and counter-arguments on subsidiary topics he seems, however, to have lost sight of the main purpose of these distinctions, and, as is invariably the case in the *Dialogus,* he did not provide a clear-cut statement of his own opinions. In particular, Ockham left unanswered the question whether a Pope could be tried for occult heresy as Joannes Teutonicus had asserted, or only for publicly admitted heresy as the theory of Huguccio required, though he did remark that when a bishop " detained " the Pope for heresy the bishop had to prove, in order to justify his action, that the Pope was a manifest heretic at the time of the denunciation.[77] More sig-

[74] *Octo Quaestiones, ed. cit.,* I, 61, " Universalis enim ecclesia, licet in hiis quae iuris sunt, praesertim divinae, errare non possit, tamen errare potest in hiis quae facti sunt." The same point of view was put forward by the contemporary canonist Henricus Bohic, *Distinctiones ad* X. V.xxxix.1, fol 131va, " Aut queris de ecclesia generali simul congregata et illa nunquid errare potest . . . . Quod credo verum in errore iuris . . . . Sed in errore facti maxime probabile ecclesia generalis errare potest."

[75] *Octo Quaestiones,* I, 61, " Sed quaeret aliquis coram quo iudice possit vel debeat papa de haeresi accusari. Huic respondent quidam dicentes quod papa coram diocesano in cuius diocesi commoratur potest de haeresi accusari . . . sicut alii episcopi, qui, si invenirentur haeretici, in diocesi alicuius episcopi iudicari possent ab ipso, quamvis non solempniter degradari, ita etiam papa, si efficiatur haereticus, praesertim notorius . . . . Si autem moratur in Romana diocesi, vel episcopus in cuius diocesi manet aut non vult aut non potest audire accusatores papae haeretici, alii episcopi fidei zelo accensi ipsos debent audire . . . . Si autem episcopi vel noluerint vel nequiverint papam haereticum iudicare, alii catholici, maxime imperator si catholicus fuerit, ipsum iudicare valebit . . . . "

[76] *Dialogus,* I.vi.c.83, 602.

[77] *Dialogus,* I.vi.c.90, 608.

nificant than this was Ockham's acceptance of the principle that not only a General Council but any Catholic authority was competent to depose a heretical Pope, and his defense of this principle in the *Dialogus* by precisely the same argument that Huguccio had first employed.

Papa haereticus non sit maior sed minor omni episcopo quia omnis haereticus minor est omni catholico.[78]

It is not difficult to suggest practical reasons why Ockham should have thought it thus worth while to re-construct an early canonistic opinion that had been often ignored by the canonists themselves. The prevailing canonistic doctrine, with its latent implications of Conciliar supremacy, might have seemed theoretically attractive to him, but after all there was no practical possibility in the 1330's of summoning a General Council that would have been prepared to take action against a reigning Pope. On the other hand, Ockham's great adversary, John XXII, fulfilled (at any rate in the eyes of his opponents) all the somewhat exacting conditions that Huguccio required to justify action against the Pope.[79] To the dissident Franciscans he seemed not only a heretic but a self-proclaimed heretic. His doctrine on the Beatific Vision might indeed appear as a new heresy (which Huguccio did not admit as a valid ground of accusation), but his teaching on evangelical poverty ran counter to previous papal pronouncements on the subject, and so, for Ockham, reduced the Pope automatically to the status of one who followed " a heresy previously condemned "; and a considerable part of the *Opus Nonaginta Dierum* was devoted to proving the point.

The practical necessities that inspired Ockham's polemics are again in evidence when we turn to the second main topic in which his theories were indebted to those of the early Decretists and especially to those of Huguccio—his discussion on the structure of the whole Church and on the location of unerring authority within it.

Ockham belonged not only to a minority in the Church as a whole, but also to a small and dissident minority within his own Order. To make such a position tenable at all it was necessary for him to maintain that all the established ecclesiastical authorities might err in their

---

[78] *Dialogus*, I.vi.c.90, 607.

[79] L. Baudry has recently argued that the first book of the *Dialogus* was composed during the pontificate of John XXII (*Guillaume d'Occam*, I, 160–163). In any case, Ockham of course attributed to John's successor, Benedict XII, most of the heresies of which he had accused John himself. See his *Tractatus contra Benedictum XII*, ed. R. Scholz, *Unbekannte kirchenpolitische Streitschriften aus der Zeit Ludwigs des Bayern* (Rome, 1914), II, 403–417.

teaching and, accordingly, that only the Universal Church, the whole *congregatio fidelium,* was the unfailing guardian of the true Faith. Huguccio, once again, was led to consider precisely the same problem, not through any exigencies of contemporary ecclesiastical politics, but by that continuing necessity to harmonize the discordant texts of the *Decretum* which inspired so much of the intellectual activity of the ·twelfth-century canonists.

On the subject of unerring authority within the Church the authorities cited by Gratian were particularly confusing. It was not only suggested in the *Decretum* that a Pope could be deposed for heresy but furthermore a specific case was cited of a Pope who was alleged to have erred in a matter of faith.

Anastasius secundus, natione Romanus, fuit temporibus Theodorici regis. Eodem tempore multi clerici et presbyteri se a communione ipsius abegerunt, eo quod communicasset sine concilio episcoporum vel presbyterorum et clerici cunctae ecclesiae catholicae diacono Thessalonicensi, nomine Photino, qui communicaverit Acacio, et quia voluit revocare Acacius occulte et non potuit, nutu divino percussus est.[80]

It was the case of Anastasius that was most frequently cited in later canonistic discussions, but Pope Marcellinus was also alleged to have committed idolatry,[81] and Gratian stated that even St. Peter himself had erred in faith.[82] On the other hand it was natural and inevitable that the ancient doctrine of the Holy See as divinely appointed guardian of the faith should also find expression in the texts of the *Decretum,* and indeed Gratian not only insisted that all disputes concerning matters of faith were to be referred to the Holy See for decision but also produced a series of texts which asserted that the " Roman church " had always remained free from the stain of sin and heresy.[83] Gratian, incidentally, made no attempt to distinguish between the powers of the Pope, of the Apostolic See, and of the Roman church; for him the three phrases could be used as interchangeable expressions.[84]

[80] *Dist.* 19 c.9.   [81] *Dist.* 21 c.7.   [82] 2 q.7 *dictum Gratiani post* c.39, " Petrus cogebat gentes iudaizare et a veritate evangelii recedere."

[83] 24 q.1 cc.9,10,11,14. " Sancta Romana ecclesia, quae semper immaculata mansit et Domino providente . . . sine ulla haereticorum insultatione firma et immobilis omni tempore persistet."

[84] Thus he could write in the course of one passage, " Sacrosancta *Romana ecclesia* ius et auctoritatem sacris canonibus impertitur, sed non eis alligatur . . . *summis* vero *pontificibus* ostenditur inesse auctoritas observandi . . . . Opportet ergo *primam sedem,* ut dicimus, observare ea, quae decernendo mandavit, non necessitate obsequendi, sed auctoritate impertiendi." 25 q.1 *dictum Gratiani post* c.16.

The Decretists were therefore presented with an unresolved antithesis between an immaculate Roman church and a Pope who might be a heretic. Huguccio was apparently the first of them to realize that the paradoxes of the *Decretum* might have their roots in an underlying confusion of thought concerning the nature of the Roman church itself; and his attempt to end that confusion was to prove of considerable significance for later theories of Church government.

To Huguccio it seemed as evident as to any fourteenth-century Conciliarist that the Roman church, understood as the Pope and the Curia, could not be that *ecclesia* that was to endure for ever, unerring in faith and unstained by sin, " sine macula et ruga." He expressed this opinion somewhat tartly, insisting that if the *Roman ecclesia* were to be identified with any particular local church, then " you will not find a Roman church in which there are not plenty of stains and wrinkles."

Maculam . . . est argumentum quod non nisi boni sunt Romana ecclesia. Ergo ubicumque sunt boni fideles, ibi est Romana ecclesia, aliter non invenes Romanam ecclesiam in qua non sint multe macule et multe ruge.[85]

. . . dicitur quod Romana ecclesia non habet maculam vel rugam . . . sed in Romana ecclesia intelligitur universitas fidelium.[86]

In the opinion of Huguccio, therefore, the term *Romana ecclesia* might be interpreted as meaning the whole body of faithful Christians, the *congregatio fidelium* of the universal Church. But Gratian had consistently used the same expression to describe a particular local church having primacy over all the others, and Huguccio did not deny that in some contexts this usage might be acceptable. His underlying thought can be illustrated from his gloss on the passage of the *Decretum* containing St. Jerome's famous phrase, " Orbis maior est urbe," where it was pointed out that the Roman church was only one local church amongst others. Huguccio accepted this definition and commented, ". . . cum maior sit orbis quam Roma, maior est auctoritas orbis quam Romae." [87] But he hastened to add that among the local churches the Roman church enjoyed a position of authority: " Sed nonne totus orbis tenetur obedire Romanae ecclesiae? Sic quo ad observationem si praecipiat aliquid observari." [88] To Huguccio the two propositions did not seem contradictory. He acknowledged that all the local churches were required to obey the Roman church in matters of Church discipline, and he upheld the same point of view

---

[85] *Summa ad Dist.* 21 c.3, Pembroke MS 72, fol 130rb.

[86] *Summa ad Dist.* 23 c.1, Pembroke MS 72, fol 132ra.

[87] *Summa ad Dist.* 93 c.24, MS 2, Lincoln Cathedral Chapter Library.   [88] *Ibid.*

in all affairs relating to judicial decisions; but he also believed that the ultimate unerring authority that Christ had promised to His Church resided in the association of all the churches. When, therefore, the term *Romana ecclesia* was used to describe the holder of this underlying authority it could only be understood as designating the Universal Church and not any particular member of it. *Romana* and *universalis* could both be used as synonyms for *catholica* so that Huguccio could define the Catholic Church as " Catholice, i.e. universalis vel catholice, i.e. Romane." [89]

In considering the opinions of Huguccio and of other contemporary canonists, one must always remember that their comments were intended as answers to specific juristic problems rather than as foundations for a generalized theory of Church government. At the least, however, Huguccio was providing very effective support for any later thinker who cared to develop his ideas into an anti-papal doctrine; and there is a consistency and clarity in his scattered glosses which suggest that Huguccio himself had formulated a coherent theory of ecclesiastical authority which was somewhat different from that of the extreme curialists of the next century.

He certainly maintained that the term *Romana ecclesia* had at least two different connotations. In one sense it signified the whole *universitas fidelium;* in another sense it described a particular local church in which was concentrated the institutional machinery that governed the affairs of the Church Universal. Huguccio, moreover, seems to have been convinced of the necessity for discriminating between the authority inherent in the whole *congregatio fidelium* and the powers that could properly be exercised by the local *Romana ecclesia.* The essence of his thought is contained in one brief but pregnant sentence in which he outlined a theory of authority within the universal Roman church.

Ecclesia romana dicitur nunquam in fide errasse . . . sed dico quod Romana ecclesia dicitur tota catholica ecclesia quia nunquam in toto erraverit, vel Romana ecclesia dicitur papa et cardinales et licet iste erraverit non tamen cardinales, vel saltem non omnes Romani . . . . [90]

The Pope was head of the ecclesiastical hierarchy with no individual superior, but Pope and Cardinals together offered a more certain guide in matters of faith, whilst only the whole Church was divinely preserved from all error.

[89] *Summa ad Dist.* 11 c.9, Pembroke MS 72, fol 123vb, commenting on the words, " Palam est quod in re dubia ad fidem valeat auctoritas ecclesiae catholicae."
[90] *Summa ad Dist.* 19 c.9, Pembroke MS 72, fol 129rb.

66

If we now turn again to Ockham's thought it may be observed that no section of his work was more influential for later Conciliar theory than the fifth book of the *Dialogus;* and the first twelve chapters of this critical book, in which Ockham demonstrated first that the Pope could err, then that the College of Cardinals could err, and finally that the "Roman church," understood in any sense other than the whole *congregatio fidelium,* could likewise err, read like a much expanded version of the doctrine that Huguccio had compressed into a few terse lines.

The core of Ockham's argument was that the term *Romana ecclesia* had several different connotations, and that only when it was used to describe the *universalis ecclesia* could the quality of unerringness properly be attributed to it.

Romana ecclesia multipliciter accipitur, aliquando enim accipitur pro universali ecclesia, aliquando pro papa, aliquando pro clero et populo Romano, aliquando pro collegio cardinalium. Illa autem Romana ecclesia quae errare non potest est universalis ecclesia.[91]

The *Discipulus,* however, expressed surprise that the term *Romana ecclesia* could be employed in this broad sense and demanded a proof that such a usage was legitimate.

Miror quod isti dicunt, totam Romanam ecclesiam aliquando congregationem fidelium importare, unde si hoc possunt trahere ex scripturis authenticis, aperire digneris.[92]

At this critical point in his argument Ockham offers us, no longer a mere reflection of Huguccio's thought, but a direct quotation from the great canonist himself, though he attributed it to a different canonistic source.

Illa ecclesia quae non habet maculam neque rugam neque aliud huiusmodi potest Romana ecclesia appellari . . . *Dist.* 22 *Quamvis* . . . Ubi dicit Glo. Ord. *quod ubicunque sunt boni est Romana ecclesia* . . . . [93]

Here, as is so often the case, one is handicapped by the absence of a critical edition of the *Dialogus.* The reference given by Goldast is in any case mistaken, for the chapter *Quamvis* occurs, not in *Dist.* 22 but in *Dist.* 21 (c.3). The *Glossa Ordinaria* on this passage has simply, "ubicunque sunt boni ibi est ecclesia," a mere platitude. It is only

[91] *Dialogus,* I.v.c.8, 478.
[92] *Dialogus,* I.v.c.12, 481.
[93] *Ibid.* The passage continues, "Ex quibus verbis datur intelligi quod tota congregatio bonorum, ubicunque sint, potest ecclesia Romana appellari, et per consequens tota congregatio fidelium potest ecclesia Romana appellari." Cf. Huguccio *ad Dist.* 23 c.1, "in Romana ecclesia intelligitur universitas fidelium."

in Huguccio's work that we find " ubicunque sunt boni ibi est *Romana ecclesia*," and of course the presence of the word *Romana* in this context was the whole point of Ockham's quotation. Huguccio's idea that the " Roman church " was unerring only when it was understood as the *congregatio fidelium* did, however, re-appear more clearly at another point in the work of Joannes Teutonicus, and Ockham did not fail to make use of the relevant gloss—his demonstration that the Apostles (and consequently all the clergy) could err in faith was based on the *Glossa Ordinaria ad* 24 q.1 c.9 [94] (wrongly cited in Goldast as 25 q.1 *A recto*).[95] Again, in another canonistic work of the same period, the apparatus *Ecce Vicit Leo*, we find an interesting anticipation of Ockham's view that the true faith might live on " even in women " since it had survived in the Mother of Christ at the time of the Passion.

Fides ecclesiae nunquam deficit quia etiam in morte domini fuit, saltem in Beata Virgine.[96]

One of the ironies of fourteenth-century thought is that the very influential Book V of the *Dialogus,* taken as a whole, provided very little justification for the Conciliar theories that were later derived from it, for Ockham went on to assert that the General Council did not embody the unfailing authority of the whole Church any more than did the Pope or the *Romana ecclesia* (understood as a local church).[97] On the contrary he maintained that no ecclesiastical institution could perfectly represent the whole *universitas fidelium* and so exercise all its inherent powers; [98] and in this he differed sharply from

[94] " Qaero de qua ecclesia intelligas quod dicitur quod non possit errare. Si de ipso papa. . . certum est quod papa errare potest ut 19 *Dist. Anastasius* et 40 *Dist. Si papa.* Respondeo, ipsa congregatio fidelium hic dicitur ecclesia . . . et talis ecclesia non potest non esse."

[95] *Dialogus,* I.v., 500.

[96] MS 0.5.17 of Trinity College, Cambridge. Gloss *ad Dist.* 21, *dictum Gratiani ante* c.1, fol 8ra. (On this manuscript see S. Kuttner, *Repertorium,* 59, and W. Ullmann, *Medieval Papalism,* 208). Cf. Ockham, *Dialogus,* 492, " dicunt quidem [fidem] posse salvari in mulieribus quemadmodum tempore passionis Christi salvata fuit in sola matre Christi," and 503, " tempore passionis Christi . . . tota fides Christianae ecclesiae in matre Christi remansit." On the origins of this belief and its diffusion in other canonistic works of the thirteenth century, see Y. M.-J. Congar, " Incidence ecclésiologique d'un thème de dévotion mariale," *Mélanges de Science Religieuse* VIII (1951), 277–292.

[97] *Dialogus,* I.v.cc.25–28, 494–498.

[98] On this aspect of Ockham's thought see G. de Lagarde, " L'idée de représentation dans les oeuvres de Guillaume d'Ockham," *Bulletin of the International Committee of Historical Sciences* IX (1937), 425–451. It seems to the present writer that de Lagarde offers a valuable appraisal of Ockham's views on the nature of a

68

Huguccio and from the prevailing canonistic tradition. A much-quoted text of the *Decretum* laid down that the first four General Councils were to be venerated "sicut quattuor evangelii," and Huguccio added that, since their decrees were established "by universal consent," they were comparable to the decrees that any corporation or city made for its own members.[99] The opinion was not challenged by his successors, and, before the time of Ockham, the canonists did not think it necessary to draw any distinction between the powers of the whole Church and those of a General Council.

Not surprisingly there were many other points at which Ockham's views differed from those of the canonists. The concept of evangelical liberty, for instance, which recurs in nearly all his works, has a peculiarly personal flavor; his opinions concerning the rôle of the Emperor in ecclesiastical affairs went far beyond what the canonists had envisaged; and his argument that no established organ of Church government was competent to give a definitive and unerring decision on a point of faith certainly seems to anticipate the later claims to private judgment, and to justify the state of affairs that one can describe according to preference as "freedom of conscience" or "spiritual anarchy."

An adequate analysis of Ockham's personal contribution to later Conciliar ideas would require a detailed examination of his debt to canonistic doctrines and also of his departures from canonistic tradition in every department of his political and ecclesiological theories; but even our preliminary survey of a few of Ockham's most characteristic and influential doctrines suggests certain interesting conclusions. It must be emphasized that Ockham's more radical and anarchic ideas held no attraction for the great publicists in the age of the Schism—their task was to restore authority in the Church, not to hasten the process of disintegration. There is no denying that the *Dialogus* provided a useful source of arguments for some of the most distinguished Conciliar writers, but to understand the nature of Ockham's influence on them it must be realized that their choice of arguments was highly selective. The personal idiosyncrasies of Ockham were largely ignored; the Conciliarists preferred to build their systems around doc-

General Council, and a useful guide through the maze of passages in the *Dialogus* touching on this subject, but that his account of earlier canonistic ideas on representation is radically at fault—de Lagarde seems to accept too uncritically the theories of Gierke.

[99] *Summa ad Dist.* 15 c.2, Pembroke MS 72, fol 125vb, "*Universali consensu . . .* arg. pro universitate et quod nulli a canonico et communi consensu sui capituli vel collegii vel civitatis recedere [licet]."

trines that Ockham himself had borrowed from earlier writers and especially from earlier canonistic writers.

Like Ockham they appealed to the principles of equity and necessity in interpreting inconvenient laws; [100] but so had the thirteenth-century canonists. They accepted Ockham's doctrine that the welfare of the whole Church should be protected at all costs, even if necessary against the Pope himself; [101] but the Decretists had put forward a very similar doctrine, and it is interesting to note that in the work of Zabarella the phrase used to describe the general welfare of the Church which even a Pope had no authority to disturb was the canonists' *status ecclesiae* [102] rather than Ockham's *bonum commune*. Again, the Conciliarists based their whole system of thought on Ockham's demonstration of the fallibility of the Roman church and its consequent inferiority to the *congregatio fidelium*,[103] which had originated

[100] On the Conciliarists' use of the principle of *epikeia*, see N. Valois, *La France et le Grand Schisme d'Occident* (Paris, 1896), IV, 83–86, 229, 496–497; E. F. Jacob, " Conciliar Thought," *op. cit.*, 1–23, at 9–10; W. Ullmann, *The Origins of the Great Schism* (London, 1948), 178–182.

[101] Conrad of Gelnhausen, *Epistola Concordiae* in Martène and Durand, *Thesaurus Novus Anecdotorum*, II, col. 1222; Henry of Langenstein, *Consilium Pacis* in von der Hardt, *Concilium Constantiense*, II, cols. 3ff.; Gerson in *Opera*, ed. Du Pin (Antwerp, 1706), II, cols. 83ff., 92ff., 205; Zabarella, *De Schismate* in Schardius, *De iurisdictione . . . imperiali et potestate ecclesiastica* (Basel, 1566), 688–711 at 703, " . . . potestatis plenitudo est in papa ita tamen quod non errat, sed cum errat habet corrigere concilium "; Pierre d'Ailly, *De Jurisdictione Ecclesiastica* in von der Hardt, *op. cit.*, VI, 44, " [papa] non habet sibi collatam potestatem super bonis ipsis nisi ad necessitatem vel communem Ecclesiae utilitatem." Dietrich of Niem, *De modis uniendi et reformandi ecclesiam in concilio universali*, ed. Heimpel (Leipzig, 1933), 15–16, " Omnes ergo constitutiones Apostolicae intelliguntur . . . ubi respublica Ecclesiastica . . . detrimento aut divisioni non videtur subesse." See also the various opinions cited by B. Hübler, *Die Constanzer Reformation* (Leipzig, 1867), 369-371.

[102] Schardius, 694, 703, " . . . papa non potest immutare universalem statum ecclesiae . . . . "

[103] Dr. Ullmann points out that Conrad of Gelnhausen's *Epistola Concordiae* " marks a turning point in the history of the Schism," and that one of Conrad's main contributions was " a late fourteenth-century conception of the *ecclesia* and her relationship with the pope and the cardinals . . . . He distinguishes clearly between the Church Universal on the one hand, the pope and the cardinals on the other. It is one of his axioms that the former is superior to the latter." (*op. cit.*, 176). E. F. Jacob mentions the importance of the same idea in the work of Dietrich of Niem, with a reference to William of Ockham, " Dietrich's distinction . . . between the *congregatio fidelium* and the Roman species of it, is a development of views that owed their inception to William of Ockham." " Dietrich of Niem," *op. cit.*, 24–43 at 41. On the ultimate authority of the whole *congregatio fidelium*, see

with Huguccio and spread from his work to that of other Decretists; but they did not accept Ockham's highly personal opinion that the General Council provided no adequate representation of the *congregatio fidelium*.[104] On the contrary they adopted the traditional canonistic viewpoint that no distinction could be drawn between the acts of a General Council and those of the whole Church. They accepted Ockham's doctrine, which was also the doctrine of the canonists, that a heretical Pope could be deposed, but they maintained that a General Council was the proper authority to depose him precisely because the Council represented the whole Church.[105] Ockham claimed that any Catholic authority had jurisdiction in such a case, and based his assertion on quite different grounds, on a twelfth-century theory that was Decretist in origin, but which had found little favor among the canonists themselves. Here, again, the Conciliarists preferred to follow the more normal canonistic tradition.

If, therefore, we exclude Ockham's ultimate influence on Reformation thought and consider only his more immediate importance for the Conciliar theories of his own century, the somewhat paradoxical conclusion emerges that Ockham was most influential precisely when he was least original. At many of the points where his influence on Conciliar thought was most direct and penetrating he was restating, and sometimes verbally repeating, arguments which had first appeared in earlier canonistic glosses; and, when Ockham parted company with the canonists, the Conciliarists in their turn usually parted company with Ockham.

Catholic University of America.

---

also Henry of Langenstein in Gerson, *Opera*, II, cols. 822–826; Dietrich of Niem, *De Modis*, 9, 39; Zabarella in Schardius, 702, 703, 708, 709; Andreas Randulf in Gerson, *Opera*, II, cols. 161–165; Pierre d'Ailly in Gerson, *Opera*, II, cols. 949ff.

[104] The Conciliarists did not envisage any distinction between the powers that could be exercised by the whole Church and those of a General Council—indeed such a distinction would have destroyed the theoretical basis of the whole Conciliar programme. Cf. Conrad of Gelnhausen's definition of a General Council in *Epistola Concordiae*, col. 1217; Gerson in *Opera*, II, col. 205; Henry of Langenstein in Gerson, *Opera*, II, col. 824; and especially Zabarella in Schardius, 689, " . . . ipsam ecclesiam universalem quae repraesentatur per concilium generale . . ." and again " universalis ecclesia, i.e. concilium."

[105] The doctrine is nowhere more clearly stated than in the famous decree, *Sacrosancta* of the Council of Constance, " Concilium generale faciens et ecclesiam catholicam repraesentans, potestatem a Christo immediate habet, cui quilibet cuiuscunque status vel dignitatis, etiamsi papalis existat, obedire tenetur in his quae pertinent ad fidem."

XII

Hermeneutics and History:
The Problem of Haec Sancta

The decree, *Haec sancta*, enacted by the Council of Constance in 1415, declared that a general council could claim the obedience of all men "of whatsoever rank, state, or dignity, even if it be the papal." A few years ago a historian could discuss this proposition with much the same happy detachment that he might bring to a consideration of the decline of feudalism or the causes of the Hundred Years' War. Quite recently, however, a lively theological controversy has grown up concerning *Haec sancta* and the historian can hardly ignore the literature it has produced without retreating into a sort of professional provincialism even though he may at first feel that the theologians' problems are no concern of his.[1]

Nowadays a historian is likely to be interested in *Haec sancta* most of all as a document of major importance in the transition from medieval to modern constitutionalism. The theologians, on the other hand, are asking whether the decree embodies a permanent truth about the nature of the Christian church. The difference is fundamental and typical. A historian's purpose is primarily to understand the past for its own sake; a theologian's is to expound a structure of religious revelation that he considers valid for the present. But although these purposes are different they are not necessarily antithetical nor mutually exclusive. The documents of religious revelation themselves – whatever else they may be – are historical

---

1 The question of *Haec Sancta*'s validity was a matter of perennial theological debate from the fifteenth century to the nineteenth. After 1870 the discussion died away for a time. Protestants were not interested in the question and, for Catholics, it seemed settled by the pronouncements of Vatican Council 1 on papal sovereignty and infallibility. The issue is still not one of denominational controversy. The scholars whose views are discussed below all write from a Catholic standpoint.

documents. The possibility of fruitful dialogue between theologians and historians exists because they have common interests as well as divergent ones.

Both disciplines are concerned in different ways with the interplay between past and present. A historian can approach objectivity only by making himself understand how the circumstances of the present tend to influence his interpretations of the past. The theologian's objectivity consists in understanding how the circumstances of the past have shaped the doctrinal structure of the present which he expounds. This implies that, while a theologian will normally appeal to modern doctrine in judging the theological pronouncements of the past, he must also be prepared to acknowledge that existing doctrinal formulations may sometimes need reconsideration in the light of a deepening understanding of historical reality.

The hermeneutical considerations involved in a theological inter-pretation of *Haec sancta* have been set out with admirable clarity in a recent study by Helmut Riedlinger.[2] A valid decree of a general council, he points out, does not necessarily express a permanent, irreformable truth of Christian faith. It may refer to some changing point of church discipline. Moreover, even those decrees that are intended as solemn dogmatic definitions will always be expressed in language and buttressed by arguments that are conditioned by the cultural climate of a particular age. This means that, even when a conciliar decree contains a permanent truth, that truth may be faultily articulated or even expressed in language that is downright misleading for a modern reader. The theologian's task is to separate the grain from the chaff, to distinguish permanent truth from time-conditioned modes of expression and argumentation.

A historian may well object that this principle opens the way to the most fanciful exegesis of historical documents. The theologian seems to be saying that he can take them to mean anything he wants them to mean. But, precisely in order to avoid mere irresponsible subjectivism, Riedlinger insists that, if theology is not to "wither away in blind isolation," theological conclusions must be supported

2 Helmut Riedlinger, "Hermeneutische Ueberlegungen zu den Konstanzer Dekreten," *Das Konzil von Konstanz*, ed. A. Franzen and W. Müller (Freiburg/Basel/Wien, 1964), pp. 214–38. An equally lucid and excellent presentation of the historical problems that arise in the exegesis of *Haec sancta* has been provided by K. A. Fink, "Zur Beurteilung des grossen abendländischen Schismas," *Zeitschrift für Kirchengeschichte*, LXXIII (1962), 335–43.

356

by convincing historical analysis. "Theology ... cannot rest content," he writes, "until it has succeeded in making its position intelligible on historical grounds." Thus it is not enough for a Catholic theologian merely to assert that the decree *Haec sancta* is invalid because it conflicts with the decree *Pastor aeternus* of Vatican Council I. If he wants to carry conviction he has to wrestle with the realities of the fifteenth century (as well as with those of the nineteeth). He has to be at least open to the possibility that there may be a good historical case for the validity of *Haec sancta* and that *Pastor aeternus* may need some re-interpretation in the light of the earlier decree. Again, if a theologian wants to argue that some particular document is to be interpreted in a sense which it only obscurely expresses, he has to show how the meaning he discerns would naturally have come to be expressed in the actual words used by an analysis of the historical context in which his document took shape.

If historical credibility is to be a criterion of sound theology, then evidently the historian has a role to play – especially as critic – in the discussions of the theologians. I propose to criticize two recent, extremely opposed, interpretations of *Haec sancta* which both use historical argumentation to reach theological conclusions, and, in so doing, to present a different interpretation of my own.

Let us begin with the text of the decree:

This holy synod of Constance, constituting a general council and lawfully assembled to root out the present schism and bring about the reform of the church in head and members ... declares that ... representing the Catholic church militant, it holds power immediately from Christ and that anyone of whatsoever state or dignity, even if it be the papal, is bound to obey it in matters which pertain to the faith, the rooting out of the said schism and the general reform of the church in head and members. Further it declares that any person of whatsoever rank, state, or dignity, even if it be the papal, who contumaciously refuses to obey the mandates, statutes, ordinances, or instructions made or to be made by this holy synod or by any other general council lawfully assembled concerning the aforesaid matters or matters pertaining to them shall, unless he repents, be subjected to fitting penance and duly punished, recourse being had, if necessary to other sanctions of the law.[3]

3 J. D. Mansi, *Sacrorum conciliorum nova et amplissima collectio* (Venice, 1784), XXVII, p. 585, "Haec sancta synodus Constantiensis, generale concilium faciens, pro extirpatione praesentis schismatis et unione ac reformatione ecclesiae Dei in capite et membris ... legitime congregata ... declarat quod ...

Haec sancta was enacted in an atmosphere of crisis: John XXIII had fled from Constance and the assembled prelates feared that he might try to dissolve the council. It is by no means a simple and straightforward decree. As Bertie Wilkinson wrote of another important constitutional document of the middle ages, "there is no plain meaning of these particular words."

The text was drafted in haste, even in panic. Moreover, although it was sponsored by the more radical members of the assembly, it had to be formulated in language that would be acceptable to the council as a whole, and the council included prelates of various shades of opinion. Not surprisingly, therefore, the decree is full of ambiguities. Probably for this reason Cardinal Zabarella opposed it. He argued for a shorter draft which claimed supremacy only for the particular council assembled at Constance and only in matters "pertaining to the faith and the ending of the present schism."[4] There seems nothing in the actual substance of *Haec sancta* that was opposed to Zabarella's own views as expressed in his *Commentaria* on the decretals – and in the end he did indeed acquiesce in the promulgation of the decree – but he probably saw that the language in which it was formulated would give rise to difficulties of interpretation in the future.

These difficulties continue to the present day. The most extreme variations of opinion have been expressed in recent work on *Haec sancta*. Joseph Gill, for instance, has restated the traditional Catholic view that the decree was a radical and invalid attempt to subvert the divinely ordained constitution of the church. Hans Küng, on the other hand, has argued that *Haec sancta* was an irreformable decree of a licit general council and as such binding on the church forever.[5]

Professor Gill, the distinguished historian of the Council of

ecclesiam catholicam repraesantans, potestatem a Christo immediate habet, cui quilibet cujuscumque status vel dignitatis, etiamsi papalis existat, obedire tenetur in his quae pertinent ad fidem et extirpationem dicti schismatis et reformationem dictae ecclesiae in capite et in membris. Item declaret quod quicumque cujuscumque conditionis, status, dignitatis, etiam si papalis, qui mandatis, statutis seu ordinationibus aut praeceptis hujus sacrae synodi et seu cujuscumque alterius concilii generalis legitime congregati, super praemissis seu ad ea pertinentibus, factis vel faciendis, obedire contumaciter contempserit, nisi resipuerit, condignae paenitentiae subjiciatur et debite puniatur, etiam ad alia juris subsidia, si opus fuerit, recurrendo."

4 Mansi, *Sacrorum conciliorum*, p. 584.

5 Hans Küng, *Strukturen der Kirche* (Freiburg/Basel/Wien, 1962). Subsequent references are given to the English translation by S. Attanasio, *Structures of the Church* (New York, 1965).

Florence, presented his views in an article published in 1964.[6] He deplored the fact that, "The principle of the superiority of council over pope, forgotten and denied in the intervening centuries (since Constance) is being revived." The issue at stake, he noted, was a theological one; but he claimed that, even without appealing to the principles of dogmatic theology, it was possible to establish the invalidity of *Haec sancta* on purely historical grounds.

His argument runs like this. The Council of Constance represented the church to the same extent that the Council of Pisa had done. Moreover, it was summoned by a "pope" whose authority was derived from Pisa. Thus, by attendance and convocation the Council of Constance had the same authority as the Council of Pisa. But Pisa is not recognized as a general council. Therefore Constance was not one either, at least in its opening stages. It became a legitimate general council when the true pope, Gregory XII of the Roman line, convoked it as such on 4 July 1415. But the decree *Haec sancta* was enacted before this, on 6 April. Therefore *Haec sancta* was not a valid decree.

Most of Gill's article is devoted to proving that, besides having been illicitly enacted in the first place, *Haec sancta* never received the papal confirmation necessary for any valid decree of a general council. The facts here are not in dispute though, as usual, the interpretation of them is. Martin V, the pope elected at Constance, declared in an unpremeditated speech toward the end of the council that he would "inviolably observe ... everything enacted *conciliariter* in matters of faith by the present Council." More importantly, in the carefully considered bull *Inter cunctas*, he required suspects accused of the Hussite heresy to affirm "that what the sacred Council of Constance, representing the universal church, has approved and approves in favor of faith and salvation of souls must be accepted and be held by all the Christian faithful." But this same Pope Martin also forbade an appeal from the pope to a future general council. The next pope, Eugenius IV, declared on one occasion, "We accept, embrace and highly respect the Council of Constance," but his attempt to dissolve the Council of Basle before it had undertaken any significant work of reform indicates a lack of any real sympathy with

---

6 Joseph Gill, "The Fifth Session of the Council of Constance," *Heythrop J.,* v (1964), 131–43. See also Gill's *The Council of Florence* (Cambridge, 1959), *Eugenius IV* (London, 1961), *Constance et Bâle-Florence* (Paris, 1965).

conciliarist doctrines; and Eugenius bitterly opposed an attempt by the dissident fathers of Basle to define the principle of conciliar supremacy as a doctrine of faith. Much ingenious theological argumentation has been deployed in attempts to prove that the papal confirmations of the Constance decrees were deliberately so worded as to exclude *Haec sancta*.[7] Gill does not rely heavily on such arguments which are indeed highly unconvincing. He is content to emphasize that no pope ever confirmed *Haec sancta* in a bull that explicitly mentioned the decree by name.

All this amounts to a moderate and reasonable argument for a widely held point of view. But it is hard to agree with Gill when he insists that his argument is a purely historical one. On the contrary, it seems to rely at every point on theological premises that would be disputed by the scholars who reach a different conclusion concerning *Haec sancta*. For example, the question whether Pisa was a valid general council seems to be essentially a theological one. There is no coherent, irrefutable historical tradition that would settle the matter beyond doubt. Lists of general councils in Catholic sources have usually omitted Pisa but lists of popes have very commonly included Alexander v, the pope elected at Pisa; and the next pope who took the name Alexander called himself Alexander vi (though of course the next John was another John xxiii).

In general Gill seems to have tacitly assumed throughout his argument that the regulations of modern canon law which lay down requirements for a legitimate general council are expressions of universal truth, valid for all time; and he never seems to realize that this is a theological presupposition, not a historically demonstrable fact. (In fact, judged by these modern criteria, the canons of the Council of Nicea are more certainly invalid than those of the Council of Constance.) One might argue that the requirements of papal convocation and papal confirmation had been clearly formulated before the fifteenth century so that it is entirely proper and not anachronistic to condemn Pisa and Constance for failing to conform to these requirements. But this is not altogether true. The canonists of the twelfth century who formulated the medieval conception of a "papal

---

7 For a typical statement of these arguments see A. Baudrillart's article, "Constance (Concile de)" in *Dictionnaire de théologie catholique* and, for a recent criticism of them, Paul De Vooght, "Le conciliarisme à Constance et à Bâle," *Le Concile et les conciles* (Paris, 1960), pp. 143–81.

general council" had clearly recognized that in time of schism a legitimate council could be assembled without formal papal convocation and that, in certain grievous emergencies (as when a pope was suspected of heresy), a council without the pope could enact valid decrees.[8] One can make a very good case for the legitimacy of Pisa and Constance in terms of medieval canon law. Cardinal Zabarella did so, of course.

In determining whether a given assembly (like Constance) was a true general council it is legitimate to enquire whether it was accepted as such by the whole church, including the pope. But it is anachronistic to make the validity of the particular decree, *Haec sancta*, depend on explicit papal ratification. From the terms of the decree itself it is self-evident that if *Haec sancta* were valid at all it was valid from the moment of its enactment, "this holy synod ... holds power immediately from Christ." This was obvious to contemporaries. The idea that *Haec sancta* should be presented to the pope for his *ex post facto* approval never presented itself to Martin v or to the fathers of the council or to anyone else.[9] The assumption that papal ratification is a necessary condition for the validity of all conciliar decrees involves the assumption that *Haec sancta* was invalid (precisely because its terms exclude the necessity for such ratification); but the initial assumption is derived from theology and not from history.

8 See my *Foundations of the Conciliar Theory* (Cambridge, 1955), pp. 57–67, 76–7 and "Pope and Council: Some New Decretist Texts," *Mediaeval Studies*, xix (1957), 197–218.

9 This was pointed out long ago by B. Hübler, *Die Constanzer Reformation* (Leipzig, 1867), but the point was usually forgotten until Fink insisted on it again, "Zur Beurteilung," 339. Gill was justified in devoting so much attention to the question of papal approbation since he was replying directly to De Vooght who also treated the matter at length. De Vooght's own position is ambiguous. In the article cited above (n.7), he maintained that (1) it is doubtful whether the Council of Constance represented the universal church adequately in the opening sessions because it consisted of only one obedience (p. 150), but that (2) none the less Pope Martin and Pope Eugene lent the weight of their authority to *Haec sancta* (pp. 160, 171) although (3) these papal approbations were not infallible decrees (p. 180). In a subsequent article, "Le conciliarisme aux conciles de Constance et de Bâle (compliments et précisions)," *Irenikon*, xxxvi (1963), 61–75, De Vooght maintained that (1) the ecumenicity of the fifth session of Constance was recognized by the other two obediences (p. 61) and that (2) in a strict sense no papal ratification took place because contemporaries did not regard it as necessary (pp. 64–5). He also warmly approved Küng's view that (3) the definitions of Constance were "definitions sans appel, qui engageaient l'avenir de l'église" (p. 73).

Gill's view that the legitimate papacy remained always with the Roman line is important to his argument for, if this is accepted, one can maintain that Gregory XII's resignation made possible the ending of the schism without any need for conciliar action against a true pope. But once again, while the persistence of the papacy in the Roman line is an interesting theological theory, it is quite impossible to demonstrate its truth as a matter of historical fact. The one thing that a historian can affirm with reasonable assurance is that it was impossible in 1415 to know with certainty who was the true pope. The possibilities are endless. The election of Urban VI in 1378 may have been invalid because the cardinals acted under coercion. The election may have been valid in form but the candidate mad.[10] (He certainly acted like a madman.) In either case, however, it does not follow that the cardinals could legitimately proceed to a second election without any judicial process against the man whom they had solemnly crowned as Roman pontiff and who was recognized as pope by the whole of Christendom. It may well be that the elections of Urban VI and of Clement VII were both carried out illicitly. It may also be the case that the sentences of deposition pronounced at Pisa against the popes of the Roman and Avignonese lines were canonically valid. Again, the canonists and theologians of the middle ages commonly taught that a pope could divest himself of his office if he cut himself off from the church by persistence in heresy or schism. The argument that all the "popes" of 1415 had so degraded themselves by willfully prolonging the schism has to be taken seriously and it applies with special force to John XXIII after his flight from Constance. Perhaps there was no true pope at the time when *Haec sancta* was enacted. If there was one it was quite impossible for contemporaries – as it is for us – to know whether he was John or Gregory or Benedict.

The historical event which broke the deadlock of the Great Schism and made possible the restoration of a legitimate papacy was the enactment of *Haec sancta*. Moreover, the historian can reasonably

---

10 On the dubious nature of the election see M. Seidlmayer, *Die Anfänge des grossen abendländischen Schismas* (Münster, 1940), O. Přerovsky, *L'elezione di Urbano VI e l'insorgere dello scisma d'occidente* (Rome, 1960), and K. A. Fink, "Zur Beurteilung." Walter Ullmann, *Origins of the Great Schism* (London, 1949), argued in favour of the claims of Urban VI, but his analysis of the juridical literature of the fourteenth century shows how impossible it was for men of that time to resolve the issue without appealing to a general council.

assert that the schism could not have been ended in any other way than by the enactment of a decree asserting authority over the legitimate pope, whoever he might be. The question whether Gregory XII was pope in the eyes of God is not really relevant to the issue. The point is that, short of a miracle – which was not vouchsafed – he could never have been established as such in the eyes of man. For a judgment in favour of any one of the competing "popes" to have been accepted by the adherents of the other two was plainly out of the question. The ideal solution of a simultaneous resignation by the rival pontiffs had proved unattainable in twenty years of tortuous negotiations before Pisa when there were only two "popes" to deal with. It passed out of the realm of practical possibility after Pisa when there were three. The only possible way out of the impasse was for some qualified body to assert jurisdiction over all three claimants.

Theologians teach that the church is indefectible, that it will endure through all the ages, and for Catholic theologians this implies the continuity of a visible church in communion with the pope. To deny the validity of *Haec sancta* is to deny the validity of the only means by which, in a real historical situation, such continuity could be preserved. The greatest flaw in Gill's argument is that this fact does not seem to interest him in the least.

Hans Küng, in presenting the opposing argument in favour of *Haec sancta*, appeals like Gill to "the most recent research in church history." He naturally emphasizes the importance of the decree as a decisive step towards the ending of the schism and, following Fink, he correctly points out that Martin v never explicitly granted or withheld approbation of *Haec sancta* because his approval was never asked for. For Küng the universal acceptance of Constance's work of re-unification and the acceptance of its decrees in general terms by Martin v and Eugenius IV are sufficient to establish that those decrees "had the authority of the whole church and of the pope behind them" and that, accordingly, "to drop the definitions of the Council of Constance ... is not allowable to a Catholic."[11]

Küng's major contribution was to set *Haec sancta* in the context of a far-ranging theological discussion on the intrinsic nature of general councils. His argument in favour of the validity of the decree seems to me very persuasive. As De Vooght observed, Küng is the first Catholic theologian in modern times who has been prepared to con-

11 *Structures of the Church*, pp. 253, 257.

sider seriously all the historical circumstances surrounding the enactment of *Haec sancta,* and his views provide a valuable and refreshing corrective to many old-fashioned opinions. But Küng overlooked one possibility (later suggested by Riedlinger) – the possibility that *Haec sancta* might well be a licit enactment of positive constitutional law without being in the technical sense "irreformable." There have been many such canons in the history of the church – canons relating to episcopal and papal elections for instance. Such laws have profoundly changed the constitutional structure of the church. They are not without theological significance. They were intended by their framers to be permanently valid and some of them have been in force for centuries. But they are not technically "irreformable." If we regard *Haec sancta* as such a decree we can preserve the substance of Küng's argument while avoiding certain objections that have been made to it, above all the objection that, in order to reach his conclusions, Küng had to rely on a strained interpretation of the text of *Haec sancta.*

Arguments about which particular ecclesiastical enactments (if any) are infallible and so irreformable usually lead into swampy terrain. A historian can contentedly leave its exploration to the dogmatic theologians (provided that the dogmatists get their history right). But all theologians would agree that the quality of irreformability, if it exists at all, inheres only in dogmatic definitions on faith and morals. And the main difficulty in Küng's argument is that *Haec sancta* is not cast in the form of a solemn dogmatic definition.[12] It does not demand belief, like a dogmatic definition; it exacts obedience, like a decree of positive law. In its preamble, *Haec sancta* does not purport to define an article of faith. It does not appeal to scripture or tradition. It does not pronounce anathemas against unbelievers. We cannot be sure that it was intended as an immutable dogmatic decree, and in such cases it would surely be wise to adopt a variation of Ockham's razor and abide by the principle that "Infallibilities are not to be multiplied without necessity."

One can well understand why Küng did consider it a necessity to classify *Haec sancta* as irreformable. He discerned a principle of

12 On this point see A. Franzen, "Das Konzil der Einheit," in *Das Konzil von Konstanz,* pp. 69–112, here 103. Hubert Jedin, in his finely balanced study, *Bischöfliches Konzil oder Kirchenparlament* (Basel/Stuttgart, 1963), notes that, when the Council of Basle tried to define the principle of conciliar supremacy as an article of faith, it was raising a new issue and that contemporaries were well aware of the fact.

permanent value in the decree and wanted to reply in advance to the argument that it had been implicitly repealed by subsequent legislation which emphasized the doctrine of papal primacy in a one-sided fashion. But we can defend the view that *Haec sancta* has a permanent theological relevance without insisting – against the evidence of the text – that it was deliberately promulgated as an irreformable dogmatic decree. It is impossible, for instance, to accept *Haec sancta* as any kind of valid decree and also to accept the extreme doctrine of papal power that was fashionable in the Roman curia for half a century before the Great Schism and that, unfortunately, was revived soon after the Schism had ended. This doctrine is crystallized in a phrase of Augustinus Triumphus, "The pope who can be called the church. ..." As developed by Augustinus himself and by other theologians of the fourteenth century it maintained that Christ originally conferred on Peter alone a divine right to rule the church. Peter in turn conferred authority on the other apostles. Similarly, in later ages, no licit jurisdiction existed in the church except jurisdiction derived directly or indirectly from the pope.[13] The fathers of Constance, at the time of the enactment of *Haec sancta*, obviously did not act by virtue of a jurisdiction derived from the pope. Therefore, on the curialist theory they had no authority to act at all. To accept *Haec sancta* as licit is to reject the fourteenth-century curialist doctrine of the church.

An alternative theology of the church existed in the fourteenth century. It had been developed mainly by the canonistic commentators on Gratian's *Decretum* and by the theologians who defended the episcopalist position in the medieval conflicts between mendicants and seculars.[14] According to this second doctrine Christ conferred jurisdiction on all the apostles and not on Peter alone. Subsequent bishops, created by election and consecration, also received

13 M. J. Wilks describes these "high papalist" theories and provides a good guide to the modern literature on them in his *The Problem of Sovereignty in the Later Middle Ages* (Cambridge, 1963). Hervaeus Natalis explained that bishops did not hold a status in the church similar to that of feudal lords in a secular kingdom. Rather they stood to the pope like stewards and bailiffs to a king, *De iurisdictione*, ed. L. Hödl (Munich, 1959), pp. 28, 29, 34. Johannes de Torquemada went further and held that the pope stood in relation to the bishops as God did to his creatures, *Oratio Synodalis de Primatu* ed. E. Candal (Rome, 1954), p. 85.

14 See Y. Congar, "Aspects ecclésiologiques de la querelle entre mendiants et séculiers," *Archives d'histoire doctrinale et littéraire du moyen âge*, xxxvi (1961), 35–151.

their authority directly from Christ. Episcopal authority was normally exercised under the presidency of the pope but, if the papal headship temporarily failed, the episcopal office was still qualified by its intrinsic nature to represent both God and the Christian people. This second theory would evidently justify legislation by a council in time of emergency when the papacy was prevented from functioning. The first theory seems tenable only on the assumption that such an emergency never has arisen and never can arise.

To sum up then: If *Haec sancta* had not been enacted, the Great Schism could not have been ended; *Haec sancta* could not have been licitly enacted if the more extreme medieval theories of papal power were valid. These facts never ceased to be true. It became convenient for a later school of theologians to forget them.

There remains one final question to consider. What was the actual nature of the claim for the general council embodied in *Haec sancta*? Here again Gill and Küng are far apart. Gill, regarding the decree as in any case invalid, asserts that it proclaimed the doctrine of conciliarism in a most extreme and radical form.[15] Küng, committed to accepting not only the validity but also the irreformability of the decree, has to advance a decidedly minimalist interpretation of its content.[16] In his view, *Haec sancta* did not claim for the general council a regular role in the government of the church but only a "control authority" in time of emergency. That is to say, the fathers of Constance foresaw that a crisis like the Great Schism might arise again at some time in the future and they wished to make provision for such a contingency. But, as Küng's critics have pointed out,[17] this is not an easily defensible interpretation of the actual text of *Haec sancta*. The decree did not merely assert a right to "control" dubious claimants to the papacy in time of schism. It also claimed a permanent superiority for future councils in all matters "which pertain to the faith ... and the general reform of the church."

It is easy to understand how these provisions came to be written into *Haec sancta*. The claim to obedience in matters of faith had to be made, not only because of the possibility that a charge of heresy might be framed against John xxiii, but above all because of the

---

15 *Constance et Bâle-Florence*, p. 51, "C'était le conciliarisme sous sa forme la plus extrême."

16 *Structures of the Church*, p. 255, "Conciliar parliamentarism (along the lines of a radical conciliarism) was *not* defined."

17 E.g. H. Hürten, "Zur Ekklesiologie der Konzilien von Konstanz und Basel," *Theologische Revue*, LIX (1963), 362–71.

impending trial of John Hus. (*Haec sancta* was enacted at the fifth session of the council on 6 April; the commission to investigate Hus was set up at the sixth session on 17 April.) A claim for the authority of future general councils, and not merely for the particular synod assembled at Constance, had to be put forward – so the majority decided – because at the time when *Haec sancta* was drafted it seemed altogether possible that the Council of Constance would dissolve before the schism had been brought to an end.[18] And once it had been agreed that this general claim for future councils had to be included because of the very nature of the immediate crisis it was hardly possible to exclude some reference to the reform of the church. To have ignored the reform issue would have tacitly conceded in advance to the papacy a right which the fathers of Constance were determined to claim in some form for the council. In the two weeks of intrigue and emotional debate that preceded the enactment of *Haec sancta* it naturally proved impossible to frame a lucid and detailed statute on such a difficult point of church law. Perhaps if the fathers of the council had had ample time for cool deliberation they would have worded their decree differently. But it is with the actual text which they adopted that we have to deal.

In interpreting this text it seems possible once again to find a middle ground between the two extremely opposed views that we have mentioned. Küng observed that the framers of *Haec sancta* never meant to reduce the pope "to a subordinate executive organ of the conciliar Parliament." This is true enough. Even if *Haec sancta* had always been held in honour and *Frequens* fulfilled to the letter, the pope, controlling all the central machinery of church government, could hardly have become a mere executive agent of a council that met only once every ten years. Probably no one at Constance had any such intention. But it was entirely possible, without any such intention, to claim for the general council a regular role, in association with the pope, in the great task of reforming the church that lay ahead. This was one of the purposes of *Haec sancta*.

The all-important point to grasp in interpreting *Haec sancta* – a

18 *Haec sancta* did not make any reference to possible future schisms. It mentioned only "the present schism" and required future popes to obey future councils in all matters pertaining to "the rooting out of the said schism." No doubt the fathers of Constance would have upheld the right of a general council to settle any other schism that might arise, but the wording of the decree makes it plain that the immediate crisis was uppermost in their minds when they framed the clause relating to future councils.

point that has been overlooked in modern interpretations – is that the decree used the word "council" in an ambiguous fashion and that the ambiguity was probably deliberate. *Haec sancta* certainly did not state, and its framers probably never intended to state, that the members of a council, acting in opposition to a certainly legitimate pope, could licitly enforce their will on such a pope in any circumstances. As regards the immediate situation, the prelates at Constance claimed authority for themselves at a time when there were three "popes," all of doubtful legitimacy.[19] As regards the future, *Haec sancta* laid down that all popes were to be subject to the decrees of lawfully assembled general councils in certain defined spheres. But in normal circumstances, once the schism was ended, a lawfully assembled council would not consist of the members alone – bishops and other representatives – but of pope and members together. The decrees of future councils, which were to be binding on the pope, would, in normal times, be decrees of pope-and-council acting jointly, not decrees of the members acting against the head. There was nothing revolutionary in claiming supremacy for such an assembly. For two hundred years before *Haec sancta* every young canon-law student, plodding through his elementary course on the *Decretum* and its *Glossa ordinaria*, had been taught that, "Where matters of faith are concerned a council is greater than a pope."[20] All the major conciliar theorists who were present at Constance affirmed that, when a legitimate pope existed, supreme authority in the church inhered in a general council that included the pope – not simply in the pope alone and not simply in the members of a council separated from the pope. And they intended that this supreme authority of pope-and-council should carry through the programme of reform envisaged in *Frequens*. The claim of the members to over-ride a legitimate head was of course put forward at Basle, but it is a radically different claim from that of *Haec sancta*.[21]

19 Some members believed that they were claiming authority for the council at a time when no true pope existed. See H. Zimmerman, "Die Absetzung der Päpste auf dem Konstanzer Konzil; Theorie und Praxis," in *Das Konzil von Konstanz*, pp. 113–37, here 120–2. This position was provided for in the rather roundabout wording of *Haec sancta* with its reference to any rank, state, or dignity, "even if it be the papal."

20 *Glossa ordinaria ad Dist.*, 19, c.19, "Videtur ergo quod papa tenetur requirere concilium episcoporum, quod verum est ubi de fide agitur, et tunc synodus maior est papa. ..."

21 The distinction we are emphasizing was brought out with great clarity by Pierre d'Ailly, *Tractatus de materia*, ed. F. Oakley: *The Political Thought of*

The distinction that we have drawn between the term "council," understood as pope-and-members together, and "council," as the members alone separated from the pope, is not an over-ingenious refinement of modern scholarship. On the contrary this distinction had been employed in debates about conciliar supremacy ever since the twelfth century. Among the canonists there was a universally held opinion that a general council, understood in the first sense of the term, possessed supreme authority in matters concerning the faith and the universal state of the church. But the canonists differed sharply among themselves concerning the authority of a council understood in the second sense of the term. At the end of the twelfth century, for instance, the French author of the *Summa, Et est sciendum* suggested that, if the members of a council disagreed with a pope, the decision of the members should be accepted. Huguccio, on the other hand, taught that, even if all the bishops of the church stood in oppostion to the pope, the judgment of the pope should prevail. Alanus held that the opinion of the members of a council in opposition to the pope was to be accepted in matters of faith but not in any other matter. Johannes Teutonicus, in his *Glossa ordinaria*, presented the various opinions and favoured the ultimate authority of the pope. A century later John of Paris hedged on the issue. There existed in the church, he wrote, an authority "equal to or greater than" the pope's. At the time of the Great Schism itself Zabarella held that the judgment of the members should prevail against that of the pope in matters of faith and he was inclined to extend their authority also to matters touching the general state of the church.[22]

This is not the place for a history of the whole problem. The point is that the leaders of the Council of Constance, men who had devoted years of study and debate to these questions, could not have been unaware of its existence. By simply decreeing that, in certain circum-

Pierre d'Ailly (New Haven, 1964), p. 304, "Secunda ad praedictam objectionem dicitur quod minor rationis non est vera, scilicet quod Papa est major et superior concilio, *licet sit major et superior in concilio cum sit caput omnium membrorum*. Et ad hanc probandum videtur esse ratio evidens, quia omne totum sua parte majus est. Sed Papa est pars concilii, sicut caput pars corporis. Ergo totum concilium majus est Papa, et per consequens auctoritas totius concilii major auctoritate Papae." The argument presents both a vindication of *Haec sancta* and a denial in advance of the claims of Basle.

22 On these various opinions see Tierney, *Foundations of the Conciliar Theory*, pp. 55, 67, 171, 232, 250–4 and "Pope and Council." All the authors used the word *concilium* sometimes to mean pope-and-members together and sometimes (especially in discussions on the trial of a heretical pope) to mean the members alone.

stances, popes were to be bound by the decisions of general councils without defining exactly what was meant by the term "council" they were deliberately leaving the issue unresolved.[23] Perhaps some of the prelates at Constance believed in the doctrine later asserted at Basle. But they did not define it. Moreover it is most improbable that a majority could have been found at Constance for any such definition. Two years after *Haec sancta* it was proposed that a decree be prepared affirming the right of the members of a council to depose a pope for crimes other than heresy, but the suggestion attracted only minority support and the decree was never enacted.

A historian might sum up the position of the fathers of Constance by suggesting that they had reached the same stage of constitutional thought as the leaders of the English parliament in 1641, at the point where they were vigorously asserting the sovereignty of king-in-parliament but had not yet advanced a claim for the supremacy of the members of parliament separated from the king. A Catholic theologian, accepting the criteria of Riedlinger set out above, might well maintain that *Haec sancta* was an attempt – a premature, imperfect attempt, perhaps – to formulate a constitutional law for the church that would be in keeping with the ancient and never-forgotten doctrine of "collegiality," the doctrine that eventually found a formal definition at Vatican Council II. He could explain the "imperfection" of the formula which was actually adopted by pointing out that, for reasons which are historically intelligible, *Haec sancta* had to combine in one long tangled sentence both an assertion of the council's authority at moments of crisis and a proposal for future co-operation between pope and council in more normal times.

These considerations can help us to understand the aftermath of the Council of Constance. For a generation after the enactment of *Haec sancta* everyone, including the popes, understood very clearly that an overt attack on the decree would re-open all the wounds of the Great Schism. For practical purposes the decree *had* to be valid. But Pope Martin, and still more Pope Eugenius, lacked any sympathetic understanding of the theology of the church underlying *Haec sancta*, and they were obdurately opposed to the line of moderate

23 Most of Hürten's criticism of Küng and De Vooght is invalidated by his failure to grasp this point. Hürten argues in various ways that the lack of universal approval for the principle of conciliar supremacy enunciated at Basle proves that there was never a consensus in favour of *Haec sancta*. But it was entirely possible to reject Basle and accept Constance.

constitutional development suggested by that theology. The inconsistencies in their attitudes led to a new period of tension and frustration. The conciliarists were driven to assert the extreme claims of Basle. Their opponents came to favour, in opposition to those claims, a variety of extreme but highly unstable papalism which was not supported by a consensus of Catholic opinion, which was dependent for its continued existence on the goodwill of secular monarchs, and which was singularly ill-adapted to carry through the necessary reform of the church. The explosion that came in the next century was as inevitable as anything in history can be.

XIII

"Divided Sovereignty" at Constance: A Problem of Medieval and Early Modern Political Theory

Recent work on the Council of Constance has dealt with two major themes — the relevance of medieval conciliarism for modern ecclesiology, and the significance of conciliar thought for the developing tradition of Western political theory. In the following discussion we shall be concerned with the second problem.

Figgis long ago argued that fifteenth century conciliar ideas provided a model for later theories of secular constitutionalism. The conciliarists, he wrote, had "discerned more clearly than their predecessors the meaning of the constitutional experiments, which the last two centuries had seen in considerable profusion, to have thought out the principles that underlay them, and based them upon reasoning that applied to all political societies." Hence, in their works, "The theory of a mixed or limited monarchy was set forth in a way which enabled it to become classical"[1]. In a series of recent articles Francis Oakley has traced out various strands of argument connecting fifteenth century conciliar ideas with the secular constitutional theories of the sixteenth and seventeenth centuries. He concluded that Figgis was basically right in his views about the influence of conciliar thought on early modern political theory. Oakley also noted, however, that Figgis was basically wrong in his account of the origins of conciliar ideas[2]. For Figgis there was a radical discontinuity between medieval and modern constitutional concepts. "When all is said and done . . . there remains a great gulf fixed between medieval and modern thought." Figgis thought that

---

[1] J. N. FIGGIS, Studies of Political Thought from Gerson to Grotius, 1414—1625, 2nd ed., Cambridge 1923, 35—36, 48.

[2] F. OAKLEY, On the Road from Constance to 1688, in: Journal of British Studies 1 (1962) 1—31; From Constance to 1688 Revisited, in: Journal of the History of Ideas 27 (1966) 429—432; Jacobean Political Theology, in: JHI 29 (1968) 323—346; Almain and Major: Conciliar Theory on the Eve of the Reformation, in: American Historical Review 70 (1965) 675—690; Figgis, Constance, and the Divines of Paris, in: AHR 75 (1969) 368—386. The last article discusses the handling of Figgis' thesis in modern works on medieval and modern political theory.

"Divided Sovereignty" at Constance

the theories of the conciliarists were derived from reflections on contemporary experimentation in secular government. They marked a sharp break with the preceding ecclesiastical tradition by "striving to turn into a tepid constitutionalism the Divine authority of a thousand years". They were above all a reaction against "the Canonist theory of sovereignty (substantially the same as Austin's)"[3].

It now seems clear that the truth is just the opposite. The central doctrines of the conciliarists had already been formulated in the canonistic writings of the twelfth and thirteenth centuries[4]. The problem of reconciling a theory of effective sovereignty with a defense of the rights of the community is a perennial one in Western political experience; it arises in twelfth century law, in fifteenth century ecclesiology, and in seventeenth century political theory. Moreover, many of the leading conciliarists were well acquainted with the views of the canonists and used them in developing their own positions. Since the arguments of the conciliarists were in turn repeated by the constitutional theorists of the sixteenth and seventeenth centuries, interesting problems of historical periodization arise concerning continuities and discontinuities in the whole period from the twelfth century to the seventeenth. We shall return to this general problem after considering, by way of illustration, one particular constitutional issue that was debated at Constance and that has not been widely discussed in the modern literature, the problem of "divided sovereignty". The central question involved can be stated simply. Is it theoretically possible — or logically impossible — for sovereignty to be divided between a ruler and his subjects or between a monarch and an assembly of estates? This problem became of central importance in early modern political theory because of the great emphasis given to it by Jean Bodin and his critics. Bodin argued that all theories of divided sovereignty, all systems in which sovereign authority was conceived of as being shared between a ruler and his people or a ruler and an assembly of estates, were intrinsically self-contradictory. If a sovereign prince shared his sovereignty with another, he wrote, "the latter could use it against his prince, who would become a mere cipher, and the subject would command his lord, the servant his master, which is manifestly absurd...". Bodin was particularly concerned to emphasize that the form of government in France was a pure monarchy and not a "mixed constitution" in which power was shared between king and estates. "This is an opinion not only absurd but treasonable", he wrote, "for it is treason to make subjects the colleagues of a sovereign prince". And again, "This is an impossible thing, impossible even to imagine"[5]. Bodin's underlying thought seems to have been that divided sovereignty was equivalent to mere anarchy. If, *per impossibile*,

---

[3] FIGGIS, 12, 31, 50.

[4] This argument was developed in my Foundations of the Conciliar Theory, Cambridge 1955. It seems to have found general acceptance in the recent literature on medieval conciliarism.

[5] J. BODIN, Les six livres de la Republique, Paris 1583, 123, 263, 254.

one were to imagine a sovereign power divided between prince and subjects the two powers would, in effect, cancel each other out. "If sovereignty is indivisible as we have shown, how could it be shared by a prince, lords, and people at the same time? The first mark of sovereignty is to give the law to subjects, but who will be the subjects who obey if they themselves also have the power to make law? And who will be the one who can give law if he himself is compelled to take it from those to whom he gives it"[6]. From the argument that sovereignty was inherently indivisible it followed for Bodin that there could be no juridical right of resistance to a sovereign prince, however grievous his offenses might be. "As regards legal procedure (against the Prince), the subject has no jurisdiction over his prince, for all power and authority to command derive from him . . ."

Bodin's assertion that sovereignty was, of its intrinsic nature, indivisible and illimitable has always been regarded as one of his major contributions to modern political theory and often, indeed, as marking the dividing line between medieval and modern thought. A recent detailed discussion of his arguments, by Julian Franklin, suggests that there were fallacies in them which were soon perceived by Bodin's critics but which were concealed from Bodin himself by the circumstances of the times in which he wrote[7]. For example, Christopher Besold pointed out that sovereignty could inhere in a king and a group of inferiors associated with him provided that the whole assembly was conceived of as a single corporate body within which the king presided as head[8]. As for a right of resistance to a sovereign ruler, Franklin suggested that the problem here was more subtle and that it was first adequately analysed by Pufendorf. According to Pufendorf a true monarch, who was subject to no earthly jurisdiction, might forfeit his office if he violated the rules according to which he held it. "Nor do we by this means subject the Prince to the judgement of the people . . . Such an act of the people, whereby they take notice of the Prince's miscarriage and forfeiture, doth not

---

[6] op. cit., 255. Bodin concluded that a regime in which a king was said to share power with his subject would be a democracy "l'etat sera tousjours populaire". In the Latin version he significantly changed the sentence to say that a mixed constitution would be equivalent to anarchy.

[7] J. FRANKLIN, Jean Bodin and the Rise of Absolutist Theory, Cambridge 1973, 26—29. A useful collection of modern views on Bodin's theory of sovereignty can be found in Proceedings of the International Conference on Bodin in Munich, ed. H. Denzer (Munich, 1970). A extensive bibliography is provided at pp. 501—513.

[8] C. BESOLD, Operis politici, editio nova, Strasbourg 1641, 176. "Numquam (inquit ille) fieri per naturam et ne quidem imaginatione perfici potest ut summa potestas sive majestas cum inferiori commisceatur, ut tamen maneat summa. Respondeo, summa manet, sed non in uno, verum in corpore seu collegio archonton universo: ita tamen ut non sit aequaliter inter eos distributa, sed Principi quaedam eminentia magna concedatur . . . alias enim fieret Aristocratia . . . licet in illo collegio caput plerumque modis prae reliquis membris excellet, non tamen in solidum omni iure Imperii fruatur. Et ita majestas haec, quam tale collegium habet, Deo immediate subest.

"Divided Sovereignty" at Constance

carry in it the semblance of a judicial proceeding for the taking cognizance of a subject's offense, but is no more than a bare declaration ..."

The sixteenth and seventeenth century views on sovereignty that we have mentioned will not seem unfamiliar to students of medieval church history and church law. The arguments for unitary sovereignty were very fully developed by the canon lawyers of the twelfth and thirteenth centuries in their discussions on papal *plenitudo potestatis*. And the same is true of the various "constitutionalist" positions. Julian Franklin, referring to the argument of Pufendorf quoted above, observed that "The logic of limited supremacy required considerable ingenuity. It was not developed until late in the seventeenth century, and even then it seemed extremely odd"[9]. Franklin found it easily understandable that Bodin, "writing in a less sophisticated era" could not conceive of any such theory. But in fact, from the twelfth century onward, the idea that Franklin calls "limited supremacy" was commonly applied to the problem of dealing with a heretical or criminal pope. According to one widely held opinion, formulated in intricate detail by Huguccio at the end of the twelfth century, a pope was subject to no human judgement, since he himself was the supreme judge; but if a pope became a heretic or a notorious criminal he ipso facto ceased to be pope and could be replaced without any formal judicial proceedings or sentence of condemnation rendered by his inferiors[10]. Huguccio's views were transmitted to the canonists of the late Middle Ages by Guido de Baysio and to political theorists by William of Ockham. They were well known at the time of the conciliar movement[11].

It is the same with Christopher Besold's argument about collegiate sovereignty. The idea that supreme authority in the church normally resided in a collegiate association of pope and cardinals was formulated by Laurentius in the *glossa palatina* at the beginning of the thirteenth century, was repeated by major canonists like Hostiensis and Johannes Monachus, and was restated at Constance by conciliarists like d'Ailly and Zabarella, along with the common view that, in time of general council, supreme authority resided in a corporative association of pope, cardinals, and council fathers. In the following discussion we shall consider the debates at the Council of Constance concerning the meaning of the decree *Haec sancta*, the most important constitutional enactment of the council, with the

---

[9] FRANKLIN, 50—53, referring to Pufendorf, Of the Law of Nature and Nations, vii. 6.10. The quotation above is from the translation of Basil Kennet, London 1717, 698.

[10] Huguccio's text is printed in Foundations of the Conciliar Theory, 248—250. Pufendorf observed that the evidence whether a prince had in fact forfeited his office "usually consists of such matters as are clear and obvious to sense, and therefore not easily liable to doubt or dispute". Huguccio insisted that a pope could be replaced only when the evidence of his transgression was so clear and evident that no formal judicial process was necessary to establish his guilt.

[11] Ockham, the Conciliar Theory, and the Canonists, in: Journal of the History of Ideas, 15 (1954) 40—70.

purpose of showing how those debates led on to a detailed analysis of the precise issue raised by Bodin, the problem of whether sovereignty is, by its inherent nature, divisible or indivisible.

Modern scholars disagree about the meaning of *Haec sancta*. The most important phrases of the decree defined the doctrine of conciliar supremacy in these terms:

> This holy synod of Constance . . . declares that . . . representing the church militant, it holds its power directly from Christ and that anyone of whatsoever state of dignity, even if it be the papal, is bound to obey it in matters which pertain to the faith, the rooting out of the schism, and the general reform of the church in head and members. Further it declares that any person of whatsoever rank, state or dignity who contumaciously refuses to obey the mandates . . . made by this holy synod or by other general council lawfully assembled concerning the aforesaid matters or matters pertaining to them shall, unless he repents, be subjected to fitting penance and duly punished[12].

According to Joseph Gill "This was conciliarism in its most extreme form". According to Hans Küng, "Conciliar parliamentarism (along the lines of a radical conciliarism) was *not* defined"[13]. My own view is that the words were ambiguous and that they were known to be ambiguous when the decree was enacted. In early April, 1415 there was a desperate need for the Council of Constance to enact a measure affirming its own authority. John XXIII had fled from the council and it was feared that he would try to dissolve it. But it seemed that the dissolution of the council would destroy the last hope of

---

[12] COD 385.

[13] The debates on the meaning of *Haec sancta* have been stimulated mainly by modern problems of ecclesiology. The most important contributions are HANS KÜNG, Strukturen der Kirche, Freiburg - Basel - Wien 1962; J. GILL, The Fifth Session of the Council of Constance, in: Heythrop Journal 5 (1964) 131—143 and Constance et Bale-Florence, Paris 1965; H. HÜRTEN, Zur Ekklesiologie der Konzilien von Konstanz und Basel, in: Theologische Revue 59 (1963) 361—372; H. JEDIN, Bischöfliches Konzil oder Kirchenparlament, Basel 1963; the articles, especially those of H. ZIMMERMANN, H. RIEDLINGER and W. MÜLLER, in: Das Konzil von Konstanz: Beiträge zu seiner Geschichte und Theologie, ed. A. FRANZEN and W. MÜLLER, Freiburg 1964; A. FRANZEN, The Council of Constance: Present State of the Problem, in: Conc(USA) 7 (1965) 29—68; P. DE VOOGHT, Les pouvoirs du concile et l'autorité du pape, Paris 1965; W. BRANDMÜLLER, Besitzt das Konstanzer Dekret "Haec sancta" dogmatische Verbindlichkeit?,in: RQ 62 (1967) 1—17; I. H. PICHLER, Die Verbindlichkeit der Konstanzer Dekrete, Vienna 1967. This literature is summarized and discussed in F. OAKLEY, Council over Pope? Towards a Provisional Ecclesiology, New York 1969, and P. DE VOOGHT, Les controverses sur les pouvoirs du concile et l'autorité du pape au Concile de Constance, in: Revue théologique de Louvain 1 (1970) 45—75.

reuniting the church after forty years of schism. There was widespread agreement at Constance that, in a time of desperate emergency, when there were three contenders for the papacy and no certainly legitimate pope, supreme authority in the church rested with the fathers of the council. But there was sharp disagreement at Constance, which was expressed in the debates preceding the enactment of *Haec sancta*, about the relationship of a pope to a general council in more normal times. This division of opinion reflected a disagreement in the preceding canonical tradition of the church. A universally accepted canonistic teaching (formulated in the Ordinary Gloss of Johannes Teutonicus to Gratian's Decretum) affirmed that "In matters of faith a council is greater than a pope". Also the canonists often taught that popes were bound by statutes of general councils which pertained to "the general state of the church". (This could be taken as justifying *Haec sancta*'s language about "the general reform of the church".) But canonistic tradition also maintained clearly that in normal circumstances a general council consisted of a pope and fathers acting together. The canonists had clearly taught that the decrees of such councils were binding on future popes in matters touching the faith and the general state of the church. But the canonists had also discussed a separate problem, the situation which would arise within a council if a pope disagreed with the council fathers. As one of them posed the question, *Sed numquid potius stabitur sententiae Apostolicae vel omnium episcoporum?* On this point no agreement had been reached. Some opinions favored the pope, some the fathers of a council. Both opinions could be read in different contexts of the Ordinary Gloss to the Decretum. The prelates at Constance were aware of these differences. It seems to me that, when they obliged future popes to obey the decrees of future councils without explaining whether the word *concilium* referred, in its normal sense, to pope-and-fathers acting together or to the fathers alone acting against the pope they were deliberately leaving the whole question open for further discussion when the immediate crisis had passed[14].

Francis Oakley has suggested that this point of view is "far from convincing" and, in any case, unproven[15]. To me it seems that a convincing proof of the

---

[14] See my Hermeneutics and History. The Problem of Haec Sancta, in: Essays in Medieval History for Presentation to Bertie Wilkinson, ed. T. A. SANDQUIST and M. R. POWICKE, Toronto 1969. For references to disagreements among the canonists see Pope and Council: Some New Decretist Texts, in: Mediaeval Studies 19 (1957) 197—218. The divergent opinions presented in the *glossa ordinaria* to the Decretum were discussed by Pierre d'Ailly at Constance in 1416 (below n. 25).

[15] F. OAKLEY, The 'New Conciliarism' and Its Implications: A Problem in History and Hermeneutics, in: JES 8 (1971) 815—840 at 831—833. Oakley was concerned to argue that *Haec sancta* has as much claim to be considered an infallible dogmatic pronouncement as the decree *Pastor aeternus*, enacted at Vatican Council I. Since the two decrees obviously contradict one another, he argues, the whole principle of infallibility is called into question. I have no

deliberate ambiguity of *Haec sancta* can be found in the content of the debates at Constance after the enactment of the decree. In those debates the most widely divergent opinions were expressed concerning the relationship between a legitimate pope and a future general council by men who had been present at the enactment of *Haec sancta* and who all accepted the validity of the decree. But the fact that quite extreme papalist views were advocated at Constance after the enactment of *Haec sancta* has been noted before[16]. It would hardly be worth pursuing the matter in further detail except that the arguments advanced are intrinsically interesting, and most especially interesting in connection with our problem concerning the theoretical divisibility or indivisibility of sovereignty.

None of the moderate conciliarists at Constance denied that, in some sense, sovereignty *(plenitudo potestatis)* resided in the pope. (All the leaders of the Council of Constance were papalists just as all the leaders of the English parliament in 1641 were royalists. The whole point and purpose of the council was to elect a new pope who could unify the church.) But the conciliarists also insisted that sovereignty inhered in some other sense in the universal church and in a general council representing it. Thus, the whole conciliar theory as it was developed by its principal exponents was based on an acceptance of the idea of "divided sovereignty". It seemed clear that, when there was no true pope, the whole power of the church could be exercised by the fathers of a council. It was not so clear where the balance of power would lie once a new pope was elected. Stephan of Prague tried to explain how the same power could reside, sometimes in a pope, sometimes in the fathers of a council by an analogy with a measure of wine. "Just as wine, divided into two vessels remains whole materially, because quantitatively all of its parts persist... though it does not remain whole formally, so it is to be imagined concerning that power (i. e. the papal *plenitudo potestatis*), when the see is vacant"[17]. Gerson wrote that ecclesiastical power was given "to Peter as monarch and to his legitimate successors, but more

---

quarrel with Oakley's general conclusion, but would suggest a different approach to *Haec sancta*. If the fathers of a general council reached a consensus concerning a point of doctrine, if they were truly "of one heart and one mind", then it would seem reasonable for scholars centuries later to inquire (in exquisite detail if necessary), what precisely the fathers had intended to define. But if no consensus existed at the council, if a verbal formula open to many different interpretations was promulgated precisely because there was no unanimity of heart and mind, then it seems futile for scholars to inquire what was the "real" meaning of the formula promulgated or to the claim for the "real" meaning a permanent normative value. Such verbal statements have no "real" meaning. This argument seems to me to apply to *Haec sancta*. It is conceivable that it also applies to *Pastor aeternus*.

[16] DE VOOGHT, Les pouvoirs, 58—67.

[17] J. D. MANSI, Sacrorum conciliorum nova et amplissima collectio, 28, Venice 1785, col. 587.

principally to the church"[18]. Cardinal Zabarella, writing before Constance, declared, "The pope has plenitude of power not alone but as the head of a corporate body so that the power is fundamentally in the corporation and in the pope as the principal minister through which this power is made explicit, provided that he rules discreetly"[19]. Maurice of Prague, addressing the Council of Constance in 1416, suggested that plenitude of power resided in the Roman pontiff "separably", in the universal church "inseparably", and in the general council "representatively".

These words were quoted by Pierre d'Ailly in his *Tractatus de potestate ecclesiastica* which, in October 1416, opened a major debate at Constance about the relationship between pope and council[20]. One point at issue was whether the decrees of the council (once a true pope was elected) should be promulgated by the pope with the formula *Nos, sacro approbante concilio statuimus . . .* or by the council as a whole with the formula *Sacrosanctum concilium statuit . . .*[21]. The two different formulas implied two different theories of conciliar authority. According to the first formula, conciliar statutes derived their authority from the pope who promulgated them, with the members of the council acting essentially as advisers who acquiesced in the promulgation. According to the second formula the council (acting as a collegiate body conjoined with the pope) itself possessed an intrinsic power to legislate. As is so often the case, this fifteenth century dispute had its roots in thirteenth century canon law, specifically in the law of corporations. Innocent IV had held that, in an ecclesiastical corporation, all jurisdiction resided in the head. Hostiensis maintained the contrary opinion, that jurisdiction inhered in the corporate body as a whole. Their views had been noted by Cardinal Zabarella in his discussion of the authority of general councils[22]. In discussing this question, Pierre d'Ailly provided a very explicit definition of the theory of collegiate or corporate sovereignty which Christopher Besold would later formulate for the secular sphere in his criticism of Bodin's position. Besold argued that in a mixed monarchy, although ultimate sovereignty could reside in a collegiate body, the monarch had to possess a certain preeminence within that body — otherwise the regime would be a simple aristocracy. D'Ailly, arguing that a general council possessed an authority greater than

---

[18] De potestate ecclesiastica, ed. P. GLORIEUX in Oeuvres completes, 6, Paris 1965, 217, *. . . Petro tamquam monarchae legitimisque successoribus suis, principalius tamen ecclesiae*. At this point Gerson was commenting directly on *Haec sancta*.

[19] Tractatus de Schismate in Schardius, De iurisdictione . . . imperiali ac potestate ecclesiastica, Basel 1566, 703.

[20] Joannis Gersonii Opera Omnia, ed. E. DUPIN, II, Antwerp 1706, col. 950.

[21] The problem had come up earlier at the council before the deposition of John XXIII. In his work of 1416 d'Ailly repeated the view he had expressed in the previous debate.

[22] See Foundations of the Conciliar Theory, 106—131, 229—230.

that of the pope acting alone, likewise emphasized the headship of the pope within the council.

> It is not true that the pope is greater and higher than a general council although *he is greater and higher within the council,* since he is the head of all the members ... Every whole is greater than its part ... The pope is a part of the council as the head is a part of the body ... therefore the authority of the whole council is greater than the authority of the pope[23].

Elsewhere he wrote that, according to some persons, it was "not only false but fatuous" to assert that a part (the pope) was greater than the whole (a general council)[24]. D'Ailly concluded that the general council as a whole — and not the pope alone — held the authority to "judge and define".

But this argument did not in itself settle the question of which party was to be obeyed if the pope and the members of a council disagreed. D'Ailly noted that the problem had been raised in the Ordinary Gloss to Gratian's Decretum but not definitively solved there. His own solution was based on the argument that a pope's plenitude of power was granted to him for the "edification" of the church, not for its "destruction". If a pope used his power for the "destruction" of the church then he forfeited his claim to obedience and could be judged by a council. In developing this argument d'Ailly had to contend with a well-known text of the Decretum stating that the supreme judge could be judged by no one, not even by all the clergy. D'Ailly explained that the phrase *ab omni clero* was to be taken "distributively" not "collectively". The pope was superior to any individual cleric or particular college of clerics but not to "all the clergy" as a whole[25]. This principle, subsequently expressed in the "lapidary phrase", *Princeps maior singulis minor universis,* was widely used in later political theory[26]. It was first stated in its medieval form by the civilian glossators of Justinian's Code at the beginning of the thirteenth century and passed from the civilian glosses into ecclesiastical thought. Although d'Ailly thought that the principle clearly justified the deposition of a pope who used his power for the destruction of the

---

[23] DUPIN II col. 957, "... *Non est vera, scilicet quod papa est major et superior concilio generali, licet sit major et superior in concilio, cum sit caput omnium membrorum ... quia omne totum sua parte majus est ... Sed papa est pars concilii sicut caput pars corporis: ergo totum concilium majus est papa, et per consequens authoritas totius concilii major authoritate papae.*"

[24] DUPIN II col. 953.

[25] DUPIN II col. 956. For another statement at Constance that the pope was greater than each individual "particularly" but not to the whole church "legitimately assembled" see H. FINKE, Forschungen und Quellen zur Geschichte des Konstanzer Konzils, Paderborn 1889, 293.

[26] E. H. KANTOROWICZ, The King's Two Bodies, Princeton, 1957, 231. On the use of this principle in late medieval and early modern political theory see O. GIERKE, Das Deutsche Genossenschaftsrecht, Berlin 1816—1913, III, 577 n. 165, IV, 299 n. 68. Neither Gierke nor Kantorowicz explored the earlier medieval origins of the principle.

church he still left rather vague the relationship between a true, unerring pope and the other members of a general council.

D'Ailly's views were representative of a broad range of moderate conciliar opinion, both in their affirmations and in their ambiguities. Gerson presented essentially similar arguments in his *De potestate ecclesiastica*, read at Constance in February 1417. But, for us, two more extreme views presented during the debates of late 1416 — one papalist, one conciliarist — are of greater interest, since it was the confrontation of these extreme views that led to the overt argument concerning indivisibility of sovereignty. There is one marked difference between these discussions and the debates of Bodin's time. Bodin wanted to argue that sovereignty inhered in the king of France, and that it was logically impossible for the king's sovereignty to be shared with an assembly of estates. After *Haec sancta* it was impossible for any speaker at Constance to deny that ecclesiastical power resided in some sense in the general council. Accordingly it was the partisan of papal monarchy who argued for a theory of divided sovereignty, seeking to define the mode of division in such a fashion that all effective power of action would rest in the hands of the pope. And it was the partisan of conciliar supremacy who argued that the concept of divided sovereignty was inherently self-contradictory, that there could be only one seat of ultimate sovereignty in the church, and that therefore sovereignty must be vested unambiguously in the fathers of a general council[27].

The papalist point of view was put forward by the master-general of the Dominicans, Leonard Statius de Datis, and was opposed by a spokesman for conciliar supremacy whose name has not come down to us[28]. Statius summarized his views in four propositions about "the supreme power of the spiritual sword". (1) This supreme power resided in the church inseparably as regards jurisdiction and separably as regards exercise. (2) It resided in the pope separably as regards both jurisdiction and exercise. (3) The exercise of "supreme power" resided wholly in a pope "legitimately presiding and residing" and in no way in a general council. (4) Accordingly the pope alone and not the general council had to define what was to be approved or disapproved in the church[29]. The first two propositions would have been acceptable to any moderate conciliarist; the last two were highly controversial. After the first attacks on his position, Statius carefully explained that he was in no way challenging the executive power of the

---

[27] AZO, Ad. singulas leges... Codicis Iustinianei commentaria, Paris 1599, ad 8.53.2 p. 671, *Unde non est maioris potestatis imperator quam totus populus, sed quam quilibet de populo.*

[28] The contributions of Leonard Statius to the debates at Constance were described by W. MULDER, Leonard Statius auf dem Konstanzer Konzil, in: Festschrift H. Finke, ed. R. d'Alos-Moner etc., Münster i. W. 1925, 257—269. In the above discussion we are more concerned with the views of Statius' anonymous adversary.

[29] H. FINKE, Acta Concilii Constanciensis II, Münster i. W. 1923, 705.

Council of Constance as it actually existed in 1416. At that time, he agreed, there was no pope "legitimately presiding and residing" in the church. Pope John XXIII had been "illegitimated" by his flight from the council and therefore the council had rightly deposed him[30]. Also, Statius conceded, if any future pope became vehemently suspected of heresy or if he sought to destroy the "ecclesiastical polity" he would not be "legitimately residing" in the church, and in those circumstances the exercise of supreme power would fall to the council. It would be the same, he added, if a pope became mad or was held as a prisoner by the infidels and so was unable to carry out the duties of his office[31]. Thus Statius conceded that a general council would always retain a certain residuary power to act in grievous emergencies against a pope who became "illegitimated" or incapacitated. After *Haec sancta* it would have been impossible to deny that. But Statius was really interested in the normal, everyday situation that would exist after a pope of unity had been elected. It was not very likely after all that the new pope would turn out to be a heretic or a destroyer of the church or a madman or that he would go crusading and be captured by the infidels. Unless one of these things happened, then according to Statius' argument, the new pope would be the sole wielder of all effective power in the church. In a later speech Statius insisted that it was neither false nor fatuous to assert that the executive power of such a pope was greater than the power of a general council[32].

The interesting aspect of Statius' argument is that he based it on the commonly accepted premise that plenitude of power could inhere, in different ways, in the pope and in the universal church. The most significant point about his adversary's reply is that it rejected as inherently self-contradictory this whole principle of divided sovereignty which had hitherto provided the principal foundation for the claims of the Council of Constance. Statius' adversary argued thus. If the supreme power that was said to inhere in the pope and in the church was one "in number" (i. e. if it was one and the same power) the absurdity followed that one and the same power could exist in two subjects that were not only separate from one another but at times opposed to one another[33]. If, on the other hand, the two powers were diverse then they differed either only in number or also in species (i. e. there were two identical powers or there were two powers of different kinds). In either case difficulties arose. If the powers were identical,

---

[30] Acta, II, 719, ... *presens concilium potuit dictum Johannem velud illegitimatum post fugam eius de dicto concilio a papatu deponere* ...

[31] Acta, II, 720.

[32] Acta, II, 723.

[33] Acta, II, 705, *Et primo circa primam et secundam queritur: Utrum ista suprema potestas sit eodem numero in ecclesia militante et in papa vel diverso? Si eodem, quomodo potest esse in diversis subiectis adequate et non solum diversis, ymmo eciam aliquando contrariis ac intendentibus eodem tempore penitus contraria* ...

then the pope would have a power of dominion over all church property (since the universal church held this power), and could alienate in at will. But this was not the case. If the powers were different in kind in the sense that the universal church was like a lord and the pope its minister then the church could lay down the law for the pope and remove him from office at will (but Statius had denied this)[34].

Again, if the powers were diverse, they were either equal or unequal. If they were unequal the greater was superior to the less and so it was incorrect to call each a "supreme power". To say that each side possessed "its own plenitude of power" was to say nothing. If the powers were equal then, just as the council or the church could take away jurisdiction from a pope (as had happened at Constance), so too the pope could take away jurisdiction from the whole church. But Statius' argument asserted that jurisdiction inhered "inseparably" in the church[35]. Therefore the two powers were not really equal. If it was said that supreme power existed in the church *in habitu* but not *in actu* then again a contradiction was implied. The power thus attributed to the church could not really be "supreme" since inability to act was itself a defect in a power; and so again there would not really be two "supreme powers"[36].

The anonymous spokesman next argued that Statius' theory was inconsistent with the actual procedures used by the council against John XXIII. If by the words "legitimately presiding" Statius meant that a pope who was justly and rightfully administering the church possessed in himself the sole right to exercise all ecclesiastical power, then who could decide whether in fact a pope was

---

[34] Acta, II, 705—706, *Si sunt diverse, tunc vel tantum numero differunt vel eciam specie. Si tantum numero, sequitur, quod, sicut ecclesia est principalis domina rerum ecclesiasticarum in terra, ita eciam papa; et consequens papa poterit similiter vendere vel donare aut quomodolibet alienare pro libito suo temporalia omnium ecclesiarum, quod tamen iuriste negant . . . Si vero eciam specie differunt, quia videlicet una est tamquam potestas domine, alii vero sicut ministri seu administratoris, tunc, sicut domina habet [potestatem] prescribere legem ministro et revocare administracionem eius, quando vult, ita poterit ecclesia facere de papa . . .*

[35] Acta, II, 706, *Preterea, si sunt diverse iste potestates, sive differant numero tantum sive non, tunc vel sunt equales vel inequales; si inequales, illa, que est maior, est superior: ergo non est in utroque "suprema", quod non est in utroque plenitudo potestatis, nisi dicatur, quod in utroque plenitudo sue potestatis, quod nihil est dicere . . . Si vero sunt equales, sequitur, quod, sicut concilium potest separare et iurisdictionem et execucionem a papa, quemadmodum factum est ab hoc concilio Constanciensi . . . ita papa potest separare a concilio sive ab ecclesia et iurisdictionem et execucionem, quod est contra primam assercionem. Preterea nullo tempore sunt equales iste potestates.*

[36] Acta, II, 707, *Et si dicatur, quod illa potestas est in habitu, licet non in actu, respondeo, quod frustra est calceamentum, cuius non est calciator; et non posse exire in actum, defectus est potestatis. Quando, si papa potest prohibere, et ecclesia seu concilium non potest hoc de papa, manifestum est, quod maior est potestas in papa quam in ecclesia et consequenter non est in utroque suprema, quod est contra asserciones.*

justly and rightly administering? If it was the pope himself, he would always decide in his own favor. But if the power to judge resided with the council then it could depose the pope whenever it saw fit. On Statius' theory a council could never really depose a pope; it could only declare that a pope had forfeited his office by his own behavior. But the Council of Constance actually had deposed John XXIII[37]. Again, it might happen that a pope was accused of heresy by many enemies, when in fact he adhered to the true faith. But if a pope was widely accused of heresy it was necessary for a general council to judge his case. Therefore a council could exercise jurisdiction over a man who was in fact a true pope. Statius replied that a pope who was vehemently suspected of heresy was not "legitimately residing" in the church and he conceded that, in those circumstances, the exercise of jurisdiction fell to a council[38]. But he still maintained that all exercise of power inhered in the pope alone so long as he was "legitimately presiding and residing". His adversary brushed the argument aside. He kept returning to the point that, in principle, the members of a council had to possess jurisdiction over a legitimate pope because the guilt of an accused pope could not be established until he had in fact been tried by the council (and of course he might prove innocent)[39]. The underlying argument was always the same. It was impossible that "supreme power" could exist simultaneously in the pope and in the members of a council. One power had to be superior to the other. And the anonymous conciliarist had no doubt that superiority inhered in the fathers of the council.

Even Statius conceded that the Council of Constance, in the actual circumstances of 1416, had the power to make laws. Would then those laws be binding on future popes, asked his adversary. If so the power of future popes would be subject to limitation by the council and so their power could not be called a "supreme power". If it was argued that the pope would not be bound because the new pope's power would be equal to that of the council and "an equal has no power over an equal" then new difficulties arose. How could a new pope take away the exercise of power from an existing council if he was only equal to it[40]? (Statius, it will be recalled, had argued that all executive power would pass to the new pope as soon as he was elected.) Again, if the council decided to retain

---

[37] Acta, II, 709, *Unde sequitur, quod nullo casu concilium potest ferre sentenciam deposicionis contra papam, ita quod ipsum deponat, sed solum declaracionis, per quam declarat, ipsum esse verum papam vel non aut esse depositum vel non, quod est contra determinata et practicata in isto concilio, in quo Johannes primo fuerit suspensus ab administracione papatus et postea depositus a papatu.*

[38] Acta, II, 720.

[39] Acta, II, 709, 714—716, 725—726.

[40] Acta, II, 710, *Si autem dicatur, quod par in parem non habet imperium, tunc quero, quomodo poterit papa futurus privare concilium invitum vel separare ab eo execucionem, quam nunc habet . . .*

"Divided Sovereignty" at Constance

the exercise of power and the pope decided to assume it how could the issue be resolved? Once more the anonymous spokesman was arguing that division of sovereignty was inherently impossible, that any detailed investigation of the implications of such a theory led to impossible paradoxes. His own views were expressed very clearly in the later stages of the debate. By natural law, he declared, no one could rule over a free people except by consent of the people[41]. The pope exercised power only within the limits prescribed by the council. The fact that the decree *Haec sancta* had limited the pope's power in certain areas specified by the council showed that the council had the capacity to limit papal power in any way[42]. The pope could judge individuals but not the whole church. And finally, referring specifically to the fathers of a council separated from the pope, he wrote "The executive power of the council is absolutely greater than that of the pope"[43].

It would be easy to point in the earlier Middle Ages to theories of unitary sovereignty. But the debate at Constance, it seems to me, provides the first overt discussion on the problem whether the very idea of divided sovereignty was basically defensible or inherently self-contradictory. The formidable attack of the anonymous spokesman made little impression on the more moderate conciliarists. They would neither abandon their claims for the council nor court the charge of heresy by relinquishing the established formula which attributed plenitude of power to the pope. The argument in favor of indivisibility was, however, taken up by later papalists who were quite happy to argue that the very idea of a divided sovereignty in the church was inherently self-contradictory, provided that undivided sovereignty was attributed to the pope and not to the council. One papal spokesman denounced the idea that supreme power could reside in the whole church as a *universitas* and in the pope as its minister in language reminiscent of Bodin. "It follows that a council could impose law on the pope. But, if so, the pope does not have the power to impose law on the whole church, which is to destroy the whole body of the law..."[44]. Johannes de Turrecremata used the same terminology as the anonymous of Constance in arguing against a division of sovereignty between pope and church (but of course he used the argument in favor of the pope). "It is impossible that in one corporate body the prelates and subjects should have the same plenitude of power... The plenitude attributed to the church is either one and the same in number as that attributed

---

[41] Acta, II, 724.

[42] Acta, II, 716—717.

[43] Acta, II, 729, *Ergo absolute maior est potestas executiva concilii generalis quam pape. Consequencia patet; et antecedens pro prima parte, quia, quamvis papa potest iudicare singulos, tamen non potest iudicare universos, quia sic posset iudicare totam ecclesiam, quam generale concilium representat...*

[44] H. FINKE, Forschungen und Quellen (above, n. 25), 293.

to the pope or it is different, but it cannot be said that it is different because then there would be two supreme powers or plenitudes of power, which cannot be . . . The plenitude of power cannot be one and the same in number because then neither would the pope be superior and prelate, nor could it be said that the church was superior in power to the Roman pontiff . . . because if 'an equal does not have power over an equal' it is still less so where there is identity of power"[45]. At the end of the fifteenth century this argument of Johannes de Turrecremata was incorporated into the *Commentaria* of the Decretum of Johannes Antonius de Sancto Giorgio[46], and it was repeated by Cajetanus in his important theological treatise *De auctoritate pape et concilii* (1511)[47].

As a final example of the interest in the problem of indivisibility of sovereignty at the end of the Middle Ages we can glance at some arguments advanced by Cardinal Jacobazzi in his *De conciliis*, published posthumously in 1538[48]. Jacobazzi was primarily concerned to argue, with a wealth of supporting authorities, that Christ had not in fact conferred jurisdiction on the whole church, but on Peter alone. Occasionally, however, he pointed out that the very idea of divided sovereignty was intrinsically implausible. To argue that the pope was head of all the individual churches but not of the totality was mere trifling, he wrote, for the universal church was nothing other than the sum of all the churches[49]. It was foolish even to ask the question whether the council was above the pope for the question itself involved a contradiction, namely that the supreme pontiff was not supreme[50]. The legists to be sure held that jurisdiction over the people could reside in a plurality of magistrates, but they referred to inferior magistrates. As regards the supreme power, if it was given equally to the pope and the church, it was given to two opposing parties. The result would be neither monarchy nor aristocracy but mere discord[51]. To assert that plenitude of power inhered in the church "fundamentally" and in the pope as its minister was to deny the existence of a usable plenitude of power, a power that could be

---

[45] Summa de ecclesia, Venice 1561, fol. 198r, quoted in A. J. BLACK, Monarchy and Community, Cambridge 1970, 169—170.

[46] Commentaria super distinctionibus, Lyons 1522, fol. 58vb.

[47] Printed in J. T. ROCABERTI, Bibliotheca maxima pontificia XIX (Rome, 1699), 463—561 at 455.

[48] Printed in J. T. MANSI, Sacrorum conciliorum . . . collectio, Vol. O, 1—580. On Jacobazzi's work see J. KLOTZNER, Kardinal Dominicus Jacobazzi und sein Konzilswerk, Rome 1948.

[49] JACOBAZZI, 554, *Item dicere papam caput singularium ecclesiarum orbis, & non omnium collective, videtur una trupha . . . ecclesia universalis non sit aliud quam omnes ecclesiae Catholicae in una fide Christi unitae.*

[50] JACOBAZZI, 499.

[51] JACOBAZZI, 504, *. . . non esset in uno suprema potestas, sed in uno aeque principaliter cum universitate; & sic duo repugnantia, per quae nec esset status monarchicus nec Aristocraticus, & pareret dissensionem.*

exercised continuously in the church, for on this theory the church itself could exercise its power only rarely when a general council was assembled but it could always impede the pope in his exercise of power; and when pope and church disagreed the plenitude of power could not be exercised at all[52]. To assert that there were two supreme powers in the church smacked of heresy. The church was one body and it had to have one head, not two heads like a monster[53]. These last assertions were supported by references to Gratian's Decretum and to Boniface VIII's *Unam sanctam*. The phrase, "The church is one body and so it shall have only one head or it will be a monster" goes back (at least) to the canonist Alanus, writing c. 1202[54].

Jacobazzi was a professional jurist. He used every possible kind of authority to buttress his position — Scripture, church Fathers, Aristotle, scholastic theologians; but most of all he relied on the works of the medieval canonists. From them he drew both the arguments for conciliar authority which he intended to refute and the affirmations of undivided papal sovereignty which he sought to defend. His work is essentially a survey of the canonistic tradition of the church from the twelfth century to the sixteenth. This observation can lead us back to the broader problem of historical periodization which we raised at the outset.

The recent work concerning the influence of the conciliarists on later political theory has consisted mainly in collecting direct references by later political thinkers to the conciliarist writings of the fifteenth century. This work is of course necessary, significant, and important. But it does not exhaust the interest of the subject matter. The truth is that, very often, even when there are striking resemblances between earlier and later thinkers, no direct influence of the earlier ideas upon the later ones can be traced. We have tried to show above that there were plenty of late medieval precedents for discussions on the indivisibility of sovereignty. The point has not been altogether overlooked in modern work and two recent authors have called attention to the very close resemblance between Bodin's arguments and those of Johannes de Turrecremata[55]. But both of the modern authors doubted whether Bodin was influenced by Johannes' text or

---

[52] JACOBAZZI, 511, *Et si ista plenitudo potestatis esset in ecclesia fundamentaliter, & in papa tanquam in ministro ... Et si per ecclesiam esset exercenda, raro vel nunquam exerceretur: cum raro sint concilia. Et si papa est solum minister, posset impediri in ejus exercitio; & si esset discordia, cessaret usus istius plenitudinis.*

[53] JACOBAZZI, 245, *Igitur ecclesiae unius & unicae unum corpus, unum caput, non duo capita, quasi monstrum.*

[54] A. STICKLER, Alanus Anglicus als Verteidiger des monarchischen Papsttums, in: Salesianum 21 (1959) 346—406 at 362.

[55] BLACK, 84. FRANKLIN, 112—113.

even know of its existence. And, indeed, there is no reason to suppose that he did so.

The resemblances between seventeenth century secular constitutional thought and fifteenth century ecclesiastical constitutional thought are too frequent and too close to be mere coincidences. The idea of an indivisible sovereignty inhering in the ruler, the alternative concept of a dual sovereignty co-existing in both ruler and community, the relevance of this concept for arguments about rights of resistance, the idea of collegiate sovereignty, the further technical problems about the distribution of authority within a collegiate sovereign — these are all themes common to medieval canon law, to fifteenth century conciliarism and to seventeenth century constitutional thought. But more often than not the existence of such a tradition would not be apparent if we read only the later works that are its end products. The themes that we have mentioned were not characteristic of ancient political thought. But the constitutional theorists of the early modern period, even when their ideas most clearly reflected the legal tradition of the medieval church, would often prefer to quote a classical author rather than a medieval one in support of their chosen positions. The point is that they were often thinking medieval thoughts even when they clothed their ideas in classical dress. When they wrote of "mixed monarchy" they would cite Aristotle or Polybius or Cicero; but what they had in mind was a collegiate sovereign of king, lords, and elected commons, or pope, cardinals, and council presiding over a national kingdom or over an international church. Such arrangements have little in common with the ancient polis. Rather evidently, both the institutions, and the ideas which explained their functioning, were derived from medieval practice and theory. But, as we have noted, it is often impossible to establish the specific influence of medieval thought on some particular "early modern" theorist. Bodin was not really propounding a novel theory when he presented his arguments about indivisibility of sovereignty, for similar arguments had often been advanced earlier in connection with ecclesiastical government; but Bodin probably was not consciously using the arguments of this earlier tradition when he framed his own doctrine. Sometimes we can trace threads of influence, sometimes not. Oakley tells us that "William Warmington certainly had read Almain". Christopher Besold, I suppose, might have read d'Ailly, though Besold did not refer to him (or to any conciliarist) in propounding his doctrine of collegiate sovereignty. Pufendorf, we can be reasonably sure, had not read Huguccio. Yet Huguccio's theory (propounded c. 1190) of a pope who removed himself from the papacy by virtue of his own criminal or heretical aberration is strikingly similar to Pufendorf's theory of a monarch who deprived himself of his office by violating the terms of tenure by which he held it.

The purpose of these observations is to suggest that resemblances which cannot be explained as a result of the influence of one writer on another may be at least

"Divided Sovereignty" at Constance

as important for the historian as those that can be so explained. They indicate a continued pre-occupation of many thinkers with essentially similar problems of constitutional theory through more than five centuries of Western history, centuries which produced radical change in many areas of life and thought including, most obviously, changes in the actual practice of government. The same questions concerning the juridical relationship between ruler and ruled were asked over and over again from the twelfth century to the seventeenth century. Often the same answers were given. Sometimes an answer was the same because it had been borrowed from an earlier author. Sometimes it was the same because a later writer, addressing himself to a similar question and working within a common tradition of thought, was led independently to the same conclusion as a predecessor. In either case the resemblances are significant. They suggest that, so far as constitutional theory is concerned, we should try to see the period from the late twelfth century to the late seventeenth century as a single historical epoch. During this period the distinctive patterns of western constitutional thought emerged. Their emergence is intelligible only when the period is considered as a whole; it becomes unintelligible if we try to erect some artificial boundary between "the Middle Ages" and "the modern world". It follows also that the task of a historian is not simply to pursue threads of influence from one author to another down the course of the centuries. The further, more difficult task for future research will be to understand what elements of continuity existed in social, political and religious life (during a period of such incessant change) which might explain the continued pre-occupation of so many different thinkers with the same constitutional problems over such a long period of time.

Figgis was merely repeating the conventional wisdom of his age when he wrote that a deep gulf separated medieval from modern thought. He was influenced especially by Gierke who had written of an "antique-modern theory" of the state that was sharply different from medieval theories. And yet, in numerous passing remarks, Figgis revealed that the results of his own research were not really in accord with the traditional system of periodization that he felt obliged to present[56]. That system rested on a deep-seated conviction, still cherished by

---

[56] "No subject illustrates more luminously the unity of history than the record of political ideas" (p. 2). "Yet even the claims of the sovereign state were no new discovery..." (p. 11). "To understand Rousseau you must read Rossaeus and to appreciate the latter you must go back to Aquinas..." (p. 30). Figgis' book is filled with such obiter dicta. Also, when contrasting medieval and modern theories, Figgis started out from a positivistic conception of the intrinsic nature of the modern state which would not nowadays command universal assent. "We in the twentieth century think of the State as essentially one, irresistible in theory and practice with a uniform system of law and a secure goverment" (p. 12). Again Figgis was repeating the conventional wisdom of his generation. But, again, his innate common-sense broke through and made

some modern historians, that the ideas of the state and of legislative sovereignty did not exist in the Middle Ages, but were created in the sixteenth century (perhaps by Bodin, perhaps by Machiavelli, or even, perhaps, by Thomas Cromwell). The great body of technical scholarship on medieval law and political theory that has grown up in the past fifty years has shown that this deep-seated conviction was mistaken[57]. But contemporary work on "early modern" theories of government seldom seems to take into account the recent findings of medievalists[58]. Figgis called his pioneering book F r o m G e r s o n t o G r o t i u s . To understand fully the growth of Western constitutional thought we shall eventually need a broader study. Perhaps it should be called F r o m G r a t i a n t o G r o t i u s .

---

him note in passing that his abstract definition did not really correspond with reality. "At last indeed, with the growth of federalism in idea and fact . . . we are going back to a state of things in some ways analagous to the medieval" (p. 13).

[57] J. R. Strayer provides a brilliant brief introduction to the whole subject, On the Medieval Origins of the Modern State, Princeton 1973, For discussions of the problem of periodisation from the medievalist's standpoint see Post op. cit. 241—247 and my article "The Prince is not Bound by the Laws'. Accursius and the Origins of the Modern State", in: Comparative Studies in Society and History, 5 (1963) 378—400.

[58] It seems superfluous to heap up references to illustrate the point. We may mention two studies in the proceedings of the Bodin conference held in Munich (above n. 12). J. H. Franklin contributed a paper called "Jean Bodin and the End of Medieval Constitutionalism" without mentioning any work on medieval constitutionalism written after 1941. Ralph Giesey illustrated in detail Bodin's use of late medieval jurisprudence, but he too concluded that Bodin's ideas differed radically from medieval ones essentially on three grounds. (1) In medieval theory "(The ruler) was given c e r t a i n powers and no more. Bodin contrariwise granted the sovereign a l l power except such and such". (2) "The king as judge is medieval; the king as legislator modern". (3) Bodin's idea of natural law was different from medieval ones because "Bodin did not have to consider God's creation of the world order as final and complete, but rather still amenable to change. If true that u t d e u s , s i c p r i n c e p s , then the innovative and generally creative role of the sovereign is vouchsafed" (pp. 182—184). Each of these three conventional assertions requires substantial modification. (1) The first assertion is not true of either emperor or pope. It will suffice to quote two phrases that were the subject of endless commentary among medieval legists and canonists. ". . . *Populus ei et in eum o m n e imperium suum et potestatem contulerit*" (Institutes, 1.2.6). ". . . *N i h i l excipiens qui dixit Quodcunque (ligaveris super terram erit ligatum et in coelis)*" (Decretales 1.33.6). As regards other rulers, we may remember the common medieval expression, *rex in regno suo est imperator*. (2) This statement seems to ignore the wide-spread legislative activity of kings and popes from the thirteenth century onward. See e. g. T. F. T. Plucknett, Legislation of Edward I, Oxford 1949, 2—3. (3) This is a more subtle point. But the idea that the creative legislative activity of the ruler was necessitated precisely by incessant change in the natural order of things was common to medieval Roman and canon law. It was expressed in Justinian's Codex, Proemium and 1.17.2.18, . . . *multas etenim formas edere natura novas deproperat*. The words of the Codex were taken over into the Ordinary Gloss to the Decretales of Gregory IX and into the body of canon law itself in the Proemium to the Liber Sextus. There is a long tradition of medieval Romanist and canonist commentary on these texts.

XIV

"Only the Truth Has Authority": The Problem of "Reception" in the Decretists and in Johannes de Turrecremata

William of Ockham, in the introduction to his *Dialogus,* suggested that his readers should consider not *who* expressed a particular opinion but *what* opinion was expressed ("non quis est alicuius sententiae auctor, sed quid dicitur attendentes.")[1] Ockham thought that theologians ought to decide disputed questions concerning the faith by right reason applied to Scripture. Christians could know that the truth of a doctrine was definitively established when it was accepted by the church without any dissent. (Ockham held that one single dissenter might maintain the true faith against all other members of the church.) Ulrich Bubenheimer has called this approach to truth and authority an "Ekklesiologie der Sachautorität"—an ecclesiology based on the internal authority of the fact itself rather than on the external authority of a defining institution.[2] Yves Congar, in a far-ranging article on reception of doctrine by the church expressed the same idea in the words, "Au fond, dans le domaine doctrinal, seule la vérité a autorité."[3]

Modern scholars have noted that this way of thinking occurs quite frequently in late medieval ecclesiology. The great canonist Panormitanus usually supported the conciliar position in the fifteenth-century disputes over the constitution of the church, but on one occasion he wrote that the opinion of a single private individual was to be preferred to that of either a pope or a council if the individual was "moved by better reasons from the Old or New Testament." Knut Nörr described this argument as a "foreign body" in Panormitanus's juridical thought. He discerned in it an attack on the whole institutional structure of the medieval church and an anticipation of Luther's ecclesiology.[4] Remigius Bäumer, on the other hand, has pointed out that Panormitanus's argument, slightly modified, enjoyed a certain popularity among the extreme papalists of the fifteenth century—for, if one single individual could be right and a whole council wrong, then that one single individual might well be the pope.[5]

The most interesting late-medieval variation of Panormitanus's argument was presented by the eminent theologian, Johannes de Turrecremata. Although he was a staunch papalist, Turrecremata conceded that the members of a council should normally be regarded as of greater authority than the pope

70

in deciding a disputed question of faith. This was because the council could normally be assumed to possess a greater capacity for discerning the truth, a greater "reason." But Turrecremata also argued that in exceptional cases a single individual, the pope, might have greater reason on his side and that then the pope's opinion was to be accepted by the church. This seems like a pure "Ekklesiologie der Sachautorität." Remigius Bäumer found it "astonishing" that Turrecremata should have put forth such an argument and Ulrich Horst, in discussing the same point, also referred to Turrecremata's "erstaunlicher Weitherzigkeit."[6]

The position does indeed seem paradoxical. Turrecremata was a conservative defender of the visible institutions of the church. Ockham is usually considered a radical critic of them. Yet apparently Turrecremata argued, just like Ockham, that in receiving a given doctrine as true, the church ought to consider the content of the doctrine rather than the source of the definition. The paradox is partly resolved in Congar's article. Congar pointed out that reception based on the substantive content of a doctrine was a normal mode of establishing authority during the first thousand years of the church's history. Evidently then we are not dealing merely with a late-medieval aberration when we find a similar idea in either Ockham or Turrecremata. Congar suggested further, however, that this way of thinking fell into the background in the period after the papal reform movement of the eleventh century as the universal church came to be conceived of, not as a community of local churches, but as a single society subjected to a single monarchical authority. Other modern scholars (especially De Luca and Munier whose works are discussed below) have suggested that the earliest commentators on Gratian's *Decretum* turned away from an emphasis on substantive content in determining the validity of church law to an emphasis on the authority of the legislator. Our own purpose, in the following study, is to carry a little further Congar's discussion on truth and reception in the church by exploring the teachings of the medieval decretists in this area.[7] We wish to argue especially that the position of Turrecremata outlined above was no eccentricity in his thought but rather an intrinsic part of his whole system of ecclesiology, a system that gave great emphasis to the substantive content of a pronouncement and its reception by the church as decisive criteria for determining the validity of church law and church doctrine. Further we would maintain that, in this respect, Turrecremata did not depart from the central canonical tradition of the church as it had been expounded earlier by the decretist commentators of the twelfth and thirteenth centuries. We might quote as an introductory comment (and as a counterpart to the words of Ockham given above) some phrases from the thirteenth-century *Glossa ordinaria* to the *Decretum*. "We are to consider not who speaks but what is said as at D.19 c. *Secundum* . . . the truth is always to be preferred whoever expresses it . . . reason is equivalent to canon law."[8]

Stephan Kuttner has written finely on the tensions in the life of the church which are necessarily reflected in the church's law, and on the canonists' ways of resolving those tensions. "Only he who is blind to the mystery of the church could find that the bond of law and the bond of love are mutually exclusive." It is another tension that we have to consider, not one between law and love but between law and truth. This too arises out of the intrinsic nature of the church as the canonists perceived it, "a social body which is also the mystical body of Christ . . . a supernatural mystery which manifests itself in the structural forms of social life."[9] As lawyers, the canonists were concerned to define a structure of institutions whose laws and teachings could bind the faithful together into an ordered community. As Christians they knew that no law or teaching could bind the faithful if its content was repugnant to Christian truth. They were certain that the church as a whole could never err from the true faith. But, since the rulers of the church were human and prone to error, a possibility existed that a licit authority might promulgate a ruling that was unacceptable because of its inherent content. It was the canonists' constant awareness of this situation that led to their continuing concern over our problem of truth and reception. Not every truth of faith and morals needed to be defined authoritatively by the church; but, especially when disputes arose, some of them had to be so defined in order to maintain the integrity of the church as a community. A doctrine could thus be true but not authoritatively defined, as the author of the *Summa Induent sancti* observed in discussing the teachings of the church fathers, "Although the things they say are true, still they are not 'authentic' unless confirmed by the supreme pontiff." On the other hand, a pronouncement that was authentic in the sense of being promulgated by a duly constituted public authority (even a supreme pontiff) could not have enduring force if its content was inherently false. Such a statement could not be received; it would have to be repudiated. Thus one canonist wrote of Pope Anastasius II who, allegedly, was rejected by his clergy and condemned by his successor for having favored the Acacian heresy, "Here the pope defended Acacius and so was convicted of erring himself . . . I think nevertheless that at the time of Anastasius this decretal was 'authentic', but his successor presumed him a heretic . . . and judged his letter iniquitous." Another writer suggested that Anastasius' doctrine was rejected because it was not "received" by a council.[10]

For the canonists then, reception was an important criterion of the validity of law. Much of their discussion on this point is found in comments on D.15–D.20 of the *Decretum* where Gratian discussed the sources of canon law. The *Glossa ordinaria* accurately described Gratian's intention in a summarizing comment at D.15 *ante* c.1. "So far the Master has discussed natural law. Now he begins to discuss canon law . . . and he shows which works are received by the church and which are not." For the decretists the structure of law actually in force, the law that guided the life of the church, was precisely the law that the church had chosen to "receive." This was true even of the legislation of general councils, the highest "instance" of ecclesiastical authority known to the decretists. At D.15 c.2 Gratian presented a very influential text of Gregory I. "I receive and venerate four councils like the four gospels." Gregory gave two reasons why he received these particular councils (Nicaea, Ephesus I, Constantinople I, and Chalcedon). Firstly, they provided a firm foundation of faith and right norms of living for the church. Secondly, their decrees were established "by universal consent."[11] The decretists used similar criteria in evaluating other councils. They taught that a general council consisted of a pope "with all the bishops"[12] but they did not assert that an assembly could be known as a general council, whose definitions were permanently binding on the church, simply from the composition of its membership or from the formal mode of its convocation. The actual content of the council's legislation was also important. The decretists knew that an assembly which seemed to have the external characteristics of a true council might err in its pronouncements on the faith. The councils of Ephesus II and Rimini were known to have erred.[13] (These same two assemblies were often cited as examples of erring councils by the anti-conciliarists of the fifteenth century.) The legislation of such councils was not "received."

This was pointed out explicitly in another text included in D.15. After quoting the words of Gregory the Great, Gratian presented a letter attributed to Pope Gelasius which set out in detail the authorities received by the church. "After the writings of the Old and New Testaments which we regularly receive, the holy Roman church also does not forbid the following to be received." There followed a list of the first four general councils as given in the preceding chapter. Other councils celebrated by the holy fathers were to be received after these four. The argument continued: "And now there is set out below which books of the holy fathers are received in the Catholic church." After a long list of orthodox writings of the fathers the author continued, "For the rest, the Catholic and apostolic Roman church in no wise receives things written by heretics." The ensuing list of condemned writings began with the decrees of the Council of Rimini (which had approved a version of the Arian heresy in 359), and continued with numerous apocryphal works falsely attributed to apostles or church fathers.[14] Throughout the letter of "Gelasius" the essential criterion for determining which writings should be received by the church was their intrinsic orthodoxy—whether they proceeded from orthodox fathers or from heretics.

The problem of apocryphal writings was explored further in D.16 in connection with the so-called "canons of the apostles." One text declared that this collection possessed no canonical authority because it was composed "by heretics under the name of the apostles"; but another text held that the collection was authoritative since it was "received by many" and confirmed by a council. Other texts of this *Distinctio* repeatedly stressed the importance of reception in determining the validity of a disputed authority. Johannes Teutonicus observed that Gratian had presented a contradiction here but had not resolved it. The solution, Johannes suggested, was simple. "The canons put forth by true apostles are to be received, but not those put forth by pseudo-apostles."[15] But the author of the *Summa Animal est substantia* distinguished more carefully. Some writings were called apocryphal because the author was unknown although the writings were certainly true. Such works could properly be received by the church. Other writings were called apocryphal because there was doubt concerning both their authorship and their truth. Such writings were not received. Here again reception depended on the intrinsic truth of the doctrine involved, not solely on the reputation of the author.[16] The problem was complicated by the fact that different chapters of D.16 mentioned different numbers of genuine "canons of the apostles." There were fifty, sixty, or eighty-five genuine canons according to c.3, c.2, and c.4 respectively. It could be argued that thirty-five of the original eighty-five canons had fallen into disuse. Alternatively, by invoking a process that might be called "progressive reception" a canonist could argue that the church, faced with a mixture of genuine and apocryphal canons had accepted first fifty, then sixty, then eighty-five of them as genuine.[17]

Similar problems arose when Gratian discussed the authority of papal decretals. The question was first mentioned in D.12, which was devoted primarily to the authority of licit customs, especially those approved by the Roman See. The key text seems clear enough, "Quae a sancta Romana ecclesia et apostolica authoritate iussa sunt salutifere impleantur." But Huguccio discerned an ambiguity. The text might mean that commands which were not "healthful" were not to be obeyed. (Huguccio's text was incorporated into Guido de Baysio's *Rosarium* and copied out almost word for word in William of Ockham's *Breviloquium*.)[18] Gratian's principal treatment of papal decretals came at D.19. Again the initial affirmations seem clear enough. "We have shown that Leo and Gelasius commanded . . . that all the decretals of our predecessors . . . are to be respectfully received and held." "All the sanctions of the apostolic see are to be received as if confirmed by the divine voice of Peter."[19] But then at D.19 c.6 a text of Augustine introduced a new theme. After observing that the letters of the apostolic see were included among the canonical writings of the church, Augustine wrote, "The enquirer should follow this method with canonical writings, namely that he should prefer those that are received by all the churches to those that some do not receive."[20] Among those that were not received by all the churches the enquirer was to prefer those that were received by more numerous and more important ("graviores") churches. If one writing was received by a greater number of churches, another by the more important churches they were to be regarded as of equal authority. (On this Huguccio commented tersely, "I understand this to be true if they are supported by equal reason, otherwise not."[21]) Augustine's text introduced a considerable complication into the argument. At first we are told that decretals must be received by all the churches because of the intrinsic authority of the apostolic see. Then we are told that the authority of the decretals is to be measured by the extent to which the churches receive them.

Gratian compounded the difficulty by citing next the case of Anastasius II, the pope who allegedly erred in faith in his letter to the heretic Acacius.

This letter, Gratian wrote, was issued "illicitly and not canonically" and so it was "repudiated" by the Roman church. The case of Anastasius gave rise to a great body of comment among the canonists concerning the problems of dealing with a heretical pope. The canonistic arguments on this point have been adequately discussed in modern works on medieval ecclesiology and we need not pursue them here.[22] It will suffice to quote Johannes Faventinus who closely paraphrased the words of Gratian himself and expressed the common opinion of the decretists, "Decretal letters . . . are to be observed devotedly unless they are found to differ from the precepts of the Gospel or the decrees of the holy fathers, like the letter of Anastasius."[23] Here again it was not only *who* said a thing but *what* he said that counted for the canonists. We shall next consider how this preoccupation influenced the decretists' treatment of certain problems (which would assume a major importance in fifteenth-century ecclesiology) concerning conflict of laws.

When the issues of "Sachautorität"—the authority of the truth itself—arose in fifteenth-century ecclesiology it was usually in connection with three problems, all of which were considered in detail by Johannes de Turrecremata. The problems can be posed thus: which authority was to be received (1) if a pope disagreed with all the fathers of a council? (2) if a church father disagreed with a pope or a council? (3) if two general councils disagreed with one another? We can best explain further the decretist background of Turrecremata's thought by considering some earlier treatments of these same questions.

The first question arose early in the *Decretum* at D.4 *post* c.3 which posed the general problem of reception of laws. Here Gratian wrote, "Laws are instituted when they are promulgated; they are confirmed when they are approved by the practice of those using them." And the *Glossa ordinaria* raised the further question whether a papal decree was to be accepted when all the bishops were opposed to it. Luigi de Luca devoted a lengthy article to the doctrines of reception elaborated by the decretists in commenting on Gratian's words.[24] He concluded that Gratian himself did not intend to propound a doctrine of popular sovereignty (as some later commentators suggested). Rather Gratian was adhering to an older way of thought, common among the church fathers, which saw law as a norm of conduct rather than as the command of a sovereign legislator and which judged the validity of law according to its objective content. De Luca did not, however, choose to investigate in any detail the persistence of this older idea in the numerous canonistic commentaries that he explored. Instead he concentrated on the canonists' treatment of legislation in its formal aspect, dealing with the problems of *consuetudo contra legem* and *approbatio utentium* primarily by dicussing the canonists' views on the respective législative authorities of the ruler and the people. Although De Luca no doubt did not intend this, his article could give the impression that, while Gratian still adhered to a patristic mode of thought which emphasized the objective content of law, his commentators were interested primarily in the formal aspects of legislative sovereignty. But this is not in fact the case. Gratian was interested in both the authority of the legislator and the substantive content of law. So were the twelfth-century decretists. So too were the fifteenth-century commentators on the *Decretum.*

It would be superfluous to explore once again in the present context all the well-known body of canonistic argumentation based on Gratian's assertion that a human law contrary to natural law was "vain and void."[25] But we may note that, just before introducing his doctrine of reception, Gratian set out at D.4 c.2 (a text of Pseudo-Isidore) the substantive qualities that a law had to possess in order to be valid (including the provision that the law had to be "secundum naturam"). The great majority of decretist commentators accordingly presented observations on the substantive content of valid law at D.4 c.2 and then turned to the formal criteria of validity in comments on D.4 *post* c.3, where they discussed the relative authorities of "princeps" and "populus." But the two areas could not be separated completely. Canonists who supported the authority of a *consuetudo contra legem* acknowledged that the *consuetudo* had to be "rationabilis" (following the definitions given by Gratian).[26] Occasionally, moreover, a concern for the substantive content of law was expressed precisely in connection with the problem of reception and the related problem of possible conflict between pope and bishops raised at D.4 *post* c.3.[27] De Luca, for instance, printed in rather fragmentary form some remarks of Huguccio on this dictum. But if more of the context of Huguccio's comment is restored a different area of interest becomes apparent. (We have àdded the italics in the following passage.)

> Certain canons cannot be abrogated by the pope as for instance those promulgated *concerning the faith and the general state of the church* . . . But cannot the clergy or people be compelled to carry out what the pope or prince wills since the pope has plenitude of power and all power is conferred on the prince? I believe that it can [be compelled] *if it wishes to deviate from reason or faith* . . . otherwise it ought not to be. Again, can the pope establish anything without or against the will of his cardinals . . .? He may do so *provided it is not contrary to reason or to the Old or New Testament.* But whatever is said, if they [i.e. pope or emperor] establish anything *that is just* it is valid and others are bound to obey.[28]

Evidently, in considering whether a law was to be received by the church, Huguccio was just as interested in the content of the law as in the authority of the legislator. (In the present discussion we have emphasized the views of Huguccio because they exercised a particular influence on the work of Turrecremata.)

The decretists also raised the problem of possible conflict between a pope and the members of a council in their intricate discussions on the problem of a heretical pope. They reached no agreement on the point. Some favored the pope, some the fathers of a council. Alanus suggested that the council fathers should be followed in matters of faith, the pope in all other matters.[29] But, again, the most relevant comment from our point of view was one of Huguccio's. Huguccio consistently maintained that, where a real doubt existed, the opinion of the pope was to be preferred; but he also made it clear that the issue could not be settled simply by weighing the authority of the pope against that of the council fathers. If the opinion of either was clearly iniquitous, then the opinion of the other was to be accepted.

> But see, a council is gathered together from the whole world; a doubt arises; the pope alone renders one decision, all the others another: which is to be preferred to the other? It is argued here that the pope is. But I distinguish and I say that if either contains iniquity it is to be rejected. But if neither contains iniquity and it is doubtful which contains the truth they may be considered equal and both held and one or the other can be chosen at will, for they are of equal authority, since on the one side is greater authority and on the other greater numbers as at D.19, *In canonicis* (c.6).[30]

Huguccio added that the pope was to be obeyed if he commanded that his decision be accepted in a matter of faith (provided of course that the decision did not contain "iniquity.") Much of his gloss was copied verbatim into Johannes de Turrecremata's commentary on the *Decretum*. Elsewhere Huguccio considered the relative authority of conciliar canons and papal decretals and wrote succinctly "If either has established anything contrary to reason the other derogates from it."[31] The idea that in case of conflict between pope and council the more "reasonable" view was to be preferred, which recurs in the fifteenth-century sources, had already been clearly expressed by the end of the twelfth century.

After discussing the authority of councils and of papal decretals, Gratian ended his review of the sources of canon law by considering the authority of the church fathers. Charles Munier discussed the whole canonistic hierarchy of laws in commenting on Gratian's treatment of this point,[32] and it will be convenient for us to consider here, in connection with Gratian's doctrine and Munier's treatment of it, the two further problems that arose in fifteenth-century ecclesiology—conflict between a church father and a pope or council, and conflict between two general councils.

Gratian began his discussion of the first problem by stating that anyone's words would seem to have greater authority the more they were supported by reason, "Quo enim quisque magis ratione nititur, eo maioris auctoritatis eius verba esse videntur." But, he continued, many church fathers such as Jerome and Augustine, "more filled with the grace of the Holy Spirit" showed more wisdom and adhered more to reason in expounding the Scriptures than some popes. It seemed therefore that the *dicta* of the fathers should be preferred to the decrees of such popes as canonical authorities. But then Gratian introduced a crucial distinction. "It is one thing to decide legal cases, another to expound the sacred Scriptures diligently. In settling legal affairs not only knowledge is required but also power." Peter, he continued, had received two keys from Christ, both a "key of knowledge" and a "key of power." This led Gratian to the conclusion that, "In expositions of sacred Scripture they [the church fathers] are to be preferred to the pontiffs; in deciding cases they deserve to be placed after them."[33]

The decretist discussion of Gratian's *dictum* led on to a clear distinction between the authority of private doctors, which was derived from their own

"ONLY TRUTH HAS AUTHORITY"   77

expertise, and the authority of prelates with power to judge cases, which was derived from their holding public office in the church. A canonist of the Anglo-Norman school put the point crisply, "Peritissimi nisi habeant potestatem causas decidere non possunt."[34] This principle was generally accepted, but it raised further problems. The difficulty in the simple statement of the Anglo-Norman canonist was that figures like Jerome and Augustine were not just private doctors. They were teachers "filled with the Holy Spirit" whose *dicta* had been accepted as *auctoritates* by the whole church for many centuries. Hence the decretists soon realized that Gratian's rather simple solution—namely that the fathers were greater in "sacrarum scripturarum expositionibus," the popes in "causis diffiniendis"—was not entirely adequate. The two spheres could not be so neatly divided. Often they overlapped. Some sayings of the fathers were accepted as authoritative in canon law. Some judgments of the pope involved the interpretation of disputed texts of Scripture. The decretists often noted that if the pope, in his official capacity as pope, promulgated a decree interpreting some dubious point of faith where Scripture was ambiguous, his decision would normally be preferred in the church courts to a text of Jerome or Augustine.[35]

Charles Munier, in his book on the patristic sources of canon law, especially emphasized this point. Munier saw in Gratian's *dictum* a turning point in the history of canonistic doctrine on the sources of law. Until this time it had been widely assumed that all *auctoritates* received by the church were essentially equal to one another. The task for a commentator was to reconcile apparently divergent texts by deploying the well-known techniques of medieval scholastic argumentation. Gratian himself, Munier noted, adhered for the most part to this method. But in the dictum at D.20 *ante* c.1 he did plainly note that, in church courts, one type of source (papal decretals) took precedence over another type (church fathers). This inspired the decretists to attempt for the first time to arrange all the sources of law in an ordered hierarchy. And, Munier suggested, in doing so they subordinated the writings of the fathers to "properly legislative documents." Already within twenty years of the *Decretum's* appearance, Stephen of Tournai had produced an ordered list of authorities. "This is to be diligently observed in the decision of ecclesiastical cases, that evangelical precepts hold the first place and after them the words of the apostles, then the four councils mentioned above, then other councils, then decrees and decretal letters, and in the last place come the words of the holy fathers Ambrose, Augustine, Jerome and others."[36] Munier argued that, in producing such lists of authorities, the decretists decisively reoriented the treatment of legal sources "toward modern solutions." He was arguing, in effect, that the canonists moved away from the older way of thought, which paid attention primarily to the substantive content of *auctoritates* in seeking to reconcile them, toward a more modern, positivist approach which resolved conflicts of law by constructing a hierarchy of legislative authorities and assigning priority to the law promulgated by the higher authority. If this were true—or, rather, if this were the whole truth—our problem of "truth" and "reception" would have disappeared from canonistic thought.

Munier's approach resembles De Luca's. Each sees the *Decretum* as standing at a mid-point between patristic and modern conceptions of law. But each has chosen to pursue a particular strand of argumentation in isolation from the whole web of canonical jurisprudence into which the individual strands were woven. Hence, although each study is valuable in itself and valid within its limits, either of them, taken in isolation, could give a misleading impression of the development of canonistic ecclesiology from the twelfth century onward. As soon as we begin to examine the network of glosses surrounding Gratian's *dictum* at D.20 *ante* c.1 we find that, for the decretists, there was no simple rule that the validity of a law could be determined merely by referring to the legislative authority of the promulgator. (This is sometimes clear from the texts that Munier himself cites.) The decretists' hierarchies of sources provided only the vaguest of guidelines which proved to be full of anomalies and exceptions whenever difficult cases had to be considered. The anomalies and exceptions are important because, in discussing them, the decretists were led to reaffirm their underlying doctrine that, whatever the legislative source of a pronouncement, the ultimately decisive criteria for determining its validity were its substantive content (its conformity with divine truth) and its reception by the church. If we view the *Decretum* and the works of the decretists not simply as collections of ecclesiastical regulations but as sustained reflections on the nature of authority in the church—and the works of Gratian and his greater commentators deserve to be so considered—this principle will seem at least as important as the more positivist doctrines in their works which were emphasized by De Luca and Munier.

The anomalies that we have mentioned arose for the canonists when they discussed conflicts between different levels of authority in the hierarchy of laws (e.g. when a church father disagreed with a council) and also when they discussed conflicts within each level (e.g. when two general councils conflicted with one another). As for the first class of problems, we may note that the gospels, the apostles, and the councils were all accorded greater authority than the pope in Stephen's list and in other similar ones. Yet in fact the decretists commonly held that the pope could dispense against the gospels in matters of church discipline and sometimes argued that he was greater than the apostles since he succeeded to the office of Peter who was prince of the apostles. But then the decretists also remembered that Peter had erred in faith in the matter of "judaizing" and that Paul had had to rebuke him. They accordingly held that the pope was strictly bound by all the teachings of Scripture including those of "the Apostle" in matters of faith.[37] Similar problems arose in connection with general councils. All the lists of ordered authorities put the general councils before the popes. But the decretists all agreed that the popes could override the positive legislation of general councils either by dispensation or abrogation (except in very grave matters touching the general state of the church). It was just the opposite where matters of faith were concerned. If a pope promulgated a decretal which contradicted the faith already defined in an earlier council, his decretal was to be repudiated (as happened in the case of Anastasius).[38] Thus one cannot say simply that the pope was above or below Scripture, above or below a general council. The decision whether he was or was not depended in each case on the substantive content of a specific papal pronouncement.

Among the possible conflicts between different levels of the hierarchy of laws the case of a conflict between the authority of an individual church father and that of a pope or council has a special significance for our enquiry because it raised the precise point later discussed by Turrecremata—whether the view of a single individual could sometimes be accepted in preference to that of the established legislative organs of the church. Gratian himself noted one striking exception to the general principle that he had formulated in the *dictum* at D.20 *ante* c.1. At C.36 q.2 he produced a whole series of texts attributed to popes and councils which asserted that a rapist could not licitly enter into a marriage with his victim. Specifically, according to Gratian, a council of Meaux and a council of Aachen has forbidden such marriages. Against all these authorities Gratian cited only one contrary opinion, that of Jerome. Then he concluded that Jerome took precedence over all the other authorities since Jerome was "supported by the testimony of divine law."

The decretists often asserted that the Council of Meaux did in fact support Jerome's position, but this conclusion could be reached only by straining the words of the council and in any case it merely opposed one local council to another of equal authority.[39] The fact was that Jerome's view really did find support in Scripture and, moreover, it had been accepted in the common practice of the church. These considerations were enough to outweigh any contrary authority of popes or councils. One glossator wrote that when Jerome contradicted a council or a decretal letter three things were to be considered—equity, the cause of the law, and the custom of the place. If Jerome's view was more consonant with any of these it was to be accepted. In the particular case under discussion Jerome's view prevailed because it was in accordance with the custom of the church.[40] The *Summa Tractaturus magister* observed that the decision of the Council of Aachen opposing Jerome's view was rejected because it was "contrary to the authority of the Old Testament and the church," while Jerome's opinion was accepted because it was supported "by the witness of divine law" (even though his texts normally lacked legislative authority).[41] For Alanus, Jerome's view acquired canonical authority "because of the approbation of the church" (or because the Council of Meaux upheld the same position). He added that, if the force of an authority could be deduced simply from the order in which it was placed in a list of authorities, then Jerome's *dicta* would have to be preferred to papal decretals, for the writings of Jerome were listed before the decretals of the popes at D.15 c.2.[42] On the general principle that papal decretals were to be preferred to the *dicta* of the fathers "in causis diffiniendis," the author of the *Summa*

Animal est substantia observed briefly, "Unless [the fathers] say things more consonant with the Old and New Testaments."[43] But this simple reservation undermines the whole principle of a hierarchy of authorities based essentially on positive legislative power.[44] What really mattered in considering the value of any *auctoritas* was its conformity with scriptural truth. A lengthy gloss by Huguccio drew together all the threads of decretist argumentation on this point.

> *Preponuntur.* So that it is not permitted to supreme pontiffs to recede from [the fathers'] expositions . . . in such matters they are called to a part of the solicitude and not to a plenitude of power . . . and this is an argument that one greater in some thing can be less in another. . . . This is true generally that in the settling of cases the authority of a canon or of a pope is greater than the authority of Augustine and Jerome . . . unless the authority of Augustine . . . should be corroborated and supported by the authority of the Old or New Testament or by a canon or by the general custom of the church; for a council that was celebrated at Aachen declares that a rapist and the woman raped cannot be joined in matrimony . . . yet the authority of Jerome prevails, not of itself but because it is supported by the Old Testament and the Council of Meaux and by the general custom of the church. . . . For the same reason the authority of one father is preferred to that of another.[45]

Huguccio's view that a pope could not depart from the teachings of the fathers was incorporated into the *Rosarium* of Guido de Baysio composed about a century later and was repeated by Aegidius de Bellemera. Eventually it found a place in the ecclesiology of Johannes de Turrecremata. The argument about Jerome was also used by late-medieval writers, including Turrecremata, when they considered the possibility that the opinion of one individual might be preferred to that of a whole council. Huguccio had already made the important point that would be reiterated by fifteenth-century canonists and theologians. It was not the personal authority of Jerome that was important here but the intrinsic truth of the doctrine he stated and its reception by the church.

Let us turn now to the final type of conflict of laws that we need to consider, conflict between two general councils. In discussing Munier's hierarchy of laws we noted that disagreements could arise, not only between different levels of the hierarchy, but also within each level. This was noted already by Huguccio. In the passage just cited he mentioned not only differences between church fathers and councils but also differences among the fathers themselves. His argument continued, "Among the pontiffs one is preferred to another as Peter to Linus, Gelasius to Lucius; and likewise among the fathers Ambrose to Isidore, Augustine to Bede."[46] When conflicts arose between authorities of the same class it was necessary for the canonists to have recourse to such criteria as *scientia, veritas* and *ratio* in determining which should be received by the church.[47]

The most extreme example of such a conflict would arise if two general councils conflicted with one another. The decretists did not doubt that some general councils had to be regarded as more authoritative than others. Thus the author of the *Summa Elegantius* wrote "Among the universal councils eight are preeminent and of these four have superlative authority" and, again, when discussing the hierarchy of laws, "next come the four councils mentioned, after them the other universal councils."[48] The general rule laid down in the *Decretum* was that, in case of conflict between two councils, "the opinion of that council is to be preferred of which the authority is more ancient or more powerful" [antiquior aut potior].[49] But this was rather vague. Stephanus suggested "sapientia" and Rufinus "pietas" as the decisive criterion in weighing the authority of councils.[50] The *Summa Elegantius* commented, "Therefore, among the canons, neither the earlier prevails over the later nor the later over the earlier but the more authoritative and more useful for deciding cases prevails." The author decided, however, that this interpretation had "more words than sense" and continued, "The authority of that council is preferred which is more powerful because more ancient," with specific reference to the eight general councils.[51]

The problem remained of explaining why the "more ancient" councils should be considered "more powerful." There was a conflict here between the Roman law principle that later legislation superseded earlier and the actual words cited by Gratian (which were perhaps reinforced by the general medieval prejudice in favor of "good old law"). Alanus pointed out that canon law differed from civil because the former was based on immutable texts—the gospels, the precepts of the Apostle, and the four councils. He added that "potior" could be taken to mean "benignior" or it could refer to the greater authority of general councils as compared with local ones.[52] Huguccio developed similar arguments at greater length. In general, he wrote, a council of greater "pietas" prevailed. The word "antiquior" meant that if two councils were of equal "pietas," then the more ancient was preferred (unless the more recent one was widely received). Alternatively the word "antiquior" could refer specifically to the first four general councils, which possessed a special dignity and authority. But even they could be modified by later legislation except as regards articles of faith and "general statutes of the church." The early general councils possessed a special authority in matters of faith because such matters were discussed in the early church 'more fully" and "more diligently" than in later times.[53]

Johannes Teutonicus also had no simple solution to this problem. He proposed that the "better" council should be preferred, not the more ancient one, and noted that the Council of Ancyra was more ancient than the Council of Nicea but that, nevertheless, Nicea was of greater authority.[54] Commenting specifically on the words "cuius aut antiquior aut potior existat auctoritas," Johannes asked, "Is not rather that opinion to be followed which is of greater 'pietas' . . . ? Because although a canon of the apostles may be more powerful because more ancient than other canons, nevertheless later ones are preferred to it." But this argument applied only when two particular, local councils were compared with one another, he noted. In the case of two general councils the later one was always to be preferred.[55] But presumably Johannes must have had in mind here only acts of positive legislation.

The decretists' treatment of this whole question seems rather confused. They do not seem to have analysed the most difficult problem, a conflict between two general councils in a matter touching the faith or the general state of the church. They did not always distinguish as clearly as one might expect between disciplinary and doctrinal decrees, between councils approved by the pope and those not so approved, or even between the authority of local and general councils. But this last ambiguity was perhaps not due to mere oversight. The decretists possessed no officially approved list which distinguished all the general councils of the past from all other synods. (It may be recalled that the author of the *Summa Elegantius* wrote of Gratian's eight general councils as being "among the universal councils," though without specifying any others.) We may note at any rate the frequent concern of the decretists to establish a criterion based on the substantive content of legislation—its "pietas," "sapientia," "benignitas"—in weighing the authority of two conflicting councils.

Evidently decretist theory on the sources of law was complex. As Congar wrote, there was "a certain dialectic" involved. In receiving a law the ecclesiastical community had to weigh its objective content (as, for instance, in accepting Jerome's opinion against that of popes and councils). But, as a complementary principle, the validity of the objective content seemed established from the fact that a given enactment had been universally received. Moreover certain sources of law, certain persons or institutions, possessed an intrinsic right to have their pronouncements received—or at any rate deferentially considered by the church—because of an authority inhering in the source itself. The pope was the successor of Peter, bishops in council were successors of the apostles, the church fathers were "filled with the grace of the Holy Spirit." Yet still the words of such persons were valued, not simply on account of some external principle of authority which they embodied, but because of an underlying presumption that the content of their pronouncements would normally be in accord with divine truth. Popes were said to legislate "pro catholica fide, pro sanis dogmatibus . . . et fidelium moribus." The four councils were especially venerated because they had so faithfully expounded the truths of Scripture. The writings of the church fathers, according to Gratian, were informed with "ratio" and "scientia."[56] A final corollary of all this was that, if the underlying presumption was invalidated, if any pronouncement from any source failed to conform to the truths of faith, it was not to be received by the church, however great the prestige of the promulgating authority.

If we turn now to the later Middle Ages we shall see that this tension between the authority of the legislator and the role of the church in receiving or rejecting legislation on the basis of its substantive content persisted in an extreme form in the ecclesiology of Johannes de Turrecremata.

Johannes de Turrecremata faced a difficult task when he undertook, in the mid-fifteenth century, to defend the unity and authority of the church and the sovereign power of the papacy within it.[57] The Council of Constance had restored unity to the church after a generation of schism. But the claim of Constance, formulated in the decree *Haec sancta,* that a general council was superior to a pope, gave rise to new problems once a universally acknowledged pontiff was elected. Extreme papalists revived old arguments going back to the mendicant disputes of the thirteenth century which asserted that bishops were mere vicars of the pope and that, accordingly, the pope and bishops assembled together in a council possessed no more authority than the pope alone. Extreme conciliarists asserted that sovereign authority inhered in the fathers of a council separated from the pope. All participants in the discussion were aware of Ockham's argument holding that neither pope nor council could adequately represent the church, that pope and council together might err, and that the true faith might survive in a few other Christians or even in one single person. Meanwhile, on different grounds, the Hussite movement was calling into question the authenticity of the whole established structure of church institutions.

Turrecremata was the first major theologian to deny the validity of *Haec sancta,* the crucial decree of the Council of Constance. But, as he moved from mere polemical writings to sustained reflections on the nature and structure of the church, he realized that merely to dispute the claims of Constance was not enough. To provide an adequate defense against them, it was necessary to rethink the whole ecclesiology underlying the conciliar doctrines. Turrecremata was discerning enough to see that this meant reappraising the whole structure of *auctoritates* assembled in Gratian's *Decretum.* All the polemicists in the conciliar disputes of the fifteenth century used selected excerpts from Gratian's work to support their various positions. Turrecremata was the only one who undertook a massive commentary on the whole of the *Decretum.* He was trained as a theologian rather than a canonist and, as he himself wrote, he found the task an arduous one, but he summoned up enough courage and persistence to carry it through to completion.

Turrecremata is usually regarded as an extreme papalist and the reputation is not undeserved. He certainly defended the supremacy of the Roman see staunchly against the attacks of contemporary conciliarists. And he also taught a personal and highly nuanced theory of papal infallibility. This did not, however, exclude the possibility that disputes might arise concerning particular papal decrees. In Turrecremata's theory, as in most theories of papal infallibility, not all teachings of the pope were considered to be defined infallibly. The problem could still arise, therefore, of deciding which particular pronouncements of a pope were to be received by the church.

The problem of reception did not arise for Turrecremata because of any doubts about the pope's legislative sovereignty. For him the pope was "prince of the laws." In the Roman pontiff there resided, "the totality and plenitude of ecclesiastical power." All other jurisdiction in the church was derived from him. Hence a pope was superior in jurisdiction to all the members of a council acting apart from the pope or against him. There could be no appeal from pope to council. A council could not judge "a true and undoubted pope."[58] A general council with the pope at its head was not greater in jurisdiction than the pope alone, just as a king with his subordinate officials was not greater in jurisdiction than the king alone, or God with his creatures was not greater in goodness than God alone.[59] In the order of juridical sovereignty, Turrecremata's doctrine was quite clear-cut. The pope was indeed sovereign. The point we wish to make is that Turrecremata's understanding of right order in the church was not bounded by the concept of juridical sovereignty. Like the early decretists he was deeply concerned with the substantive content of laws and, even more than them, with relating this concern to a very explicit and detailed theory of reception by the church.

In commenting on D.19, Turrecremata expanded Augustine's view that writings received by all the churches were to be accorded the highest authority with a series of quotations from Aristotle, "Things that all men assert cannot altogether lack truth as the Philosopher says." "A common saying is not altogether false as the Philosopher says." "What is said by the many and the wise is probably true as the Philosopher says." But he did not forget to add Huguccio's caveat on the words, "equalis auctoritatis": "I understand this to be true if they are supported by equal reason; otherwise it is not true."[60]

Also Turrecremata laid a firm foundation for his doctrine of reception by distinguishing carefully between the different ways in which the church could "receive" authorities. The question posed was whether all works of the fathers received by the church were necessarily approved by the church. It would seem, Turrecremata wrote, that this must be the case since the church itself was unerring. "The church cannot err since it is ruled and guided by the Holy Spirit, the teacher of truth. Therefore the works of the fathers that the church receives should be acknowledged without any suspicion of falsity." But Turrecremata then distinguished between three different types of reception. Some works, he wrote, were received by the church with an approbation that prohibited the contrary of their teachings to be held. The four councils, for instance, were received in this way. Others were received *ad usum lectionis*. Such were commentaries on Scripture, sermons, lives of saints and martyrs, sacred histories. These were to be treated with respect but it was not forbidden to dissent from their teachings on particular points. Finally some writings were received "through dispensation," that is to say the faithful were merely permitted to read them, as was the case with pagan authors like Plato, Aristotle, and Cicero. After further discussion Turrecremata concluded that teachings of the fathers were to be held for catholic truth only to the extent that they were approved by the church. "The works of the holy fathers do not receive authority from the authority of the authors, but from the approbation of the church because they are found consonant with canonical wisdom or reason."[61] Here the twin criteria of reception and objective truth were neatly bracketed together in one short sentence.

The concrete problem of reception of papal decretals by the church first arose for Turrecremata at D.4 c.3 where the *Glossa ordinaria* posed the question whether the decision of a pope ought to prevail if all the bishops of the church were opposed to it. Here Turrecremata showed little interest in the problems of popular sovereignty and *consuetudo contra legem* discussed in many of the canonistic quotations presented by De Luca. His discussion focussed almost entirely on the substantive content of a papal law. According to the text of Pseudo-Isidore quoted by Gratian at D.4 c.2, every law ought to be "honesta, iusta, possibilis, secundum naturam, secundum consuetudinem patriae . . . necessaria, utilis . . . nullo privato commodo sed pro communi utilitate civium conscripta." If a pope promulgated a law that conformed to these criteria, Turrecremata wrote, his decision was to be preferred to that of all others opposing it, since the pope, as vicar of Christ, possessed a superior authority which all were bound to obey. If, on the other hand, the pope promulgated a law which did not have the required qualities but rather their opposites, his law was not to be received. Turrecremata provided a far more detailed and systematic discussion of this question than any of the early decretists. If, for instance, a papal law was "inhonesta" because contrary to the Christian faith or "iniusta" because contrary to natural law, it was not to be received according to Turrecremata. It was the same if a law was not "possibilis." This could happen in two ways, either from the point of view of the legislator or from that of the subjects. From the point of view of the legislator it was impossible, for instance, for the pope to grant dispensations in things prohibited by divine law. From the point of view of the subjects it might be impossible for them to accept a law contrary to their customs and way of life. As an example Turrecremata mentioned that the oriental churches did not receive the law concerning celibacy of priests. If a papal law was harmful rather than useful (as for instance if the pope tried to depose all bishops) it was not to be received. If a law was promulgated for private convenience rather than public welfare (as for instance if the pope tried to name his own successor) it was not to be received. Finally, Turrecremata summed up his argument and reached the conclusion that the bishops might on occasion licitly contradict the pope, not because they possessed a greater authority than him but because of "the bad quality of the law itself."[62]

After this discussion Turrecremata raised tentatively for the first time the question whether in matters of faith a general council was greater than a pope. We can best follow his further discussions on truth and reception by considering in turn his treatment of the three possible conflicts of authorities that arose earlier, as we have seen, in the works of the decretists—conflict between a pope and the members of a council, conflict between a father of the church and a council, and, most difficult of all, conflict between two general councils. In his initial discussion of the first problem at D.4 c.3 Turrecremata suggested that the words of the *Glossa ordinaria*, "In matters of faith

. . . a council is greater than a pope," should be interpreted as meaning that the council was greater in "discretion of judgement" (though not in "power of jurisdiction") and that, accordingly, the judgment of all the bishops should be preferred to that of the pope in a doubtful matter of faith.[63] He returned to the question at D. 15 c.2, where Gregory I's text stating that the four councils were to be venerated "like the four gospels," was presented. Gregory did not mean, Turrecremata wrote, that the councils were equal in authority to the Gospels. The wisdom of God was preferred to any human authority. Rather Gregory referred to the content of the councils' teachings concerning the faith; they were revered because they conformed to evangelical truth. Accordingly, the pope was bound by them in matters pertaining to the faith and the general state of the church.[64] But, in his comment on the following chapter, Turrecremata's characteristic emphasis on the supreme authority of the pope appeared again. All laws derived their vigor and coercive force from the authority of the prince. But the pope received the principate over the whole church from God. Therefore the acts of a general council representing the community of the church received their authority from the approbation of the pope.[65] Just as the pope approved councils that were good and holy, so he rejected those that were evil and pernicious and subversive of the faith.

Turrecremata's comments so far seem to suggest contradictory answers to the question whether the pope or the fathers of a council were to be followed in case of conflict between them in a matter of faith. At C.9 q.3 c.17 he noted Huguccio's discussion of the point[66] and at D.19 c.8 presented his own solution. It was his comment here that some modern authors have found "astonishing"; yet Turrecremata's position was firmly grounded on earlier decretist thought, especially on Huguccio's (though Turrecremata's argument was probably derived immediately from the corresponding text of Panormitanus). Turrecremata first repeated his view that the words of the *Glossa ordinaria,* "A council is greater than a pope," could not be taken to refer to the pope's power of jurisdiction when "a true and undoubted pope" existed, for the pope possessed all power of rulership over the church. Then he continued:

> But regularly this is true [i.e. that a council is greater than a pope] concerning greatness of authority of discernment in judging (just as we say that 'the more one uses reason, the more authority his words seem to have') and this is presumed to be greater in the whole council than in one man. But I say 'regularly' because it may happen that even in a matter of faith the pope may be moved by better reasons and authorities than the council and then the definition of the pope should be supported. For a council can err like those of Rimini and Ephesus II and many others; also the council of which we read in 27 q.2 c. *placuit* and c. *tria* which determined that there could be no marriage between a rapist and his victim. Yet Jerome says the contrary, moved by better reasons and authorities of divine law, and his opinion is preferred to the determination of a whole council.[67]

Here again the issue could not be settled by any appeal to a formal power of jurisdiction. The decisive authority resided in the intrinsic truth of the doctrine maintained, even if the truth was maintained by one single person, and that person might be the pope or it might be a private doctor. Turrecremata concluded his argument by noting that, if a pope attempted to contradict a doctrine of faith already defined by a general council and approved by the apostolic see, the pope's opinion would not be followed but rather he would be presumed to err. Elsewhere Turrecremata held that if a pope was seen to err in faith his error was to be shown to him "from sacred Scripture or the determination of the universal church."[68] If he refused to recant he was to be considered as self-deposed from the papacy.

Turrecremata's attitude to the authority of church fathers is indicated by the reference to Jerome given above. When he discussed in detail the problem of a conflict between a church father and a pope or council, he distinguished carefully between "magisterial approval"—the expert opinion of a specialist in his own field, and "authoritative approval"—the decision of the one holding supreme public authority in the church. This distinction had been made in comments on Gratian's *dictum* at D.20 *ante* c.1 ever since the twelfth century. But, as we have seen, it did not automatically solve all outstanding problems. When Turrecremata came to comment on D.20, he relied heavily on the exposition of Huguccio. In the decision of cases, the popes were preferred to those expositors of Scripture who were "only expositors," and canons of councils were also preferred to the doctors of the church. But then came the crucial reservation. "This conclusion is regularly true, unless the decision of the doctor is confirmed and strengthened by the authority of the New or Old Testament, or by a canon, or by the general custom of the church." And he went on to quote the inevitable example of Jerome and the council of Aachen. Again, still following Huguccio and developing his thought, Turrecremata wrote that, in interpreting Scripture, the opinion to be preferred was the one "more consonant with reason." According to Gratian the fathers often "adhered more to reason" in their expositions. Hence it was not permitted even to supreme pontiffs to depart from certain opinions of the fathers, "namely those which concern the faith or the universal state of the church . . . or which are already received and approved by the universal church."[69] Once more we have the juxtaposition of objective truth and reception by the universal church as the ultimate criteria in determining the validity of canonical texts.

The final problem that we have to consider was the most difficult one for Turrecremata. If two general councils conflicted with one another which decision should the church accept? Here again Turrecremata provided a more adequate treatment of this problem than any of the early decretists while continuing the main lines of their thought. He carefully brought into play the relevant distinctions between general councils and local councils and between canons concerning the faith and those concerning church discipline. These distinctions produced straightforward solutions to many problems. Thus, a general council was always preferred to a local council in matters of faith. But, in matters of discipline the canon of a general council was not assumed to override the local legislation of provincial councils unless the canon expressed a specific intent to do so in a *clausula derogatoria*. When two provincial councils disagreed in a matter of faith the one to be preferred was the one supported "by the authority of sacred Scripture or of the holy fathers." If two local councils disagreed in a matter of church discipline the legislation of each was to be observed in its own district (provided it was not contrary to natural or divine law). If two local councils of the same province disagreed the later was preferred to the earlier one. If it was not clear which was prior in time the sentence "of greater piety" was preferred.[70]

When two general councils disagreed in a matter of positive law the later one took precedence over the earlier one. There remained a theoretical possibility that two general councils, legitimately summoned and confirmed by papal authority, might differ from one another on a question of faith. In spite of his devotion to the papacy Turrecremata accepted the common opinion of his day that an individual pope could fall into heresy. But, in the case that he had now envisaged, a whole council acting with the pope would have to be condemned as "not Catholic." Turrecremata was reluctant to admit that such a case could arise, but he did not neglect to provide a solution for it. Every effort should be made to harmonize the teachings of the two councils, he urged; but in the last resort, if their doctrines clearly conflicted, the later council was to be rejected, since the doctrine of the earlier one "had already been approved by the acceptance of the universal church."[71] Once again, even in this extreme case, reception by the church was the decisive criterion in deciding problems of conflicting authorities.

We began with a tension in the life of the church between "law" and "truth." It is a permanent and necessary tension. The church needs law to define its way of living as an ordered community. Law can on occasion conflict with truth. But the church must persist in the truth if it is to maintain its identity as a true church. When Stephan Kuttner wrote of a similar tension between "the bond of law" and the "bond of love" he explained that the canonists reconciled the apparent opposites in the ideal of canonical equity "which permeated their analytical thought and their solution of cases at every step."[72] Our tension between law and truth was resolved in the canonists' teaching on reception, which likewise permeated their thought whenever they had to deal with apparent dissonances in the area of ecclesiology. Here they looked for another kind of harmony. A word one often encounters in their discussions is *consona*. Always that authority was to be received by the church which was consonant with Scripture, consonant with truth.

There is one final point to be considered. The classical canonists—and, following them, Johannes de Turrecremata—held that in some circumstances the teaching of a single individual was to be preferred to that of any other authority in the church. Did the holding of this view really imply an attitude of persistent distrust toward the established institutions of the church, an anticipation of the ecclesiology of Luther? William of Ockham certainly used the canonists' arguments to defend his assertion that the whole institutional church of his own day had fallen into heresy. But this attitude was not typical of the mainstream of canonistic thought and it was entirely untypical of Johannes de Turrecremata. When a Huguccio or a Turrecremata wrote that the views of a single individual were to be preferred to those of any other ecclesiastical authority if the individual was supported by divine law, their underlying attitude was not one of skepticism toward the visible institutions of church government. Rather they were expressing a serene assurance that in actual fact, in the ongoing life of the church, the truth always would come to be accepted by the church as a whole (whatever its immediate source) and would eventually be proclaimed through the church's institutions. Their doctrine of reception was rooted in faith, not in doubt. Temporary distortions might occur, but the visible church, they thought, would always remain the vehicle of man's salvation precisely because it would always remain open to the reception of saving truth. Huguccio wrote, "The bark of Peter may be storm-tossed but never submerged."[73] Johannes de Turrecremata observed that the church had often erred but not in matters essential to man's salvation, not in ways that compromised her essential sanctity. "Not every error is damnable . . . in many things the church deceives and is deceived . . . and yet such error in no way derogates from the church's holiness."[74] The crisis of the sixteenth century came only when the actual conduct of ecclesiastical institutions gave rise to a widespread belief that the church was no longer holy, that it was no longer showing the way of salvation, that it could no longer be relied upon to receive the truth— whoever expressed it.

Cornell University

Notes

1. *Dialogus Magistri Guillermi de Ockham,* in M. Goldast, *Monarchia S. Romani Imperii* (Frankfurt, 1614), II: 398, "non quis est alicuius sententiae auctor sed quid dicitur attendentes."

2. U. Bubenheimer, *Consonantia theologiae et iurisprudentiae: Andreas Bodenstein von Karlstadt als Theologe und Iurist* (Th.D. dissertation, Tübingen, 1971), cited by S. Hendrix, "In Quest of the *Vera Ecclesia:* The Crises of Late Medieval Ecclesiology," *Viator* VII (1976), n. 64.

3. Y. Congar, "La 'Reception' comme Réalité ecclésiologique," *Revue des Sciences philiosophiques et théologiques* LVI (1972), 369–403, at p. 392.

4. K. Nörr, *Kirche und Konzil bei Nicolaus de Tudeschis (Panormitanus)* (Cologne-Graz, 1964), p. 133. See also H. Schuessler, "The Canonist 'Panormitanus' and the Problem of Scriptural Authority," *Concordia Theological Monthly* XXXVIII (1967), 234–41, and M. Watanabe, "Authority and Consent in Church Government: Panormitanus, Aeneas Sylvius, Cusanus," *Journal of the History of Ideas* XXXIII (1972), 217–36. Schuessler and Watanabe both mention Luther's references to Panormitanus. On this see especially C. T. Johns, *Luthers Konzilidee in ihrer historischen Bedingtheit und ihrem reformatorischen Neuansatz* (Berlin, 1966), pp. 28, 127, 130, 132–34.

5. R. Bäumer, *Nachwirkungen des konziliaren Gedankens in der Theologie und Kanonistik des frühen 16. Jahrhunderts* (Münster Westf., 1971), pp. 184–203.

6. Bäumer, *Nachwirkungen,* p. 190, "Erstaunlicherweise nimmt er Gedanken von Ockham und Nicholaus de Tudeschis auf, um sie für seine papalistischen Theorien zu verwerten." U. Horst, "Grenzen der päpstlichen Autorität. Konziliare Elemente in der Ekklesiologie des Johannes Torquemada," *Freiburger Zeitschrift für Philosophie und Theologie* XIX (1972), 361–88, at pp. 366, 378. As for Ockham's influence on Panormitanus and Turrecremata: Panormitanus, like Ockham, argued that councils could err since the true faith might survive in only one person as it had survived in Mary alone at the time of the Passion. Modern authors have often pointed out that the theme of Mary as sole guardian of the faith was no invention of Ockham. But Ockham, I think, was the first to use this old belief as an argument against the authority of general councils and so he did play a major role in its development as an ecclesiological argument. Turrecremata applied Ockham's argument to the members of a council separated from the pope but explicitly denied that it could apply to a general council united with the pope, *Summa de ecclesia* (Venice, 1561), III c.60. However, he was not quite consistent on this point. See below n. 70.

7. Congar was basically concerned to argue that the idea of "reception" has enduring validity in the life of the church but that its full meaning cannot be expressed in terms of juridical sovereignty (i.e. as an expression of popular sovereignty opposed to monarchical sovereignty). Reception, he suggests, is rather a recognition by the community of the truth proposed to it. This point, it seems to me, is true and can be demonstrated even from the "juridical" writings of the canonists themselves.

8. *Decretum Gratiani . . . una cum glossis* (Venice, 1550), *Gl. ord. ad* D.9 c.5 s.v. *Quantamlibet,* "Arg. quod non est considerandum quis dicat sed quod dicatur ut 19 dist. secundum (c.8) . . . quia veritas a quocumque prolata semper praeferenda est." s.v. *Probabiles,* "ratio aequivalet canoni." D.19 c.8 dealt with the case of the supposedly heretical pope Anastasius.

9. S. Kuttner, *Harmony from Dissonance* (Latrobe, Pa., 1960), pp. 41, 50.

10. *Summa Induent sancti ad* D.20 *ante* c.1, Douai MS 649, fol. 71ra, "Licet enim sunt vera que dicunt non tamen sunt autentica nisi a summo pontifice confirmata." *Summa Et est sciendum ad* D.19 c.8, Barcelona MS S. Cugat 55, fol. 70r, "Credo tamen tempore Anastasii hanc decretalem fuisse autenticam, eius vero successor presumpsit ille hereticus quia est fulmine percussus . . . quare et eius scripta iniqua iudicavit." *Summa Omnis qui iuste ad* D.19 *ante* c.9, Rouen MS 743, fol. 7ra, "Dici potest quod non erat receptum capitulum istud a concilio et ideo reprobatur." The texts are printed more fully in my "Pope and Council: Some New Decretist Texts," *Mediaeval Studies* XIX (1957), 197–218.

11. "Sicut sancti evangelii quatuor libros, sic quatuor concilia suscipere et venerari me fateor . . . quia in his velut in quadrato lapide sanctae fidei structura consurgit et cuiuslibet vitae atque actionis norma consistit . . . dum universale sunt consensu constituta."

12. *Gl. ord.* ad. D.17, *ante* c.1, "Universale est quod a papa vel eius legato cum omnibus episcopis statuitur."

13. Ibid., *ad* D.15 c.1 s.v. *Ephesina prima,* "Hoc dicit ad differentiam secundae quae fuit reprobata." For Rimini see the following note.

14. D.15 c.3, "Caeterum, quae ab haeriticis sive schismaticis conscripta vel praedicata sunt, nullatenus recipit catholica et apostolica ecclesia Romana . . . In primis Ariminensem synodum."

15. See D.16 c.1, c.4 and *Gl. ord. ad* D.16 *ante* c.1 s.v. *Apostolorum,* "Solutio brevis est quia illi canones sunt recipiendi qui a veris apostolis sunt editi, sed illi non qui a pseudoapostolis sunt editi."

16. At D.16 c.1, Bamberg MS Can 42, fol. 103vb, "Et sciendum quod quandoque apocrifum dicitur illud cuius veritas certa est, auctor vero incertus . . . et tale apocrifum bene recipitur . . . quandoque dicitur apocrifum quando nec scitur auctor nec veritas et talis liber non recipitur."

17. See *Summa Parisiensis,* ed. T. P. McLaughlin (Toronto, 1952), p. 14, and Rufinus, *Summa Decretorum.* ed. H. Singer (Paderborn, 1902), p. 36, "Vel forte illa xxxv capitula olim

a quibusdam patribus apocripha habebantur, moderno autem tempore, cum ab omnibus recepta fuerint, pro auctoritate summa observantur."

18. See my "Ockham, the Conciliar Theory and the Canonists," *Journal of the History of Ideas* xv (1954), 40–50, at p. 45.

19. D.19 c.1, c.2.

20. "Tenebit igitur hunc modum in scripturis canonicis, ut eas quae ab omnibus recipiuntur ecclesiis praeponat eis quas quaedam non accipiunt."

· 21. *Summa ad* D.19 c.6, Admont MS 7, fol. 24, "*Equalis auctoritatis.* Hoc intelligo esse verum si equali ratione nitantur, aliter non."

22. See my *Foundations of the Conciliar Theory* (Cambridge, 1955), "Pope and Council" (above n. 10), H. Zimmermann, *Papstabsetzungen des Mittelalters* (Graz-Vienna-Cologne, 1968). On Anastasius' legendary reputation and on the confusions between him and other allegedly heretic popes in the Middle Ages, see H. Fuhrmann, "Die Fabel von Papst Leo und Bischof Hilarius," *Archiv für Kulturgeschichte* xliii (1962), 125–62.

23. Quoted in Guido de Baysio, *Rosarium Decretorum* (Strasbourg, 1473), *ad* D.19 *ante* c.1 (unpaginated).

24. L. de Luca, "L'Accettazione popolare della Legge canonica nel Pensiero di Graziano e dei suoi Interpreti," *Studia Gratiana* iii (1955), 193–276.

25. For texts and literature on this see R. Weigand, *Die Naturrechtslehre der Legisten und Decretisten von Irnerius bis Accursius und von Gratian bis Johannes Teutonicus* (Munich, 1967). For an excellent introduction to the cluster of canonical ideas surrounding the words "iustitia," "aequitas," "ratio" see E. Cortese, *La norma giuridica* (Milan, 1964). Another valuable discussion is that of L. Buisson, *Potestas und Caritas* (Cologne-Graz, 1958).

26. D.1 c.5, D.12 c.7. For a brief survey, with bibliography, see G. Le Bras, C. Lefebvre, and J. Rambaud, *L'Âge classique.* Histoire du Droit et des Institutions de l'Église en Occident vii (Paris, 1965), pp. 214–19, 533–57.

27. See the comments of the *Summa Reginensis* and of Ricardus Anglicus cited by De Luca, "Accettazione popolare," pp. 212, 235. The *Summa Parisiensis* required that the "general will" which could abrogate law by non-reception should be "prudens." *Summa ad* D.4 *post* c.3 s.v. *Mores,* "i.e. voluntas generalis omnium et sciens et prudens" (p. 5). The *Summa Animal est substantia* offered a particularly interesting argument. Since the legislator and the law itself intended to promote the common utility, a people did not really act against the will of the legislator when they abrogated an unacceptable law. *Summa ad* D.4 *post* c.3, Bambe: MS Can. 42, fol. 101ra, s.v. *Abrogare,* "Verum est dicunt quidam accedente consensu legis latoris tacito vel expresso . . . Set dico quod etiam sine consensu domini pape potest lex abrogari. Set consensus eius generalis et consensus etiam legis et ad hoc tendunt ut fiat communis populi utilitas. Unde si rate inspiciamus non sit hic contra voluntatem legis vel legis latoris scilicet quod aliqua lex abrogetur, cum lex velit fieri ad communem omnium utilitatem." This should be compared with the fifteenth-century view of Dominicus de Sancto Gemignano discussed by De Luca, "Accettazione popolare," p. 219. De Luca mentioned the text of the *Summa Animal est substantia* (p. 236) but was misled as to its significance by a faulty transcription.

28. *Summa ad* D.4 *post* c.3, Admont MS 7, fol. 6vb, "Set nonne clerus vel populus posset compelli ut impleret quod papa vel princeps vult cum papa habeat plenitudinem potestatis et omnis potestas sit in principe collata? Credo quod posset si a ratione vel fide [posset] vellet deviare . . . aliter non deberet. Item posset papa preter vel contra voluntatem suorum cardinalium aliquod statuere vel imperator preter vel contra voluntatem suorum baronum? Respondeo, non debeat si eorum consensum posset habere, alias posset dummodo non sit contrarium rationi vel veteri vel novo testamento. Set quidquid dicatur, si sic aliquid quod iustum est constituunt ratum erit et alii tenebuntur obedire." Cf. De Luca, "Accettazione popolare," p. 214, n. 38 (referring to Guido de Baysio's use of this passage), and p. 233, n. 74.

29. For the text of Alanus and other decretist comments see "Pope and Council," pp. 210–18.

XIV

30. *Summa ad* c.9 q.3 c.17, Admont MS 7, fol. 214vb, "Set ecce congregatum est concilium de toto orbe, oritur dubitatio, fertur una sententia a solo papa alia ab omnibus aliis. Que ergo cui est preponenda? Arg. hic quod sententia pape. Distinguo tamen et dico, si altera continet iniquitatem illi preiudicatur. Si vero neutra videtur continere iniquitatem et dubium est que veritatem contineat, pares debent esse et ambe teneri et hec vel illa pro voluntate potest eligi quia paris sunt auctoritatis dum hinc sit maior auctoritas, inde maior numerus, arg. di. xviiii In canonicis (c.6)." The most detailed presentation of Huguccio's views is provided by M. Fernández Ríos, "El Primado del Romano Pontifice nel Pensiamento de Huguccio de Pisa Decretista," *Compostellanum* VI (1961), 47–97; VII (1962), 97–149; VIII (1963), 65–99; XI (1966), 29–67.

31. *Summa ad* D.19 *ante* c.1, Admont MS 7, fol. 22ra, "et quidem si alterum illorum statuit contra rationem et ei derogatur per alterum."

32. C. Munier, *Les Sources patristiques du Droit de l'Église* (Mulhouse, 1957). See also S. Chodorow, *Christian Political Theory and Church Politics in the Mid-Twelfth Century* (Berkeley-Los Angeles, 1972), pp. 96–153.

33. D.20 *ante* c.1, ". . . absolutio vero vel condemnatio non scientiam tantum sed etiam potestatem praesidentium desideret; apparet quod divinarum tractores scripturarum et si scientia pontificibus praeemineant, tamen quia dignitatis eorum apicem non sunt adepti, in sacrarum quidem scripturarum expositionibus eis praeponuntur, in causis vero definiendis secundum post eos locum merentur." Gratian's text gave rise to a considerable body of canonistic commentary on the power of the keys. On this L. Hödl, *Die Geschichte der scholastischen Literatur und der Theologie der Schlüsselgewalt* (Münster-Westf., 1960).

34. Cambridge, Caius College MS 676, cited by John Watt, "The Early Medieval Canonists and the Formation of Conciliar Theory," *Irish Theological Quarterly* XXIV (1957), 13–31, at p. 28.

35. See B. Tierney, *Origins of Papal Infallibility* (Leiden, 1972), pp. 41–43.

36. J. F. von Schulte (ed.), *Die Summa des Stephanus Tornacensis über das Decretum Gratiani* (Giessen, 1891), p. 30. See Munier, *Sources,* pp. 190–91, 198–99.

37. These problems are explored in illuminating detail by S. Kuttner, "Pope Lucius III and the Bigamous Archbishop of Palermo," *Medieval Studies Presented to Aubrey Gwynn S.J.* (Dublin, 1961), pp. 409–53.

38. Tierney, "Pope and Council," pp. 210–12.

39. E.g. Rufinus *ad* C.36 q.2 *post* c.11, "Sed verbum Ieronimi et capitulo Meldensis concilii nititur et in veteris testamenti auctoritate fundatur," cited by Munier, *Sources* p. 203, n. 102. (Munier also quoted in part the texts of Alanus and Huguccio given below, but with some inaccuracies.) Rufinus' view was echoed by the author of the *Summa Omnis qui iuste,* "Set verbum ieronimi et canon meldensis concilii veteris testamenti autoritate fundatur" (Rouen MS 743, fol. 133ra). See also *Gl. ord. ad* D.20 c.1 s.v. *Illorum.*

40. Cited by Munier, *Sources,* p. 202, n. 96, p. 203, n. 106, *Gl. ad* D.20 c.1 s.v. *Illorum,* "Cum scripta Ieronimi inveniantur contraria consilio vel decretali epistolae, tria considerantur, aequitas, constitutionis causa, consuetudo loci, ut si Ieronimus magis consonat alteri istorum . . . standum sit dictis Ieronimi." "Nam quia ecclesiae est consuetudo, ut raptor post peractam paenitentiam raptam ducit, optinet Ieronimus." Munier quotes these glosses from Paris, Bibl. nat., MS lat. 3903, which I have not been able to see. He attributes them to Johannes Teutonicus but they do not occur in the *Glossa ordinaria.* Presumably they are derived from one of the other sets of glosses in MS 3903 described by Kuttner, *Repertorium der Kanonistik, (1140–1234),* Studi e Testi LXXI (Vatican City, 1937), pp. 39–40.

41. *Summa ad* D.20 c.1, Paris, Bibl. nat., MS lat. 15994, fol. 16ra, 86vb s.v. *Ieronimi,* "Contra tamen, auctoritas que est infra xxxvi Q. ult. Tria (c.8) prefertur constitucioni concilii ut causa eadem c. ult. Set illud ideo reprobatur quia contrarium est auctoritati veteris testamenti et ecclesie." Ad C.36 q.2 *post* c.11 s.v. *Hanc auctoritatem,* "Set hoc quia testi divine legis innititur, non quia Ieronimus legitur et sententia diffinienda."

42. *Summa ad* D.20 c.1, Paris, Bibl. nat., MS lat. 3909, fol 4ra, 53va s.v. *Conciliorum,* "Infra xxxvi Q.ii in fine [?] § ult. contra, ubi auctoritas ieronimi contra concilium aquisgranis

dicitur obtinere, set hoc est propter ecclesie approbacionem vel quia illud est contrarium concilio meldensi ut eadem, q. eadem, Si autem (c. 10) licet Gratianus aliter senserit." *Ad* C. 36 q. 2 *post* c. 11 s. v. *Nitatur,* "Nec est contra supra di. xx De libellis (a. c. 1) ubi dicitur quod in questionibus iuris ad concilia et pape decreta debemus primo recurrere et tandem ad sanctorum patrum dicta, quod ideo dicitur quia huiusmodi questiones sepius per decreta quam per sanctorum scripta soluuntur. Si enim vis fiat in ordine erunt ieronimi scripta decretalibus preferenda, arg. supra di. xv Sancta romana (c. 3)."

· 43. *Summa ad* D. 20 *ante* c. 1, Bamberg MS can. 42, fol. 105ra s. v. *Merentur,* ". . . nisi ipsi dicant aliqua magis consona veteri vel novo testamento xxxvi q. ult. Placuit (c. 11)."

44. Munier's argument on this point seems to rest on a presupposition that Scripture was regarded simply as a body of legislation essentially similar to, though higher than, canons of councils, decrees of popes etc. He emphasizes that patristic texts had juridical authority only when they were supported by Scripture or were generally accepted by the church, but fails to note that similar considerations were applied to the "properly legislative" texts also.

45. *Summa ad* D. 20 *ante* c. 1, Admont MS 7, fol. 24rb s. v. *Preponuntur,* "Adeo etiam quod summis pontificibus non licet recedere ab eorum expositionibus ut xxv q. i Sunt quidam (c. 6) set preter eos. Sunt enim huiusmodi vocati in partem sollicitudinis non in plenitudinem potestatis ut ii q. vi Decreto (c. 11) et est arg. quod maior in aliquo potest esse minor in alio . . . Hoc verum est generaliter, scilicet quod in negotiis diffiniendis maior est auctoritas canonis sive apostolici quam auctoritas Augustini vel Ieronimi et huiusmodi nisi auctoritas Augustini vel huiusmodi corroberetur et iuvetur auctoritate veteris vel novi testamenti vel canone vel generali ecclesie consuetudine. Concilium enim quod fuit celebratum apud aquisgrani dicit quod raptor et rapta nullo modo possunt coniungi matrimonialiter ut xxxvi qu. ii Placuit (c. 11). Ieronimus contradicit quod sic ut xxxvi q. ii Tria (c. 8) et obtinet auctoritas Ieronimi non ex se sed quia nititur auctoritate veteris testamenti et meldensis concilii et generali consuetudine ecclesie . . . Hac autem causa auctoritas unius patrum preiudicet alteri."

46. Ibid., "Nam et inter apostolicos unus preponitur alteri ut Petrus Lino et Gelasius Lucio. Sic inter ipsos patres ut Ambrosius Isidoro, Augustinus Bede."

47. The problem often arose in discussions on D. 20 *ante* c. 1 when Gregory the Great's authority as a private doctor was compared to that of other church fathers. Gregory's authority was said to prevail when his words were "profundioris scientie" (Sicardus, Augsburg MS 1, fol. 80va; *Summa Antiquitate et tempore,* Göttingen MS iur. 159, fol. 25vb); "magis consona veritati" (*Summa Et est sciendum,* Barcelona MS S. Cugat 55, fol. 70v; *Summa Omnis qui iuste,* Rouen MS 743, fol. 7rb); "magis consona rationi" (Huguccio, Admont MS 7, fol. 24ra).

48. G. Fransen and S. Kuttner, eds. *Summa 'Elegantius in iure divino' seu Coloniensis,* Monumenta iuris canonici, Series A: Corpus glossatorum I (New York, 1969), chapts. 51, 52, p. 15.

49. D. 50 c. 28, "quotiescumque in gestis conciliorum discors sententia invenitur, illius concilii magis teneatur sententia cuius aut antiquior aut potior extat auctoritas."

50. Stephanus, ed. Schulte, p. 71, "Cuius antiquior et sanctior. Ut haec duo concurrant; nec enim sufficit antiquiorem cum saepe priora trahantur ad posteriora. Vel antiquiorem dicit non tempore sed sapientia et auctoritate." Rufinus, ed. Singer, p. 122, *"Antiquior* tempore *et potior* maxime pietate . . . non sufficit ut sit antiquior."

51. Eds. Fransen and Kuttner, p. 40. "Verum quia hec interpretatio plus verborum quam sensus habet, potest non incongrue sic accipi ut eius concilii preferatur auctoritas que inde potior quod antiquior est, ut sic ad viii. universalia concilia referatur. Eorum enim conciliorum auctoritas potior est quorum auctores potiores." The *Summa Parisiensis,* ed. McLaughlin, p. 45, also referred to the early general councils in this context, "Dicimus ergo hoc intelligendum de illis octo universalibus synodis, vel de quatuor principalibus, quia si in aliquo sibi obvient, prior et quae potiores habuit patres praeiudicabit."

52. *Summa ad* D. 50 c. 28, Paris, Bibl. nat. MS lat. 3909, fol. 9vb, s. v. *Antiquior,* "Secus in canonibus quam in legibus . . . in canonicis enim scripturis quedam sunt que mutari non possunt ut evangelium et apostoli precepta et iiii concilia . . . de quibus potest hoc intelligi, vel intelligatur de provincialibus conciliis in quibus habet locum quod dicitur supra, di. xix,

94

In canonicis (c.6). *Potior* id est benignior et est arg. pro misericordia . . . vel potior id est maior sicut generale concilium maiorem habet aúctoritatem provinciali."

53. *Summa ad* D.50 c.28, Admont MS 7, fol. 70ra, "*Antiquior* tempore et *pocior* presertim pietate ut hec duo concurrant . . . Sufficit autem si est pocior pietate vel dignitate . . . Set quid facit antiquitas cum idem sit, scilicet quod sententia modernorum conciliorum vel canonum prefertur si nitatur maiori pietati? Respondeo ad hoc. Potest valere quod si ambe sententie concurrunt et sint equalis pietatis et contradicant, sententia antiquioris concilii preferatur nisi sententia novi contra a pluribus observetur . . . Vel antiquior dignitate et auctoritate, ideo preponenda ut arg. di.xviiii, In canonicis (c.6). Priora trahuntur ad posteriora . . . nisi priora sunt summe dignitatis ut quatuor generalia concilia que vicem obtinent quatuor evangeliorum . . . Set et hec trahuntur in multis . . . Nota quod si papa ex certa scientia statuat contra statutum alicuius concilii vel pape vel augustini vel alterius prevalebit eius constitutio . . . exceptis articulis fidei et preceptis utriusque testamenti et ille que spectant ad generale statutum ecclesie, contra que papa statuere non potest . . . Set queras quare ille iiii^{or} vel octo generalia concilia sint maioris auctoritatis quam alia. Dico quia plenius ibi de fide tractatam est quam in aliis . . . et plenius in antiquis quam in modernis quia tunc pauci erant fideles et multi infideles . . . et ideo diligentior erat tunc inquisitio de talibus quam nunc."

54. *Gl. ord. ad* D.16 c.11 s.v. *Maiorem,* "Arg. quod non quia prior est tempore prior est iure sed melior praeferendus est." *Ad* D.16 c.4 s.v. *Praeponimus,* "licet Ancyrana synodus fuerit prior Nicaena, tamen propter maiorem auctoritatem Nicaena praeponitur."

55. *Gl. ord. ad* D.50 c.28 s.v. *Discors,* "Nonne ille sententia est potius sequenda quae maiorem continet pietatem? . . . Licet tamen canon apostolorum potior sit quia antiquior sit aliis canonibus, tamen praeiudicatur . . . Quod ergo dicitur hic intellige cum ambae constitutiones sunt particulares et locales et de illis loquitur 19 dist. In canonicis (c.6) . . . Sed si ambae sunt generales semper posterior praeiudicat." s.v. *Cuius aut antiquior,* "Si ambo sunt aequalis pietatis, 19 dist. In canonicis (c.6)."

56. D.19 c.1, D.15 c.2, D.20 *ante* c.1.

57. On Turrecremata see K. Binder, *Wesen und Eigenschaften der Kirche bei Kardinal Juan de Torquemada* (Innsbruck-Vienna-Munich, 1955). Binder, however, does not deal much with the problems we are investigating. P. Massi, *Magistero infallible del Papa nella Teologia di Giovanni da Torquemada* (Turin, 1957), is a simplistic treatment which emphasizes only the strongly papalist texts in Turrecremata. More balanced appraisals are provided by U. Horst,, "Grenzen," and P. de Vooght, *Les Pouvoirs du Concile et l'Autorité du Pape* (Paris, 1965), pp. 137–62. The fullest account of Turrecremata's ecclesiology is presented in Thomas Izbicki, *The Ecclesiology of Cardinal Johannes de Turrecremata* (Ph.D. dissertation, Cornell University, 1973).

58. These phrases are all taken from Turrecremata's *Summa de ecclesia,* III c.64, II c.83, III c.43, III c.50.

59. *Oratio synodalis de primatu,* ed. E. Candal (Rome, 1954), p. 86. In the following notes, because of the particular emphasis of this paper, we have illustrated Turrecremata's views from his commentary on the *Decretum.* Often the same views were expressed in virtually the same words in this work and in the *Summa de ecclesia.*

60. *In Gratiani Decretorum primam . . . commentaria* (Venice, 1578), D.19 c.6, p. 169, "et quae ab omnibus asseruntur non possunt omnino carere veritate ut dicit Philosophus primo rethorices et 7 ethicorum . . . sermo communis non est omnino falsus ut Philosophus dicit primo rethorices . . . ut dicit Philosophus primo topicorum, probabile verum est, quod a pluribus et sapientibus dicitur . . . *Aequalis authoritatis.* Hoc intelligo esse verum si aequali ratione nitantur, alias non est verum. Hu."

61. *Com. ad* D.15 c.3, p. 141, "opuscula sanctorum patrum habent authoritatem non ab ipsis authoritatibus, sed ab approbatione ecclesiae quae ideo approbatae sunt quia canonicae sapientiae aut rationi consonat reperta, secundum quod ait Augustinus in epistola ad Hieronymum et habetur in c. Ego solis (c.5) supra di. 9." At D.9 c.5 Turrecremata repeated the words of Johannes Teutonicus, "non est considerandum quis dicat sed quid dicatur." (p. 91).

62. *Com. ad* D.4 c.3, p. 62, "Respondeo dicendum quod si papa constituat leges aliquas habentes qualitates illas in superiori capitulo, Erit autem lex (c.2) . . . sententia papae praeferenda est omnium aliorum contradicentium sententiae . . . Si vero contingat quod lex posita a domino papa sive constitutio non habeat qualitates praedictas sed contrarias, recipienda non est, ut puta: Primo si non sit honesta utpote non conveniens religioni sive fidei Christianae . . . iudicio et sententiae episcoporum magis standum esset iuxta c. Anastasius (c.9) di. 19, et c. Si papa (c.6) di. 40. Item secundo, si lex aut constitutio papae esset iniusta, ut puta contra ius naturale, recipienda non esset . . . Tertio si constitutio papae non est possibilis et hoc sive respectu potestatis suae, quia excederet facultatem potestatis suae, ut puta si vellet dispensare in prohibitis lege divina . . . sive etiam sit impossibilis ex parte subditorum, ut si vellet constituere aliqua quae non convenirent moribus et consuetudini subditorum . . . de quo exemplum habemus in statuto de continentia non recepto ab episcopis orientalis ecclesiae . . . Quarto, si lex et constitutio papae non sit necessaria, id est expediens reipublicae . . . Quod enim contradicere possint huiusmodi subditi suo superiori, non ex maioritate autoritatis, sed ex ipsa mala qualitate legis."

63. *Com. ad.* D.4 c.3, p. 63, "Gl. illa dicens quod cum materia fidei ventilatur synodus maior sit quam papa loquitur de maioritate iudicii discretionis et non de maioritate potestatis iurisdictionis. . . . Et ideo ubi papa aliquid contra fidem instituere vellet, synodus ei contradicere posset et deberet, unde Paulus resistit in faciem Petri, ad Gal. 2, unde nobis videtur quod in dubiis quae circa fidem oriuntur, magis standum esset iudicio omnium episcoporum simul in synodo aggregatorum, quam iudicio solius papae, sed de hoc duce Deo, in alio loco plenius dicere intendimus."

64. *Com. ad* D.15 c.2, p. 136, "Sed denotare voluit (Gregorius) quia in hiis quae ex fide determinant conformia sunt doctrinae evangelicae quo ad veritatem. . . ." p. 137, ". . . non possit . . . immutare quae pertinent ad articulos fidei, ad generalem statum universalis ecclesiae."

65. *Com. ad* D.15 c.3, p. 139, "Patet leges non habent vigorem et virtutem coactivam nisi principis authoritate, sive ex eo quo totius communitatis principatus est collocatus. Sed Romanus pontifex est in quo Deus rex regum et dominus dominantium totius ecclesiae posuit principatum . . . Ergo ad ipsum spectabit approbatio gestorum per concilia universalia quae communitatem ecclesiasticam repraesentant."

66. *Com. ad* C.9 q.3 c.17, p. 369. Turrecremata quoted here from the gloss of Huguccio given above (n. 31).

67. *Com. ad* D.19 c.8, p. 176, "Quod vero consequenter dicit gl. quod tunc synodus est maior papa, videtur quod hoc non sit verum de maioritate potestatis iurisdictionis existente vero et indubitato papa . . . Sed bene regulariter verum est de maioritate authoritatis discretivi iudicii, secundum quod dicimus quod qui magis ratione utitur eo maioris authoritatis eius verba esse videntur ut in di. se. 1 (D.20 *ante* c. 1), quae praesumitur maior est in toto concilio quam in uno homine. Dico autem regulariter, quia potest esse quod etiam in facto fidei papa moveretur melioribus rationibus et authoritatibus quam concilium unde tunc standum esset diffinitioni pape. Nam concilium errare potest, sicut Arimense, sicut Ephesinum secundum et plura alia, et concilium de quo in c. Placuit (c.11) 36 q.2 et c. Tria (c.8) quod disposuit ut inter raptam et raptorem non posset consistere matrimonium, et tamen Hieronymus dicit contrarium, motus melioribus rationibus et authoritatibus iuris divini, et dictum eius praefertur dispositioni totius concilii. . . . Bene tamen verum est quod ubi papa velit statuere in causa fidei contra statuta sacrorum conciliorum non esset standum papae, quia in hoc casu praesumeretur errare."

68. *Com. ad* D.17 *ante* c.1, p. 149, "ostendo per sacram scripturam aut per universalis ecclesiae determinationem errorem esse quod tenet."

69. *Com. ad* D.20 *ante* c.1, p. 177, "Si primo modo, scilicet in causis decidendis sit ista conclusio, pontifices praeeminent et praeferuntur sacrae scripturae expositoribus qui tantum sunt expositores . . . Canones conciliorum etiam praeferuntur doctoribus in decisione causarum . . . quae conclusio vera regulariter est, nisi decisio doctoris roboretur vel iuvetur autoritati novi vel veteris testamenti vel canone vel generali ecclesiae consuetudine. Concilium enim fuit apud Aquisgranum et dicit quod raptor et rapta nullo modo possunt coniungi matri-

monialiter . . . Hieronymus tamen dicit quod sic . . . et obtinet authoritas Hieronymi . . . In expositione sacrae scripturae praefertur qui rationi consona magis dixerit . . . unde a quibusdam dictis sanctorum doctorum sive expositionibus non licet etiam summis pontificibus discedere ut puta in his quae de fide sunt aut de universali statu ecclesiae . . . aut quae iam per ecclesiam universalem sunt recepta et approbata."

70. *Com. ad* D.50 c.28, pp. 417–18.

71. *Com. ad* D.50 c.28, p. 417, "Quod credimus standum esset sententiae antiquioris sive prioris concilii universalis, dum tamen fuerit authoritate Romani pontificis et approbatione fultum et roboratum . . . Aut ergo controversia vera non est, quod magis credendum est, aut aliquod illorum catholicum non esset, quod magis de posteriori praesumendum esset, cum antiquum iam totius ecclesiae acceptatione fuisset approbatum."

72. Kuttner, *Harmony from Dissonance,* p. 50.

73. *Summa ad* 9 q.3 c.17, Admont MS 7, fol. 214va, "Fluctuare potest petri navicula set non submergi."

74. *Summa de ecclesia,* III c.64, "non omnis error est damnabilis aut obvius sanctitati ecclesiae, ecclesia enim in multis fallit et fallitur . . . et nihilominus talis error non derogat sanctitati militantis ecclesiae."

XV

MEDIEVAL CANON LAW AND WESTERN CONSTITUTIONALISM

Any scholar who sets out to discuss the state of canonistic studies in these middle decades of the twentieth century finds himself faced at once with a disconcerting paradox. Enthusiasts for the modern ecclesiastical reform movement have been attacking the evils of excessive legalism in the Church with such uninhibited glee that, in some quarters, the very word "juridical" has come to be accepted as a conventional term of abuse. (It is as though the authorities had declared an open season on canonists.) Yet, at the same time, historians of the Middle Ages have become so impressed by the subtlety and profundity of medieval canonical thought that the study of church law has now emerged as a respected and indeed internationally fashionable branch of medieval studies.

Our paradox is perhaps only an apparent one. It is not law as such that the true reformer needs to fight against but only bad law. The Church is, among other things, a visible society of men here on earth. She needs a juridical structure. She always has had a juridical structure. She always will have a juridical structure. And this should not really be regarded as a matter for argument. The great distinguishing characteristic of the twelfth-century canonists (in contrast

* This paper was read as the presidential address at the annual meeting of the American Catholic Historical Association in San Francisco on December 29, 1965. Mr. Tierney is professor of history in Cornell University.

to some more recent ones) was their vivid appreciation of the fact that—ideally—the Church ought to have a *sensible* juridical structure. The medieval Decretists lived in a time of "renaissance," of brilliant pioneering in many spheres of life and thought, and they were eager to press into service all the newest and boldest ideas of their age in accomplishing the great task that they set themselves. That task was nothing less than to express in appropriate juridical terms the ancient theological concept of the Church as the people of God— and the canonists addressed themselves to it with such learning and skill and wit that their writings influenced the whole subsequent tradition of Western government.

During the past twenty years an extensive literature has grown up concerning the ecclesiology and political theories of the Decretists and Decretalists.[1] We are beginning, not only to understand the general outlines of their thought, but to appreciate the individual characteristics of many particular teachers, of men like Huguccio, Alanus, Laurentius, Hostiensis, great masters in their own day, whose names are just beginning to creep into the textbooks on medieval history. My own intention is not to present yet another technical paper on some detailed point of canonical scholarship but rather to attempt a broad survey of the significance of all this recent work for a central problem of Western history—the emergence of the constitutional state in the Middle Ages.[2] I should be especially happy if I could succeed in conveying to you that the objective of modern canonistic studies is not simply to add a few additional esoteric footnotes to the standard works on constitutional history, but rather to find fresh answers for the new problems concerning the nature and origins of constitutionalism that are posed inescapably by the circumstances of our own age.

I am using the word "constitutionalism" to signify simply the most basic, taken-for-granted ideas that are implied by the most familiar platitudes of our political discourse, by phrases like "gov-

---

[1] The literature for the period 1945-1955 was discussed in my article, "Some Recent Works on the Political Theories of the Medieval Canonists," *Traditio,* X (1954), 594-625. For the years since 1955 a convenient guide is provided by the bibliographies of the Institute of Medieval Canon Law published annually in *Traditio.*

[2] My debt to two recent works will be especially apparent. They are Ernst H. Kantorowicz, *The King's Two Bodies* (Princeton, 1957), and Gaines Post, *Studies in Medieval Legal Thought* (Princeton, 1964).

ernment under law" or "government by consent." We mean, I take it, a system in which the citizen is guaranteed due process of law and in which law itself is not merely the arbitrary will of a despot but rather reflects the moral outlook of the whole society, at least in its broad principles. And "government by consent," of course, means to us not just that the majority imposes its will on the minority but that machinery exists for eliciting a consensus of opinion, for formulating courses of action that all the citizens are prepared to accept, even though with differing degrees of enthusiasm. The characteristic institutional machinery for eliciting a consensus in modern constitutional states is the elected representative assembly with effective rights of consent to legislation and taxation.

The point which must strike a contemporary historian most forcefully at the outset is the extreme improbability of this kind of system ever emerging anywhere or persisting if by chance it has emerged. During my own lifetime ancient European peoples that might have known better have willingly handed themselves over to the most revolting forms of despotism and new nations that, a few years ago, were everywhere embarking on brave adventures in constitutional government have usually abandoned the system after a brief period of unsuccessful experimentation. Adlai Stevenson once observed that, "The natural government of man is servitude. Tyranny is the normal pattern of human government." And the historian cannot fail to discern that the normal story of human government is indeed one of alternation between different forms of tyranny with occasional interludes of anarchy. All this is not to say that our political system must necessarily be dismissed as a mere freakish aberration in the general history of mankind. Perhaps things will be different in the future. Constitutionalism is the distinctive contribution of Western civilization to the art of government, and, in India, the leaders of half a billion people are still striving—not unsuccessfully so far, though the outcome is unpredictable—to adapt our Western institutions to the needs of an Asiatic society. Constitutionalism may after all represent the main axis of development in the growth of human government for the next thousand years. Or it may not. The historical problem of how constitutional structures of government could first grow into existence is a fascinating one for the scholar precisely because the practical issue of whether such structures can survive and expand is poised so delicately in the modern world.

Now nations first began to organize themselves into constitutional states during the Middle Ages. We can indeed trace an interesting and most important chapter in the pre-history of constitutionalism in the life of certain classical city-states; but the problems of government by consent become so much more complex when one moves from the intimate society of a single little city to an area the size of a nation or a whole continent that they become essentially different in kind and necessitate for their solution a different kind of institutional machinery from any that existed in the ancient world. Individual city-states lacked the principle of representation in anything like its modern form. The occasional leagues of city-states that arose lacked the principle of sovereignty in anything like its modern form.

In a quite different sphere the anthropologists could point out to us dozens of primitive societies that experience limited government in the sense that they have tribal councils and customary laws. Such institutions are in no way peculiar to the Teutonic peoples of northern Europe. One can find them among West Africans or Red Indians, almost anywhere indeed where the appropriate research has been conducted; and this is the most obvious reason why the mere exploration of primeval Teutonic folkways—a once popular pursuit among medievalists—can provide no adequate explanation for the rise of medieval constitutionalism. Primitive societies provide no real analogue for the constitutional state because they lack most of the essential attributes of the state iself—ordered departments of government, written records, the idea of legislation as a deliberate product of reason and will; and when primitive peoples have outgrown their tribal customs to develop a civilization and a state it has normally taken the form of a despotism, most commonly a theocracy. Many examples were classified in Wittfogel's book, *Oriental Despotism.*

In Western Europe, from the twelfth century onward, events took a different turn. A great revival of classical Roman law re-introduced into the feudal world of the West with its countless petty jurisdictions the idea of strong central government exercising broad powers of legislation and taxation for the public welfare. Moreover, the example of the Roman *Corpus Iuris* stimulated the monk Gratian to undertake a major systematization of the law of the Church and, about 1140, he completed his Decretum, an immensely influential work that created an ordered synthesis for the first time out of the chaos of conflicting canons, decretals, and patristic texts that had been accumulating in the Church for a thousand years. The next two centuries saw a great growth of governmental activity, first in the ecclesiastical sphere, then in the secular. Kingdoms built up more sophisticated bureaucracies. There was increased taxation, judicial centralization and, by 1300, a great upsurge of legislative activity. But this growth of centralized government coincided precisely with a growth of constitutional theories and practices. Administrative structures were emerging that we can reasonably call states but for the first time they were constitutional states. It was a major turning point in the history of human government.

Not everyone, to be sure, agrees with this way of looking at the Middle Ages. One can still encounter books on the origins of Western constitutionalism that dwell lovingly on the Athenian democracy and the Roman republic—and then leap over the intervening centuries to take up the story again with Hobbes and Locke and the Glorious Revolution. Indeed some scholars seem disposed to turn the study of medieval institutions into a mere recondite branch of anthropology by arguing that medieval men, like other primitive peoples, lacked any sophisticated conception of sovereignty and the state. The most common error in this approach is for an author to start out from a nineteenth-century theory of sovereignty, usually Austinian or Hegelian, and then demonstrate that there was no state in the Middle Ages (which can accordingly be shrugged aside as irrelevant to his subject) because the organization of medieval political life did not conform to the chosen stereotype. It is true enough of course. The point is that these nineteenth-century theories are just as inapplicable to contemporary constitutional states as to medieval ones. The study of such doctrines can perhaps help us to understand some modern forms of absolutist government, but that is precisely because they are aberrations from the central tradition of Western constitutionalism. They have little relevance for the historian who seeks to explore either the origins of that tradition or its modern manifestations.

The discussion of these problems can become extremely complex, but the immediate point that I am concerned to make is not over-subtle. A modern institution of representative government like the American senate has no meaningful connection whatsoever with the ancient Roman senate. On the other hand its whole nature and mode of functioning is rooted in an antecedent tradition of parliamentary government—and parliament did not come into existence in ancient Greece or ancient Rome but in medieval England. The fact of the matter is that in 1200 there were no national representative assemblies anywhere and there never had been any, while by 1400 the whole Western Church was engaged in trying to replace papal monarchy with conciliar government, and almost every country from Scandinavia to Spain and from England to Hungary had produced constitutional documents stating that the ruler was under the law and had experimented with representative assemblies seeking to give effect to that principle. This is the phenomenon of medieval constitutionalism. It is, as I have emphasized, a rare, perhaps a unique phenomenon. There is no general work of synthesis that would explain the whole phenomenon satisfactorily. It is surely interesting enough to deserve an explanation.

Medievalists have always been aware of the importance of constitutional history. It has always been a central theme of our discipline. But they have not always approached it from the point of view that I have been suggesting. On the contrary, when the subject first began to be studied scientifically in the nineteenth century, there was a widespread assumption that a constitutional, representative system was a kind of natural norm of human government, which the English had come to exemplify first because of their innate Anglo-Saxon virtue, but toward which all societies could be expected to progress in due course given a little goodwill and a modicum of elementary education. With that preconception the whole task of explaining the origins of constitutionalism became one of merely documenting the stages by which medieval men pursued this normal and natural course of development from Teutonic tribesmen to members of the House of Commons. This in itself presented some problems, and it is widely held nowadays that William Stubbs, the greatest of the early constitutional historians, presented the stages of development wrongly. Around 1900 revisionists like Maitland and McIlwain began to criticize him. The argument proliferated, and it is still going on. We now have a fantastically elaborate bibliography of hundreds of books and articles devoted to this one question and all the fascinating subsidiary issues that arise out of it—whether the English Parliament was already some kind of representative legislature in 1297 or whether we are so radically to modify our whole view of human progress as to suppose that this felicitous state of affairs did not begin to come about until, say, 1327. The material that has been unearthed in the course of the controversy is invaluable. If there is ever to be a satisfactory account of medieval constitutionalism as a whole the interpretation of English parliamentary records will play a major part in it. But this can hardly come about so long as parliamentary studies are conducted in an insular spirit and are dominated to such an extraordinary degree by the discussion of technical problems arising out of an academic dispute of sixty years ago. They need to be set in a broader perspective.

The study of the law of the universal Church can provide such a perspective. If we set out from the terms of reference that impose themselves in the 1960's, from the surely self-evident premise that constitutionalism is not a normal stage in the evolution of societies but extremely abnormal—its emergence improbable, its extension most difficult, its survival always precarious—then we must ask a new kind of question of the age that first produced it. The obvious question is this. What was abnormal about the Middle Ages? What elements of social organization or economic life were common to all the countries of Western Europe between 1200 and 1400 but peculiar to that medieval civilization as a whole compared to the others that we know of? This kind of question leads straight to the topics for which medieval canonists provide the primary source material. For there is nothing very out of the way about the medieval economy— a primitive agrarian basis diversified by a little commerce. Nor is the technology especially striking—more advanced than we used to think but not really remarkable. Nor is the basic social structure, with prestige accorded to a military aristocracy, highly unusual. It is only when we turn to the ecclesiastical aspects of medieval culture that we encounter situations that are indeed extremely abnormal by the standards of most other civilizations.

When students first come to consider the conflicts of popes and kings in the Middle Ages they are sometimes surprised at the pretensions of both sides. They find it remarkable that popes should claim to depose kings or kings to appoint bishops; but there is really nothing unusual in one ruler aspiring to exercise supreme spiritual and temporal power. That again is a normal pattern of human government. Innumerable societies have been ruled by a god-emperor, a divine king or a chieftain of magical potency. The unusual thing in the Middle Ages was not that certain emperors and popes aspired to a theocratic role but that such ambitions were never wholly fulfilled. There remained always two structures of government, ecclesiastical and secular, intricately interlinked but dedicated ultimately to different ends, often in conflict with one another, each constantly limiting the other's power. Evidently the very existence of such a situation would enhance the possibilities for a growth of human freedom by preventing medieval society from congealing into a rigid despotism, and Lord Acton pointed this out long ago. "To that conflict of four hundred years," he wrote, "we owe the rise of civil liberty."

But, although important, this is only part of the story. We have to deal with two societies that were not only frequently in conflict with each other but that were also in a state of constant interaction. Throughout the Middle Ages there was a very frequent interchange of personnel and also of ideas and institutional techniques between the spheres of ecclesiastical and secular government. Kings were anointed like bishops and bishops became feudal lords like kings. Secular laws relating to the ancient Senate were used to define the status of cardinals in the Roman church, and canonical rules regarding the choice of bishops were used to regulate the elections of emperors. The pope assumed the imperial tiara, and the emperor the episcopal mitre. One could multiply such examples endlessly.

To understand the distinctive characteristics of medieval government, therefore, we have to consider two sets of problems—problems of conflict and problems of interaction between Church and State. On the whole the problems of interaction are more complex and more important, and these are the ones that I want particularly to consider. It is quite easy to see in the abstract that a very duality of Church and State in any society would produce a situation of exceptional flexibility. It is very difficult to explain in the concrete how that particular ecclesiastical organization interacted with that particular system of secular government to produce the new forms of constitutional organization whose origins we are trying to explore. Merely to mix ecclesiastical autocracy with feudal anarchy does not sound very promising, and it was widely assumed until recently that all canonical theories of papal authority were indeed starkly autocratic. But a major conclusion arising out of all the recent research is that medieval canon law was not merely, as it was once called, "a marvellous jurisprudence of spiritual despotism." On detailed investigation we find that the great canonistic glosses and *summae* of the age of

Innocent III contain, not only the familiar and expected passages exalting papal authority, but also other sections that are filled with constitutional concepts, with sophisticated discussions on representation and consent and on the due limits to lawfully constituted authority, even papal authority.

Before we turn to this structure of ideas we ought to consider a preliminary question that inevitably presents itself. How could medieval canon lawyers, of all people, have been led to pioneer in the development of constitutional principles, of all things? To understand this we must consider one more way in which Western history has pursued an unusual course—I mean in the extraordinary convolutions of its chronological structure. Perhaps no other civilization, through the centuries of its existence, has enjoyed so many and such varied love affairs with its own past as those of the Western world, ranging as they do from the most prolific unions to the merest illicit flirtations. From the twelfth century onward there were all those Renaissances of ancient culture that historians delight in multiplying until, the wheel coming full circle, the Middle Ages themselves became an object of flirtatious advances from the Romantics of the nineteenth century. To the historian, for whom time is the very raw material of his craft, the situation is one of intriguing complexity. For us the essential point is that, in the first great encounter of Western man with his past, the "Renaissance of the twelfth century," a revival of classical Roman law coincided precisely with a new systematic study of all the ancient Christian sources assembled in Gratian's Decretum. Roman law re-introduced the ideas of sovereignty and the state into the Western world but the canonical texts had a distinctive contribution to make too. Early Christianity was not just a belief, but a body of believers, a communion, a community. The earliest references to Christian life are full of community meetings, community sharings, community participation in decisions, community election of officers. Something of this had persisted down to the twelfth century in that the Church was still a structure of elective offices, and the early tradition was reflected very strongly in many of the texts assembled by Gratian.

It would be tempting to assert simply that the first formulation of the basic concepts of Western constitutionalism was stimulated by an encounter between the Roman law idea of a sovereign state and the patristic ideal of a corporate Christian community in the works of the medieval canonists. But this would not be quite the whole truth. After all there was classical law and Christian doctrine in the ancient world and they led on only to Byzantine absolutism. We have to deal with ancient law and early Christian institutions as they were perceived by the eyes of medieval men. The canonists had grown up in a world soaked in the preconceptions of feudalism and of Teutonic customary law, preconceptions that inevitably helped to shape their own personalities and temperaments. Moreover, men of the twelfth and thirteenth centuries did not have the advantage of knowing that they were living in the Middle Ages. They thought they were living in the latest age of the Roman Empire. They were hardly conscious of the great gulf between their own culture and that of the ancient world. This led them to assimilate classical ideas the more readily but almost inevitably to read into them new interpretations of their own. One finds the same pattern in many activities of medieval men. They read Vitruvius—and built Gothic cathedrals. They read Ovid—and wrote about courtly love. They read Justinian—and founded the constitutional state.

One of the most familiar platitudes of our textbooks is the assertion that Western culture was formed from a fusion of classical and Christian elements. It is true of course like most platitudes. But the textbooks do not always emphasize sufficiently that often the fusion took place in the Middle Ages, and still less that in the fields of law and government the works of the medieval canonists played a crucially important role in the whole process. Yet it could hardly have been otherwise. The canonists were the only group of intellectuals in Western history who were professionally concerned with classical law and with Christian doctrine to an equal degree. They delighted in applying to the papal office all the exalted language which Roman law used in describing the majesty of the emperor. They called the pope a supreme legislator whose very will was law, a supreme judge from whom there could be no appeal, a "lord of the world," "loosed from the laws." But these same canonists never forgot St. Paul's reminder that in the Church all power is given "for edification, not for destruction." Moreover, although they lacked the critical insights of a modern historian, there was a profoundly historical dimension to their thought. Gratian's Decretum depicted for the canonists all the ages of the Church's past—and depicted them "warts and all." The misdeeds of several popes who had sinned and erred in former times were recounted in the Decretum and such examples apparently had a sobering effect on the canonists. One of Gratian's texts (Dist. 40 c.1) suggested that all popes were to be considered holy. The Ordinary Gloss, written about 1215, commented somewhat drily, "It does not say that they are holy but that they are to be presumed holy—until the contrary becomes apparent." The Decretists were fascinated by the potentialities for reform of a papacy wielding vast power but at the same time appalled by the dangers for the Church if all that power should fall into evil hands. They were up against the very nub of the problem of sovereignty. It is easy enough to avoid a despotism if one is content to tolerate an anarchy. The difficult task is to concede to a ruler all the very great powers needed for effective government while guarding against the dangers of arbitrary tyranny.[3]

The canonists' aproach to this problem was to seek in the consensus of the whole Christian community, in the indefectible Church guided by the Holy Spirit, norms of faith and order which could define the limits within which the pope's supreme legislative and judicial powers were to be exercised. (The English parliamentary leaders of a later age would set themselves an analogous task in relation to the political community and the limitations of secular kingship.) A juridical basis for the canonists was provided by a text of Pope Gregory the Great, incorporated in the Decretum at Dist. 15 c.2, which declared that the canons of the first four General Councils were always to be preserved inviolate because they were established "by universal consent" or "by a universal consensus" (*universali consensu*). The canonists gave a more precise meaning to Gregory's vague dictum by interpreting it in terms of their own categories of corporation law. They glossed it with phrases like these. "No man can withdraw from the common consent of his community," or "What touches all should be approved by all"—this latter text being used to defend the right of lay representatives to attend General Councils when matters of faith were to be discussed. In the years around 1200 it was commonly maintained that even the pope was bound by the canons of General Councils, representing the whole Church, "in matters pertaining to the faith and the general state of the Church." Such a doctrine could

---

[3] The following discussion of Decretist theories on church government is based on my *Foundations of the Conciliar Theory* (Cambridge, 1955) and "Pope and Council: Some New Decretist Texts," *Medieval Studies,* XIX (1957), 197-218.

be developed without any attack on the ancient principle of papal primacy because of course the pope himself was normally the presiding head of a General Council. Its canons could be regarded as manifestations of the papal will expressed in its highest, most sovereign form and so as binding on the pope himself considered as an isolated individual. The English canonist who, toward 1200, declared that "the authority of a pope with a council is greater than that of a pope without one" was expressing the same idea that King Henry VIII of England would apply to the secular sphere some three centuries later when he said, "We be informed by our judges that we at no time stand so highly in our estate royal as in time of Parliament wherein we as head and you as members are conjoined and knit together in one body politic."

There remained the possibility of an irreconcilable conflict between the pope and the representatives of the Christian community assembled in a General Council. The canonists of the early thirteenth century were deeply divided over this question but the more radical of them taught that a pope could be corrected and even deposed by a council if his conduct endangered the "state of the church." Fifty years later we find the barons of England claiming the right to oppose their king in defense of the "state of the realm." Long ago historians came to realize that the canonists influenced the history of Western political thought in that their theories of papal sovereignty provided an archetype for later theories of divine right monarchy. We are just beginning to understand the importance of their work for theories of representative government also.

It is a complicated task to reconstruct all the constitutionalist elements in the canonists' thought from their voluminous but scattered glosses, and still more complicated to explain in detail how their ideas influenced the growth of secular government. Basically there were two processes at work. Most obviously the canonists offered reflections on the constitutional law of the Church which could and did influence subsequent speculations on the right ordering of the State. But they also formulated a series of doctrines in the sphere of private law which eventually proved of the utmost importance in the growth of representative government although, at first, they had nothing to do with high matters of state. These private-law doctrines again reflected the collegial structure of the medieval Church. Much of the canonists' day-to-day business dealt with the affairs of ecclesiastical communities. They were therefore led to develop an elaborate jurisprudence concerning the representation of corporate groups, the prerogatives of the head of a juridical society in relation to its members, and the rights of individual members in relation to the whole community before such matters began to be discussed as overt issues of political theory.

Just as in some primitive economies there is a shortage of good currency, so too in the medieval polity there was a shortage of good law, especially of constitutional law. When the need for more sophisticated structures of public law came to be urgently felt men naturally turned to the legal rules that were already available in the province of private law—especially in the well-developed canonical law of corporations—and applied them in the constitutional sphere also. A typical line of development was the assimilation of technical rules of Roman private law into canon law, the subsequent inflation of such rules into general principles of church government by the canonists, and the eventual transfer of those principles to the public law of the growing states by the usual medieval process of osmosis. For instance the already mentioned phrase, *Quod omnes tangit ab omnibus approbetur* (What touches all is to be approved by all), was developed from a mere technicality of the Roman law of co-tutorship into a juristic theory about the right relationship between popes and General Councils in the works of the canonists who were writing around 1200. Then, moving from legal theory to real life, we find it in official documents convoking church councils and, finally, by the end of the thirteenth century, it occurs in writs of summons to secular representative assemblies.

This is not the occasion for a detailed exploration of all the maze of arguments that has grown up around the phrase *Quod ommes tangit* and around other terms that underwent a similar development—*plena potestas, status, necessitas.* Let me rather try to summarize the over-all effect of the quite exceptional interplay between all the diverse influences that were at work in thirteenth-century legal thought. The most striking result of their interaction was to produce a peculiar ambivalence in all the concepts commonly used in medieval political discourse. The ruler's power was conceived of as flowing from both God *and* the people. It was held to be in some ways above the law and in some ways below it. The medieval term *status,* the origin of our "state," was used to extend the authority of rulers by justifying extraordinary or extra-legal actions undertaken by them for the defense of the community, but it also served to define a condition of public welfare that the ruler himself was not permitted to disrupt. Representation could mean either the symbolizing of a community in its head, with absolutist implications, or a delegation of authority from the subjects, with constitutionalist implications. The doctrine of natural law provided both a stimulus to new legislation and a criterion for judging its value. It is not that we find popes and princes, intent on building up centralized power, using one set of concepts, and subjects, intent on limiting that power, using another. The very concepts that all had in common were ambivalent; every building block of sovereignty had a constitutional face; Western political thought was already beginning to revolve around the central problem, or paradox, that has fascinated its greatest exponents ever since, the problem of reconciling the idea of sovereignty with the ideal of limited government, of government "under the law."

Some scholars will think that ideas and ideals have little enough to do with the growth of governmental institutions. One young expert has recently observed that, "It did not matter too much what one or another theorist said. . . ." And, certainly, we could all agree that, when medieval kings summoned representative assemblies, they were not normally inspired to do so by protracted meditations on the subtleties of canonical jurisprudence. Kings needed help or counsel or money. They wanted assent to their policies and political support for them. These obvious facts should indeed receive due emphasis in any institutional history of the Middle Ages, but it is a delusion to suppose that, by merely calling attention to them, we are providing a sufficient explanation for the rise of medieval constitutionalism. The problem of maximizing assent to governmental policies arises for all rulers in all societies. It is not normally solved by the development of representative assemblies. Our argument is not that hard-headed medieval statesmen behaved in such-and-such a way because some theorist in a university had invented a theory saying that they ought to do so. The argument is rather that all men behave in certain ways in part at least because they adhere to certain ways of thinking. No doubt the ideas that are most influential in shaping actions are ones that the agent is hardly conscious of at all—he takes them so much for granted. But the historian has to make himself conscious of those ideas if he is to understand the men of a past age and the institutions that they created. The works of the medieval canonists provide invaluable source material for the constitutional historian precisely because they can help him to become aware of the implicit presuppositions about man and society that lay below the surface of medieval political thought and political action.

There is one final and most important point to be made. The ways of arguing that we have used in seeking to understand the origins of the constitutional state can also help us to understand the history of the Catholic Church. Ecclesiastical government too has been shaped throughout the centuries by the incessant interplay between Church and State and, more subtly, between past and present that characterizes our history. The problems of Catholic ecclesiology parallel those of Western political theory, and, in nearly all the ages of the Church's past, it was simply taken for granted that ecclesiastical and secular patterns of government could be expected to exert a mutual influence on one another. This was true in the Middle Ages. It remained true through all the centuries of throne-and-altar Catholicism that followed the medieval period. (James I of England understood the matter well enough when he said, "A Scotch presbytery agree-eth as well with monarchy as God with the Devil.") A decisive break with this way of thinking did not come until the nineteenth century when vast Catholic populations became irrevocably committed to political democracy at a time when the Roman see had committed itself to the improbable task of governing the affairs of a world-wide Church through the institutional apparatus of a petty baroque despotism. It then became the fashion for theologians to distinguish very sharply indeed between the theoretical basis and institutional structure of the Church on the one hand and of the State on the other. Right norms of government for the Church, they pointed out, were to be arrived at by the explication of divine revelation, right norms of government for the State by the exercise of natural human reason; and they seem to have viewed with total equanimity the prospect that, in this particular sphere, reason and revelation might lead to radically opposed conclusions, apparently regarding the Roman curia of their own day as a sort of earthly embodiment of a Platonic ideal laid up immutably in Heaven—complete, presumably, with papal chamberlains and protonotaries apostolic.

During the past five years the theological fashion has changed yet again. Nowadays one can hardly pick up a Catholic journal without reading that the structure of the Church has been in a state of incessant flux throughout the ages. There was a Roman imperial church, a decentralized barbarian church, a medieval feudal church, a baroque absolutist church and so, the argument concludes, why not a twentieth-century democratic church for the age of democracy? This picture of a chameleon-like church wriggling its way down the centuries is no more satisfying than the immediately preceding one. A historian might be forgiven nowadays for occasionally thinking that theology is too important to be left to the theologians—at any rate the theology of the church.[4]

Within the Catholic tradition there have always been these three, Peter, the Apostles, and the people of God—pope, bishops, and faithful. In expressing the constitutional relationships between them the Church has never stood wholly aloof from the world, uninfluenced by the legal and political presuppositions of the societies in which she has existed. But nor has the Church ever been a mere passive entity, molded by external secular forces. In the shaping of Western institutions down the centuries she has given more than she has received. The Church never did become merely "the ghost of the Roman empire sitting crowned on the grave thereof." The principles of Roman law that she assimilated in the twelfth century were transmuted in accordance with the needs of her own intrinsic nature and given back to the secular state charged with a new dynamism. And if the Church should now choose to assimilate into her own structure the constitutional practices of the modern world, that would be no embrace of an alien system but a return to a tradition that drew its own initial inspiration in part from the works of the great jurists who first gave a unified law to the Church in the twelfth century.

From the study of medieval law we can learn above all to appreciate the profound intellectual stresses amid which Western constitutionalism came to birth. Apart from all else the revived classical studies produced an acute tension between the intellectual's symbol structure, the set of concepts available for sophisticated political discourse, and the actual forms of society in which he had to live. (The intrusion of the classical idea of the State into the feudalized, decentralized, Christianized world of the Middle Ages was not unlike the intrusion

---

[4] The problem of the changing structure of the church in time has been handled with admirable sophistication by theologians like Yves Congar and Hans Küng—these are theologians who are also good historians.

of the modern idea of the State into various tribal societies nowadays.) It may be that such a state of tension that breaks old stereotypes and creates sufficient fluidity for experiment is an indispensable precondition whenever the perennial idea of human freedom is to find expression in the institutions of constitutional government. The grievous problem is that, if the stresses within a society become too acute, the society disintegrates altogether. The ideals of the twelfth-century canonists were never realized in the later Middle Ages, and medieval society perhaps came close to disintegration from the tensions that had grown up within it by the age of the Great Schism. A deeper understanding of this chapter of our own past might give us a more perceptive sympathy with some developments of the present in both Church and State. There can be few more fascinating tasks for the historian than to pursue such understanding.

INDEX